Elizabethan Popular Culture

Elizabethan Popular Culture

Leonard R.N. Ashley

Morris Dancers
From a picture at Richmond Palace
by Vincenboom

Bowling Green State University Popular Press
Bowling Green, Ohio 43403

Library of Congress Catalogue Card No.: 88-071063

ISBN: 0-87972-426-9 Clothbound
0-87972-427-7 Paperback

Cover design by Greg Budgett and Gary Dumm

In Memoriam

Albert Edwin Graham

obit 18 May 1986

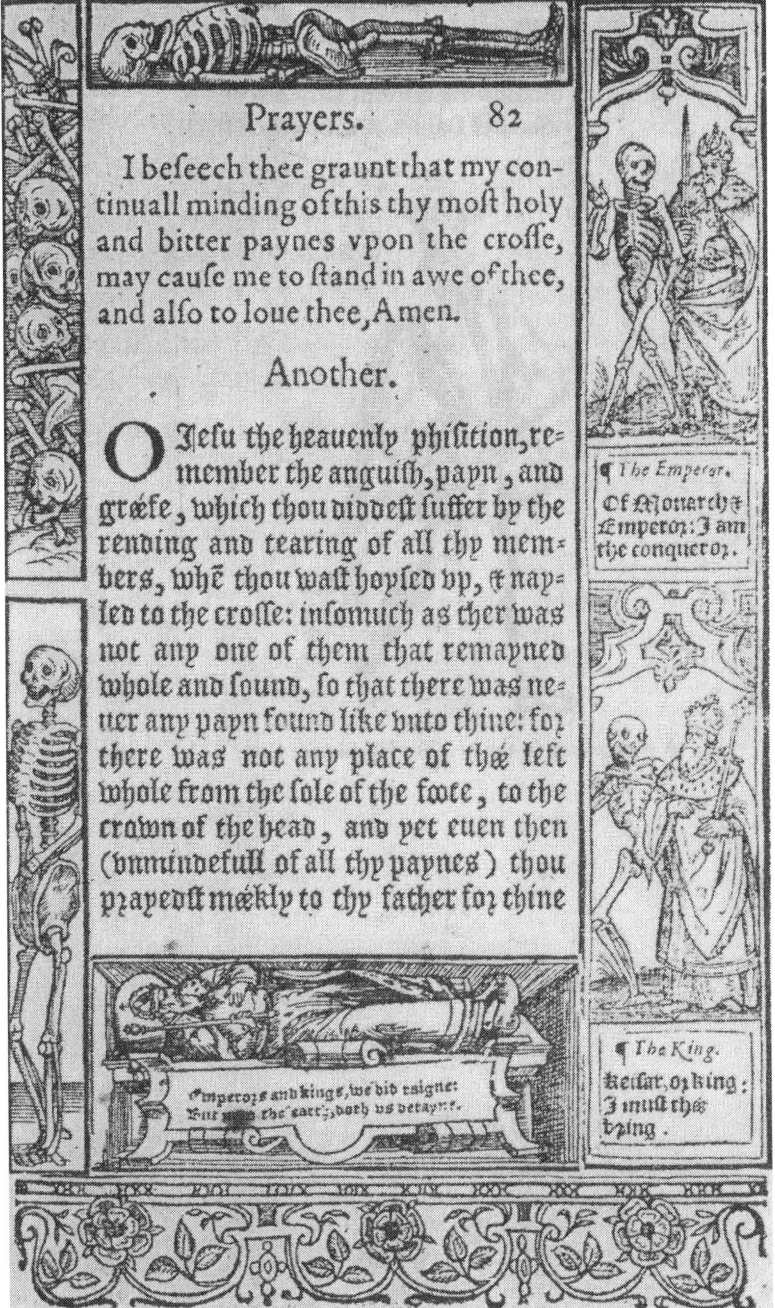

Prayers. 82

I beſeech thee graunt that my continuall minding of this thy moſt holy and bitter paynes vpon the croſſe, may cauſe me to ſtand in awe of thee, and alſo to loue thee, Amen.

Another.

O Ieſu the heauenly phiſition, remember the anguiſh, payn, and græfe, which thou diddeſt ſuffer by the rending and tearing of all thy members, whē thou waſt hoyſed vp, & nayled to the croſſe: inſomuch as ther was not any one of them that remayned whole and ſound, ſo that there was neuer any payn found like vnto thine: for there was not any place of thæ left whole from the ſole of the fœte, to the crown of the head, and yet euen then (vnmindefull of all thy paynes) thou prayedſt mækly to thy father for thine

¶ The Emperor.

Of Monarchy & Emperor: I am the conqueror.

¶ The King.

Keiſar, or king: I muſt thæ bring.

Emperors and kings, we did raigne:
But … the earth, doth vs detayne.

Prayers with *momenti mori* resembling an illuminated manuscript from the *Book of Christian Prayers* (1578).

And who, in time, knows whither may be sent
The treasure of our tongue, to what strange shores
This gain of our best glory shall be lent,
T'inrich unknowing nations with our stores?
—Samuel Daniel, *Musophilus* (1602)

A young man in the height of fashion *c.* 1580.

Contents

Preface

The Master Gunner. From Edward Webbe's Travels (1590).

Though I would not willingly be classed with Lyly for style, I may begin with one of that affected gentleman's sweeping bows and thank all those who have encouraged or assisted my labors on this anthology of Elizabethan popular culture. And I might add something of what Lyly puts in one of his prefaces, that to Euphues, or The Anatomy of Wit:

I was driven into a quandary, gentlemen, whether I might send this my pamphlet to the printer or to the pedlar. I thought it too bad for the press, and too good for the pack. But seeing my folly in writing to be as great as others', I was willing my fortune should be as ill as any man's. We commonly see the book that at Christmas lieth bound on the stationer's stall, at Easter to be broken in the haberdasher's shop, which sith it is the order of proceeding, I am content this winter to have my doings read for a toy that in summer they may be ready for trash. It is not strange whenas the greatest wonder lasteth but nine days, that a new work should not endure but three months. Gentlemen use books as gentlewomen handle their flowers, who in the morning stick them in their heads, and at night straw them at their heels. Cherries be fulsome when they be through ripe, because they be plenty, and books be stale when they be printed, in that they be common. In my mind printers and tailors are bound chiefly to pray for gentlemen: the one hath so many fantasies to print, the other such diverse fashions to make, that the pressing iron of the one is never out of the fire, nor the printing press of the other at any time lieth still. But a fashion is but a day's wearing and a book but an hour's reading: which seeing it is so, I am of a shoemaker's mind who careth not so the shoe hold the plucking on, nor I, so my labours last the running over. He that cometh in print because he would be known, is like the fool that cometh into the market because he would be seen. I am not he that seeketh praise for his labour, but pardon for his offence, neither do I set this forth for any devotion in print, but for duty which I owe to my patron. If one write never so well, he cannot please all, and write he never so ill, he shall please some. Fine heads will pick a quarrel with me if all be not curious, and flatterers a thank if any thing be current. But this is my mind: let him that findeth fault amend it, and him that liketh it use it. Envy braggeth, but draweth no blood: the malicious have more mind to quip, than might to cut. I submit myself to the judgment of the wise, and I little esteem the censure of fools. The one will be satisfied with reason: the other are to be answered with silence. I know gentlemen will find no fault without cause, and I bear with those that deserve blame, as for others I care not for their jests, for I never meant to make them my judges.

Elizabethan Popular Culture *is an anthology which attempts to provide a more recent and specific account of what Professor G. B. Harrison attempted in a book published the year I was born,* England in Shakespeare's Day. *In that he selected Elizabethan (and some later) passages from literature to reveal "the mind of the nation, especially as revealed in its everyday life...the inner life of those who wrote and read its books." Later John Dover Wilson compiled* Life in Shakespeare's England.

My book inevitably repeats many of their selections and quotes familiar material which lies scattered elsewhere. However, I have tried not so much to be original as to give the reader what is essential to form a clear idea of how the ordinary Elizabethan thought and lived, what his or her concerns were from religion to entertainments. I have had to omit much the Elizabethans liked, even sermons, then a form of popular entertainment and instruction, like plays.

I have excluded Shakespeare's plays, readily available elsewhere, although it might be argued that in his work there is the very essence and totality of Elizabethan life. In fact I have deliberately excluded the Elizabethan drama, though I have myself been reading it for forty years and boast I have read nearly all of it that is extant (only very occasionally and temporarily rejoicing that about 80 percent of it is lost). The drama, with its direct appeal and its varied, popular audience, is a good place to find out a great deal about the life of the common man in England of Elizabeth's day, however much Elizabethans enjoyed the stories of exotic locales and battles long ago. But that can wait for another book. Many dramatists do appear in this book, but as poets or writers of prose fiction, not of plays. I make an exception for some few dramatic things of particular popular culture interest, giving (for example) the text of one of the Lord Mayor's Shows. These were, with royal progresses and other free celebrations of the period, a source of much joy and instruction to those who saw them pass by.

I make an occasional exception and include something written outside the limits of Elizabeth's reign (1558-1603) but usually because the material was popular in reprint in Elizabeth's time or definitely a remembrance of her reign though published in the reign of her successor. Just outside my limits there are plenty of memories of the times of James I's predecessor, but they can wait to be collected as Memories of The Spacious Days of Queen Elizabeth, *or some such thing. I had to make this collection you have in hand, not another.*

An anthologist must make choices—and face the critics:

> For what there was none cared a jot;
> But all were wroth with what was not.

I hope you will approve my collections and not miss all the things I had regretfully to cut—or failed to find in the first place.

Leonard R.N. Ashley
Brooklyn College of
The City University of New York

Printed at London by John Danter for William Barley, 1591.

London:

The Chamber of the King

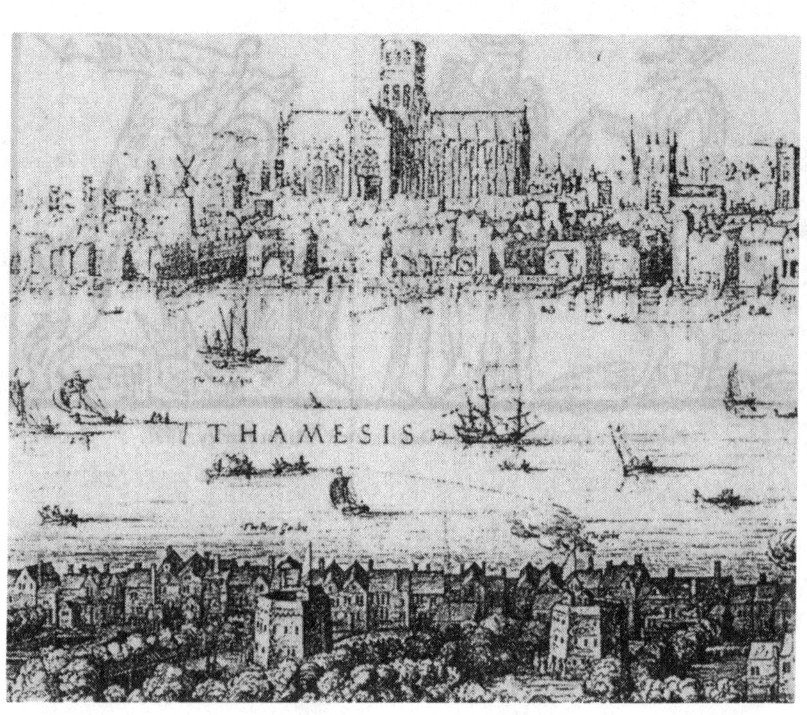

Strangers often notice things that the locals miss (which is why the best book about America was written by Alexis de Tocqueville, who came, and saw, and caught us). These are travelers' reports of Elizabethan London. These tourists did, of course, see all the tourist sights, but sometimes they saw more of what John Norden (1593) called "populous, rich and beautiful" London. Foreign travelers came to London as Englishmen went to Venice and Paris, etc.

Georg Braun and Franz Hogenberg (1572):

London, a most ancient city in the county of Middlesex, the most fertile and salubrious region in all England, is situated on the River Thames, 60,000 paces from the sea, at 52 degrees latitude and 19 degrees, 15 minutes longitude. Its founder is claimed by countless chroniclers to have been Brutus.... The noble River Thames, which is at first called the Isis, springs not far above the village of Winchcomb, and then, augmented by brooks and rills, near Oxford it joins waters with the River Thames, and so the names are joined too. After flowing by London, it empties into the sea through a broad and navigable estuary, which, says Gemma Frisius, in 25 hours fluctuates 80,000 paces with the ebb and flow of the tides. This city is great in itself, but also has spacious suburbs and a magnificently built castle, called The Tower. It is adorned with worthy buildings and temples, and with 120 churches, which they call parishes. A stone bridge leads over to the other side of the river, a long and amazing work constructed on a series of arches, with houses on both sides of it, arranged so that it does not look like a bridge but a continuous street.... According to Polydore Vergil, London has continually been, from ancient times, a royal seat and head of the realm, most crowded with citizens and foreigners, abounding in riches and goods, and most famous in its market. In London, kings are crowned in style and inaugurated in splendid ceremonies. In London the council (they call it Parliament) meets; and moreover, London is administered according to an ancient privilege of the British realm by 24 citizens whom the English call Aldermen, or elders, as it were. From whose number they elect a city 'praetor,' called Mayor in their language; and two 'tribunes,' called Sheriffs in alternating years apply municipal laws and justice. It is a wonder for learned men, who shine famously among writers and who come forth abundantly, from the whole of England but from London especially.

Lupold von Wedel (1584-1585):

I again stepped into my boat, sailing down the river thirty miles towards London, where I arrived at twelve o'clock. All the time the river was full of tame swans, who have nests and breed on small islands formed by the river. They are exclusively used for the Queen's table, and it is on pain of death forbidden to meddle with them.

...The Thames is crossed by a bridge, leading to another town on the other side of the water called Sedorck [Southwark]. This bridge is built of stone, 470 paces long, but its upper part has not the appearance of a bridge, being entirely set with fine houses filled with all kinds of wares, very nice to look at....

On the 23rd we went across the bridge to the above-mentioned town. There is a round building three storeys high, in which are kept about a hundred large English dogs, with separate wooden kennels for each of them. These dogs were made to fight singly with three bears, the second bear being larger than the first, and the third larger than the second. After this a horse was brought in and chased by the dogs, and at last a bull, who defended himself bravely. The next was, that a number of men and women came forward from a separate compartment, dancing, conversing, and fighting with each other; also a man who threw some white bread among the crowd, that scrambled for it. Right over the middle of the place a rose was fixed, this rose being set on fire by a rocket: suddenly lots of apples and pears fell out of it down upon the people standing below. Whilst the people were scrambling for the apples, some rockets were made to fall down upon them out of the rose, which caused a great fright but amused the spectators. After this, rockets and other fireworks came flying out of all corners, and that was the end of the entertainment....

Thomas Platter (1599):

London is the capital of England and so superior to other English towns that London is not said to be in England, but rather England to be in London, for England's most resplendent objects may be seen in and around London: so that he who sees the sights of London and the royal courts in its vicinity may assert without impertinence that he is properly acquainted with England. The town is called in Latin *Londinium,* in French *Londres,* by the ancients *Trinovantum,* and is situated on the river Thames (*Thamesis*) 60 Italian miles or 60,000 paces from the sea, which ebbs and flows as far as London and yet further.... For which reason ocean-craft are accustomed to run in here in great numbers as into a safe harbor, and I myself beheld one large galley next the other the whole city's length from St. Katherine's suburb to the bridge, some hundred vessels in all, nor did I ever behold so many large ships in one port in all my life....

And while a very fine long bridge is built across this stream, it is customary to cross the water or travel up and down the town as at Lyons and elsewhere by attractive pleasure craft, for a number of tiny streets lead to the Thames from both ends of the town; the boatmen wait there in great crowds, each one eager to be first to catch one, for all are free to choose the ship they find most attractive and pleasing, while every boatman has the privilege on arrival of placing his ship to best advantage for people to step into....

This city of London is so large and splendidly built, so populous and excellent in crafts and merchant citizens, and so prosperous, that it is not only the first in the whole realm of England, but is esteemed one of the most famous in all Christendom; especially since the wars in the Netherlands and France it has increased by many thousands of families who have settled in this city for religion's sake....

Most of the inhabitants are employed in commerce; they buy, sell and trade in all the corners of the globe, for which purpose the water serves them well, since ships from France, the Netherlands, Germany and other countries dock at this city, bringing goods with them and loading others in exchange for exportation. For which reason they allow some 10 percent interest, because through shipping much may be effected and attained with money.

There are also many wealthy merchants and moneychangers in this city, some of whom sell costly wares while others only deal in money for wholesale transactions.

In one very long street called Cheapside dwell almost exclusively goldsmiths and moneychangers on either hand so that inexpressibly great treasures and vast amounts of money may be seen here.

The Exchange [built by Sir Thomas Gresham] is a great square place like the one in Antwerp,...a little smaller, though, and with only two entrances and only one passage running through it, where all kinds of fine goods are on show; and since the city is very large and extensive, merchants having to deal with one another agree to meet together in this place, where several hundred may be found assembled twice daily, before lunch at eleven, and again after their meal at six o'clock, buying, selling, bearing news, and doing business generally....

On September 21st after lunch, about two o'clock, I and my party crossed the water, and there in the house with the thatched roof witnessed an excellent performance of the [Shakespearian] tragedy of the first Emperor Julius Caesar with a cast of some fifteen people; when the play was over, they danced very marvellously and gracefully together as is their wont, two dressed as men and two as women.

On another occasion not far from our inn, in the suburb at Bishopsgate, if I remember, also after lunch, I beheld a play in which they presented diverse nations and an Englishman struggling together for a maiden.... Thus daily at two in the afternoon, London has two, sometimes three plays running in different places, competing with each other, and those which play best obtain most spectators. The playhouses are so constructed that they play on a raised platform, so that everyone has a good view. There are different galleries and places, however, where the seating is better and more comfortable and therefore more expensive. For whoever cares to stand below only pays one English penny but if he wishes to sit he enters by another door, and pays another penny, while if he desires to sit in the most comfortable seats, which are cushioned, where he not only sees everything well, but can also be seen, then he pays yet another English penny at another door. And during the performance food and drink are carried around the audience, so that for what one cares to spend one may also have refreshment. The actors are most expensively and elaborately costumed; for it is the English custom for eminent lords or knights at their decease to bequeath and leave almost the best of their clothes to their serving men, which it is unseemly for the latter to wear, so that they offer them then for sale for a small sum to the actors....

There are a great many inns, taverns, and beer gardens scattered about the city, where much amusement may be had with eating, drinking, fiddling, and the rest, as for instance in our hostelry, which was visited by players almost daily. And what is particularly curious is that the women as well as the men, in fact more often than they, will frequent the taverns or ale-houses for enjoyment..

In the ale-houses tobacco or a species of wound-wort are also obtainable for one's money, and the powder is lit in a small pipe, the smoke sucked into the mouth, and the saliva is allowed to run freely, after which a good draught of Spanish wine follows. This they regard as a curious medicine for defluctions and as a pleasure; and the habit is so common with them, that they always carry the instrument on them, and light up on all occasions, at the play, in the taverns or elsewhere, drinking as well as smoking together, as we sit over wine, and it makes them riotous and merry, and rather drowsy, just as if they were drunk, though the effect soon passes—and they use it so abundantly because of the pleasure it gives, that their preachers cry out against them for their self-destruction, and I am told the inside of one man's veins after death was found to be covered in soot just like a chimney....

At the fishmarket, in a long street, I saw a quantity of pike up for sale; they are very fond of this...and eat it with needle-fish (*aiguilles*), eels and other tiny fish. And I noticed that each of these fishermen and fishwives kept a copper or brass needle and thread in the tub, with a sharp knife. And when the purchasers desired a pike the salesmen and saleswomen slit open its belly at their bidding, placing the guts on their hands to show whether the pike was sufficiently fat, and then sewed it up again: if the pike proved fat enough, then the purchaser took it, but if the guts looked thin and poor the fishmonger kept it, throwing it back into the basin among the tenches, against which they rub themselves and recover enough to keep fresh for at least another week, in fact according to them, fish could keep fresh for some months. Indeed, they kept tench ready in the fish tanks with the pike, so that they would get used to them; all this I witnessed in London with my own eyes, nor is it otherwise.

Wound-wort was of the goldenrod family. Platter was a Swiss physician. A grander visitor was "his princely Grace" Philip Julius, Duke of Pomerania, who visited in 1602:

On arriving in London we heard a great ringing of bells in almost all the churches going on very late in the evening, also on the following days until 7 or 8 o'clock in the evening. We were informed that the young people do that for the sake of exercise and amusement, and sometimes they lay considerable sums of money as a wager, who will pull a bell the longest or ring it in the most approved fashion.

Parishes spend much money on harmoniously-sounding bells, that one being preferred which has the best bells. The old queen is said to have been pleased very much by this exercise, considering it as a sign of the health of the people. They do not ring the bells for the dead, but when a person lies in agony, the bells of the parish he belongs to are touched with the clappers until he either dies or recovers again.

As soon as this sign is given, everybody in the street, as well as in the houses, falls on his knees offering prayer for the sick person....

On the 15h his princely Grace intended to see the Exchange, where the merchants are used to assemble in a square, covered space. Round the top is a fine broad vaulted gallery, where may be bought almost everything a man may imagine in the way of costly wares.

At eleven o'clock, at noon, and at five o'clock in the evening, the lower part becomes so filled with people that only by force are you able to make your way. It is a pleasure to go about there, for one is not molested or accosted by beggars, who are elsewhere so frequently met with in places of this kind. For in all England they do not suffer any beggars, except they be few in number and outside the gates.

Every parish cares for its own poor; strangers are brought to the hospital, but those that belong to the kingdom or have come from distant places, are sent from one parish to the other, their wants being cared for, until at last they reach their home.

Every city has its traffic problems. Those of Elizabethan London were exacerbated by narrow old streets, overcrowding, and vehicles that were said to have been invented in Poland in a town called Kocz. John Stow:

The number of cars, drays, carts and coaches more than hath been accustomed, the streets and lanes being straitened, must needs be dangerous, as daily experience proveth.

The coachman rides behind the horse tails, lasheth them, and looketh not behind him; the drayman sitteth and sleepeth on his dray and letteth his horse lead him home. I know that by the good laws and customs of this city, shod carts are forbidden to enter the same, except upon reasonable causes, as service of the prince or such like, they be tolerated. Also that the fore-horse of every carriage should be led by hand; but these good orders are not observed. Of old times, coaches were not known in this island, but chariots or whirlicotes, then so called, and they only used of princes or great estates, such as had their footmen about them.... But now of late years, the use of coaches, brought out of Germany, is taken up and made so common, as there is neither distinction of time nor difference of persons observed; for the world runs on wheels with many whose parents were glad to go on foot.

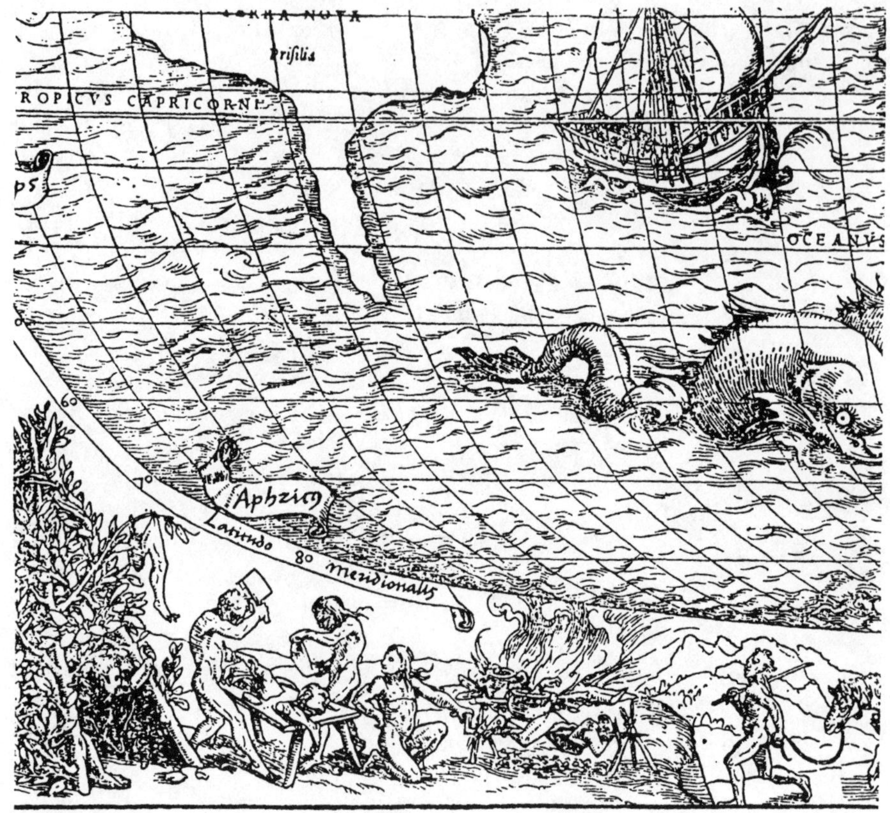

Cannibals decorate a map made before the Elizabethan voyagers set out. Grynaeus, *Novus Orbis* (1532).

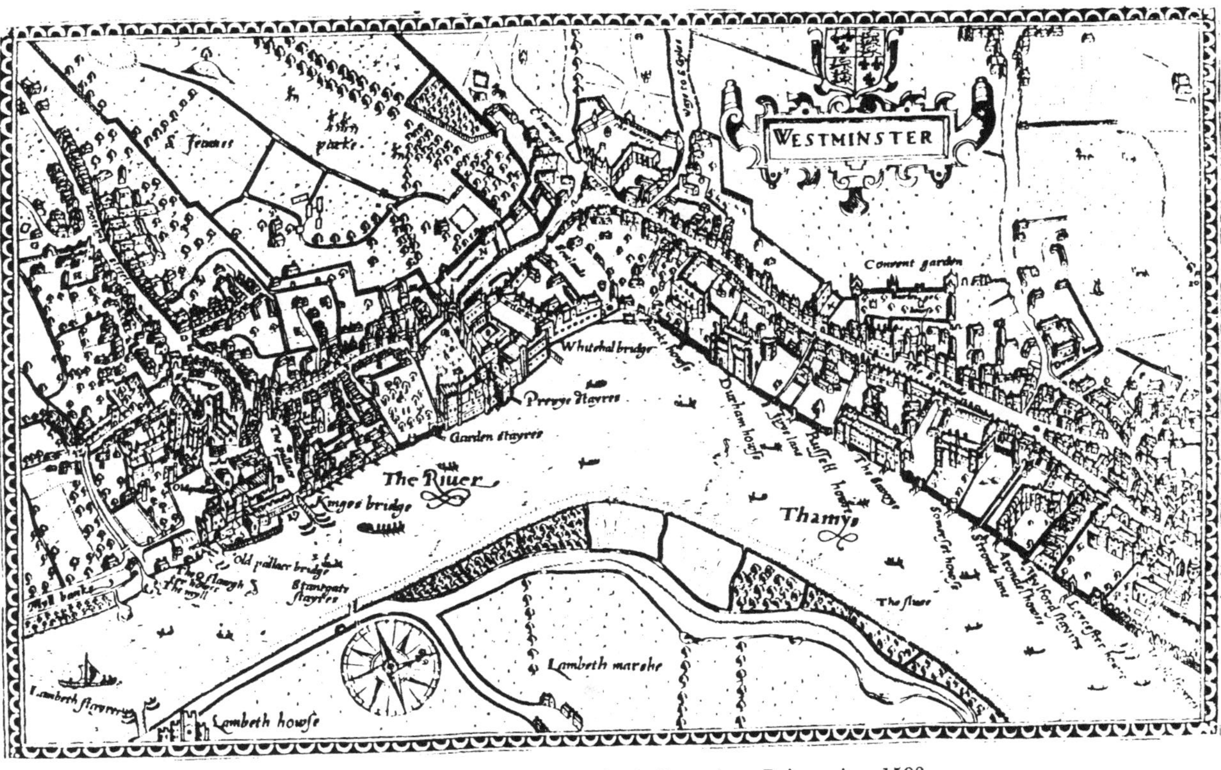

Map of Westminster from John Norden's Speculum Britanniae, 1593.

City People and Country People

A noble lady and a middle-class wife (*c.* 1580).

The medieval practice of electing a Lord Mayor of London each year had, by Elizabeth's time, become one of the principal ways by which the rich merchants of the city's livery companies (or trade guilds) exercised some authority over the one-mile-square area of the ancient City of London. Even the Queen could not enter The City without meeting its bourgeois officials at Temple Bar.

In 1574, Thomas Norton (1532-1584), a member of the Grocers' Company and of the Inner Temple, Remembrancer of The City of London (1571), presumed to instruct the Lord Mayor on his duties.

There be many reasons, which I ought not to doubt, that you do daily call to mind the weight of your charge in the office of the Lord Mayor of London. You are to remember how great a thing is the Lord Mayor, and of London so great a City, the imperial chamber of so great a prince, of our sovereign lady, the immediate lieutenant of the most great and mighty God. You are to think what trust Her Majesty and her progenitors have, and repose, in the corporate and politic body of her City of London, as to commit to ourselves the naming and choice of her deputed chief magistrate here and of our own governor. And how upon Her Highness' pleasure well known, you have been in one and honourable form received and allowed, and your care and fidelity is from and for Her Majesty committed to the keeping of the place, the preservation of the estate, and the government of her people of London, a most dear precious jewel in the crown of England. You are to have in mind what strength of the prince is here kept for her service and for the realm's defence; what polity, what wealth, and what order to be maintained for her use and honour for the common good; what multitudes of subjects, as well inhabiting as repairing, are to be provided for. You are not to forget what care Her Majesty and her council have showed themselves to have, that London be in the charge of a trusty man, and what particular proceedings have brought you and left you in your good acceptation and confidence, for which you are highly to thank God and His ministers. You must thereof gather what necessity is laid unto you to answer good expectation....

Yourself is blessed of God with sufficiency for that experience which the honour of the place requireth; by reason whereof you are not subject to such need as might make a man apt to corruption, or to contempt. You bring, I doubt not, an upright mind to serve God and the Queen sincerely; you have been noted a man of good charitable disposition and a tender heart to your poor; you are not young; you have not lived obscurely; you have had long experience and been in place of knowledge, and of both politic and judicial understanding. You are joined with a sufficient number of wise and grave brethren and commons, being companions of a great part of your charge; some of them have passed the way before you, and the rest have [assayed] of others, and all together shall sit with you, shall advise you, shall strengthen you, shall ease your travails, shall supply your lacks, shall defend your doings, shall to you, with you, and for you give, establish, and maintain direction, power and countenance....

You must be careful for provision of victual, fuel, and all things necessary; and that of all things there be true and wholesome stuff, good assize [regulation], just weight and measure, and prices reasonable; wherein your best policies shall be by encouragement to permit, and by good foresight not to let slip, the best times of providing or bringing.

Among all your cares do justice with discretion, execute laws uprightly, and keep order. Have ever still a pitiful eye to the poor, and whensoever you see the poor, craving needing, you aid them in any thing, saving to do wrong....

Now, lastly, my Lord, you must not forget that God is the giver of all good things. You must resort to Him daily by prayer, and to pray with heart; not suffered to say over 'Our Father' but to weigh every petition and join thereto a most affectuous [earnest] desire to obtain it according to His will. In that the Lord's Prayer, so oft as you say it, when you come to this place, 'our daily bread,' you must remember that there is not comprised bread only, but therein is meant all things that are necessary for this present life; and among other things His blessing, that you may answer your charge in governing.

Every freeman of the city of London swore this oath (1580):

Ye shall swear that ye shall be good and true to our sovereign Lady Queen Elizabeth, etc., and to the heirs of our said sovereign Lady the Queen. Obeisant and obedient ye shall be to the Mayor and to the ministers [officials] of the City. The franchises and customs thereof ye shall maintain...[and pay various charges and taxes], bearing your part as a freeman ought to do. Ye shall colour no foreign's goods whereby the Queen might lose her customs or advantages.

Ye shall know no foreigner to buy or sell any merchandise within the City or the franchise thereof, but ye shall warn the Chamberlain thereof, or some minister of the chamber.

Ye shall emplead or sue no free man out of this City whiles ye may have right and law within this same City.

Ye shall take none apprentice but if he be free born, that is to say, no bond man's son, and for no less term than for seven years. Within the first year ye shall cause him to be enrolled, and at his term's end ye shall make him free of this City, if he have well and truly served you.

Ye shall also keep the Queen's peace in your person; ye shall know no gatherings, conventicles, nor conspiracies made against the Queen's peace, but ye shall warn the Mayor thereof, or let it to [stop it insofar as it is in] your power.

All these points and articles ye shall well and truly keep, according to the laws and custom of this City to your power. So God you help, and by the holy contents of this Book.

Walled cities inevitably produced suburbs outside the walls; suburbs often were outside the bounds of propriety, too, because outside the control of the Lord Mayor and other authorities. Across the Thames from London one was no longer in Middlesex but in Surrey and free of the puritanical burghers of The City. There were the playhouses and also the whorehouses, the "stews," some on land owned by the Bishop of Winchester and so prostitutes were called "Winchester geese." Like the geese the Romans kept on their walls to warn of attack, these whores of the suburbs constituted a caveat to the pious of the direction society might take. It was good journalistic business to point the finger, combining the sensational with the moral, and Thomas Nashe (1592) was eloquent in his popular pamphlets.

London, what are thy suburbs but licensed stews? Can it be so many brothel houses of salary sensuality and sixpenny whoredom (the next door to the magistrate's) should be set up and maintained, if bribes did not bestir them? I accuse none, but certainly justice somewhere is corrupted. Whole hospitals of ten-times-a-day dishonested strumpets have we cloistered together. Night and day the entrance unto them is as free as to a tavern. Not one of them but hath a hundred retainers. Prentices and poor servants they encourage to rob their masters. Gentlemen's purses and pockets they will dive into and pick, even whiles they are dallying with them....

Every one of them is a gentlewoman, and either the wife of two husbands or a bed-wedded bride before she was ten years old. The speech-shunning sores and sight-irking botches of their insatiate intemperance they will unblushingly lay forth and jestingly brag of wherever they haunt....

Ere they come to forty you shall see them worn to the bare bone. At twenty their lively colour is lost, their faces are sodden and parboiled with French surfeits. That colour you behold on their cheeks superficialized is but Sir John White's or Sir John Red-cap's livery. The alchemist of quicksilver makes gold. These (our openers to all comers) with quickening and conceiving get gold. The souls they bring forth, at the latter day, shall stand up and give evidence against them.

Houses of Elizabethan London are more or less familiar from old pictures and nostalgic Victorian imitations, but what country houses were like is probably less known to the reader, so here is a description from Gervase Markham's The English Husbandman *(1613):*

Here you behold the model of a plain country man's house, without plaster or imbosture [ornamentation], because it is to be intended that it is as well to be built of stud and plaster, as of lime and stone, or if timber be not plentiful it be built of coarser wood, and covered with lime and hair; yet if a man would bestow cost in this model, the four inward corners of the hall would be convenient for four turrets, and the four gavel [gable] ends, being thrust out with bay windows might be formed in any curious manner: and where I place a gate and a plain pail [paling fence], might be either a terrace, or a gatehouse, of any fashion whatsoever; besides all those windows which I make plain might be made bay windows, either with battlements, or without: but the scope of my book tendeth only to the use of the honest husbandman, and not to instruct men of dignity, who in architecture are able wonderfully to control me; therefore that the husbandman may know the use of this facsimile, he shall understand it by this which followeth.

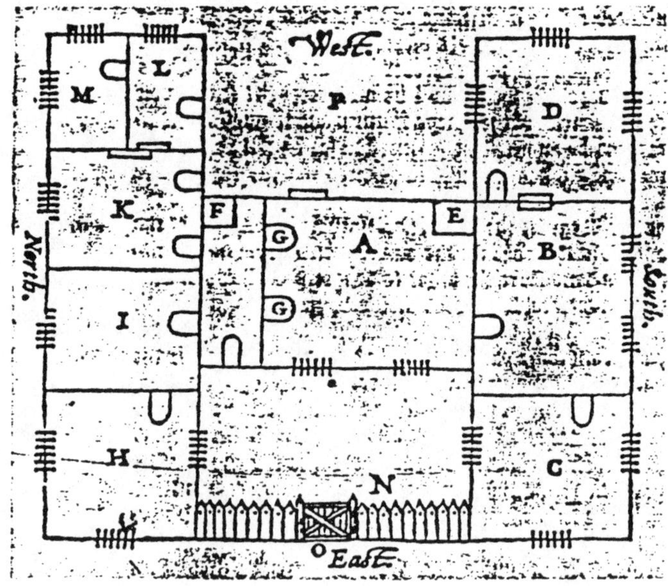

A. Signifieth the great hall.
B. The dining parlour for entertainment of strangers [visitors].
C. An inward closet within the parlour for the mistress' use, for necessaries.
D. A stranger's lodging within the parlour.
E. A staircase into the rooms over the parlour.
F. A staircase into the goodman's rooms over the kitchen and buttery.
G. The screen in the hall.
H. An inward cellar within the buttery, which may serve for a larder.
I. The buttery.
K. The kitchen, in whose range may be placed a brewing lead, and convenient ovens, the brewing vessels adjoining.
L. The dairy house for necessary business.

M. The milkhouse.
N. A fair sawn pale before the foremost court.
P. A place where a pump would be placed to serve the offices of the house.

This figure signifieth the doors of the house.
This figure signifieth the windows of the house.
This figure signifieth the chimneys of the house.

Now you shall further understand that on the South side of your house, you shall plant your garden and orchard, as well for the prospect thereof to all your best rooms, as also your house will be a defence against the northern coldness, whereby your fruits will much better prosper. You shall on the west side of your house, within your inward dairy and kitchen court, fence in a large base court, in the midst whereof would be a fair large pond, well stoned and gravelled in the bottom, in which your cattle may drink, and horses when necessity shall urge be washed; for I do by no means allow washing of horses after instant labour. Near to this pond you shall build your dovecote, for pigeons delight much in the water; and you shall by no means make your dove house too high, for pigeons cannot endure a high mount, but you shall build it moderately, clean, neat, and close, with water pentisses [over-hanging eaves] to keep away vermin. On the north side of your base court you shall build your stables, ox-house, cow-house, and swinecotes, the doors and windows opening all on the south. On the south side of the base court, you shall build your hay barns, corn bars, pullen-houses for hens, capons, ducks, geese; your French kiln, and malting floors, with such like necessaries: and over cross betwixt both these sides you shall build your bound hovels [connected sheds], to carry your pease, of good and sufficient timber, under which you shall place when they are out of use your carts, wains [wagons], tumbrels [dung carts], ploughs, harrows, and such like, together with plough timber and axletrees [frames and axles], all which should very carefully be kept from wet, which of all things doth soonest rot and consume them. And thus much of the husbandman's house, and the necessaries thereto belonging.

Elizabethan gardens were of many sorts (some people introducing Italian and other foreign designs as well as imported plants and specimen bushes and trees) and of many uses. Everyone with a garden also grew herbs and spices and "simples" for medicine. Some "wise women" grew plants for use in witchcraft, perhaps providing borders of red flowers as soldiers to protect their treasures. Flowers and vegetables, decoration and use, were combined, and things were planted in strict accordance with the phases of the moon as well as the change of the seasons: there was a bit of folklore to instruct one on how and when to plant each and every thing, which plants ought to be planted together, and so on. Some plants, according to the popularly-held Doctrine of Signs, bore evidence of their medicinal properties. For instance, heart-shaped leaves told one that the plant might be useful to treat heart disease.

Many of the common (rather than the botanical) names of plants we still use today were in use in Elizabethan times and tell us of the folk beliefs of our ancestors.

In every way, even in their lush profusion and extravagant mixing of kinds and colors, Elizabethan gardens revealed, as all gardens do, the tastes and ideas of the period, the combination in Elizabethan England of the old and the new, the fanciful and the practical, the hierarchical and meticulously arranged and the exuberant.

In addition the Elizabethans maintained orchards, and they were as likely to welcome a new tree as they were to follow age-old customs such as wassailing the appletrees or keeping on the right side of the bees by telling them of any births and deaths in the family.

William Harrison on Elizabethan gardens and orchards:

If you look into our gardens annexed to our houses, how wonderfully is their beauty increased, not only with flowers...and variety of curious and costly workmanship, but also with rare and medicinable herbs sought up in the land within these forty years: so that, in comparison of this present, the ancient gardens were but dunghills and laystows to such as did possess them. How art also helpeth nature in the daily colouring, doubling and enlarging the proportion of our flowers, it is incredible to report: for so curious and cunning are our gardeners now in these days that they presume to do in manner what they list with nature, and moderate her course in things as if they were her superiors. It is a wonder also to see how many strange herbs, plants and annual fruits are daily brought unto us from the Indies, Americas, Taprobane, Canary Isles, and all parts of the world: the which, albeit that in respect of the constitutions of our bodies they do not grow for us, because that God hath bestowed sufficient commodities upon every country for her own necessity, yet, for delectation sake unto the eye and their odoriferous savours unto the nose, they are to be cherished, and God to be gloried also in them, because they are His good gifts, and created to do man help and service. There is not almost one nobleman, gentleman or merchant that hath not great store of these flowers, which now also do begin to wax so well acquainted with our soils that we may almost account of them as parcel of our own commodities. They have no less regard in like sort to cherish medicinable herbs fetched out of other regions nearer hand, insomuch that I have seen in some one garden to the number of three hundred or four hundred of them, if not more, of the half of whose names within forty years past we had no manner knowledge. But herein I find some cause of just complaint, for that we extol their uses so far that we fall into contempt of our own, which are in truth more beneficial and apt for us than such as grow elsewhere, sith (as I said before) every region hath abundantly within her own limits whatsoever is needful and most convenient for them that dwell therein....

The writing of "characters" or brief portraits of types was common in the Renaissance. Here is Sir Thomas Overbury on the yeoman:

His outside is an ancient yeoman of England, though his inside may give arms (with the best gentlemen) and ne'er see the herald. There is no truer servant in the house than himself. Though he be master, he says not to his servants, "Go to the field," but "let us go"; and with his own eye doth both fatten his flock, and set forward all manner of husbandry. He is taught by nature to be contented with a little; his own fold yields him both food and raiment: he is pleased with any nourishment God sends, whilst curious gluttony ransacks, as it were, Noah's Ark for food, only to fee the riot of one meal. He is ne'er known to go to law; understanding, to be law-bound among men, is like to be hide-bound among his beasts; they thrive not under it: and that such men sleep as unquietly, as if their pillows were stuffed with lawyers' pen-knives. When he builds, no poor tenant's cottage hinders his prospect: they are indeed his almshouses, though there be painted on them no such superscription. He never sits up late, but when he hunts the badger, the vowed foe of his lambs: nor uses he any cruelty, but when he hunts the hare; nor subtlety, but when he setteth snares for the snipe, or pitfalls for the blackbird; nor oppression, but when in the month of July, he goes to the next river, and shears his sheep. He allows of honest pastime, and thinks not the bones of the dead any thing bruised, or the worse for it though the country lasses dance in the churchyard after evensong. Rock Monday, and the wake in summer, shrovings, the wakeful ketches on Christmas Eve, the hockey or seed cake, these he yearly keeps, yet holds them no relics of popery. He is not so inquisitive after news derived from the privy closet, when the finding an aerie of hawks in his own ground, or the foaling of a colt come of a good strain are tidings more pleasant, more profitable. He is lord paramount within himself, though he hold by never so mean a tenure; and dies the more contentedly (though he leave his heir young) in regard he leaves him not liable to a covetous guardian. Lastly, to end him; he cares not when his end comes, he needs not fear his audit, for his quietus is in heaven.

John Stephens (Satyrical Essays, Characters, and others, 1615) *on the shepherd:*

An honest shepherd is a man that well verifies the Latin piece, *qui bene latuit bene vixit*: he lives well that lives retired: for he is always thought the most innocent because he is least public: and certainly I cannot well resolve you whether his sheep or he be more innocent. Give him fat lambs and fair weather, and he knows no happiness beyond them. He shows, most fitly among all professions, that nature is contented with a little. For the sweet fountain is his fairest alehouse: the sunny bank his best chamber. Adam had never less need of neighbours' friendship; nor was at any time troubled with neighbours' envy less than he: the next grove or thicket will defend him from a shower: and if they be not so favourable, his homely palace is not far distant. He proves quietness to be best contentment, and that there is no quietness like a certain rest. His flock affords him his whole raiment, outside and linings, cloth, and leather; and instead of much costly linen, his little garden yields hemp enough to make his lockram shirts: which do preserve his body sweetened against court-itch and poxes, as a sear-cloth sweetens carcasses. He gives the just epitome of a contented man: for he is neither daunted with lightning and thunder, nor overjoyed with springtime and harvest. His daily life is a delightful work, whatsoever the work be; whether to mend his garments, cure a diseased sheep, instruct his dog, or change pastures: and these be pleasant actions, because voluntary. He comprehends the true pattern of a moderate wise man: for as a shepherd, so a moderate man hath the supremacy over his thoughts and passions: neither hath he any affection of so wild a nature, but he can bring it into good order, with any easy whistle. The worst temptation of his idleness teaches him no further mischief, than to love entirely some nut-brown milkmaid, or hunt the squirrel, or make his cosset wanton. He may turn many rare esteemed physicians into shame and blushing: for whereas they, with infinite compounds and fair promises, do carry men to death the furthest way about; he with a few simples preserves himself and family to the most lengthened sufferance of nature. Tar and honey be his mithridates and syrups; the which, together with a Christmas carol, defend his desolate life from cares and melancholy. With little knowledge and a simple faith, he purifies his honest soul, in the same manner as he can wash his body in an obscure fountain, better than in the wide ocean. When he seems lazy and void of action, I dare approve his harmless negligence, rather than many approved men's diligence. Briefly he is the perfect allegory of a most blessed governor: and he that will pursue the trope's invention, may make this character a volume.

Sir Thomas Overbury on the milkmaid such as Princess Elizabeth envied "singing pleasantly" when she herself was a prisoner in the country as a girl:

A fair and happy milkmaid is a country wench, that is so far from making herself beautiful by art, that one look of hers is able to put all face-physic out of countenance. She knows a fair look is but a dumb orator to commend virtue, therefore minds it not. All her excellencies stand in her so silently, as if they had stolen upon her without her knowledge. The lining of her apparel (which is herself) is far better than outsides of tissue: for though she be not arrayed in the spoil of the silkworm, she is decked in innocency, a far better wearing. She doth not, with lying long abed, spoil both her complexion and conditions. Nature hath taught her too immoderate sleep is rust to the soul. She rises therefore with chanticleer, her dame's cock, and at night makes the lamb her curfew. In milking a cow, and straining the teats through her fingers, it seems that so sweet a milk-press makes the milk the whiter or sweeter; for never came almond glove or aromatic ointment on her palm to taint it. The golden ears of corn fall and kiss her feet when she reaps them, as if they wished to be bound and led prisoners by the same hand that felled them. Her breath is her own, which scents all the year long of June, like a new-made hay-cock. She makes her hand hard with labour, and her heart soft with pity: and when winter evenings fall early (sitting at her merry [spinning] wheel) she sings a defiance to the giddy wheel of fortune. She doth all things with so sweet a grace, it seems ignorance will not suffer her to do ill, being her mind is to do well. She bestows her year's wages at next fair; and in choosing her garments, counts no bravery in the world like decency. The garden and beehive are all her physic and chirurgery, and she lives the longer for it. She dares go alone and unfold sheep in the night, and fears no manner of ill, because she means none; yet to say truth, she is never alone, for she is still accompanied with old songs, honest thoughts and prayers, but short ones: yet they have their efficacy, in that they are not palled with ensuing idle cogitations. Lastly, her dreams are so chaste, that she dare tell them; only a Friday's dram is all her superstition; that she conceals for fear of anger. Thus lives she, and all her care is she may die in the springtime, to have store of flowers stuck upon her winding-sheet.

To tell the story of the common man whom history in the Elizabethan period (as in most others) more or less ignored is difficult, though in this book I have tried to catch echoes of his inarticulate life in the works of literature from the period. One other source that needs at least a nod of recognition is diaries or account books. For our example we take the Diary and Family Book of Robert Furse, *Yeoman of 1593, published in part in* Devonshire Transactions *26 (1894).*

In modern spelling here, Robert Furse of Devon prepared for his posterity a record that says that his ancestors were men of "small possession and ability, yet have they by little and little...so run their course...that by these means we are come to much more possessions, credit and reputation than ever any of them had." A kinsman, John Furse, was "for his manhood and good qualities" employed by a "Mr. Shylston" and "after him, he served a worthy knight with whom he went to Scotland, and lastly in service with Henry Courtney, Earl of Devon." John Furse, however, married a yeoman's daughter and put together some farms. Robert Furse set down all the rights by which he held property and recommended his heirs continue this, because "it will be to those that come after you...great quietness, perfect knowledge, and a true means to understand all their evidences and titles." What they won hard they held fast. Some did very well. "When this John and Mary were first married they had but little, but God did so prosper them that before she died they had 400 bullocks and great store of money and other such stuff and were as well furnished of all things in their house as any one man of their degree [the yeomanry] was in all their country." Robert Furse himself built "the porch and entry and sealed the hall and glassed all the windows" in his house, though Robert Carew as late as 1602 noted that glass in the windows of private persons' houses was still unusual, and Robert Furse wrote in an earlier decade. The yeomen worked hard but also enjoyed themselves. It was said that "when hospitality died in England" it perished last "among the yeomen of Kent." In Devon the old pastimes and Merry England lasted longer than in most places. Robert Furse writes that his grandfather "was lusty and given to all pleasure as to hunt, dice, cards and all other pastime but especially to shooting." At dusk ("between the lights," they said in Devon) the yeoman ended his long work day. On holidays he celebrated with liberality. He worked hard, played hard, hoped to leave his children well provided for when he was (as they put it) "brought home" to his grave. He went about getting richer by toil and Robert Furse advised his children to look after themselves and "let every man shoot his own bow," be responsible for himself and his family.

*Too much ignored was the simple artisan, the farmer, the factory worker. Jack of Newbury, of whom Thomas Deloney wrote, set up one of the earliest sweatshops—or ideal weaving factory. He certainly "gave employment to the artisan." (*Silly = *simple,* broachs = *roasting spits.)*

Within one room being large and long,
There stood two hundred looms full strong:
Two hundred men the truth is so,
Wrought in these looms all in a row.
By every one a pretty boy,
Sat making quills with mickle joy.
And in another place hard by,
An hundred women merrily,
Were carding hard with joyful cheer,
Who singing sat with voices clear.
And in a chamber close beside,
Two hundred maidens did abide
In petticoats of stammell red,
And milk-white kerchers on their head:
Their smock-sleeves like to winter snow,
That on the Western mountains flow,
And each sleeve with a silken band,
Was neatly tied at the hand.
These pretty maids did never lin,
But in that place all day did spin:
And spinning so with voices meet,
Like nightingales they sung full sweet.
Then to another room came they,
Where children were in poor array:
And every one sat picking wool,
The finest from the coarse to cull:
The number was seven score and ten,
The children of poor silly men;
And these were shearmen every one,
Whose skill and cunning there was shown:
And hard by them there did remain,
Full fourscore rowers taking pain.
A dye-house likewise had he then,
Wherein he kept full forty men:

And likewise in his fulling mill,
Full twenty persons kept he still.
Each week ten good fat oxen he
Spent in his house for certainty:
Beside good butter, cheese, and fish,
And many another wholesome dish.
He kept a butcher all the year,
A brewer eke for ale and beer;
A baker for to bake his bread,
Which stood his household in good stead.
Five cooks within his kitchen great,
Were all the year to dress his meat.
Six scullion boys unto their hands,
To make clean dishes, pots and pans,
Beside poor children that did stay,
To turn the broachs every day.
The old man that did see this sight,
Was much amazed, as well he might:
This was a gallant clothier sure,
Whose fame for ever shall endure.

Alfred Harbage makes the point that there were not enough "knights, baronets, and temporal lords" (the lords spiritual were the episcopacy) in all England to fill The Globe, so an occasional one there paid handsomely, as he did for everything in a time when 40 shillings (two pounds) a year were (with "all found" as regards board and lodging and probably livery) a servant's wages.

Here is the account book for the Earl of Rutland with some items for 1598-1599 in the original form:

Item for Sir Ph. Sidneys *Arcadia* [3d ed.?], ixs.
Item for my Lorde's supper at Courte, 28 *Octoberis,* isx. *iid.*

....the cooke in the pryvy kitchen, xs...tobacco pipes, viiid.
Item, 28 September, my Lorde's boatehier to Lambeth and back againe, xviid....boatehire I October, for his Lordship and his men, and the play, and James his going to Lambeth to see Capten Whitlock, viiis.

Item the foteman's boatehire to Lambeth and to the play howse sondry tymes, iis. iiid.

Item, 28 *Julii,* an oz. of ball tobacco, vs.; boatehier for his Lordship that day, xiid.; to the buttery at Nonesuch, vs.

Item, 18 November, for an oz of tobacco, iis. vid....boatehier and a play, vis.

It is extremely difficult to say in modern terms what people paid for various things in Elizabeth's time—and remember that prices rose over so long a period as 1558-1603—but we can say that the public theatre near the end of her reign cost 1, 2, or 3 pence (depending on whether you were prepared to stand in The Pit or wanted to sit in the gallery or even on the stage itself), while one could buy a quart of small beer for a penny and a quart of good ale for 4 pence, two broadsides (usually containing songs) for a penny and a printed play or 180 pages of prose romance for a shilling or less, and for 3 pence one had one's choice of a pipeload of tobacco, a wherry ride on The Thames from Paul's Wharf to Westminster, or a really cheap meal "for your London Usurer, your stale Bachelor, and your thrifty Attorney" in an ordinary or low tavern with (as Thomas Dekker wrote) "rooms as full of company as a Jail."

The famous Sidney family has left us accounts of the 1560s and 1570s which give a hint as to prices in those days. For instance:

1572: For making a pair of crimson satin hose for Mr. Robert Sidney [aged 9], 10 s[hillings].

1574: Gowns of purple and white purled mockadoes and petticoats of frysadoes [imitation velvet and woollen cloth] for Mary Sidney [aged 13] and her sister Ambrosia [9], £6.

1576: 2 pairs long white hose, 16 s[hillings]. Velvet hat with a gold band and gold feather, 40 s[hillings]. (All this for Robert Sidney as Oxford undergraduate.)

1577: Black velvet, 25 s[hillings] a yard. White satin, 13 s[hillings] 4d [pence] a yard. Carnation velvet, 20 s[hillings]. carnation satin, 15 s[hillings]. For making a doublet of the carnation satin, 4 s[hillings]. Carnation lace, 4 s[hillings] 6d [pence] a yard, and 2 1/2 dozen carnation [covered] buttons, 2 s[hillings] and 6d [pence].

From servants (whom great lords overpaid then):
1573-1574: Cleaning your lordship's pew at Penshurst, 1 s[hilling]. Cleaning your lordship's boots at Canterbury, which he lent your lordship, 6 d [pence]. 'To them that played Robin Hood' in private theatricals, 3 s[hillings]. Various other prices are suggestive: 62 1/2 shillings for a c.1570 portrait painted of Sir Henry Sidney, 46 shillings for two volumes of Foxe's Book of Martyrs *in 1573-1574, three pounds for a falcon in 1571-1572, 8 shillings "to a tooth drawer that plucked out Mr. Robert his teeth" in 1573, one pound for a "Brasse graven for my Mistresses Marie and Margaret's grave stone" in 1563-1564, a schoolboy's pen and inkhorn in 1574 a shilling.*

William Harrison on the lower orders:

As for slaves and bondmen, we have none; nay, such is the privilege of our country by the especial grace of God and bounty of our princes, that if any come hither from other realms, so soon as they set foot on land they become so free of condition as their masters, whereby all note of servile bondage is utterly removed from them, wherein we resemble (not the Germans, who had slaves also, though such as in respect of the slaves of other countries, might well be reputed free), but the old Indians and the Taprobanes, who supposed it a great injury to Nature to make or suffer them to be bond, whom she in her wonted course doth product and bring forth free.

This fourth and last sort of people, therefore, have neither voice nor authority in the commonwealth, but are to be ruled and not to rule other; yet they are not altogether neglected, for in cities and corporate towns, for default of yeomen, they are fain to make up their inquests of such manner of people. And in villages, they are commonly made churchwardens, sidesmen, aleconners, now and then constables, and many times enjoy the name of headboroughs [constables]. Unto this sort, also, may our great swarms of idle serving-men be referred, of whom there runneth a proverb, "Young serving-men, old beggars," because service is non heritage. These men are profitable to none; for, if their masters, to their friends, and to themselves; for by them, oftentimes their masters are encouraged unto unlawful exactions of their tenants, their friends brought into poverty by their rents enhanced, and they themselves brought to confusion by their own prodigality and errors. . . .

Sir Thomas Wilson's The State of England *(1600) states that*

there are many yeomen in divers Provinces in England which are able yearly to despend betwixt 3 or 5 hundred pound yearly by their lands and Leases and some twice and some thrice as much.

John Ballyston of Norfolk was described in Elizabethan archives as

very rich in stock and offereth to buy the farm he useth at 2,050 pounds.

William Scarlet of Shropshire bought his lands for 2000 pounds. Richard Elmhurst of Yorkshire was so rich he had Sir George Ratcliffe in debt to him to the tune of 2200 pounds. These were exceptions. A yeoman was comfortable at 40 or 50 pounds a year and rich at 100 or 200. A nobleman with 2000 pounds was thought to be very well off indeed.

Jean de Beau Chesne's book on handwriting was translated by John Baildon (1571) and gives us examples of the English Secretary Hand and the fashionable new Italic handwriting which Venetian printers had made the basis of Italic type. (Most Elizabethan handwriting was not so neat!)

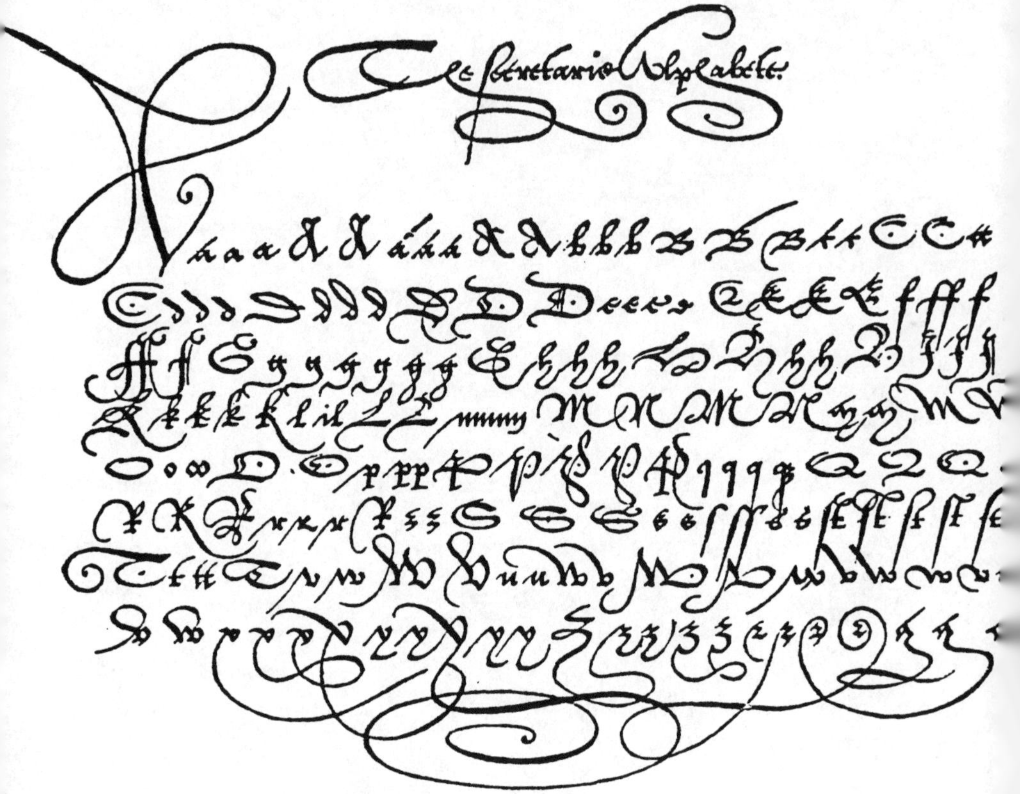
The secretarie Alphabete:

And the Italian handwriting:

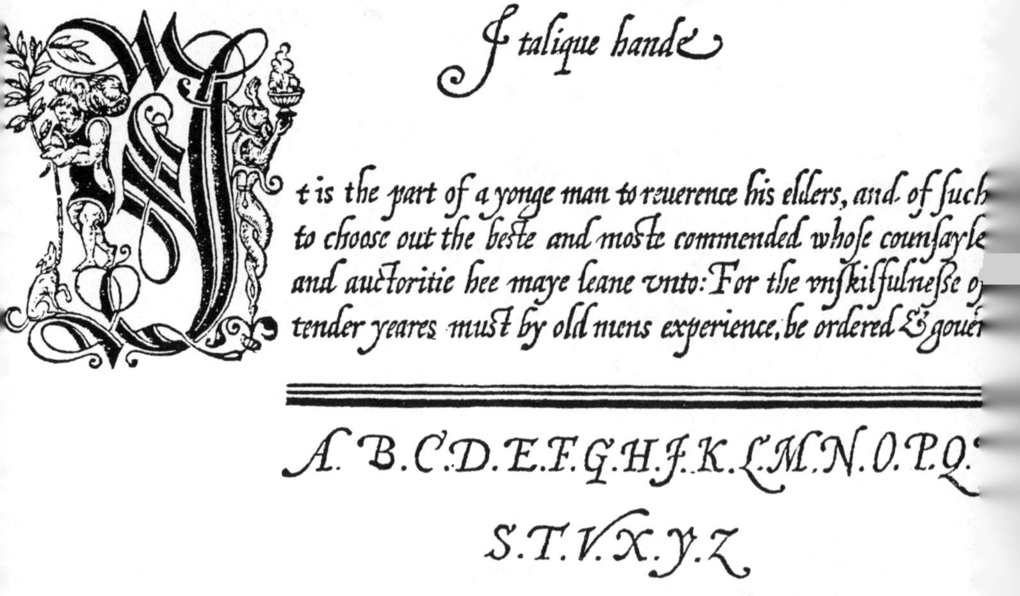
Italique hande

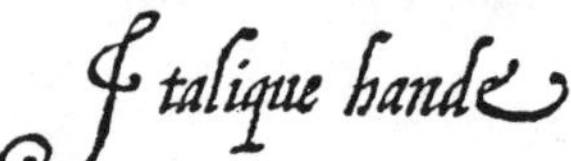

It is the part of a yonge man to reuerence his elders, and of such
to choose out the beste and moste commended whose counsayle
and auctoritie hee maye leane vnto: For the vnskilfulnesse o
tender yeares must by old mens experience, be ordered & gouer

A. B. C. D. E. F. G. H. J. K. L. M. N. O. P. Q.
S. T. V. X. Y. Z.

A stocks to stay sure, and safely detain
Lazy lewd loiterers, that laws do offend,
Impudent persons, thus punished with pain,
Hardly for all this, do mean to amend.

Fetters or shackles serve to make fast
Male malefactors that on mischief do muse,
Until the learned laws do quit or do cast
Such subtle searchers as all evil do use.

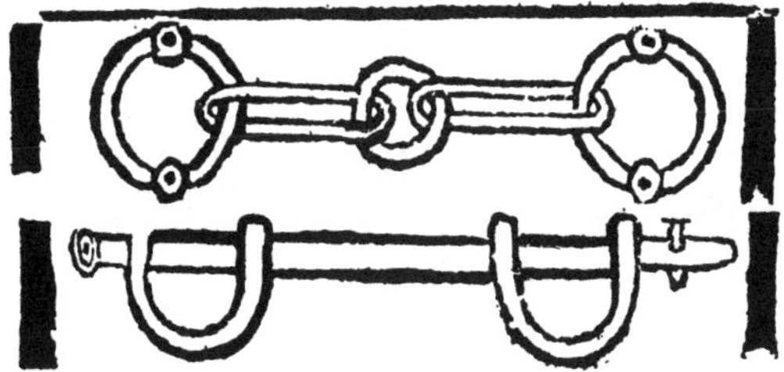

Criminals in the stocks in an old pamphlet, with warning verses and shackles.

The Underclasses

"There are cozeners abroad," says someone in The Winter's Tale, *"therefore it behooves men to be wary." Many were the popular pamphlets that warned people of cozenage, cony-catching, the danger of being gulled. They were the beginning of a whole school of popular literature which is not extinct even in our day. This section will give you some idea of some of the contents of pamphlets about the criminal classes and the poor.*

"I see this is the time that the unjust man doth thrive," says Shakespeare's Autolycus, that "snapper-up of unconsidered trifles." He avers that "every lane's end, every shop, church, [court] session, hanging" gives opportunity to the rogue.

In truth wars and other social dislocations had filled the Elizabethan streets and highways with rogues and vagabonds and various Poor Laws and attempts to put down "masterless men" (such as touring actors not enjoying some noble's patronage) were passed by an ever more worried government. William Harrison refers to a law of 1572:

With us the poor is commonly divided into three sorts, so that some are poor by impotency, as the fatherless child, the aged, blind and lame, and the diseased person that is judged to be incurable: the second are poor by casualty, as the wounded soldier, the decayed householder, and the sick person visited with grievous and painful diseases: the third consisteth of thriftless poor, as the rioter that hath consumed all, the vagabond that will abide nowhere but runneth up and down from place to place, and finally the rogue and the strumpet.... Such as are idle beggars through their own default are of two sorts, and continue their estates either by casual or mere voluntary means. Those that are such by casual means are in the beginning justly to be referred either to the first or second sort of poor aforementioned, but, degenerating into the thriftless sort, they do what they can to continue their misery, and, with such impediments as they have, to stray and wander about, as creatures abhorring all labour and honest exercise. Certes I call these casual means in the respect of the original of their poverty, but the continuance of the same, from whence they will not be delivered, such is their own ungracious lewdness and forward disposition. The voluntary means proceed from outward causes, as by making of corrosives and applying the same to the more fleshy parts of their bodies, and also laying of ratsbane, spearwort, crowfoot and such like unto their whole members, thereby to raise pitiful and odious sores and move the hearts of the goers by such places where they lie, to yearn at their misery, and thereupon bestow large alms upon them. How artificially they beg, what forcible speech, and how they select and choose out words of vehemency whereby they do in manner conjure or adjure the goer-by to pity their cases, I pass over to remember, as judging the name of God and Christ to be more conversant in the mouths of none and yet the presence of the heavenly Majesty further off from no men than from this ungracious company. Which maketh me to think that punishment is far meeter for them than liberality or alms, and sith Christ willeth us chiefly to have a regard to Himself and His poor members.

Unto this nest is another sort to be referred, more sturdy than the rest, which, having sound and perfect limbs, do yet notwithstanding sometime counterfeit the possession of all sorts of diseases. Divers times in their apparel also they will be like serving-men or labourers: oftentimes they can play the mariners and seek for ships which they never lost. But in fine they are all thieves and caterpillars in the commonwealth, and by the word of God not permitted to eat, sith they do but lick the sweat from the true labourer's brows, and bereave the godly poor of that which is due unto them, to maintain their excess, consuming the charity of well-disposed people bestowed upon them, after a most wicked and detestable manner.

It is not yet full threescore years since this trade began: but how it hath prospered since that time it is easy to judge, for they are now supposed, of one sex and another, to amount unto above 10,000 persons, as I have heard reported. Moreover, in counterfeiting the Egyptian rogues, they have devised a language among themselves, which they name 'canting,' but others 'pedlar's French,' a speech compact thirty years since of English and a great number of odd words of their own devising, without all order or reason, and yet such it is as none but themselves are able to understand. The first deviser thereof was hanged by the neck—a just reward, no doubt, for his deserts, and a common end to all of that profession.

Having given the actual names of various wandering criminals, including "above a hundred of Irishmen and women that wander about and beg for their living, that hath come over these two years" as a result of the depridations following the failure of the Desmond Rebellion, and having gone into some detail about the itinerant thieves and beggars of Essex, Middlesex, Sussex, Surrey, and Kent, the author of A Caveat for Common Cursetors *provides an extraordinary insight into their "pelting speech," finishing with the story of one of these underworld characters.*

Here I set before the good reader the lewd, lousy language of these loitering lusks and lazy lorels, wherewith they buy and sell the common people as they pass through the country; which language they term pedlars' French, an unknown tongue only but to these bold, beastly, bawdy beggars and vain vagabonds, being half mingled with English when it is familiarly talked. And first placing things by their proper names as an introduction to this peevish speech:

nab, a head

nab-cheat, a hat or cap

a fambling-cheat, a ring on thy hand

glaziers, eyes
a smelling-cheat, a nose
gan, a mouth
a prattling-cheat, a tongue
crashing-cheats, teeth
hearing-cheats, ears
fambles, hands

stampers, shoes
a muffling-cheat, a napkin
a belly-cheat, an apron
duds, clothes
a lag of duds, buck of clothes
a slate or *slates,* a sheet or sheets
libbege, a bed
bung, a purse
lour, money
mint, gold
a bord, a shilling
half-a-bord, sixpence
flag, a groat
a win, a penny
a make, a halfpenny
booze, drink
bene, good
beneship, very good
queer, nought
a gage, a quart pot
a skew, a cup
pannam, bread
cassan, cheese
yarrum, milk
lap, buttermilk or whey
peck, meat

quarroms, a body

prat, a buttock
stamps, legs
a caster, a cloak
a togman, a coat
a commission, a shirt
drawers, hosen

grannam, corn
a lowing-cheat, a cow
a bleating-cheat, a calf or sheep
a prancer, a horse
autem, a church
Solomon, a altar or mass
patrico, a priest
nosegent, a nun
a gybe, a writing
a jark, a seal
a ken, a house
a stalling-ken, a house that will receive stolen ware
a boozing ken, a ale-house
a libken, a house to lie in
a libbege, a bed
glimmer, fire
Rome-booze, wine
lage, water
a skipper, a barn
strummel, straw
a gentry cove's ken, a noble or gentleman's house
a jigger, a door
bufe, a dog
the lightmans, the day
the darkmans, the night

From a ballad sung in a Jonson play (to the old tune of Pagginton's Pound):

Repent then, repent you, for better, for worse,
And kiss not the gallows for cutting a purse.
Youth, youth, thou hadst better been starv'd by thy nurse,
Than live to be hanged for cutting a purse.

Robert Greene sold a lot of pamphlets fulminating against lowlife persons of all sorts. Here he is after the ballad singers who draw crowds which cutpurses and pickpockets "work."

This trade, or rather unsufferable loitering quality, in singing of ballets and songs at the doors of such houses where plays are used, as also in open markets and other places of this city where is most resort, which is nothing else but a sly fetch [clever ruse] to draw many together, who, listening unto a harmless ditty, afterward walk home to their houses with heavy hearts: from such as are hereof true witnesses to their cost, do I deliver this example. A subtle fellow, belike emboldened by acquaintance with the former deceit, or else, being but a beginner to practise the same, calling certain of his companions together, would try whether he could attain to be master of his art or no, by taking a great many of fools with one train. But let his intent and what else beside remain to abide the censure after the matter is heard, and come to Gracious Street, where his villainous prank was performed. A roguing mate and such another with him, were there got upon a stall singing of ballets, which belike was some pretty toy, for very many gathered about to hear it, and divers buying, as their affections served, drew to their purses and paid the singers for them. The sly mate and his fellows, who were dispersed among them that stood to hear the songs, well noted where every man that bought put up his purse again, and to such as would not buy, counterfeit warning was sundry times given by the rogue and his associate, to beware of the cut-purse, and look to their purses, which made them often feel where their purses were, either in sleeve, hose, or at girdle, to know whether they were safe or no. Thus the crafty copesmates were acquainted with what they most desired, and as they were scattered, by shouldering, thrusting, feigning to let fall something, and other wily tricks fit for their purpose, here one lost his purse, there another had his pocket picked, and to say all in brief, at one instant, upon the complaint of one or two that saw their purses were gone, eight more in the same company found themselves in like predicament. Some angry, others sorrowful and all greatly discontented, looking about them, knew not who to suspect or challenge, in that the villains themselves that had thus beguiled them, made show that they had sustained like loss. But one angry fellow, more impatient than all the rest, he falls upon the ballad singer, and beating him with his fists well favouredly, says, if he had not listened to his singing, he had not lost his purse, and therefore would not be otherwise persuaded but that they two and the cut-purses were compacted together. The rest that had lost their purses likewise and saw that so many complain together, they jump in opinion with the other fellow, and begin to tug and hail the ballad singers, when one after one, the false knaves began to shrink away with the purses. By means of some officer then being there present, the two rogues were had before a Justice, and upon his discreet examination made, it was found that they and the cut-purses were compacted together, and that by this unsuspected villainy, they had deceived many. The fine food-taker himself, with one or two more that company, was not long after apprehended, when I doubt not but they had their reward answerable to their deserving, for I hear of their journey westward, but not of their return. Let this forewarn those that listen to singing in the streets.

It may surprise you to find a few very modern-sounding slang words in this Elizabethan thieves' language:

A Canter in Prose

Stow you, bene cose; and cut benar whids and bing we to Romeville to nip a bong. So shall we have lowre for the bowsing ken, and when we bing back to the Dewsaville, we will filch some duds off the ruffmans, or mill the ken for a lag of duds.

Thus in English

Stow you, bene cose: hold your peace, good fellow.
And cut benar whids: and speak better words.
And bing we to Romeville: and go we to London.
To nip a bong: to cut a purse.
So shall we have lowre: so shall we have money.
For the bowsing ken: for the alehouse.
And when we bing back: And when we come back.
To the Dewsaville: into the country.
We will filch some duds: we will steal some clothes.
Off the ruffmans: from the hedges.
Or mill the ken: or rob the house.
For a lag of duds: for a lot of clothes.

A sketch of one of the many kinds of Elizabethan criminals. From such humble beginnings the novel had one of its principal wellsprings.

A Abraham Man

These Abraham men be those that feign themselves to have been made, and have been kept either in Bethlem or in some other prison a good time, and not one amongst twenty that ever came in prison for any such cause. Yet will they say how piteously and most extremely they have been beaten and dealt withal. Some of these be merry and very pleasant; they will dance and sing. Some others be as cold and reasonable to talk withal. These beg money. Either when they come at farmers' houses, they will demand bacon, either cheese, or wool, or anything that is worth money. And if they espy small company within, they will with fierce countenance demand somewhat. Where for fear the maids will give them largely, to be rid of them.

If they may conveniently come by any cheat, they will pick and steal, as the upright man or rogue, poultry or linen. And all women that wander be at their commandment. Of all that ever I saw of this kind, one naming himself Stradling is the craftiest and most dissemblingest knave. He is able with his tongue and usage to deceive and abuse the wisest man that is. And surely for the proportion of his body, with every member thereunto appertaining, it cannot be amended. But as the proverb is, 'God hath done His part.' This Stradling saith he was the Lord Sturton's man; and when he was executed, for very pensiveness of mind he fell out of his wit, and so continued a year after and more; and that with the very grief and fear, he was taken with a marvellous palsy, that both head and hands will shake when he talketh with any and that space or fast, whereby he is much pitied, and getteth greatly. And if I had not demanded of others, both men and women that commonly walketh as he doth, and known by them his deep dissimulation, I never had understand the same. And thus I end with these kind of vagabonds.

There were many busy pamphlet writers of the late Elizabethan period but probably the best and most various of them all was Robert Greene, author of The Black Book's Messenger. *It was one of many pamphlets from a tireless University Wit who tried his hand at almost all the commercial genres of his time and whose name sold his plays, romances, pamphlets, etc., to an appreciative public, making him famous, but never rich. Note the lively style—and the moral at the end.*

To the Courteous Reader, Health

Gentlemen, I know you have long expected the coming forth of my *Black Book* I commit to your courteous censures, being written before I fell sick, which I thought good in the meantime to send you as a fairing, discoursing Ned Browne's villainies, which are too many to be described in my *Black Book.*

I had thought to have joined with this treatise a pithy discourse of the repentance of a cony-catcher lately executed out of Newgate, yet forasmuch as the method of the one is so far differing from the other, I altered my opinion, and the rather for that the one died resolute and desperate, the other penitent and passionate. For the cony-catcher's repentance, which shall shortly be published, it contains a passion of great importance, first, how he was given over from all grace and godliness, and seemed to have no spark of the fear of God in him; yet, nevertheless, through the wonderful working of God's spirit, even in the dungeon at Newgate the night before he died, he so repented him from the bottom of his heart, that it may well beseem parents to have it for their children, masters for their servants, and to be perused of every honest person with great regard.

And for Ned Browne, of whom my *Messenger* makes report, he was a man infamous for his bad course of life and well known about London. He was in outward show a gentlemanlike companion, attired very brave, and to shadow his villainy the more would nominate himself to be a marshal-man, who when he had nipped a bung or cut a good purse, he would steal over into the Low Countries, there to taste three or four stoups of Rhenish wine, and then come over forsooth a brave soldier. But at last he leapt at a daisy for his loose kind of life. And therefore imagine you now see him in his own person, standing in a great bay window with a halter about his neck ready to be hanged, desperately pronouncing this his whole course of life, and confesseth as followeth.

Yours in all courtesy, R[obert]. G[reene].

A Table of the Words of Art Lately Devised by Ned Browne and his Associates to Crossbite the Old Phrases Used in the Manner of Cony-Catching

He that draws the fish to the bait, *the beater.*
The tavern where they go, *the bush.*
The fool that is caught, *the bird.*
Cony-catching to be called *bat-fowling.*
The win to be called *the shrap.*
The cards to be called *the lime-twigs.*
The fetching in a cony, *beating the bush.*
The good ass if he be won: *stooping to the lure.*
If he keep aloof: *a haggard.*
The verser in cony-catching is called *the retriever.*
And the barnacle *the pot-hunter.*

[I'll translate the Vergilian tag in the following, but try the Elizabethan slang and allusions on your own!]

The Life and Death of Ned Browne,
a Notable Cutpurse and Cony-Catcher

If you think, Gentlemen, to hear a repentant man speak, or to tell a large tale of his penitent sorrows, ye are deceived. For as I have ever lived lewdly, so I mean to end my life as resolutely, and not by a cowardly confession to attempt the hope of a pardon. Yet, in that I was famous in my life for my villainies, I will at my death profess myself as notable, by discoursing to you all merrily the manner and method of my knaveries, which, if you hear without laughing, then after my death call me base knave, and never have me in remembrance.

Know therefore, Gentlemen, that my parents were honest, of good report and no little esteem amongst their neighbours, and sought (if good nurture and education would have served) to have made me an honest man. But as one self same ground brings forth flowers and thistles, so of a sound stock proved an untoward scion; and of a virtuous father, a most vicious son. It boots little to rehearse the petty sins of my nonage, as disobedience to my parents, contempt of good counsel, despising of mine elders, filching, pettilashery, and such trifling toys. But with these follies I injured myself, till, waxing in years, I grew into greater villainies. For when I came to eighteen years old, what sin was it that I would not commit with greediness, what attempt so bad, that I would not endeavour to execute! Cutting of purses, stealing of horses, lifting, picking of locks, and all other notable cozenages. Why, I held them excellent qualities, and accounted him unworthy to live, that could not, or durst not, live by such damnable practices. Yet, as sin too openly manifested to the eye of the magistrate is either sore revenged or soon cut off, so I, to prevent that, had a net wherein to dance, and divers shadows to colour my knaveries withal, as I would title myself with the name of a fencer, and make gentlemen believe that I picked a living out by that mystery, whereas, God wot, I had no other fence but with my short knife and a pair of purse strings, and with them in troth many a bout have I had in my time. In troth? Oh, what a simple oath was this to confirm a man's credit withal! Why, I see the halter will make a man holy, for whilst God suffered me to flourish, I scorned to disgrace my mouth with so small an oath as *In faith;* but I rent God in pieces, swearing and forswearing by every part of his body, that such as heard me rather trembled at mine oaths, than feared my braves, and yet for courage and resolution I refer myself to all them that have ever heard of my name.

Thus animated to do wickedness, I fell to take delight in the company of harlots, amongst whom, as I spent what I got, so I suffered not them I was acquainted withal to feather their nests, but would at my pleasure strip them of all that they had. What bad woman was there about London, whose champion I would not be for a few crowns, to fight, swear, and stare in her behalf, to the abuse of any that should do justice upon her! I still had one or two in store to crossbite withal, which I used as snares to trap simple men in. For if I took but one suspiciously in her company, straight I versed upon him, and crossbite him for all the money in his purse. By the way, with sorrow cannot help to save me, let me tell you a merry jest how once I crossbite a maltman, that would needs be so wanton as when he had shut his malt to have a wench, and thus the jest fell out.

A Pleasant Tale how Ned Browne Crossbite a Maltman

This *senex fornicator*, this old lecher, using continually into Whitechapel, had a haunt into Petticoat Lane to a trugging-house there, and fell into great familiarity with a good wench that was a friend of mine, who one day revealed unto me how she was well thought on by a maltman, a wealthy old churl, and that ordinarily twice a week he did visit her, and therefore bade me plot some means to fetch him over for some crowns. I was not to seek for a quick invention, and resolved at his coming to crossbite him, which was, as luck served, the next day. Monsieur the maltman, coming according to his custom, was no sooner secretly shut in the chamber with the wench, but I came stepping in with a terrible look, swearing as if I meant to have challenged the earth to have opened and swallowed me quick, and presently fell upon her and beat her. Then I turned to the maltman, and lent him a blow or two, for he would take no more. He was a stout stiff old tough churl, and then I railed upon them both, and objected to him how long he had kept my wife, how my neighbours could tell me of it, how the Lane thought ill of me for suffering it, and now that I had myself taken them together, I would make both him and her smart for it before we parted.

The old fox that knew the ox by the horn, was subtle enough to spy a pad in the straw, and to see that we went about to crossbite him, wherefore he stood stiff, and denied all, and although the whore cunningly on her knees weeping did confess it, yet the maltman faced her down, and said she was an honest woman for all him, and that this was but a cozenage compacted between her and me to verse and crossbite him for some piece of money for amends, but sith he knew himself clear, he would never grant to pay one penny.

I was straight in mine oaths, and braved him with sending for the constable, but in vain. All our policies could not draw one cross from this crafty old car, till I, gathering my wits together, came over his fallows thus. I kept him still in the chamber, and sent, as though I had sent for the constable, for a friend of mine, an ancient cozener, and one that had a long time been a knight of the post. Marry, he had a fair cloak and a damask coat, that served him to bail men withal. To this perjured companion I sent to come as a constable, to make the maltman stoop, who, ready to execute any villainy that I should plot, came speedily like an ancient wealthy citizen, and, taking the office of a constable in hand, began very sternly to examine the matter, and to deal indifferently, rather favouring the maltman than me. But I complained how long he had kept my wife. He answered, I lied, and that it was a cozenage to crossbite him of his money. Mas[ter] Constable cunningly made this reply to us both:

'My friends, this matter is bad, and truly I cannot in conscience but look into it. For you, Browne, you complain how he hath abused your wife a long time, and she partly confesseth as much. He, who seems to be an honest man, and of some countenance amongst his neighbours, forswears it, and saith it is but a device to strip him of his money. I know not whom to believe, and therefore this is my best course because the one of you shall not laugh the other to scorn. I'll send you all three to the Counter, so to answer it before some justice that may take examination of the matter.'

The maltman, loath to go to prison, and yet unwilling to part from any pence, said he was willing to answer the matter before any man of worship, but he desired the constable to favour him that he might not go to ward, and he would send for a brewer a friend of his to be his bail.

'In faith,' says this cunning old cozener, 'you offer like an honest man, but I cannot stay so long till he be sent for, but if you mean, as you protest, to answer the matter, then leave some pawn, and I will let you go wither you will while tomorrow, and then come to my house here hard by at a grocer's shop, and you and I will go before a justice, and then clear yourself as you may.' The maltman, taking this crafty knave to be some substantial citizen, thanked him for his friendship and gave him a seal-ring that he wore on his forefinger, promising the next morning to meet him at his house.

As soon as my friend had the ring, away walks he, and while we stood brabbling together, he went to the brewer's house with whom this maltman traded and delivered the brewer the ring as a token from the maltman, saying he was in trouble, and that he desired him by that token to send him ten pound. The brewer, seeing an ancient citizen bringing the message, and knowing the maltman's ring, stood upon no terms, sith he knew his chapman would and was able to answer it again if it were a brace of hundred pounds, delivered him the money without any more ado; which ten pound at night we shared betwixt us, and left the maltman to talk with the brewer about the repayment.

Tush, this was one of my ordinary shifts, for I was holden in my time the most famous crossbiter in all London.

Well, at length as wedding and hanging comes by destiny, I would, to avoid the speech of the world, be married forsooth, and keep a house. But, Gentlemen, I hope you that hear me talk of marriage, do presently imagine that sure she was some virtuous matron that I chose out. Shall I say, my conscience, she was a little snout-fair, but the commonest harlot and hackster that ever made fray under the shadow of Coleman Hedge. Wedded to this trull, what villainy could I devise but she would put in practice, and yet, though she could foist a pocket well, and get me some pence, and lift now and then for a need, and with the lightness of her heels bring me in some crowns, yet I waxed weary, and stuck to the old proverb, that change of pasture makes fat calves. I thought that in living with me two years she lived a year too long, and therefore, casting mine eye on a pretty wench, a man's wife well known about London, I fell in love with her, and that so deeply that I broke the matter to her husband, that I loved his wife, and must needs have her, and confirmed it with many oaths, that if he did not consent to it, I would be his death. Whereupon her husband, a kind knave, and one every way as base a companion as myself, agreed to me, and we bet a bargain, that I should have his wife, and he should have mine, conditionally that I should give him five pounds to boot, which I promised, though he never had it. So we, like two good horse-coursers, made a chop and change, and swapped up a roguish bargain, and so he married my wife and I his. Thus, Gentlemen, did I neither fear God nor his laws, nor regarded honesty, manhood, or conscience.

But these be trifles and venial sins. Now, sir, let me boast of myself a little, in that I came to the credit of a high lawyer, and with my sword freebooted abroad in the country like a cavalier on horseback, wherein I did excel for subtlety. For I had first for myself an artificial hair, and a beard so naturally made, that I could talk, dine, and sup in it, and yet it should never be spied. I will tell you there rests no greater villainy than in this practice, for I have robbed a man in the morning, and come to the same inn and baited, yea, and dined with him the same day; and for my horse that he might not be known I could ride him one part of the day like a goodly gelding with a large tail hanging to his fetlocks, and the other part of the day I could make him a cut, for I had an artificial tail so cunningly counterfeited, that the ostler when he dressed him could not perceive it. By these policies I little cared for hues and cries, but straight with disguising myself would outslip them all, and as for my cloak, it was tarmosind, as they do term it, made with two outsides that I could turn it how I list, for howsoever I wore it the right side still seemed to be outward. I remember how prettily once I served a priest, and because one death dischargeth all, and is as good as a general pardon, hear now I served him.

Robert Greene's A Notable Discovery of Cozenage *(1591) is another of his very popular works, addressed to "Young Gentlemen, Merchants, Apprentices,*

Farmers, and Plain Country Men" who want the inside story on London's "roguish arts." Greene knew his subject and his audience equally well.

After a disquisition on the art of cony-catching, Greene provides the cant:

A Table of the Words of Art Used in the Effecting These Base Villainies, Wherein is Discovered the Nature of Every Term, Being Proper to None But to the Professors Thereof

1. High Law: robbing by the highway side.
2. Sacking Law: lechery.
3. Cheating Law: play at false dice.
4. Cross-Biting Law: cozenage by whores.
5. Cony-Catching Law: cozenage by cards.
6. Versing Law: cozenage by false gold.
7. Figging Law: cutting of purses and picking of pockets.
8. Barnard's Law: a drunken cozenage by cards.

These are the eight laws of villainy, leading the high way to infamy: In High Law

The thief is called a high lawyer.
He that setteth the watch, a scripper.
He that standeth to watch, an oak.
He that is robbed, the martin.
When he yieldeth, stooping.

In Sacking Law

The bawd, if it be a woman, a pander.
The bawd, if a man, an apple squire.
The whore, a commodity.
The whorehouse, a trugging place.

In Cheating Law

Pardon me, gentlemen, for although no man could better than myself discover this law and his terms and the name of their cheats, barred dice, flats, forgers, langrets, gourds, demies, and many others, with their nature, and the crosses and contraries to them upon advantage, yet for some special reasons herein I will be silent.

In Cross-Biting Law

The whore, the traffic.
The man that is brought in, the simpler.
The villains that take them, the cross-biters.

In Cony-Catching Law

The party that taketh up the cony, the setter.
He that placeth the game, the verser.
He that is cozened, the cony.
He that comes in to them, the barnacle.
The money that is won, purchase.

In Versing Law

He that bringeth him in, the verser.
The poor country man, the cousin
And the drunkard that comes in, the suffer.

In Figging Law

The cutpurse, a nip.
He that is half with him, the snap.
The knife, a cuttle-bung.
The pickpocket, a foist.
He that faceth the man, the stale.
Taking the purse, drawing.
Spying of him, smoking.
The purse, the bung.
The money, the shells.
The act doing, striking.

In Barnard's Law

He that fetcheth in the man, the taker.
He that is taken, the cousin.
The landed man, the verser.
The drunken man, the barnard.
And he that makes the fray, the rutter.

Cum multis aliis quae nunc praescribere longum est.
[With many others it would take a long time to set down.]

These quaint terms do these base arts use to shadow their villainy withal, for *multa latent quae non patent* [many things are hidden which are not obvious]—obscuring their filthy crafts with these fair colors, that the ignorant may not espy what their subtlety is. But their end will be like their beginning, hatched in Cain and consumed in Judas. And so, bidding them adieu to the devil and you farewell in God, I end. And now to the art of crossbiting.

The art of Cross-Biting

The cross-biting law is a public profession of shameless cozenage, mixed with incestuous whoredoms, as ill as was practiced in Gomorrah or Sodom, though not after the same unnatural manner. For the method of their mischievous art (with blushing cheeks and trembling heart let it be spoken) is that these villainous vipers, unworthy the name of men, base rogues (yet why do I term them so well?) being outcasts from God, vipers of the world and an excremental reversion of sin, doth consent—nay, constrain—their wives to yield the use of their bodies to other men, that, taking them together, he may crossbite the party of all the crowns he presently can make. And that the world may see their monstrous practices, I will briefly set down the manner.

They have sundry preys that they call simplers, which are men fondly and wantonly given, whom for a penalty of their lust they fleece of all that ever they have: some merchants, prentices, serving-men, gentlemen, yeomen, farmers, and of all degrees.

And this is their form: There are resident in London and the suburbs certain men attired like gentlemen, brave fellows but basely minded, who, living in want, as their last refuge fall unto this crossbiting law and to maintain themselves either marry with some stale whore or else forsooth keep one as their friend. And these persons be commonly men of the eight laws before rehearsed: either high lawyers, versers, nips, cony-catchers, or such of the like fraternity. These, when their other trades fail (as the cheater when he hath no cousin to grime with his stop dice, or the high lawyer when he hath not set match to ride about [no one to rob on the highway] and the nip when there is no term, fair, nor time of great assembly) then to maintain the main chance, they use the benefit of their wives or friends to the cross-biting of such as lust after their filthy enormities. Some simple men are drawn on by subtle means, which never intended such a bad matter.

In summer evenings and in winter nights these traffics—these common trulls, I mean—walk abroad, either in the fields or streets that are commonly haunted, as stales to draw men unto hell. And afar off, as their attending apple squires, certain cross-biters stand aloof, as if they knew them not. Now, so many men, so many affections. Some unruly mates that place their content in lust, letting slip the liberty of their eyes on their painted faces, feed upon their unchaste beauties till their hearts be set on fire. Then come they to these dishonest minions and court them with many sweet words. Alas, their loves need no long suits, for they are forthwith entertained; and either they go to the tavern to seal up the match with a pottle of hippocras [spiced wine] or straight she carries him to some bad place and there picks his pocket. Or else the cross-biters comes swearing in and so outface the dismayed companion that rather than he would be brought in question he would disburse all that he present hath, or possible may get, to their content.

But this is but an easy cozenage. Some other meeting with one of that profession in the street will question if she will drink with him a pint of wine. Their trade is never to refuse, and if for manners they do, it is but once. And then scarce shall they be warm in the room but in comes a terrible fellow with a side hair and a fearful beard, as though he were of Polyphemus' cut. And he comes frowning in and saith, "What hast thou to do, base knave, to carry my sister (or my wife) to the tavern? By his 'ouns [By God's wounds] you infamous whore, 'tis some of your companions, and I will have you both before the justice, deputy, or constable to be examined."

The poor servingman, apprentice, farmer, or whatsoever he is, seeing such a terrible huff-snuff, swearing with his dagger in his hand, is fearful both of him and to be brought in trouble, and therefore speaks kindly and courteously to him and desires him to be content; he meant no harm. The whore, that hath tears at command, falls aweeping and cries him mercy. At this submission of them both, he triumphs like a braggart and will take no composition. Yet at the last, through the entreaty of other his companions that comes in like strangers, he is pacified with some forty shillings; and the poor man goes sorrowful away, sighing out that which Solomon said in his proverbs:

> A shameless woman hath honey in her lips and her throat as sweet as honey, her throat as soft as oil. But the end of her is more bitter than aloes, and her tongue is more sharp than a two-edged sword. Her feet go unto death, and her steps lead unto hell. [*Proverbs* V, 3-5.]

Again, these trulls, when they have gotten in a novice then straight they pick his purse. And then have they their cross-biters ready, to whom they convey the money, and so offer themselves to be searched. But the poor man is so outfaced by these cross-biting ruffians that he is glad to go away content with his loss. yet are these easy practices. Ah, might the justices send out espials [spies] in the night, they should see how these streetwalkers will jet [strut] in rich-guarded gowns, quaint periwigs, ruffs of the largest size (quarter and half deep) gloried richly with blue starch, their cheeks dyed with sulfuring water. And thus are they tricked up, and either walk like stales up and down the streets or else stand like the devil's *siquis* [advertisement] at a tavern or alehouse, as if who should say, "If any be so minded for to satisfy his filthy lust, to lend me his purse and the devil his soul, let him come in and be welcome."

Now, sir, comes by a country farmer, walking from his inn to perform some business. And seeing such a gorgeous damsel, he, wondering at such a brave wench, stands staring her on the face. Or perhaps doth but cast a glance and bid her good speed (as plain, simple swains have their lusting humors as well as others). The trull, straight beginning her *exordium* with a smile, saith, "How now, my friend, what want you? Would you speak with anybody here?"

If the fellow hath any bold spirit, perhaps he will offer the wine. And then he is caught; 'tis enough. In he goes, and they are chambered. Then sends she for her husband or her friend, and there either the farmer's pocket is stripped or else the cross-biters fall upon him and threaten him with Bridewell [the workhouse] and the law. Then, for fear, he gives them all in his purse and makes them some bill to pay a sum of money at a certain day.

If the poor farmer be bashful and passeth by one of these shameless strumpets, then will she verse it with him and claim acquaintance of him and by some policy or other fall aboard on him and carry him into some house or other. If he but enter in at doors with her, though the poor farmer never kissed her, yet then the cross-biters, like vultures, will prey upon his purse and rob him of every penny. If there be any young gentleman that is a novice and hath not seen their trains, to him will some common filth that never knew love feign an ardent and honest affection till she and her cross-biters have versed him to the beggar's estate.

Ah, gentlemen, merchants, yeomen, and farmers, let this to you all and to every degree else be a caveat to warn you from lust, that your inordinate desire be not a means to impoverish your purses, discredit your good names, condemn your souls, but also that your wealth, gotten with the sweat of your brows or left by your parents as a patrimony, shall be a prey to those cozening cross-biters. Some fond men are so far in with these detestable trugs that they consume what they have upon them and find nothing but a Neapolitan favor [syphillis] for their labor. Read the seventh of Solomon's proverbs and there at large view the description of a shameless and impudent courtezan.

Yet is there another kind of cross-biting which is most pestilient, and that is thus: there lives about this town certain householders, yet mere shifters and cozeners, who, learning some insight in the civil law, walk abroad like paritors, summoners, and informers, being none at all either in office or credit. And they go spying about where any merchant or merchant's prentice, rich citizen, wealthy farmer, or other of good credit, either doth accompany with any woman familiarly or else hath gotten some maid with child. As men's natures be prone to sin, straight they come over his fallows thus: they send for him to a tavern and there open the matter unto him which they have cunningly learned out and tell him he must be presented to the [Court of ecclesiastical] Arches, and the citation shall be peremptorily served in his parish church. The party, afraid to have his credit cracked with the worshipful of the city and the rest of his neighbors, and grieving highly his wife should hear of it, straight takes composition with this cozener for some twenty mark—nay, I have heard of three-score pound cross-bitten at one time. And then the cozening informer or cross-biter promiseth him to wipe him out of the court and discharge him from the matter when it was neither known nor presented. So go they to the woman and fetch her off, if she be married. And though they have this gross sum, yet oftentimes they cross-bite her for more. Nay, thus do they fear citizens, prentices, and farmers that they find but any way suspicious of the like fault.

These cross-biting bawds, for no better I can term them, in that for lucre they conceal the sin and smother up lust, do not only enrich themselves mightily but also discredit, hinder, and prejudice the Court of the Arches and the officers belonging to the same. There are some purblind patches [fools] of that faculty that have their tenements purchased and their plate on their board very solemnly, who only get this gains by cross-biting, as afore is rehearsed. But leaving them to the deep insight and consideration of such as are appointed with justice to correct vice, again to the crew of my former cross-biters, whose fee simple to live upon is nothing but the following of common, dishonest, and idle trulls, and thereby they maintain themselves brave [handsomely] and the strumpets in handsome furniture.

And to end this art with an English demonstration, I will tell you a pretty tale alate performed in Bishopsgate Street. There was there five traffics, pretty but common housewives, that stood fast by a tavern door, looking if some prey would pass by for their purpose. Straight the eldest of them and most experienced in that law, named Mal B., spied a master of a ship coming all along.

"Here is a simpler," quoth she. "I'll verse him or hang me. Sir," quoth she, "Good even. What are you so liberal as to bestow on three good wenches that are dry a pint of wine?"

"In faith, fair women," quoth he, "I was never niggard for so much." And with that he takes one of them by the hand and carries them all into the tavern. There he bestowed cheer and hippocras upon them, drinking hard till the shot came to a noble, so that they three carousing to the gentleman made him somewhat tipsy; and then *Et venus in vinis, ignis in igne fuit.* [And just as Venus was in wine, so the glow of passion is in fire.] Well, night grew on and he would away, but this Mistress Mal B. stopped his journey thus: "Gentleman," quoth she, "this undeserved favor of yours makes us so deeply beholding unto you that our ability is not able any ways to make sufficient satisfaction. Yet, to show us kind in what we can, you shall not deny me this request to see my simple house before you go."

The gentleman, a little whittled [tipsy], consented and went with them. So the shot was paid and away they go. Without the tavern door stood two of their husbands, J.B. and J.R.; and they were made privy to the practice. Well, home goes this gentleman with these jolly huswives, stumbling; and at last he was welcome to Mistress Mal's house; and one of the three went into a chamber and got her to bed, whose name was A.B. After they had chatted awhile, the gentleman would have been gone, but she told him that before he went he should see all the rooms of her house and so led the gentleman up to the chamber where the party lay in bed.

"Who is here?" said the gentleman.

"Marry," saith Mal, "a good pretty wench, sir, and if you be not well, lie down by her. You can take no harm of her."

Drunkenness desires lust, and so the gentleman begins to dally. And away goes she with the candle, and at last he put off his clothes and went to bed. Yet he was not so drunk but he could after awhile remember his money; and feeling for his purse, all was gone and three links of his whistle ['s chain] were broken off. The sum that was in his purse was, in gold and silver, twenty nobles. As thus he was in a maze, though his head were well laden, in comes J.B., goodman of the house, and two other with him, and speaking somewhat loud.

"Peace, husband," quoth she, "there's one in bed. Speak not so loud."

"In bed!" saith he. "Gog's nouns [God's wounds] I'll go see."

"And so will I," said the other.

"You shall not," saith his wife, and strove against him.

But up goes he and his cross-biters with him, and seeing the gentleman in bed, out with his dagger and asked what base villain it was that there sought to dishonest his house. Well, he sent one of them for a constable and made the gentleman rise, who, half drunk, yet had that remembrance to speak fair and to entreat him to keep his credit. But no entreaty could serve, but to the Counter [jail] he must; and the constable must be sent for. Yet at last one of them entreated that the gentleman might be honestly used, and carried to a tavern to talk of the matter till a constable came.

"Tut," saith J.B., "I'll have the law upon him."

But the base cross-biter at last stooped, and to the tavern they go, where the gentleman laid his whistle to pawn for money and there bestowed as much of them as came to ten shillings and sat drinking and talking until the next tomorrow.

By that the gentleman had stolen a nap and, waking, it was daylight. And then, seeing himself compassed with these cross-biters, and remembering his night's work, soberly smiling, asked them if they knew what he was. They answered, "Not well."

"Why, then," quoth he, "you base, cozening rogues, you shall ere we part." And with that, drawing his sword, kept them into the chamber, desiring that the constable might be sent for. But this brave of his could not dismay Mistress Mal, for she had bidden a sharper brunt before. Witness the time of her martyrdom, when upon her shoulders was engraven the history of her whorish qualities. But she, replying, swore, seeing he was so lusty her husband should not put it up by no means.

"I will tell thee, thou base, cross-biting bawd," quoth he, "and you cozening companions, I serve a nobleman; and for my credit with him, I refer me to the penalty he will impose on you. For by God, I will make you an example to all cross-biters ere I end with you. I tell you, villains, I serve—" And with that he named his lord.

When the guilty whores and cozeners heard of his credit and service, they began humbly to entreat him to be good to them.

"Then," quoth he, "first deliver me my money."

They, upon that, gladly gave him all and restored the links of his chain. When he had all, he smiled and sware afresh that he would torment them for all this, that the severity of their punishment might be a caveat to others to beware of the like cozenage; and upon that knocked with his foot and said he would not let them go till he had a constable. Then, in generally they humbled themselves, and so recompensed the party that he agreed to pass over the matter, conditionally beside that they would pay the sixteen shillings he had spent in charges—which they also performed. The gentleman stepped his way and said, "You may see the old proverb fulfilled, *Fallere falentem non est fraus.*" [Cheating a cheat is no deceit.] But the poor cross-biters sat sighing a sorrowful heigh-ho.

Thus have I deciphered an odious practice not worthy to be named. And now, wishing all of what estate soever to beware of filthy lust and such damnable stales as draws men on to disordinate desires, and rather to spend their coin amongst honest company than to bequeath it unto such base cross-biters as prey upon men like ravens on dead carcasses, I end with this prayer—that cross-biting and cony-catching may be as little known in England as the eating of swine's flesh was among the Jews. Farewell....

This is a mock sermon in praise of thieves and thievery highway robbers forced a clergyman to give ex tempore *when he was made to stand and deliver both his purse and* A Sermon of Parson Haberdyne,

which he made at the commandment of certain thieves, after they had robbed him besides Hartley Row in Hampshire, in the fields there, standing upon a hill where a windmill had been, in the presence of the thieves that robbed him, as followeth.

I greatly marvel that any man will presume to dispraise thievery, and think the doers thereof to be worthy of death, considering it is a thing that cometh near unto virtue, being used of many in all countries, and commended and allowed of God himself. The which things, because I cannot compendiously show unto you at so short a warning and in so sharp a weather, I shall desire you, gentle audience of thieves, to take in good part these things that at this time cometh to my mind, not misdoubting that you of your good knowledge are able to add much more unto it than this which I shall now utter unto you.

First, fortitude and stoutness of courage and also boldness of mind, is commended of some men to be a virtue; which being granted, who is it then that will not judge thieves to be virtuous[ed]? For they be of all men most stout and hardy and most without fear. For thievery is a thing most usual among all men; for not only you that be here present, but many other in divers places, both men and women and children, rich and poor, are daily of this faculty (as the hangman of Tyburn can testify).

And that it is allowed of God himself, as it is evident in many stories of [the] Scriptures; for if you look in the whole course of the Bible, you shall find that thieves have been beloved of God. For Jacob, when he came out of Mesopotamia, did steal his uncle Laban's kids. The same Jacob did also steal his brothe[r] Esau's blessing. And yet God said, 'I have chosen Jacob and refused Esau.' The children of Israel, when they came out of Egypt, did steal Egyptians' jewels of silver and gold, as God commanded them so to do. David, in the days of Abiazar the high priest, did come into the temple and did steal the hallowed bread. And yet God said, 'David is a man after mine own heart.'

Christ himself, when he was here on the earth, did take an ass and a colt that was none of his; and you know that God said of him, 'This is my beloved Son, in Whom I delight.'

Thus you may see that God delighteth in thieves. But most of all I marvel that men can despise you thieves, whereas in all points (almost) you be like unto Christ himself. For Christ had no dwelling-place; no more have you. Christ went from town to town; and so do you. Christ was hated of all men, saving of his friends; and so are you. Christ was laid wait upon in many places;

and so are you. Christ at the length was caught; and so shall you be. He was brought before the judges; and so shall you be. He was condemned; and so shall you be. He was hanged; and so shall you be.

He went down into Hell; and so shall you do. Marry, in this one thing you differ from him, for he rose again and ascended into heaven; and so shall you never do, without God's great mercy, which God grant you! To whom, with the Father, and the Son and the Holy Ghost, be all honour and glory for ever and ever. Amen.

Thus his sermon being ended, they gave him his money again that they took from him, and two shillings to drink, for his sermon.

Edmund Spenser, in Ireland as secretary to the Lord Deputy (Lord Grey of Wilton), reported on the effects upon the Irish of the Desmond Rebellion (1579-1583):

Out of every corner of the woods and glens they came creeping forth upon their hands, for their legs would not bear them; they looked like little anatomies of death; they spoke like ghosts crying out of their graves; they did eat the dead carrions, happy where they could find them; yea and one another soon after, insomuch as the very carcasses they spared not to scrape out of their graves.... How then? Should the Irish have been quite rooted out? That were too bloody a course: and yet their continual rebellious deeds deserve little better.

Maire and Conor Cruise O'Brien's Concise History of Ireland *notes Spenser's horror at the execution of Murrough O'Brien at Limerick at which "an old woman, which was his foster-mother, took up his head whilst he was quartered, and sucked up all the blood running thereout, saying that the earth was not worthy to drink it." The O'Briens comment:*

By Spenser's standards, to behead and quarter Murrough was not barbarous, but to drink his blood *was* barbarous, and invited such further beheadings and quarterings as might be necessary to put an end to such practices and establish a civil Ireland, subdued and largely settled from England. There can be no doubt that Spenser and his friends genuinely conceived themselves to be engaged on a mission of civilization, and they felt their own landed acquisitions to be a legitimate reward for their part in this mission. The conquest of Ireland provided the psychological basis, as well as part of the material basis and training, for the colonization of a great part of the world. The young captain of 'certain bands' referred to by Lord Grey at Smerwick ["who fell straight to execution...six hundred slain"] was to be the great Walter Raleigh who planned the first English Colonies in America.

A satire in Gaelic called in English The Parliament of Clan Thomas *may or may not have been written in the Elizabethan period but certainly portrays the peasantry that* passed their lives during every king's reign waiting on the nobility, and so they lived until the time of Elizabeth, daughter of Henry, the eighth king of that name, and during her reign they were really full of spunk and had swelled heads, pride and impudence, because they were so prosperous and well off....

Clan Thomas passed their time merrily, with bodies full and minds empty, as Saint Patrick had ordained for them. They did not indulge in spicy succulent food nor sweet intoxicating drink, nor clean well-fitting clothes, but wore rough canvas shirts, slimy coarse swallow-tailed coats woven of the dirty wool of goats and other animals, stinking and untanned leather boots, crooked and shapeless caps with long flaps, shitty, bare, worn-out slippery clogs. Still, as Patrick had instructed, they watched and waited, served and ploughed and slaved for the nobility and gentry...

Illustration from the chapter "Of the Potatoes of Virginia" from John Gerard(e)'s *Herbal* (1597).

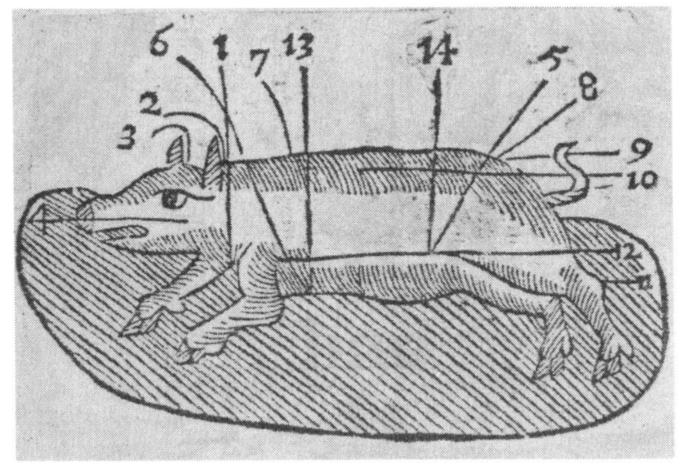

"The dissection of a sucking pig." From Giles Rose, *A Perfect School of Instructions for the Officers of the Mouth*

From the titlepage of *The Accomplished Lady's Delight in Preserving, Physick, Beautifying and Cookery*

Cakes and Ale

The food of the Elizabethan was less like "stodge" than that the English are supposed to be sustained by today. In some ways Elizabethan food was far from bland; it was, in fact, rather spiced with the preservatives that The Crusades had brought. Tourists today recall the "English breakfast" of homely "bed and breakfast" establishments of the earlier 20th century. (Now the urban "B & Bs" are full of the homeless on welfare and the parsimonious "Continental breakfast" of a roll and harsh coffee or tea is all tourists are offered.) The big breakfast was not an Elizabethan feature, and what pubs still offer as a "ploughman's lunch" (bread and cheese, perhaps a pickled onion, with some beer) was more or less like the Elizabethan's midday meal. The one big meal of the day was in the evening, meat being the main ingredient and salad and vegetables being occasional rather than inevitable accompaniments. When offered good food, however, the Englishman was a "good trencherman," cleaning his wooden plate, and for celebrations there was a "groaning board," Fynes Morrison writing that "at feasts for invited friends [the English] are so excessive in the number of dishes, as the table is not thought well-furnished, except they stand one upon another," whether they held roasts or the salad named for Elizabeth's father, "Good King Henry." Of course, in Elizabeth's time the English had plenty of ale and beer, imported wines, but no tea.

The little islands off the coast of Europe became in the Renaissance a world sea power. In consequence the newly far-flung trade and exploration brought to England a much more varied diet than England enjoyed in the Middle Ages and such exotic New World foods as potatoes. Now the ideal of a "square" or "meat and potatoes" meal could develop, "solid nourishment" to "stick to the ribs" of vigorous people in a cold and clammy island.

The situation of our region, lying near unto the north, doth cause the heat of our stomachs to be of somewhat greater force: therefore our bodies do crave a little more ample nourishment than the inhabitants of the hotter regions are accustomed withal, whose digestive force is not altogether so vehement, because their internal heat is not so strong as ours, which is kept in by the coldness of the air that from time to time (especially in winter) doth environ our bodies....

In number of dishes and change of meat the nobility of England (whose cooks are for the most part musical-headed Frenchmen and strangers) do most exceed, sith there is no day in manner that passeth over their heads wherein they have not only beef, mutton, veal, lamb, kid, pork, cony, capon, pig or so many of these as the season yieldeth, but also some portion of the red or fallow deer, beside great variety of fish and wild-fowl, and thereto sundry other delicates wherein the sweet hand of the sea-faring Portingal is not wanting:

so that for a man to dine with one of them, and to taste of every dish that standeth before him (which few use to do, but each one feedeth upon that meat him best liketh for the time, the beginning of every dish notwithstanding being reserved unto the greatest personage that sitteth at the table, to whom it is drawn up still by the waiters as order requireth, and from whom it descendeth again even to the lower end, whereby each one may taste thereof, is rather to yield unto a conspiracy with a great deal of meat for the speedy suppression of natural health, than the use of a necessary mean to satisfy himself with a competent repast to sustain his body withal. But as this large feeding is not seen in their guests no more is it in their own persons, for sith they have daily much resort unto their tables (and many times unlooked for) and thereto retain great numbers of servants, it is very requisite and expedient for them to be somewhat plentiful in this behalf.

The chief part likewise of their daily provision is brought in before them (commonly in silver vessels, if they be of the degree of barons, bishops and upwards) and placed on their tables; whereof, when they have taken what it pleaseth them, the rest is reserved and afterward sent down to their serving men and waiters, who feed thereon in like sort with convenient moderation, their reversion also being bestowed upon the poor which lie ready at their gates in great numbers to receive the same. This is spoken of the principal tables whereat the nobleman, his lady and guests are accustomed to sit; besides which they have a certain ordinary allowance daily appointed for their halls, where the chief officers and household servants (for all are not permitted by custom to wait upon their master), and with them such inferior guests do feed as are not of calling to associate the nobleman himself; so that, besides those aforementioned, which are called to the principal table, there are commonly forty or three score persons fed in those halls, to the great relief of such poor suitors and strangers also, as oft be partakers thereof and otherwise like to dine hardly. As for drink it is usually filled in pots, goblets, jugs, bowls of silver, in noblemen's houses; also in fine Venice glasses of all forms; and, for want of these elsewhere, in pots of earth of sundry colours and moulds, whereof many are garnished with silver, or at the leastwise in pewter, all which notwithstanding are seldom set on the table, but each one, as necessity urgeth, calleth for a cup of such drink as him listeth to have, so that, when he hath tasted of it, he delivereth the cup again to some one of the standers by, who, making it clean by pouring out the drink that remaineth, restoreth it to the cupboard from whence he fetched the same....

It is a world to see in these our days, wherein gold and silver most aboundeth, how that our gentility, as loathing those metals (because of the plenty) do now generally choose rather the Venice glasses, both for our wine and beer, than any of those metals or stone wherein before time we have been accustomed to drink; but such is the nature of man generally that it most coveteth things difficult to be attained; and such is the estimation of this stuff that many become rich only with their new trade unto Murano (a town near to Venice, situate on the Adriatic Sea), from whence the very best are daily to be had, and such as for beauty do well near match the crystal or the ancient *Murribina vasa* whereof now no man hath knowledge. And as this is seen in the gentility, so in the wealthy communalty the like desire of glass is not neglected, whereby the gain gotten by their purchase is yet much more increased to the benefit of the merchant. The poorest also will have glass if they may; but, sith the Venetian is somewhat too dear for them, they content themselves with such as are made at home of fern and burnt stone; but in fine all go one way—that is, to shards at the last, so that our great expenses in glasses (besides that they breed much strife toward such as have the charge of them) are worst of all bestowed in mine opinion, because their pieces do turn unto no profit....

At such time as the merchants do make their ordinary or voluntary feasts, it is a world to see what great provision is made of all manner of delicate meats, from every quarter of the country, wherein, beside that they are often comparable herein to the nobility of the land, they will seldom regard anything that the butcher usually killeth, but reject the same as not worthy to come in place. In such cases also gellifs of all colours, mixed with a variety in the representation of sundry flowers, herbs, trees, forms of beasts, fish, fowls and fruits and thereunto marchpane wrought with no small curiosity, tarts of divers hues and sundry denominations, conserves of old fruits, foreign and home-bred, suckets, codiniacs, marmalades, marchpane, sugar-bread, gingerbread, florentines, wild-fowl, venison of all sorts, and sundry outlandish confections, altogether seasoned with sugar (which Pliny called *mel ex arundinibus*, a device not common nor greatly used in old time at the table, but only in medicine, although it grew in Arabia, India, and Sicilia), do generally bear the sway, besides infinite devices of our own not possible for me to remember. Of the potato, and such venerous roots as are brought out of Spain, Portingal, and the Indies to furnish up our banquets, I speak not, wherein our mures of no less force, and to be had about Crosby-Ravenswath, do now begin to have place...except beef, bacon and pork, are not any whit esteemed, and yet these three may not be much powdered); but, as in rehearsal thereof I should commend the nobleman, merchant and frugal artificer, so I could not clear the meaner sort of husbandmen and country inhabitants of very much babbling (except it be here and there some odd yeoman), with whom he is thought to be the merriest that talketh of most ribaldry or the wisest man that speaketh fastest among them, and now and then surfeiting and drunkenness which they rather fall into for want of heed-taking than willfully following or delighting in those errors of set mind and purpose. It may be that divers of them living at home, with hard and pinching diet, small drink, and some of them having scarce enough of that, are soonest overtaken when they come into such banquets; howbeit they take it generally as no small disgrace if they happen to be cupshotten, so that it is a grief unto them, though now sans remedy, sith the thing is done and past. If the friends also of the wealthier sort come to their houses from far, they are commonly so welcome till they depart as upon the first day of their coming; whereas in good towns and cities, as London, etc., men oftentimes complain of little room, and, in reward of a fat capon or plenty of beef and mutton bestowed upon them in the country, a cup of wine or beer with a napkin to wipe their lips and an 'You are heartily welcome!' is thought to be a great entertainment....

Heretofore there hath been much more time spent in eating and drinking than commonly is in these days; for whereas of old we had breakfasts in the forenoon, beverages or nunchions after dinner, and thereto rear-suppers generally when it was time to go to rest...now these odd repasts, thanked be God, are very well left, and each one in manner (except here and there some young hungry stomach that cannot fast till dinner-time) contenteth himself with dinner and supper only.

With us the nobility, gentry and students do ordinarily go to dinner at eleven before noon, and to supper at five or between five and six at afternoon. The merchants dine and sup seldom before twelve at noon, and six at night, especially in London. The husbandmen dine also at high noon as they call it, and sup at seven or eight; but out of the term in our universities the scholars dine at ten. As for the poorest sort they generally dine and sup when they may, so that to talk of their order of repast it were but a needless matter. I might here take occasion also to set down the variety used by antiquity in their beginnings of their diets, wherein almost every nation had a several fashion, some beginning of custom (as we do in summer time) with salads at supper, and some ending with lettuce, some making their entry with eggs, and shutting up their tables with mulberries, as we do with fruit and conceits of all sorts. Divers (as the old Romans) began with a few crops of rue, as the Venetians did with the fish called *gobius,* the Belgies with butter, or (as we do yet also) with butter and eggs upon fish days. But whereas we commonly begin with the most gross food, and end with the most delicate, the Scot, thinking to leave the best for his menial servants, maketh his entrance at the best, so that he is sure thereby to leave the worst. We use also our wines by degrees, so that the hottest cometh last to the table; but to stand upon such toys would spend much time and turn to small profit. Wherefore I will deal with others things more necessary for this turn.

*Here I have followed the guidance of John Dover Wilson (*Life in Shakespeare's England) *in the choice of passages from the second edition of William Harrison's* Description of England *(1587).*

A bit of an old ballad:

Talk not of goose and capon, give me good beef and bacon,
And good bread and cheese now at hand;
With pudding, brawn and souse, all in a farmer's house,
    That is living for a husbandman.

Gervase Markham (1568-1637) was a writer on a wide variety of popular subjects. At one point he had so many of his books in print on the subject of "the diseases or cures of any cattle, as horse, ox, cow, sheep, swine, goats, etc." that the Stationers' Company made him sign a pledge not to write any more (1617). In Elizabeth's day he wrote a play, The Dumb Knight, *and was noted by Francis Meres in his* Palladis Tamia *as a respectable writer. His verses were included in* England's Parnassus *(1600). But he is famous for a book published after Elizabeth's reign,* The English Housewife, *which first appeared in 1615, much of which is Elizabethan and earlier material he collected and "polished."*

I have chosen a number of his household recipes for "waters." In those days the housewife had to distill as well as cook, bake, and perform many other household chores, for the country house had to be as self-sufficient as possible. Many of these recipes Markham got from Elizabethan and earlier sources. The first, for instance, is from Peter Levens, The Pathway to Health *(1582).*

A very principal aqua composita

Take of balm, of rosemary flowers tops and all, of dried red rose leaves, of pennyroyal, of each of these a handful, of hyssop half a handful, one root of elecampane the whitest that can be got, three quarters of a pound of liquorice, two ounces of cinnamon, two drams of great mace, two drams of galingale, three drams of coriander seed, three drams of caraway seeds, two or three nutmegs cut in four quarters, an ounce of aniseeds, a handful of borage; you must choose a fair sunny day to gather the herbs in; you must not wash them, but cut them in sunder, and not too small; then lay all your herbs in souse all night and a day, with the spices grossly beaten or bruised, and then distil it in order aforesaid; this was made for a learned physician's own drinking.

To make the imperial water

Take a gallon of Gascon wine; ginger, galingale, nutmegs, grains, cloves, aniseeds, fennel seeds, caraway seeds, of each one dram, then take sage, mints, red roses, thyme, pellitory, rosemary; wild thyme, camomile, and lavender, of each a handful, then bray the spices small, and the herbs also, and put all together into the wine, and let it stand so twelve hours, stirring it divers times, then distil it with a limbeck, and keep the first water, for it is best: of a gallon of wine you must not take above a quart of water; this water comforteth the vital spirits, and helpeth inward disease that cometh of cold, as the palsy, the contraction of sinews; also it killeth worms, and comforts the stomach; it cureth the cold dropsy, helps the stone, the stinking breath, and maketh one seem young.

To make cinnamon water

Take a pottle of the best sack, and half a pint of rose-water, a quarter and half of a pound of good cinnamon well bruised, but not small beaten; distil all these together in a glass still, but you must carefully look to it that it boil not over hastily, and attend it with cold wet cloths to cool the top of the still if the water should offer to boil too hastily. This water is very sovereign for the stomach, the head, and all the inward parts; it helps digestion, and comforteth the vital spirits.

Aqua composita *was made of a mixture of ingredients. Here are the "virtues" of various simple extracts. Watch for magical aspects:*

The virtues of several waters

The water of chervil is good for a sore mouth.
The water of calamint is good for the stomach.
The water of plantain is good for the flux and the hot dropsy.
Water of fennel is good to make a fat body small, and also for the eyes.
Water of violets is good for a man that is sore within his body, and for the reins, and for the liver.
Water of endive is good for the dropsy, and for the jaundice, and the stomach.
Water of borage is good for the stomach, and for the *iliaca passio* [consumption], and many other sicknesses in the body.
Water of both sages is good for the palsy.
Water of betony is good for the hearing and all inward sicknesses.
Water of radish drunk twice a day, at each time an ounce, or an ounce and a half, doth multiply and provoke lust, and also it provoketh the terms [menstruation] in women.

Rosemary water (the face washed therein both morning and night) causeth a fair and clear countenance: also the head washed therewith, and let dry of itself, preserveth the falling of the hair, and causeth more to grow; also two ounces of the same, drunk, driveth venom out of the body in the same as mithridate [as artridate] doth; the same twice or thrice drunk, at each time half an ounce, rectifieth the mother ['s womb], and it causeth women to be fruitful: when one maketh a bath of this decoction, it is called the bath of life; the same drunk comforteth the heart, the brain, and the whole body, and cleanseth away the spots of the face; it maketh a man look young, and causeth women to conceive quickly, and hath all the virtues of balm.

The water of sorrel drunk is good for all burning and pestilent fevers, and all other hot sicknesses; being mixed with beer, ale, or wine, it slaketh thirst; it is also good for the yellow jaundice, being taken six or eight days together; it also expelleth heat from the liver if it be drunk and a cloth wet in the same and a little wrung out, and so applied to the right side over against the liver, and when it is dry then wet another, and apply it; and thus do three or four times together.

Lastly the water of angelica is good for the head, for inward infection, either of the plague or pestilence; it is very sovereign for sore breasts; also the same water, being drunk of twelve or thirteen days together, is good to unlade the stomach of gross humours and superfluities, and it strengtheneth and comforteth all the universal parts of the body; and lastly, it is a most sovereign medicine for the gout, by bathing the diseased members much therein.

Now to conclude and knit up this chapter, it is meet that our housewife know that from the eight of the calends of the month of April unto the eight of the calends of July, all manner of herbs and leaves are in that time most in strength and of the greatest virtue to be used and put in all manner of medicines; also from the eight of the calends of July unto the eight of the calends of October the stalks, stems, and hard branches of every herb and plant is most in strength to be used in medicines; and from the eight of the calends of October, unto the eight of the calends of April, all manner of roots of herbs and plants are the most of strength and virtue to be used in all manner of medicines.

An excellent water for perfume

To make an excellent sweet water for perfume, you shall take of basil, mints, marjoram, corn-flag roots, hyssop, savory, sage, balm, lavender, and rosemary, of each one a handful; of cloves, cinnamon, and nutmegs of each half an ounce, then three or four pomecitrons [citrons] cut into slices; infuse all these into damask rose-water the space of three days, and then distil it with a gentle fire of charcoal, then when you have put it into a very clean glass, take of fat musk, civet, and ambergris of each the quantity of a scruple, and put into a rag of fine lawn, and then hang it within the water. This. being either burnt upon a hot pan, or else boiled in perfuming pans with cloves, bay leaves, and lemon peels, will make the most delicatest perfume that may be without any offence, and will last the longest of all other sweet perfumes, as hath been found by experience.

To perfume gloves

To perfume gloves excellently, take the oil of sweet almonds, oil of nutmegs, oil of benjamin *[liquidambar orientals]*, of each a dram, of ambergris one grain, fat musk two grains: mix them altogether and grind them upon a painter's stone [islor grinding] and then anoint the gloves therewith: yet before you anoint them let them be dampishly moistened with damask rose-water.

To [clean and] perfume a jerkin

To perfume a jerkin well, take the oil of benjamin a pennyworth, oil of spike [French lavender], and oil of olives half pennyworths of each, and take two sponges and warm one of them against the fire and rub your jerkin therewith; and when the oil is dried, take the other sponge and dip it in the oil and rub your jerkin therewith till it be dry, then lay on the perfume before prescribed for gloves.

To make vinegar

To make excellent strong vinegar, you shall brew the strongest ale that may be, and having tunned it in a very strong vessel, you shall set it either in your garden or some other safe place abroad, where it may have the whole summer day's sun to shine upon it, and there let it lie till it be extreme sour, then into a hogshead of this vinegar put the leaves of four or five hundred damask roses, and after they have lain for the space of a month therein, house the vinegar and draw it as you need it.

Elizabethans ate more vegetables and salads than medieval Englishmen but they continued to enjoy meat when they could get it and they ate poultry, fish, venison and game, etc. Here are some recipes you can try, though you probably will never construct the elaborate meals we describe with "the ordering of banquets" from Gervase Markham.

Pudding of a hog's liver

Take the liver of a fat hog and parboil it, then shred it small, and after, beat it in a mortar very fine; then mix it with the thickest and sweetest cream, and strain it very well through an ordinary strainer; then put thererto six yolks of eggs, and two whites, and the grated crumbs of near half a penny white loaf, with good store of currants, dates, cloves, mace, sugar, saffron, salt, and the best swine suet, or beef suet, but beef suet is the more wholesome, and less loosening; then after it hath stood a while, fill it into the farmes, and boil them, as before showed; and when you serve them to the table, first boil them a little, then lay them on a gridiron over the coals, and broil them gently, but scorch them not, nor in any wise break their skins, which is to be prevented by oft turning and tossing them on the gridiron, and keeping a slow fire.

Oyster pie

Take of the greatest oysters drawn from the shells, and parboil them in verjuice: then put them into a colander, and let all the moisture run from them, till they be as dry as is possible: then raise up the coffin of the pie, and lay them in: then put to them good store of currants and fine powdered sugar, with whole mace, whole cloves, whole cinnamon, and a nutmeg sliced, dates cut, and good store of sweet butter: then cover it, and only leave a vent hole: when it is baked, then draw it, and take white wine, and white wine vinegar, sugar, cinnamon, and sweet butter, and melt it together; then first trim the lid therewith, and candy it with sugar; then pour the rest in at the vent hole, and shake it well, and so set it into the oven again for a little space, and so serve it up, the dish edges trimmed with sugar. Now some use to put to this pie onions sliced and shred, but that is referred to discretion, and to the pleasure of the taste.

To recover venison that is tainted

Take strong ale, and put to it of wine vinegar as much as will make it sharp: then set it on the fire, and boil it well, and scum it, and make of it a strong brine with bay-salt [sea salt] or other salt: then take it off, and let it stand till it be cold, then put your venison into it, and let it lie in it full twelve hours: then take it out from that mere sauce, and press it well; then parboil it, and season it with pepper and salt, and bake it.

A chewet pie

Take the brawns and the wings of capons and chickens after they have been roasted, and pull away the skin; then shred them with fine mutton suet very small; then season it with cloves, mace, cinnamon, sugar, and salt: then put to raisins of the sun and currants, and sliced dates, and orange peels, and, being well mixed together, put it into small coffins made for the purpose, and strew on the top of them good store of caraway comfits: then cover them, and bake them with a gentle heat, and these chewets you may also make of roasted veal, seasoned as before showed, and of all parts the loin is the best.

Roasting mutton with oysters

If you will roast mutton with oysters; take a shoulder, a loin, or a leg, and after it is washed parboil it a little; then take the greatest oysters, and, having opened them into a dish, drain the gravy clean from them twice or thrice, then parboil them a little: then take spinach, endive, succory, strawberry leaves, violet leaves, and a little parsley, with some scallions; chop these very small together: then take your oysters very dry drained, and mix them with a half part of these herbs; then take your meat and with these oysters and herbs face or stop [stuff] it, leaving no place empty, then spit it and roast it; and whilst it is in roasting take good store of verjuice and butter, and a little salt, and set it in a dish on a chafing-dish and coals; and when it begins to boil, put in the remainder of your herbs without oysters, and a good quantity of currants, with cinnamon, and the yolk of a couple of eggs: and after they are well boiled and stirred together, season it up according to taste with sugar; then put in a few lemon slices, and the meat being enough, draw it and lay it upon this sauce removed into a clean dish, the edges thereof being trimmed about with sugar, and so serve it forth.

A blood pudding

Take the blood of a hog whilst it is warm, and steep in it a quart, or more, of great oatmeal grits, and at the end of three days with your hands take the grits out of the blood, and drain them clean; then put to those grits more than a quart of the best cream warmed on the fire; then take mother of thyme, parsley, spinach, succory, endive, sorrel, and strawberry leaves, of each a few chopped exceeding small, and mix them with the grits, and also a little fennel seed finely beaten: then add a little pepper, cloves and mace, salt, and great store of suet finely shred, and well beaten: then therewith fill your farmes [cleaned pig's intestines to stuff, as for sausages], and boil them....

Puddings of a calf's mugget [chitterlings]

Take a calf's mugget, clean and sweet dressed, and boil it well; then shred it as small as is possible, then take of strawberry leaves, of endive, spinach, succory, and sorrel, of each a pretty quantity, and chop them as small as is possible, and then mix them with the mugget; then take the yolks of half a dozen eggs, and three whites, and beat them into it also; and if you find it is too stiff, then make it thinner with a little cream warmed on the fire; then put in a little pepper, cloves, mace, cinnamon, ginger, sugar, currants, dates, and salt, and work all together, with casting in little pieces of sweet butter one after another, till it have received good store of butter; then put it up into the calf's bag [stomach], sheep's bag, or hog's bag, and then boil it well, and so serve it up.

Thomas Dawson adds: "And so boil it with a little mutton broth and wine, lettuce and spinach whole in the same broth"—and he *doesn't forget the bread: "the quantity of a farthing loaf grated." The result is the English answer to Scotch haggis.*

A herring pie

Take white pickled herrings of one night's watering [soaking], and boil them a little: then peel off the skin, and take only the backs of them, and pick the fish clean from the bones, then take good store of raisins of the sun, and stone them, and put them to the fish: then take a warden [pear] or two, and pare it, and slice it in small slices from the core, and put it likewise to the fish: then with a very sharp shredding knife shred all as small and fine as may be: then put to it good store of currants, sugar, cinnamon, sliced dates, and so put it into the coffin with good store of very sweet butter, and so cover it, and leave only a round vent hole on the top of the lid, and so bake it like pies of that nature. When it is sufficiently baked, draw it out, and take claret wine and a little verjuice, sugar, cinnamon, and sweet butter, and boil them together; then put it in at the vent hole, and shake the pie a little and put it again into the oven for a little space, and so serve it up, the lid being candied over with sugar, and the sides of the dish trimmed with sugar.

To strew a lamb's head and purtenance

Take a lamb's head and purtenance ["pluck," guts] clean washed and picked and put it into a pipkin with fair water, and let it boil, and scum it clean; then put in currants and a few sliced dates, and a bunch of the best farcing herbs tied up together, and so let it boil well till the meat be [tender] enough: then take up the lamb's head and purtenance, and put it into a clean dish with sippets ["soldiers" or bits of bread or toast as sops]; then put in a good lump of butter, and beat the yolks of two eggs with a little cream, and put it to the broth with sugar, cinnamon, and a spoonful or two of verjuice, and whole mace, and as many prunes as will garnish the dish, which should be put in when it is but half boiled, and so pour it upon the lamb's head and purtenance, and adorn the sides of the dish with sugar, prunes, barberries, oranges and lemons, and in no case forget not to season well with salt, and so serve it up.

The English have always loved "sweets." Elizabethans liked cakes and candy especially, dusting all deserts with sugar and (in the medieval fashion) gilding gingerbread (so that they still say to express disappointment at something having lost its original attractiveness "the gilt is off the gingerbread") and otherwise making the sweet course as extravagant as they could manage. Here are some of their recipes simple enough to make today:

A Norfolk fool

Take a pint of the sweetest and thickest cream that can be gotten, and set it on the fire in a very clean scoured skillet, and put into it sugar, cinnamon, and a nutmeg cut into four quarters, and so boil it well: then take the yolks of four eggs, and take off the films, and beat them well with a little sweet cream: then take the four quarters of the nutmeg out of the cream, then put in the eggs, and stir it exceedingly, till it be thick: then take a fine manchet, and cut it into thin shives, as much as will cover a dish bottom, and holding it in your hand, pour half the cream into the dish: then lay your bread over it, then cover the bread with the rest of the cream, and so let it stand till it be cold: then strew it over with caraway comfits, and pick up some cinnamon comfits, and some sliced dates; or for want thereof, scrape all over it some sugar, and trim the sides of the dish with sugar, and so serve it up.

A trifle

Take a pint of the best and thickest cream, and set it on the fire in a clean skillet, and put into it sugar, cinnamon, and a nutmeg cut into four quarters, and so boil it well; then put it into the dish you intend to serve it in, and let it stand to cool till it be no more than lukewarm; then put in a spoonful of the best earning [moderns should use jam or fruit preserves], and stir it well about, and so let it stand till it be cold, and then strew sugar upon it, and so serve it up, and this you may serve either in dish, glass, or other plate.

To make bread puddings

Take the yolks and whites of a dozen or fourteen eggs, and, having beat them very well, put to them the fine powder of cloves, mace, nutmegs, sugar, cinnamon, saffron, and salt; then take the quantity of two loaves of white grated bread, dates (very small shred) and great store of currants, with good plenty either of sheep's, hog's, or beef suet beaten and cut small; then when all is mixed and stirred well together, and hath stood a while to settle, then fill it into the farmes as hath been before showed, and in like manner boil them, cook them, and serve them to the table.

Rice puddings

Take half a pound of rice, and steep it in new milk a whole night, and in the morning drain it, and let the milk drop away; then take a quart of the best, sweetest, and thickest cream, and put the rice into it, and boil it a little; then set it to cool an hour or two, and after put in the yolks of half a dozen eggs, a little pepper, cloves, mace, currants, dates, sugar, and salt; and having mixed them well together, put in great store of beef suet well beaten, and small shred, and so put it into the farmes, and boil them as before showed, and serve them after a day old.

Marzipan

Marci panis *(or St. Mark's Bread) was one of the sweets the Elizabethans loved. It is mentioned in connection with a feast in* Romeo and Juliet. *This is the recipe used in the household of Sir Hugh Plat(t) (1552-1611?), who also gave recipes for preserving fruit, dyeing the hair, etc. To make what he called "marchpane" take 2 pounds of blanched, dried almonds, grind them in a stone mortar, mix them with an equal amount of sugar, add a couple of spoonfuls of rose water to make a paste, and roll it out. Then bake it and ice with sugar and rosewater mixture. Put that into the oven to dry the icing. Then (according to* Delights for Ladies, 1602):

garnish with pretty conceits and birds and beasts being cast out of standing moulds. Stick long comfits upright in it, cast biscuit and carroways in it, and so to serve it; gild it before you serve it.

Fine ginger cakes

Take of the best sugar, and when it is beaten searce it very fine, and [take] of the best ginger and cinnamon; then take a little gum dragon and lay it in rose-water all night, then pour the water from it, and put the same, with a little white of an egg well beaten, into a brass mortar, the sugar, ginger, cinnamon, and all together, and beat them together till you may work it like paste; then take it and drive it forth into cakes, and print them, and lay them before the fire, or in a very warm stove to bake. Or otherwise take sugar and ginger (as is before said), cinnamon and gum dragon excepted, instead whereof take only the whites of eggs, and so do as was before showed you.

To make suckets

Take curds, the parings of lemons, of oranges or pomecitrons, or indeed any half ripe green fruit, and boil them till they be tender, in sweet wort [malt water]; then make a syrup in this sort: take three pound of sugar, and the whites of four eggs, and a gallon of water; then swinge and beat the water and the eggs together, and then put in your sugar, and set it on the fire, and let it have an easy fire, and so let it boil six or seven walms, and then strain it through a cloth, and let it seethe again till it fall from the spoon, and then put it into the rinds of fruits.

Coarse gingerbread

Take a quart of honey clarified, and seethe it till it be brown, and if it be thick put to it a dish of water: then take fine crumbs of white bread grated, and put to it, and stir it well, and when it is almost cold, put to it the powder of ginger, cloves, cinnamon, and a little liquorice and aniseeds; then knead it, and put it into moulds and print it [stamp designs on it]; some use to put to it also a little pepper, but that is according unto taste and pleasure.

Fynes Moryson:

English Husbandmen eat Barley and Rye brown bread, and prefer it to white bread as abiding longer in the stomach, and not so soon digested with their labor.

The working classes liked food that "stuck to the ribs." Scots ate a lot of porridge. The North Country liked suet puddings and other "stodge." Beef was eaten by all who could afford it but fish was common, being then obtainable from The Thames.

Shakespeare's England *gives without further identification the "diet of a well-to-do bachelor who lived in lodgings in Warwick Lane, London, for four months in 1589" (in the original spelling):*

On May 11 he had for dinner [midday meal]:

A pece of bief	xviijd
A loyne of veale	ijs
2 chickens	xiiijd
Orenges	ijd
For dressings ye veale & chickens & sawce	xijd

and for supper [between 5 and 6 pm]

A shoulder of mutton	xvjd
2 Rabbettes	xd
For dressinge ye mutton, rabbettes & a pigges pettie toes	viijd
Colde bief	viijd
Cheese	ijd

On June 20 he evidently had friends to dinner, as several delicacies are introduced:

Butter	iijd
A pece of bief	xiiijd
A legg of mutton	xviijd
A loyne of veale	xxijd
2 pecks of Pescodes	viijd
3 Rabbettes	ijs
A quart of creame	vjd
3 quarts of Strawberries	xvjd
2 li of cheries	xxd
Di: li of muske confectes	xd
Di: li of violett confectes	xjd
Orenges	iijd
2 Lemans	vjd
Bred	viijd
Beare	ixd

One of the Friday dinners, on May 2, is interesting:

A side of hab[er]dyn & another of genre fishe	xiiijd
Foure playses	xijd
ij whitinges	viijd
Conger	viijd

Butter	iiijd
Lettise for sallett	ijd
A pynt of white wyne & another of clarett	vjd
Sugar	ijd
A pound of butter	vd
For dressinge the fishe	viijd
Oyle & suger for sallett	ijd
More for butter	ijd
A pounde of candles	iiijd

He appears to have been a moderate drinker, contenting himself with an occasional pint of claret, Rhenish, or beer for dinner.

On May 23 he has among other things a pynt of Strawberries, xijd.'— *a very early date, even in old style, for this fruit, if grown without protection. On May 29 he gets three pints of strawberries for the same price.*

FORKS. They were in use on the Continent in the 13th and 14th centuries.— Voltaire. *This is reasonably disputed, as being too early. In Fynes Moryson's* Itinerary, *reign of Elizabeth, he says, "At Venice each person was served (besides his knife and spoon) with a fork to hold the meat, while he cuts it, for there they deem it ill manners that one should touch it with his hand." Thomas Coryate describes, with much solemnity, the manner of using forks in Italy, and adds, "I myself have thought it good to imitate the Italian fashion since I came home to England," A.D. 1608.*
—Joseph Haydn, Dictionary of Dates *(1841)*

Few common people can ever have experienced, except perhaps as waiters and waitresses, the grand banquets that nobles and rich merchants enjoyed, but on occasion they would try to make the board groan as much as possible, especially at marriages or wakes. A simple country girl's wedding party might consist of a little food and she herself selling *ale to the guests, who paid as much for it as they liked, thus giving a sort of wedding present. A more elaborate dinner might be offered by the wealthier farmer or gentleman for his daughter's nuptials. Royal visits and such demanded great feasts, though Elizabeth was a small woman and did not eat like her father (or throw bones on the floor for the dogs, as Charles Laughton did portraying Henry VIII in the films), but she liked to keep the ale or wine flowing freely, especially since her host was paying for it. The servants got the leftovers (and maybe hid away a few things in the kitchen to enjoy for themselves, so supervision of a feast was essential).*

Ordering of banquets

Thus having showed you how to preserve, conserve, candy, and make pastes of all kinds, in which four heads consists the whole art of banqueting dishes, I will now proceed to the ordering or setting forth of a banquet; wherein you shall observe that marchpanes have the first place, the middle place, and last place; your preserved fruits shall be dished up first, your pastes next, your wet suckets after them, then your dried suckets, then your marmalades and goodinyakes, then your comfits of all kinds; next, your pears, apples, wardens baked, raw or roasted, and your oranges and lemons sliced; and lastly your wafer cakes. Thus you shall order them in the closet; but when they go to the table, you shall first send forth a dish made for show only, as beast, bird, fish, or fowl, according to invention: then your marchpane, then preserved fruit, then a paste, then a wet sucket, then a dry sucket, marmalade, comfits, apples, pears, wardens, oranges, and lemons sliced; and then wafers, and another dish of preserved fruits, and so consequently all the rest before: no two dishes of one kind going or standing together, and this will not only appear delicate to the eye, but invite the appetite with the much variety thereof.

Ordering of great feasts and proportion of expense

Now we have drawn our housewife into these several knowledges of cookery, in as much as in her is contained all the inward offices of household, we will proceed to declare the manner of serving and setting forth of meat for a great feast, and from it derive meaner, making a due proportion of all things for what avails it our good housewife to be never so skillful in the parts of cookery, if she want skill to marshal the dishes, and set every on in his due place, giving precedency according to fashion and custom; it is like to a fencer leading a band of men in rout, who knows the use of the weapon, but not how to put men in order. It is then to be understood, that it is the office of the clerk of the kitchen (whose place our housewife must many times supply) to order the meat at the dresser, and deliver it unto the sewer [server, butler], who is to deliver it to the gentlemen and yeomen waiters to bear to the table. Now because we allow no officer but our housewife, to whom we only speak in this book, she shall first marshal her sallats, delivering the grand sallat first, which is evermore compound; then green sallats, then boiled sallats, then some smaller compound sallats. Next unto sallats she shall deliver forth all her fricassees, the simple first, as collops, rashers, and such like; then compound fricassees; after them all her boiled meats in their degrees, as simple broths, stewed broth, and the boilings of sundry fowls. Next them all sorts of roast meats, of which the greatest first, as chine of beef or sirloin, the gigot or legs of mutton, goose, swan, veal, pig, capon, and such like. Then baked meats, the hot first, as fallow deer in pasty, chicken, or calf's-foot pie and doucet. Then cold baked meats, pheasant, partridges, turkey, goose, woodcock, and such like. Then lastly, carbonadoes both simple and compound. And being thus marshalled from the dresser, the sewer, upon the placing them on the table, shall not set them down as he received them, but, setting the sallats extravagantly about the table, mix the fricassees about them; then the boiled meats amongst the fricassees, roast meats amongst the boiled, baked meats amongst the roast, and carbonadoes amongst the baked; so that before every trencher may stand a sallat, a fricassee, a boiled meat, a roast meat, a baked meat, and a carbanado, which will both give a most comely beauty to the table, and very great contentment to the guest. So likewise in the second course she shall first prefer the lesser wild fowl, as mallard, teal, snipe, plover, woodcock, and such like: then the lesser land fowl; as chicken, pigeons, partridge, rail, turkey, chickens, young peahens, and such like. Then the greater wild fowl; as bittern, hern, shoveller, crane, bustard, and such like. Then the greater land fowls; as peacocks, pheasant, pewits, gulls, and such like. Then hot baked meats; as marrow-bone pie, quince pie, Florentine, and tarts.

Then cold baked meats, as red deer, hare pie, gammon of bacon pie, wild boar, roe pie, and such like, and these also shall be marshalled at the table as the first course, not one kind all together, but each several sort mixed together, as a lesser wild fowl and a lesser land fowl; a great wild fowl, and a great land fowl; a hot baked meat, and a cold: and for made dishes and *quelquechoses,* which rely on the invention of the cook, they are to be thrust in, into every place that is empty, and so sprinkled over all the table: and this is the best method for the extraordinary great feasts of princes. But in case it be for much more humble means, then less care and fewer dishes may discharge it; yet, before I proceed to that lower rate, you shall understand that in these great feasts of princes, though I have mentioned nothing but flesh, yet is not fish to be exempted; for it is a beauty and an honour unto every feast, and is to be placed amongst all the several services, as thus; as amongst your sallats all sorts of soused fish that lives in the fresh water; amongst your fricassees all manner of fried fish; amongst your boiled meats, all fish in broths; amongst your roast meats, all fish served hot, but dry; amongst the baked meats, all fish baked, and sea fish that is soused, as sturgeon and the like; and amongst your carbonadoes, fish that is broiled. As for your second course, to it belongeth all manner of shell-fish, either in the shell, or without; the hot to go up with the hot meat, and the cold with the cold. And thus shall the feast be royal, and the service worthy.

Now for a more humble feast, or an ordinary proportion which any goodman may keep in his family for the entertainment of his true and worthy friends, it must hold limitation with his provision, and the season of the year; for summer affords what winter wants, and winter is master of that which summer can but with difficulty have: it is good then for him that intends to feast, to set down the full number of full dishes, that is, dishes of meat that are of substance, and not empty or for show; and of these sixteen is a good proportion for one course unto one mess. As thus for example; first, a shield of brawn with mustard; secondly, a boiled capon; thirdly, a boiled piece of beef; fourthly, a chine of beef roasted; fifthly, a neat's tongue roasted; sixthly, a pig roasted; seventhly, chewets baked; eighthly, a goose roasted; ninthly, a swan roasted; tenthly, a turkey roasted; the eleventh, a haunch of venison roasted; the twelfth, a pasty of venison; the thirteenth, a kid with a pudding in the belly; the fourteenth, an olive pie; the fifteenth, a couple of capons; the sixteenth, a custard or doucets. Now to these full dishes may be added in sallats, fricassees, *quelquechoses,* and devised paste, as many dishes more, which make the full service no less than two and thirty dishes, which is as much as can conveniently stand on one table, and in one mess; and after this manner you may proportion both your second and third course, holding fullness in one half of the dishes, and show in the other, which will be both frugal in the spender, contentment to the guest, and much pleasure and delight to the beholders. And thus much touching the ordering of great feasts and ordinary entertainments. Such lavish feasts were never *ordinary* in our sense of the term. The word *ordinary* came to mean inn, tavern, restaurant. The Elizabethan inn was a centre of social life.

The Elizabethan inn was overcrowded, noisy, none too clean, and often full of waiters whose arithmetic errors seemed magically always to favor themselves, not the customer, but the English inn was hospitable and inexpensive and far and away superior to (for instance) what Erasmus found when he visited Germany early in the century:

When you have taken care of your horse you come into the Stove Room, boots, baggage, mud, and all, for that is a common room for all comers.... In the Stove Room you will pull off your boots, put on your shoes, and, if you will, change your shirt.... There one combs his head, another...belches garlic, and...there is as great a confusion of tongues as at the building of the Tower of Babel. In my opinion nothing is more dangerous than for so many to draw in the same vapor, especially when their bodies are opened with the heat...not to mention...the farting, the stinking breaths...and without doubt many have the Spanish, or, as it is called, the French, pox, though it is common to all nations.

Puritans deplored wine, women, and song (though perhaps not in that order) and Philip Stubbes' Anatomy of Abuses *had this to say of an all-too-common state, drunkenness, in what Iago called "England, where indeed they are most potent in potting":*

PHILOPONUS. I say that it is a horrible vice, and too much used in Ailgna [England]. Every country, city, town, village, and other place hath abundance of ale-houses, taverns and inns, which are so fraught with malt-worms, night and day, that you would wonder to see them. You shall have them there sitting at the wine and good-ale all the day long, yea, all the night too, peradventure a whole week together, so long as any money is left; swilling, gulling and carousing from one to another, till never a one can speak a ready word. Then, when with the spirit of the buttery they are thus possessed, a world it is to consider their gestures and demeanours, one towards another and towards every one else. How they stut and stammer, stagger and reel to and fro like madmen...and which is most horrible, some fall to swearing, cursing and banning, interlacing their speeches with curious terms of blasphemy to the great dishonour of God, and offence of the godly ears present.

SP. But they will say that God ordained wines and strong drinks to cheer the heart and to sustain the body withal, therefore it is lawful to use them to that end.

PHILO. Meats (moderately taken) corroborate the body, refresh the arteries and revive the spirits, making them apter, every member, to do his office as God hath appointed; but being immoderately taken (as commonly they be), they are instruments of damnation to the abusers of the same, and nourish not the body, but corrupt it rather, casting it into a world of diseases. And a man once drunk with wine or strong drink rather resembleth a brute than a Christian man. For do not his eyes begin to stare and to be red, fiery and bleared, blubbering forth seas of tears? Doth he not froth and foam at the mouth like a boar? Doth not his tongue falter and stammer in his mouth? Doth not his head seem as heavy as a millstone, he not being able to bear it up? Are not his wits and spirits, as it were, drowned? Is not his understanding altogether decayed? Do not his hands, and all his body vibrate, quaver and shake, as it were, with a quotidian fever? Besides these, it casteth him into a dropsy or pleurisy, nothing so soon; it enfeebleth the sinews, it weakeneth the natural strength, it corrupteth the blood, it dissolveth the whole man at the length, and finally maketh him forgetful of himself altogether, so that what he doth being drunk, he remembereth not being sober. The drunkard, in his drunkenness, killeth his friend, revileth his lover, discloseth secrets, and regardeth no man. He either expelleth all fear of God out of his mind, all love of his friends and kinfolks, all rembrance of honesty, civility and humanity; so that I will not fear to call drunkards beasts, and no men; and much worse than beasts, for beasts never exceed in any such kind of excess or superfluity, but always *modum adbibent appetitui* they measure their appetites by the rule of necessity, which, would God, we would do.

These verses which follow are Jacobean; the pub names they record often go back generations. London had many old inns, such as The George, The Tabard, The Boar's Head, all named for the signs that directed even those who could not read to refreshment within. Some of the jokes here (The Ram for cuckolds because of its horns, *the Welshmen at The Goat because that is the way—perhaps—they pronounced* God, *so that the pub sign "God Encompasses Us" became The Goat and Compasses) are a bit difficult. Nevertheless, on the whole it's easy to see the appeal of a poem that brought together a lot of well-known names.*

These are pubs that are ordinaries, that is places to eat as well as drink.

Though the Royal Exchange as I
  walked,
Where gallants in satin do shine,
At midst of the day they parted away
To several places to dine.

The gentry went to the King's Head,
The nobles unto the Crown;
The knights went to the Golden
  Fleece,
And the ploughmen unto the Clown.

The clergy will dine at the Mitre,
The vintners at the Three Tuns;
The usurers to the Devil will go,
And the friars to the Nuns.

The ladies will dine at the Feathers,
The Globe no captain will scorn;
The huntsmen will go to the
Greyhound below,
And some townsmen to the Horn.

The plumbers will dine at the
Fountain,
The cooks at the Holy Lamb;
The drunkards by noon to the Man
in the Moon,
And cuckolds to the Ram.

The roarers will dine at the Lion,
The watermen at the Old Swan;
The bawds will to the Negro go,
And whores to the Naked Man.

The keepers will to the White Hart,
The merchants unto the Ship;
The beggars they must take their way
To the Eggshell and the Whip.

The farriers will to the Horse,
The blacksmiths unto the Lock;
The butchers unto the Bull will go,
And the carmen to Bridewell Dock.

The fishmongers unto the Dolphin
The bakers to the Cheat Loaf;
The turners unto the Ladle will go,
Where they may merrily quaff.

The tailors will dine at the Shears,
The shoemakers will to the Boot;
The Welshmen they will make their
way
And dine at the sign of the Goat....

Hospitality was more openhanded in the countryside than in the city, and country people in Britain to this day complain, "Tell them you're thirsty in London and they'll give you a glass of water." From William Harrison's Description (1597):

If the friends also of the wealthier sort come to their houses from far, they are commonly so welcome till they depart as upon the first day of their coming, whereas in good towns and cities, as London, etc., men oftentimes complain of little room; and in reward of a fat capon or plenty of beef and mutton largely bestowed upon them in the country, a cup of wine or beer, with a napkin to wipe their lips and an 'you are heartily welcome', is thought to be great entertainment. And therefore the old country clerks have framed this saying in that behalf, I mean upon the entertainment of townsmen and Londoners after their days of abode, in this manner:

Primus iucundus, tollerabilis estque secundus,
Tertius est vanus, sed fetet quadriduanus.

["The first day is jovial, and tolerable the second, the third day is empty, the fourth day stinking reckoned."]

The country squires and nobles on their estates, so common in the medieval period, were fewer in Elizabethan times, and the serving class and the poor suffered, as an old ballad of The Servingman's Comfort *(1598) laments:*

When Country's causes did require
Each Nobleman to keep his house,
Then Bluecoats had what they desire,
Good cheer, with many a full carouse:
For now not as it wont to be,
For dead is Liberality.

The Hall boards-end is taken up,
No Dogs do differ for the bones,
Blackjack is left, now Glass or Cup,
It makes me sigh with many groans,
To think what was, now thus to be
By death of Liberality.

The golden world is past and gone,
The Iron Age hath run his race,
The lump of Lead is left alone
To press the poor in every place:
Nought else is left but misery,
Since death of Liberality.

Elizabethan printing presses such as this turned out great quantities of cheap, popular literature.

Popular Reading

Greene Raised From the Grave
From the title-page to John Dickenson's "Greene in Conceipt," 1598.

Someone once said that he didn't care who wrote the nation's laws if he could write its songs. If by songs we mean all that we now call the media which form the public mind, then he had a point. In Elizabethan times the public was always ready (like some people The Bible mentions) to hear a new thing, especially if it was sensational. Thomas Nashe, no mean exploiter of the public taste himself, has this to say in his Anatomy of Absurdity *(1589) about some popular writers:*

Another sort of men there are, who, though not addicted to such counterfeit curiosity, yet are they infected with a farther improbability; challenging knowledge unto themselves of deeper mysteries, whenas with Thales Milesius they see not what is under their feet; searching more curiously into the secrets of nature, whenas in respect of deeper knowledge, they seem mere naturals; coveting with the phoenix to approach so nigh to the sun, that they are scorched with his beams and confounded with his brightness. Who made them so privy to the secrets of the Almighty, that they should foretell the tokens of his wrath, or terminate the time of his vengeance? But lightly some news attends the end of every term, some monsters are booked, though not bred, against vacation times, which are straightway diversely dispersed into every quarter, so that at length they become the alehouse talk of every carter: yea, the country ploughman feareth a Calabrian flood in the midst of a furrow, and the silly shepherd committing his wandering sheep to the custody of his wrap, in his field-naps dreameth of flying dragons, which for fear lest he should see to the loss of his sight, he falleth asleep; no star he seeth in the night but seemeth a comet; he lighteth no sooner on a quagmire, but he thinketh this is the foretold earthquake, whereof his boy hath the ballad.

Thus are the ignorant deluded, the simple misused, and the sacred science of astronomy discredited; and in truth what leasings will not make-shifts invent for money? What will they not feign for gain? Hence come our babbling ballads, and our new found songs and sonnets which every rednose fiddler hath at his fingers' ends, and every ignorant ale-knight will breathe forth over the pot, as soon as his brain waxeth hot. Be it a truth which they would tune, they interlace it with a lie or two to make metre, not regarding verity, so they may make up the verse; not unlike to Homer, who cared not what he feigned, so he might make his countrymen famous. But as the straightest things being put into water seem crooked, so the crediblest truths if once they come within compass of these men's wits, seem tales. Were it that the infamy of their ignorance did redound only upon themselves, I could be content to apply my speech otherwise than to their Apuleian [asinine] ears, but sith they obtain the name of our English poets, and thereby make men think more basely of the wits of our country, I cannot but turn them out of their counterfeit livery, and brand them in the forehead, that all men may know their falsehood. Well may that saying of Campanus be applied to our English poets, which he spake of them in his time: 'They make (saith he) poetry an occupation, lying is their living, and fables are their movables; if thou takest away trifles, silly souls, they will famish for hunger.' It were to be wished that the acts of the venturous, and the praise of the virtuous were, by public edict, prohibited by such men's merry mouths to be so odiously extolled, as rather breeds detestation than admiration, loathing than liking. What politic councillor or valiant soldier will joy or glory of this, in that some stitcher, weaver, spendthrift or fiddler hath shuffled or slubbered up a few ragged rimes, in the memorial of the one's prudence, or the other's prowess? It makes the learned sort to be silent when they see unlearned sots so insolent.

One of the best anonymous plays of the Elizabethan (or any other) period of English literature is Arden of Faversham, *based on a true story from the reign of Edward VI. The* Wardmote Book *of Faversham (Kent) tells the tale of the "horrible and heinous" murder of a Mr. Ardern in 1551, and it was on true and sensational stories such as this that a good deal of popular literature, from broadsides to plays, was based. Our detective fiction began in such ways.*

This year the 15 day of February being Sunday one Thomas Ardern, of Faversham aforesaid, gentleman, was heinously murdered in his own parlour, about seven of the clock in the night, by one Thomas Morsby, a tailor of London, late servant to sir Edward North, knight, chancellor of the augmentations, father-in-law unto Alice Ardern, wife of the said Thomas Ardern; and by one Black Will, of Calyce [Calais, France], a murderer, which murderer was privily sent for to Calyce by the earnest suit, appointment, and confederacy of the said Alice Ardern, and Thomas Morsby, one John Green a tailor, and George Bradshaw, a goldsmith, inhabitants of Faversham aforesaid, to th' intent to murder the said Ardern her husband; which Alice, the said Morsby did not only carnally keep in her own house in this town, but also fed him with delicate meats and sumptuous apparel, all which things the said Ardern did well know, and willfully did permit and suffer the same, by reason whereof she procured her said husband's death, to th' intent to have married with the said Morsby, and so first she made of her said counsel the said Thomas Morsby, and one Cecily Pounder his sister, Michael Saunderson, tailor, and Elizabeth Stafford; which Michael and Elizabeth were the daily servants to the said Thomas Ardern, and the abettors and councilors to the said murder, were the aforesaid and John Green, George Bradshaw, and William Blackbourne, painter; which Bradshaw set th' aforesaid murderer at Calyce foresaid, and the same murderer came over to Faversham, and brought with him a coadjutor named Loosebagg, who also was made a counsel to th' aforesaid murder, so that he was most shamefully murdered, as is aforesaid, as he was playing at tables friendly with the said Morsby; for suddenly came out of a dark house, adjoining to th' said parlour, the 'foresaid Black Will, whom she and her complices had bestowed privily before, and came with a napkin in his hand, and suddenly came behind the said Ardern's back, threw the said napkin over his head and face, and strangled him, and forthwith the said Morsby stepped to him, and struck him with a tailor's great pressing Iron upon the skull to the brain, and immediately drew out his dagger, which was great and broad, and therewith cut the said Ardern's throat; being at the death of him the said Alice his wife, Michael Saunderson, and Elizabeth Stafford, and after that he was thus murdered, he was carried out of the said parlour into the aforesaid dark house, and when the said Black Will had helped to lay him there he returned forthwith to the said Cecily Pounder's house, and there received for his thus doing, the sum of eight pounds in money, which was there appointed for his reward, and immediately he departed from Faversham, so that he could not justly be heard of since that time, and he being thus departed with the reward, Cecily Pounder went to the said Ardern's house, and did help to bear the dead corpse out into a meadow there, commonly called the Amery Croft, on the back side of the said Ardern's garden: and about eleven of the clock the said Sunday night, the said Ardern was found where they had laid him, in the said meadow; whereupon the said Ardern's house was searched, and thereupon his blood was found, that it was manifest and well approved that he was slain in his own house. Whereupon the said Alice Ardern, Michael Saunderson, and Elizabeth Stafford, were apprehended and attached of felony, and also the said Morsby and Bradshaw, but the aforesaid John Green, William Blackbourne, and George Loosebagg, escaped at that time; and the aforesaid Alice Ardern, Thomas Morsby, Cecily Pounder, Michael Saunderson, George Bradshaw, and Elizabeth Stafford, were indicted and arraigned within the said town and liberties of Faversham, in the abbey-hall which the said Ardern had purchased, and there adjudged to die, that is, to wit, the said Alice Ardern to be burned to Cantorburye, and the said Bradshaw to be there hanged in chains by the commandment of the king's most honourable counsel, and the aforesaid Thomas Morsby and his sister judged to be hanged in Smithfield, in London; and the foresaid Michael Saunderson to be drawn and hanged in chains within the liberties of Faversham aforesaid, and the foresaid Elizabeth Stafford to be burned within the liberties of the said town; all which was accomplished and performed accordingly. And about the last end of the month of July then next following the foresaid John Green was apprehended and taken in Cornwall, and brought again by men of that country to Faversham, where shortly after he was judged to be hanged in chains, within the liberties there. And all the apparel that belonged to the said Alice Ardern, all the moveable goods of the aforesaid Thomas Morsby, Cecily Pounder, George Bradshaw, and John Green, amounted unto the sum of nine score and four pounds ten shillings and four pence halfpenny, over and above certain jewels of the said murderers, which are contained in certain Boxes delivered into the treasury house of Faversham foresaid, as by the particulars thereof more plainly doth appear; of which said nine score and four pounds ten shillings and four pence halfpenny, the accountants or sellers of the said goods ask to be allowed upon two bills of reckoning bestowed upon the said felons and their attainder, sixty-three pounds fifteen shillings and seven pence, and so they have delivered in ready money to the foresaid treasury parcel of the said money, after the old rate one hundred and twenty pounds whereof there was lost by abasing or fall of the said money sixty pounds.

The official record just does not have the drama and narrative appeal of the version so many Elizabethans read in Holinshed's Chronicles. *His French may be as bad as any other Elizabethan Englishman's (*fleur de lys *in an inn name becomes* floure de lice *by the same process by which* Chateau Vert *became* Shotover *and* Beauclerc, Buckley) *but the storyteller here has a firm grasp on the tale and the reader.*

About this time there was at Feversham in Kent a gentleman named Ardern, most cruelly murdered and slain by the procurement of his own wife. The which murder, for the horribleness thereof, although otherwise it may seem to be but a private matter, and therefore as it were impertinent to this history, I have thought good to set it forth somewhat at large, having the instructions delivered to me by them, that have used some diligence to gather the true understanding of the circumstances. This Arden was a man of a tall and comely personage, and matched in marriage with a gentlewoman, young, tall, and well favored of shape and countenance, who chancing to fall in familiarity with one Mosbie a tailor by occupation, a black swart man, servant to the Lord North, it happened this Mosbie upon some misliking to fall out with her: but she being desirous to be in favor with him again, sent him a pair of silver dice by one Adam Foule dwelling at the Floure de lice in Feversham.

After which he resorted to her again, and oftentimes lay in Arden's house: insomuch that within two years after, he obtained such favor at her hands, that he lay with her, or (as they term it) kept her, in abusing her body. And although (as it was said) Arden perceived right well their mutual familiarity to be much greater than their honesty, yet because he would not offend her, and so lose the benefit which he hoped to gain at some of her friends' hands in bearing with her lewdness, which he might have lost if he should have fallen out with her: he was contented to wink at her filthy disorder, and both permitted, and also invited Mosbie very often to lodge in his house. And thus it continued a good space, before any practice was begun by them against Master Arden. She at length inflamed in love with Mosbie, and loathing her husband, wished and after practiced the means how to hasten his end.

There was a painter dwelling in Feversham, who had skill of poisons, as was reported. She therefore demanded of him, whether it were true that he had such skill in that feat or not? And he denied not but that he had indeed. Yea (said she) but I would have such a one made, as should have most vehement and speedy operation to dispatch the eater thereof. That can I do (quoth he) and forthwith made her such a one, and willed her to put it into the bottom of a porrenger, and then after to pour milk on it. Which circumstance she forgetting, did clean contrary, putting in the milk first, and afterward the poison. Now Master Arden purposing that day to ride in Canterbury, his wife brought him his breakfast, which was wont to be milk and butter. He having received a spoonful or two of the milk, misliked the taste and color thereof, and said to his wife: Mistress Ales what milk have you given me here? Wherewithall she tilted it over with her hand, saying I ween nothing can please you. Then he took horse and rode toward Canterbury, and by the way fell into extreme purging upwards and downwards, and so escaped for that time.

After this, his wife fell in acquaintance with one Greene of Feversham, servant to Sir Anthonie Ager, from which Greene Master Arden had wrested a piece of ground on the backside of the Abbey of Feversham, and there had blows and great threats passed betwixt them about that matter. Therefore she knowing that Greene hated her husband, began to practice with him how to make him away; and concluded, that if he could get any that would kill him, he should have ten pounds for a reward. This Greene having doings for his master Sir Anthonie Ager, had occasion to go up to London, where his master then lay, and having some charge up with him, desired one Bradshaw a goldsmith of Feversham that was his neighbor, to accompany him to Gravesend, and he would content him for his pains. This Bradshaw, being a very honest man, was content, and rode with him. And when they came to Rainham down, they chanced to see three or four servingmen that were coming from Leeds: and therewith Bradshaw espied coming up the hill from Rochester, one Black Will, a terrible cruel ruffian with a sword and a buckler, and another with a great staff on his neck.

Then said Bradshaw to Greene: We are happy that here comes some company from Leeds, for here comes up against us as murdering a knave as any is in England: if it were not for them we might chance hardly to escape without loss of our money and lives. Yea thought Greene (as he after confessed) such a one is for my purpose, and therefore asked; Which is he? Yonder is he quoth Bradshaw, the same that hath the sword and buckler: his name is Black Will. How know you that, said Greene? Bradshaw answered, I knew him at Bullongne, where we both served, he was a soldier, and I was Sir Richard Cavendishe's man, and there he committed many robberies and heinous murders on such as traveled betwixt Bullongne and France.

By this time the other company of servingmen came to them, and they going all together, met with Black Will, and saluting him, demanded of him wither he went? he answered; By his blood (for his use was to swear almost at every word) I know not, nor care not, but set up my staff, and even as it falleth I go. If thou (quoth they) wilt go back again to Gravesend, we will give thee thy supper. By his blood (said he) I care not, I am content, have with you: and so he returned again with them. Then Black Will took acquaintance of Bradshaw, saying; Fellow Bradshaw how doth thou? Bradshaw unwilling to renew acquaintance, or to have aught to do with so shameless a ruffian, said; Why do ye know me? Yea that I do (quoth he) did not we serve in Bullongne together? But ye must pardon me (quoth Bradshaw) for I have forgotten you.

Then Greene talked with Black Will, and said; When ye have supped, come to mine host's house at such a sign, and I will give you the sack and sugar. By his blood (said he) I thank you, I will come and take it I warrant you. According to his promise he came, and there they made good cheer. Then Black Will and Greene went and talked apart from Bradshaw, and there concluded together, that if he would kill Master Arden, he should have ten pounds for his labor. Then he answered, By his wounds that I will if I may know him. Marry, tomorrow in Poules I will show him thee, said Greene. Then they left their talk, and Greene bade him go home to his host's house. Then Greene wrote a letter to Mistress Arden, and among other things put in these words: We have got a man for our purpose, we may thank my brother Bradshaw. Now Bradshaw not knowing anything of this, took the letter of him, and in the morning departed home again, and delivered the letter to Mistress Arden, and Greene and Black Will went up to London at the tide.

At the time appointed, Greene showed Black Will Master Arden walking in Poules. Then said Black Will, What is he that goeth after him? Marry, said Greene one of his men. By his blood (said Black Will) I will kill them both. Nay (said Greene) do not so, for he is of counsel with us in this matter. By his blood (said he) I care not for that, I will kill them both. Nay, said Greene, in any wise do not so. Then Black Will thought to have killed Master Arden in St. Poules churchyard, but there were so many gentlemen that accompanied him to dinner, that he missed of his purpose. Greene showed all this talk to Master Arden's man, whose name was Michaell, which ever after stood in doubt of Black Will, lest he should kill him. The cause that this Michaell conspired with the rest against his master, was: for that it was determined, that he should marry a kinswoman of Mosbie's.

After this, Master Arden lay at a certain parsonage which he held in London, and therefore his man Michaell and Greene agreed, that Black Will should come in the night to the parsonage, where he would find the doors left open, that he might come in and murder Master Arden. This Michaell having his master to bed, left open the doors according to the appointment. His master then being in bed, asked him if he had shut fast the doors, and he said yea; but yet afterwards, fearing lest Black Will would kill him as well as his master, after he was in bed himself, he rose again and shut the doors, bolting them fast. So that Black Will coming thither, and finding the doors shut, departed, being disappointed at that time. The next day Black Will came to Greene in a great chafe, swearing and staring because he was so deceived, and with many terrible oaths threatened to kill Master Arden's man first, wheresoever he met him. No (said Greene) do not so, I will first know the cause of shutting the doors.

Then Greene met and talked with Arden's man, and asked of him, why he did not leave open the doors, according to his promise? Marry (said Michaell) I will show you the cause. My master yesternight did that he never did before: for after I was in bed, he rose up and shut the doors, and in the morning rated me for leaving them unshut. And herewith Greene and Black Will were pacified. Arden being ready to go homewards, his maid came to Greene and said; This night will my master go down. Whereupon it was agreed that Black Will should kill him on Rainham down. When Master Arden came to Rochester, his man still fearing that Black Will would kill him with his master, pricked his horse of purpose, and made him to halt, to the end he might protract the time, and tarry behind. His master asked him why his horse halted, he said, I know not. Well (quoth his master) when ye come at the Smith here before (between Rochester and the hill foot over against Cheetam) remove his shoe, and search him, and then come after me. So Master Arden rode on: and ere he came at the place where Black Will lay in wait for him, there overtook him divers gentlemen of his acquaintance, who kept him company: so that Black Will missed here also of his purpose.

After that Master Arden was come home, he sent (as he usually did) his man to Sheppey to Sir Thomas Cheinie [Cheyney], then lord warden of the cinque ports, about certain business, and at his coming away, he had a letter delivered sent by Sir Thomas Cheinie to his master. When he came home, his mistress took the letter and kept it, willing her man to tell his master, that he had a letter delivered him by Sir Thomas Cheinie, and that he had lost it; adding that he thought it best that his master should go the next morning to Sir Thomas, because he knew not the matter: he said he would, and therefore he willed his man to be stirring betimes. In this meanwhile, Black Will, and one George Shakebag his companion, were kept in a storehouse of Sir Anthonie Ager's at Preston, by Greene's appointment: and thither came Mistress Arden to see him, bringing and sending him meat and drink many times. He therefore lurking there, and watching some opportunity for his purpose, was willed in anywise to be up early in the morning, to lie in wait for Master Arden in a certain broom close [field] betwixt Feversham and the ferry (which close he must needs pass) there to do his feat. Now Black Will stirred in the morning betimes, but missed the way, and tarried in a wrong place.

Master Arden and his man coming on their way early in the morning towards Shornelan, where Sir Thomas Cheinie lay: as they were almost come to the broom close, his man always fearing that Black Will would kill him with his master, feigned that he had lost his purse; Why said his master, thou foolish knave, couldst thou not look to thy purse but lose it? What was in it? Three pounds said he. Why then go thy way back again like a knave (said his master) and seek it, for being so early as it is, there is no man stirring, and therefore thou mayst be sure to find it, and then come and overtake me at the ferry. But nevertheless, by reason that Black Will lost his way, Master Arden escaped yet once again. At that time, Black Will yet thought he should have been sure to have met him homewards: but whether that some of the lord warden's men accompanied him back to Feversham, or that being in doubt, for that it was late to go through the broom close, and therefore took another way, Black Will was disappointed then also.

But now Saint Valentine's Fair being at hand, the conspirators thought to dispatch their devilish intention at that time. Mosbie minded to pick some quarrel to Master Arden at the Fair to fight with him; for he said he could not find in his heart to murder a gentlemen in that sort as his wife wished:

although she had made a solemn promise to him, and he again to her, to be in all points as man and wife together, and thereupon they both received the sacrament on a Sunday at London, openly in a church there. But this devise to fight with him would not serve, for Master Arden both then and at other times had been greatly provoked by Mosbie to fight with him, but he would not. Now Mosbie had a sister that dwelt in a tenement of Master Arden's near to his house in Feversham: and on the Fair even, Black Will was sent for to come thither, and Greene bringing him thither, met there with Mistress Arden, accompanied with Michaell her man, and one of her maids. There were also Mosbie and George Shakebag, and there they devised to have killed him in manner as afterwards he was. But yet Mosbie at the first would not agree to that cowardly murdering of him, but in a fury flung away, and went up the Abbey street toward the Floure de lice, the house of the aforenamed Adam Foule, where he did often host. But before he came thither now at this time, a messenger overtook him that was sent from Mistress Arden, desiring him of all love to come back again to help to accomplish the matter he knew of. Thereupon he returned to her again, and at his coming back, she fell down upon her knees to him, and besought him to go through with the matter, as if he loved her he would be content to do, since as she had divers times told him, he needed not to doubt, for there was not any that would care for his death, nor make any great inquiry for them that should dispatch him.

Thus she being earnest with him, at length he was contented to agree unto that horrible device, and thereupon they conveyed Black Will into Master Arden's house, putting him into a closet at the end of his parlor. Before this, they had sent out of the house all the servants, those excepted which were privy to the devised murder. Then went Mosbie to the door, and there stood in a nightgown of silk girded about him, and this was betwixt six and seven of the clock at night. Master Arden having been at a neighbor's house of his, named Dumpkin, and having cleared certain reckonings betwixt them, came home: and finding Mosbie standing at the door, asked him if it were supper time? I think not (quoth Mosbie) it is not yet ready. Then let us go and play a game at the tables in the mean season, said Master Arden. And so they went straight into the parlor, and as they came by through the hall, his wife was walking there, and Master Arden said; How now Mistress Ales? But she made small answer to him. In the meantime one chained the wicket door of the entry. When they came into the parlor, Mosbie sat down on the bench, having his face toward the place where Black Will stood. Then Michaell Master Arden's man stood at his master's back, holding a candle in his hand, to shadow Black Will, that Arden might by no means perceive him coming forth. In their play Mosbie said thus (which seemed to be the watchword for Black Will's coming forth) Now may I take you sir if I will. Take me (quoth Master Arden) which way? With that Black Will stepped forth, and cast a towel about his neck, to stop his breath and strangle him. Then Mosbie having at his girdle a pressing iron of fourteen pounds weight, struck him on the head with the same, so that he fell down, and gave a great groan, insomuch that they thought he had been killed.

Then they bore him away, to lay him in the counting house, and as they were about to lay him down, the pangs of death coming on him, he gave a great groan, and stretched himself, and then Black Will gave him a great gash in the face, and so killed him out of hand, laid him along, took the money out of his purse, and the rings from his fingers, and then coming out of the counting house, said; Now the feat is done, give me my money. So Mistress Arden gave him ten pounds: and he coming to Greene, had a horse of him, and so rode his way. After that Black Will was gone, Mistress Arden came into the counting house, and with a knife gave him seven or eight picks into the breast. Then they made clean the parlor, took a clout, and wiped where it was bloody, and strewed again the rushes that were shuffled with struggling, and cast the clout with which they wiped the blood, and the knife that was bloody, wherewith she had wounded her husband, into a tub by the well's side; where afterwards both the same clout and knife were found. Thus this wicked woman, with her accomplices, most shamefully murdered her own husband, who most entirely loved her all his lifetime. Then they sent for two Londoners to supper, the one named Prune, and the other Cole, that were grocers, which before the murder was committed, were bidden to supper. When they came, she said: I marvel where Master Arden is; we will not tarry for him, come ye and sit down, for he will not be long. Then Mosbie's sister was sent for, she came and sat down, and so they were merry.

After supper, Mistress Arden caused her daughter to play on the virginals, and they danced, and she with them, and so seemed to protract time as it were, till Master Arden should come, and she said, I marvel where he is so long; well, he will come anon I am sure, I pray you in the meanwhile let us play a game at the tables. But the Londoners said, they must go to their host's house, or else they should be shut out at doors, and so taking their leave, departed. When they were gone, the servants that were not privy to the murder, were sent abroad into the town; some to seek their master, and some on other errands, all saving Michaell and a maid, Mosbie's sister, and one of Mistress Arden's own daughters. Then they took the dead body, and carried it out, to lay it in a field next to the churchyard, and joining to his garden wall, through the which he went to the church. In the meantime it began to snow, and when they came to the garden gate, they remembered that they had forgotten the key, and one went in for it, and finding it, at length brought it, opened the gate, and carried the corpse into the same field, as it were ten paces from the garden gate, and laid him down on his back straight in his nightgown, with his slippers on: and between one of his slippers and his foot, a long rush or two remained. When they had thus laid him down, they returned the same way they came through the garden into the house.

They being returned thus back again into the house, the doors were opened, and the servants returned home that had been sent abroad: and being now very late, she sent forth her folks again to make inquiry for him in divers places; namely, among the best in the town where he was wont to be, who made answer, that they could tell nothing of him. Then she began to make an outcry, and said; Never woman had such neighbors as I have, and herewith wept: insomuch that her neighbors came in, and found her making great lamentation, pretending to marvel what was become of her husband. Whereupon, the mayor and others came to make search for him. The Fair was wont to be kept partly in the town, and partly in the Abbey; but Arden for his own private lucre and covetous gain had this present year procured it to be wholly kept within the Abbey ground which he had purchased; and so reaping all the gains to himself, and bereaving the town of that portion which was wont to come to the inhabitants, got many a bitter curse. The mayor going about the Fair in this search, at length came to the ground where Arden lay: and as it happened, Prune the grocer setting sight of him, first said; Stay, for me think I see one lie here. And so they looking and beholding the body, found that it was Master Arden, lying there thoroughly dead, and viewing diligently the manner of his body and hurts, found the rushes sticking in his slippers, and making further, espied certain footsteps, by reason of the snow, betwixt the place where he lay, and the garden door.

Then the mayor commanded every man to stay, and herewith appointed some to go about, and to come in at the inner side of the house through the garden as the way lay, to the place where Master Arden's dead body did lie; who all the way as they came, perceived footings still before them in the snow; and so it appeared plainly that he was brought along that way from the house through the garden, and so into the field where he lay. Then the mayor and his company that were with him went into the house, and knowing her evil demeanor in times past, examined her of the matter: but she defied them and said, I would you should know I am no such woman. Then they examined her servants, and in the examination, by reason of a piece of his hair and blood found near to the house in the way, by the which they carried him forth, and likewise by the knife with which she had thrust him into the breast, and the clout wherewith they wiped the blood away which they found in the tub, into the which the same were thrown; they all confessed the matter, and herself beholding her husband's blood, said; Oh the blood of God help, for this blood have I shed.

Then were they all attached [arrested], and committed to prison, and the mayor with others went presently to the Floure de lice, where they found Mosbie in bed: and as they came towards him, they espied his hose and purse stained with some of Master Arden's blood. And when he asked what they meant by their coming in such sort, they said; See, here ye may understand wherefore, by these tokens, showing him the blood on his hose and purse. Then he confessed the deed, and so he and all the others that had conspired the murder, were apprehended and laid in prison, except Greene, Black Will, and the painter, which painter and George Shakebag, that was also fled before, were never heard of [again]. Shortly were the sessions kept at Feversham, where all the prisoners were arraigned and condemned. And thereupon being examined whether they had any other accomplices, Mistress Arden accused Bradshaw, upon occasion of the letter sent by Greene from Gravesend (as before ye have heard), which words had none other meaning, but only by Bradshaw's describing of Black Will's qualities; Greene judged him a meet instrument for the execution of their pretended murder. Whereto notwithstanding (as Greene confessed at his death certain years after) this Bradshaw was never made privy; howbeit, he was upon his accusation of Mistress Arden, immediately sent for to the sessions, and indicted, and declaration made against him, as a procurer of Black Will to kill Master Arden, which proceeded wholly by misunderstanding of the words contained in the letter which he brought from Greene.

Then he desired to talk with the persons condemned, and his request was granted. He therefore demanded of them if they knew him, or ever had any conversation with him, and they all said no. Then the letter being shown and read, he declared the very truth of the matter, and upon what occasion he told Greene of Black Will: nevertheless, he was condemned, and suffered. These condemned persons were diversely executed in sundry places, for Michaell Master Arden's man was hanged in chains at Feversham, and one of the maids was burnt there, pitifully bewailing her case, and cried out on her mistress, that had brought her to this end, for the which she would never forgive her. Mosbie and his sister were hanged in Smithfield at London; Mistress Arden was burned at Canturbury the four and twentieth of March. Greene came again certain years after, was apprehended, condemned, and hanged in chains in the highway betwixt Ospring and Boughton against Feversham; Black Will was burnt on a scaffold at Flushing in Zeeland. Adam Foule that dwelt at the Floure de lice in Feversham was brought into trouble about this matter, and carried up to London, with his legs bound under the horse's belly, and committed to prison in the Marshalsea: for that Mosbie was heard to say; Had it not been for Adam Foule, I had not come to this trouble: meaning that the bringing of the silver dice for a token to him from Mistress Arden, as ye have heard, occasioned him to renew familiarity with her again. But when the matter was thoroughly ripped up, and that Mosbie had cleared him, protesting that he was never of knowledge in any behalf to the murder, the man's innocence preserved him.

This one thing seemeth very strange and notable, touching Master Arden, that in the place where he was laid, being dead, all the proportion of his body might be seen two years after and more, so plain as could be, for the grass did not grow where his body had touched: but between his legs, between his arms, and about the hallowness of his neck, and round about his body, and where his legs, arms, head or any other part of his body had touched, no grass grew at all of all that time. So that many strangers came in that meantime, besides the townsmen, to see the print of his body there on the ground in that field. Which field he had (as some have reported) most cruelly taken from a woman, that had been a widow to one Cooke, and after married to one Richard Read a mariner, to the great hinderance of her and her husband the said Read: for they had long enjoyed it by a lease, which they had of it for many years, not then expired: nevertheless, he got it from them. For the which, the said Read's wife not only exclaimed against him, in shedding many a salt tear, but also cursed him most bitterly even to his face, wishing many a vengence to light upon him, and that all the world might wonder on him. Which was thought then to come to pass, when he was thus murdered, and lay in that field from midnight till the morning: and so all that day, being the Fair day till night, all the which day there were many hundreds of people came wondering about him. And thus far touching this horrible and heinous murder of Master Arden.

There you have a murder story with villains, clues, a widow's curse, a bit of magic! Here is another. Thomas Deloney knew how to spin a popular crime yarn, as we can appreciate from this one even if he perpetrates some anachronisms. The plot later turned up in both English and German dramas.

How Thomas of Reading Was Murdered at His Hosts' House of Colebrook; Who Also Had Murdered Many Before Him, and How Their Wickedness Was at Length Revealed

Thomas of Reading, having many occasions to come to London, as well about his own affairs as also the king's business, being in a great office under his majesty, it chanced on a time that his host and hostess of Colebrook, who through covetousness had murdered many of their guests, and having every time he came thither great store of his money to lay up, appointed him to be the next fat pig that should be killed. For it is to be understood that when they plotted the murder of any man, this was always their team, the man to his wife and the woman to her husband.

"Wife, there is now a fat pig to be had if you want one."

Whereupon she would answer this, "I pray you put him in the hogsty till tomorrow."

This was when any man came thither alone without others in his company, and they saw he had great store of money.

This man should be then laid in the chamber right over the kitchen, which was a fair chamber and better set out than any other in the house. The best bedstead therein, though it were little and low, yet was it most cunningly carved and fair to the eye; the feet whereof were fast nailed to the chamber floor in such sort that it could not in any wise fall. The bed that lay therein was fast sewed to the sides of the bedstead. Moreover, that part of the chamber whereupon this bed and bedstead stood was made in such sort that, by the pulling out of two iron pins below in the kitchen, it was to be let down and taken up by a drawbridge, or in manner of a trap door. Moreover, in the kitchen, directly under the place where this should fall, was a mighty great caldron, wherein they used to seethe their liquor when they went to brewing. Now, the men appointed for the slaughter were laid unto this bed, and in the dead time of the night when they were sound asleep, by plucking out the foresaid iron pins, down would the man fall out of his bed into the boiling caldron, and all the clothes that were upon him. Where, being suddenly scalded and drowned, he was never able to cry or speak one word.

Then had they a little ladder ever standing ready in the kitchen, by the which they presently mounted into the said chamber and there closely took away the man's apparel, as also his money in his male or capcase. And then lifting up the said falling floor which hung by hinges, they made it fast as before.

The dead body would they take presently out of the caldron and throw it down the river, which ran near unto the house. Whereby they escaped all danger.

Now if in the morning any of the rest of the guests that had talked with the murdered man over eve [the previous night] chanced to ask for him, as having occasion to ride the same way that he should have done, the goodman would answer that he took horse a good while before day and that he himself did set him forward. The horse the goodman would also take out of the stable and convey him to a haybarn of his that stood from his house a mile or two, whereof himself did always keep the keys full charily, and when any hay was to be brought from thence, with his own hands he would deliver it. Then, before the horse should go from thence, he would dismark him, as, if he were a long tail, he would make him curtal, or else crop his ears, or cut his mane, or put out one of his eyes; and by this means, he kept himself a long time unknown.

Now Thomas of Reading, as I said before, being marked and kept for a fat pig, he was laid in the same chamber of death; but by reason Gray of Gloucester chanced also to come that night, he escaped scalding.

The next time he came, he was laid there again, but before he fell asleep or was warm in his bed, one came riding through the town and cried piteously that London was all on afire and that it had burned down Thomas Becket's house in Westcheap, and a great number more in the same street.

"And yet," quoth he, "the fire is not quenched."

Which tidings, when Thomas of Reading heard, he was very sorrowful, for of the same Becket that day had he received a great piece of money and had left in his house many of his writings and some that appertained to the king [Henry I] also. Therefore, there was no nay but he would ride back again to London presently to see how the matter stood; thereupon, making himself ready, he departed. This cross fortune caused his host to frown.

"Nevertheless, the next time," quoth he, "will pay for all."

Notwithstanding, God so wrought that they were prevented then likewise, by reason of a great fray that happened in the house betwixt a couple that fell out at dice, insomuch as the murderers themselves were enforced to call him up, being a man in great authority, that he might set the house in quietness; out of the which, by means of this quarrel, they doubted to lose many things.

Another time when he should have been laid in the same place, he fell so sick that he requested to have somebody to watch with him. Whereby also they could not bring their vile purpose to pass. But hard it is to escape the ill fortunes whereunto a man is allotted. For albeit that the next time that he came to London his horse stumbled and broke one of his legs as he should ride homeward. Yet hired he another to hasten his own death, for there was no remedy but he should go to Colebrook that night. But by the way he was so heavy asleep that he could scant keep himself in the saddle; and when he came near unto the town, his nose burst out suddenly ableeding.

Well, to his inn he came and so heavy was his heart that he could eat no meat. His host and hostess, hearing he was so melancholy, came out and said. "Never did we see you thus sad before. Will it please you to have a quart of burned sack [mulled wine]?"

"With a good will," quoth he. "And would to God Thomas Dove were here. He would surely make me merry, and we should lack no music. But I am sorry for the man with all my heart, that he is come so far behindhand. But, alas, so much can every man say, but what good doth it him? No, no, it is not words can help a man in this case; the man had need of other relief than so. Let me see: I have but one child in the world and that is my daughter, and half that I have is hers, the other half my wife's. What then? Shall I be good to nobody but them? In conscience, my wealth is too much for a couple to possess, and what is our religion without charity? And to whom is charity more to be shown than to decayed householders?"

"Good my host, lend me a pen and ink and some paper, for I will write a letter unto the poor man straight, and something I will give him. That alms which a man bestows with his own hands he shall be sure to have delivered, and God knows how long I shall live."

With that, his hostess dissemblingly answered, saying, "Doubt not, Master Cole, you are like enough by the course of nature to live many years."

"God knows," quoth he, "I never found my heart so heavy before."

By this time, pen, ink, and paper was brought; setting himself to writing, as followeth:

> In the name of God, Amen, I bequeath my soul to God and my body to the ground, my goods equally between my wife Elenor, and Isabel my daughter.
>
> Item: I give to Thomas Dove of Exeter one hundred pounds—nay, that is too little, I give to Thomas Dove two hundred pounds—in money, to be paid unto him presently upon his demand thereof by my said wife and daughter.

"Ha, how say you, my host?" quoth he. "Is not this well? I pray you read it."

His host, looking thereon, said, "Why, Master Cole, what have you written here? You said you would write a letter, but methinks you have made a will. What need have you to do thus? Thanks be to God, you may live many fair years."

" 'Tis true," quoth Cole, "if it please God, and I trust this writing cannot shorten my days. But let me see, have I made a will? Now I promise you, I did verily purpose to write a letter; notwithstanding, I have written that that God put into my mind. But look once again, my host, is it not written there that Dove shall have two hundred pounds, to be paid when he comes to demand it?"

"Yes, indeed," said his host.

"Well, then, all is well," said Cole. "And it shall go as it is for me. I will not bestow the new writing thereof any more."

Then, folding it up, he sealed it, desiring that his host would send it to Exeter. He promised that he would. Notwithstanding, Cole was not so satisfied but, after some pause, he would needs hire one to carry it. And so, sitting down sadly in his chair again, upon a sudden he burst forth aweeping. They demanding the cause thereof, he spoke as followeth:

"No cause of these tears I know. But it comes now into my mind," said Cole, "when I set toward this my last journey to London, how my daughter took on, what a coil she kept to have me stay. And I could not be rid of the little baggage a long time, she did so hang about me. When her mother by violence took her away, she cried out most mainly, 'Oh, my father, my father, I shall never see him again.' "

"Aye, it is indeed," said Cole, and with that he began to nod.

Then they asked him if he would go to bed.

"No," said he, "although I am heavy, I have no mind to go to bed at all."

With that, certain musicians of the town came to the chamber and, knowing Master Cole was there, drew out their instruments and very solemnly began to play.

"This music comes very well," said Cole. And when he had listened a while thereunto, he said, "Methinks these instruments sound like the ring of St. Mary Overy's bells, but the base drowns all the rest. And in my ear it goes like a bell that rings a forenoon's knell. For God's sake, let them leave off and and bear them this simple reward."

The musicians being gone, his host asked if now it would please him to go to bed.

"For," quoth he "it is well near eleven of the clock."

With that, Cole, beholding his host and hostess earnestly, began to start back, saying "What all you to look so like pale death? Good Lord, what have you done, that your hands are thus bloody?"

"What, my hands?" said his host. "Why, you may see they are neither bloody nor foul. Either your eyes do greatly dazzle, or else fancies of a troubled mind do delude you."

"Alas, my host, you may see," said he, "how weak my wits are. I never had my head so idle before. Come, let me drink once more, and then I will to bed and trouble you no longer."

With that he made himself unready, and his hostess was very diligent to warm a kerchief and put it about his head.

"Good Lord," said he, "I am not sick, I praise God, but such an alteration I find in myself as I never did before."

With that the screech owl cried piteously, and anon after the night raven sat croaking hard by his window.

"Jesu have mercy upon me!" quoth he. "What an ill-favored cry do yonder carrion birds make!"

And therewithal he laid him down in his bed, from whence he never rose again.

His host and hostess, that all this while noted his troubled mind, began to commune betwixt themselves thereof. And the man said he knew not what were best to be done.

"By my consent," quoth he, "the matter should pass, for I think it is not best to meddle on him."

"What, man," quoth she, "faint you now? Have you done so many, and do you shrink at this?"

Then, showing him a great deal of gold which Cole had left with her, she said, "Would it not grieve a body's heart to lose this? Hang the old churl, what should he do living any longer? He hath too much, and we have too little. Tut, husband, let the thing be done and then this is our own."

Her wicked counsel was followed, and when they had listened at his chamber door, they heard the man sound asleep.

"All is safe," quoth they.

And down into the kitchen they go, their servants being all in bed; and pulling out the iron pins, down fell the bed, and the man dropped out into the boiling caldron. He being dead, they betwixt them cast his body into the river. His clothes they hid away, and made all things as it should be. But when he came to the stable to convey thence Cole's horse, the stable door being open, the horse had got loose, and with a part of of the halter about his neck and straw trussed under his belly (as the hostlers had dressed him o'er eve). He was gone out at the backside, which led into a great field adjoining to the house; and so, leaping divers hedges, being a lusty stond [virile] horse, had got into a ground where a mare was grazing. With whom he kept such a coil that they got into the highway, where one of the town meeting them, knew the mare and brought her and the horse to the man that ow[n]ed her.

In the meanspace the musicians had been at the inn; and in requital of their evening's gift, they intended to give Cole some music in the morning. The goodman told them he took horse before day. Likewise there was a guest in the house that would have borne him company to Reading, unto whom the host also answered that he himself set him upon horseback and that he went long ago.

Anon comes the man that owed the mare, inquiring up and down to know and if none of them missed a horse. Who said no. At last he came to the Sign of the Crane, where Cole lay; and calling the hostlers, he demanded of them if they lacked none. They said no.

"Why, then," said the man, "I perceive my mare is good for something; for if I send her to field single, she will come home double."

Thus it passed on all that day and the night following. But the next day after, Cole's wife, musing that her husband came not home, sent one of her men on horseback to see if he could meet him.

"And if," quoth she, "you meet him not betwixt this and Colebrook, ask for him at the Crane. But if you find him not there, then ride to London; for I doubt he is either sick or else some mischance hath fallen unto him."

The fellow did so, and asking for him at Colebrook, they answered he went homeward from thence such a day. The servant musing what should be become of his master, and making much inquiry in the town for him, at length one told him of a horse that was found on their highway, and no man knew whence he came. He, going to see the horse, knew him presently, and to the Crane he goes with him. The host of the house, perceiving this, was blank, and that night fled secretly away. The fellow, going unto the justice, desired his help; presently after, word was brought that Jarman of the Crane was gone. Then all the men said he had surely made Cole away; and the musicians told what Jarman said to them when they would have given Cole music. Then the woman, being apprehended and examined, confessed the truth. Jarman soon after was taken in Windsor Forest. He and his wife were both hanged after they had laid open all these things before expressed. Also, he confessed that he, being a carpenter, made that false falling floor, and how his wife devised it, and how they had murdered by that means sixty persons. And yet notwithstanding all the money which they had gotten thereby, they prospered not, but at their death were found very far in debt.

When the king heard of this murder, he was for the space of seven days so sorrowful and heavy as he would not hear any suit, giving also commandment that the house should quite be consumed with fire wherein Cole was murdered and that no man should ever build upon that cursed ground.

Cole's substance at his death was exceeding great. He had daily in his house an hundred men servants, and forty maids; he maintained, beside, above two or three hundred people, spinners and carders, and a great many other householders. His wife never after married; and at her death she bestowed a mighty sum of money toward the maintaining of the new-built monastery. Her daughter was most richly married to a gentleman of great worship, by whom she had many children. And some say that the river whereinto Cole was cast did ever since carry the name of Cole, begin called the river of Cole and the town of Colebrook.

We still encounter the sensational and the salacious in popular writing excused by the idea that Vice "to be hated needs but to be seen." Jack Wilton saw murder, revenge, and execution and reformed his life. We, too, are supposed to be first titillated and then transformed by such fiction.

The speech from the scaffold, by the way, was a major feature of executions at Tyburn in Elizabeth's day and into the 18th century villains went to their deaths with farewell exhortations to the crowds that flocked to this free dramatic entertainment. Many condemned men made the most of their last speeches and were concerned with their effect upon the crowds, the final figure they cut. Even Charles I, on his way to having his head cut off in 1642, wore two shirts: he did not want to shiver with the cold and have the crowd think he was afraid. Gallows humor, so-called, has been a feature of English literature. Gallows rhetoric ought to be collected and studied as popular culture!

Thomas Deloney's life is obscure but it was almost exactly coeval with Elizabeth's reign. How a silkweaver also knew so much Latin is a trifle difficult to explain, but the combination of a workingman's outlook and a flair for writing (which seems to have first appeared with several ballads celebrating the defeat of the Spanish Armada) gave Deloney a significant place in literature and at the end of the 16th century he published Jack of Newberry, *two parts of a praise of shoemaking as* The Gentle Craft *with the history of Sir Simon Eyre (the shoemaker's apprentice who became a jovial Lord Mayor of London), and* Thomas of Reading. *From the latter Shakespeare seems to have got the idea for a scene in* Macbeth *and from* The Gentle Craft *Thomas Dekker certainly derived his hit play of* The Shoemaker's Holiday. *Deloney's* The Gentle Craft *is much quoted, but here are some stories from* Jack of Newberry.

After the King's Majesty [Henry VIII] and the Queen had heard this song sweetly sung by them, he cast them a great reward: and so departing thence, when to the fulling-mills, and dye-house, where a great many were also hard at work: and His Majesty perceiving what a great number of people were by this one man set on work, both admired, and commended him, saying further, that no trade in all the land was so much to be cherished and maintained as this, "which," quoth he, "may well be called, The life of the poor." And as the King returned from this place with intent to take horse and depart, there met him a great many of children in garments of white silk, fringed with gold, their heads crowned with golden bays, and about their arms each one had a scarf of green sarcenet fast tied, in their hands they bore silver bows, and under their girdles golden arrows.

The foremost of them represented Diana, Goddess of Chastity, who was attended on by a train of beautiful nymphs and they presented to the King four prisoners:

The first was a stern and grisly woman, carrying a frowning countenance, and her forehead full of wrinkles, her hair as black as pitch, and her garments all bloody, a great sword she had in her hand all stained with purple gore: they called her name Bellona, Goddess of Wars, who had three daughters: the first of them was a tall woman, so lean and ill-favoured, that her cheekbones were ready to start out of the skin, of a pale and deadly colour: her eyes sunk into her head: her legs so feeble, that they could scantly carry the body; all along her arms & hands through the skin you might tell the sinews, joints and bones: her teeth were very strong and sharp withal: she was so greedy, that she was ready with her teeth to tear the skin from her own arms: her attire was black, and all torn and ragged, she went barefooted, and her name was Famine.

The second was a strong and lusty woman, with a look pitiless, and unmerciful countenance: her garments were all made of iron and steel, and she carried in her hand a naked weapon, and she was called the Sword.

The third was also a cruel creature her eyes did sparkle like burning coals: her hair was like a flame, and her garments like burning brass: she was so hot, that none could stand near her, and they called her name Fire.

After this they retired again, and brought unto His Highness two other personages, their countenance was princely and amiable, their attire most rich and sumptuous: the one carried in his hand a golden trumpet, and the other a palm tree: and these were called Fame & Victory, whom the Goddess of Chastity charged to wait upon this famous prince forever. This done, each child after other with due reverence, gave unto His Majesty a sweet gilliflower, after the manner of the Persians, offering something in token of loyalty and obedience.

The King and Queen beholding the sweet favour and countenance of these children, demanded of Jack of Newbury whose children they were?

Who answered "It shall please Your Highness to understand, that these are the children of poor people, that do get their living by picking of wool, having scant a good meal once in a week."

With that the King began to tell his gilliflowers, whereby he found that there was 96. children.

"Certainly," said the Queen, "I perceive God gives as fair children to the poor as to the rich, and fairer many times: and though their diet and keeping be but simple, the blessing of God doth cherish them. Therefore," said the Queen, "I will request to have two of them to wait in my chamber."

"Fair Katharine," said the King, "thou and I have jumped in one opinion, in thinking these children fitter for the court than the country:" whereupon he made choice of a dozen more, four he ordained to be pages to his royal person, and the rest he sent to the universities, allotting to everyone a gentleman's living. Divers of the noblemen did in like sort entertain some of those children into their services, so that (in the end) not one was left to pick wool, but were all so provided for, that their parents never needed to care for them: and God so blessed them, that each of them came to be men of great account and authority in the land, whose posterities remain to this day worshipful and famous.

The King, Queen, and nobles, being ready to depart, after great thanks and gifts given to Jack of Newbury His Majesty would have made him knight, but he meekly refused it, saying, "I beseech Your Grace let me live a poor clothier among my people, in whose maintenance I take more felicity, than in all the vain titles of gentility: for these are the labouring ants whom I seek to defend, and these be the bees which I keep: who labour in this life, nor for ourselves, but for the glory of God, and to do service to our dread sovereign."

"Thy knighthood need be no hindrance of thy faculty," quoth the King.

"O my dread sovereign," said Jack, "honour and worship may be compared to the Lake of Lethe, which makes men forget themselves that taste thereof: and to the end I may still keep in mind from whence I came, and what I am, I beseech Your Grace let me rest in my russet coat, a poor clothier to my dying day."

"Seeing then," said the King, "that a man's mind is a kingdom to himself, I will leave thee to the riches of thy own content, and so farewell."

The Queen's Majesty taking her leave of the good wife with a princely kiss, gave her in token of remembrance, a most precious and rich diamond set in gold, about the which was also curiously set six rubies and six emeralds in one piece, valued at nine hundred marks: and so Her Grace departed.

But in this mean space, Will Summers kept company among the maids, and betook himself to spinning as they did, which among them was held as a forfeit of a gallon of wine, but William by no means would pay it, except they would take it out in kisses, rating every kiss at a farthing.

"This payment we refuse for two causes," quoth the maids: "the one for that we esteem not kisses at so base a rate; and the other, because in so doing we should give as much as you."

Here under the name "Will Summers" is Henry VIII's fool, Will Somers, a clown whose jokes on Wolsey convulsed the monarch and whose influence was significant. Deloney is describing a time before his own, for Somers retired from the court in 1547 and died in 1560.

The maidens consented together, seeing Will Summers was so busy both with their work and in his words, and would not pay his forfeiture, to serve him as he deserved: first therefore they bound him hands and feet, and set him upright against a post, tying him thereto: which he took in ill part, notwithstanding he could not resist them. And because he let his tongue run at random, they set a fair gag in his mouth, such a one as he could not for his life put away: so that he stood as one gaping for wind. Then one of them got a couple of dogs' droppings, and putting them in a bag, laid them in soak in a basin of water, while the rest turned down the collar of his jerkin, and put an house-cloth about his neck instead of a fine towel: then came the other maid with a basin and water in the same, and with the perfume in the pudding-bag, flapped him about the face and lips, till he looked like a tawny Moor, and with her hand washed him very orderly: the smell being somewhat strong, Will could be no means abide it, and for want of other language, cried, "Ah ha ha ha." Fain he would have spit, and could not, so that he was fain to swallow down such liquor as he never tasted the like. When he had a pretty while been washed in this sort, at the length he crouched down upon his knees, yielding himself to their favour: which the maidens perceiving, pulled the gag out of his mouth.

He had no sooner the liberty of his tongue, but that he curst and swore like a devil: the maids that could scant stand for laughing, at last asked how he liked his washing?

"God's wounds," he quoth he, "I was never thus washed, nor ever met with such barbers since I was born: let me go," quoth he, "and I will give you whatsoever you will demand," wherewith he cast them an English crown [a gold coin].

"Nay," quoth one of the maids, "you are yet but washed, but we will shave you ere ye go."

"Sweet maids," quoth he, "pardon my shaving, let it suffice that you have washed me: if I have done a trespass to your trade, forgive it me, and I will never hereafter offend you."

"Tush," said the maids, "you have made our wheels cast their bands, and bruised the teeth of our cards in such sort, as the offence may not be remitted without great penance. As for your gold, we regard it not: therefore as you are perfumed fit for the dogs, so we enjoin you this night to serve all our hogs, which penance, if you will swear with all speed to perform, we will let you loose."

"O," quoth Will, "the huge elephant was never more fearful of the silly sheep, than I am of your displeasures: therefore let me loose, and I will do it with all diligence."

Then they unbound him, and brought him among a great company of swine, which when Will had well viewed over, he drove out of the yard all the sows:

"Why how now," quoth the maids, "what mean you by this?"

"Marry," quoth Will, "these be all sows, and my penance is but to serve the hogs."

"Is it true," quoth they, "have you overtaken us in this sort? Well, look there be not one hog unserved we would advise you."

William Summers stripped up his sleeves very orderly, and clapped an apron about his motley hosen, and taking a pail served the hogs handsomely. When he had given them all meat, he said thus:

My task is duly done,
My liberty is won,
The hogs have eat their
crabs,
Therefore farewell you
drabs.

"Nay soft friend."

"Where the devil is he," said Will, "that I see him not?"

"Wrapped in a motley jerkin," quoth they, "take thyself by the nose, and thou shalt catch him by the snout."

"I was never so very a hog," quoth he, "but I would always spare from my own belly to give a woman."

"If thou do not," say they, "eat (like the prodigal child) with thy fellow hogs, we will so shave thee, as thou shalt dearly repent thy disobedience."

He seeing no remedy, committed himself to their mercy; and so they let him go. When he came to the court, he shewed to the King all his adventure among the weaver's maidens, whereat the King and Queen laughed heartily.

Finally, two tales on Deloney's favorite topic, how the talented but low born have been able to rise in the world, which was very popular indeed with ambitious young readers of two-for-a-penny broadsides and little, inexpensive books from the "stationers" and chapmen.

Of the pictures which Jack of Newbury had in his house, whereby he encouraged his servants to seek for fame and dignity.

In a fair large parlour which was wainscotted round about, Jack of Newbury had fifteen fair pictures hanging, which were covered with curtains of green silk, fringed with gold, which he would often shew to his friends and servants.

In the first was the picture of a shepherd, before whom kneeled a great king named Viriat, who sometime governed the people of Portugal.

"See here," quoth Jack, "the father a shepherd, the son a sovereign. This man ruled in Portugal, and made great wars against the Romans, and after that invaded Spain, yet in the end was traitorously slain."

The next was the portraiture of Agathocles, which for his surpassing wisdom and manhood, was created King of Sicilia, and maintained battle against the people of Carthage. His father was a poor potter, before whom he also kneeled. And it was the use of this king, that whensoever he made a banquet, he would have as well vessels of earth as of gold set upon the table, to the intent he might always bear in mind the place of his beginning, his father's house and family.

The third was the picture of Iphicrates an Athenian born, who vanquished the Lacedaemonians in plain and open battle. This man was captain general to Artaxerxes, King of Persia, whose father was notwithstanding a cobbler and there likewise pictured. Eumenes was also a famous captain to Alexander the Great, whose father was no other than a carter.

The fourth was the similitude of Aelius Pertinax, sometime Emperor of Rome, yet was his father but a weaver: and afterward, to give example to others of low condition to bear minds of worthy men, he caused the shop to be beautified with marble curiously cut, wherein his father before him was wont to get his living.

The fifth was the picture of Diocletian, that so much adorned Rome with his magnifical and triumphant victories. This was a famous emperor, although no other than the son of a bookbinder.

Valentinian stood the next, painted most artificially [artfully], who was also crowned emperor, and was but the son of a poor ropemaker: as the same picture was expressed; where his father was painted by him, using his trade. . . .

How one of Jack of Newbury's maids became a lady

At the winning of Morless in France, [1544, Thomas Howard, later second Duke of Norfolk] the noble Earl of Surrey being at the time Lord High Admiral of England, made many knights: among the rest was Sir George Rigley, brother to Sir Edward Rigley, and sundry other, whose valours far surpassed their wealth: so that when peace bred a scarcity in their purse, and that their credits grew weak in the city, they were enforced to ride into the country, where at their friends' houses they might have favourable welcome, without coin or grudging.

Among the rest, Jack of Newbury that kept a table for all comers, was never lightly without many such guests: where they were sure to have both welcome and good cheer, and their mirth no less pleasing than their meat was plenty. Sir George having lain long at board in this brave yeoman's house, at length fell in liking of one of his maidens, who was as fair as she was fond. This lusty wench he so allured with hope of marriage, that at length she yielded him her love, and therewithal bent her whole study to work his content: but in the end, she so much contented him, that it wrought altogether her own discontent: to become high, she laid herself so low, that the knight suddenly fell over her, which fall became the rising of her belly. But when this wanton perceived herself to be with child, she made her moan unto the knight in this manner.

"Ah Sir George, now is the time to perform your promise, or to make me a spectacle of infamy to the whole world forever: in the one you shall discharge the duty of a true knight, but in the other shew yourself a most perjured person. Small honour will it be to boast in the spoil of poor maidens, whose innocency all good knights ought much rather to defend."

"Why thou lewd paltry thing," quoth he, "comest thou to father thy bastard upon me? Away ye dunghill carrion, away: Hear you good housewife, get you among your companions, and lay your litter where you list: for if you trouble me any more, by heaven I swear, thou shalt dearly abide it:" and so bending his brows like the angry god of war, he went his ways, leaving the child-breeding wench to the hazard of her fortune, either good or bad.

This poor maiden seeing herself for her kindness thus cast off, shed many tears of sorrow for her sin, inveighing, with many bitter groans, against the unconstancy of love-alluring men. But in the end, when she saw no other remedy, she made her case known unto her mistress: who after she had given her many bitter checks and taunts, threatening to turn her out of doors, she opened the matter to her husband.

So soon as he heard thereof, he made no more to do, but presently posted to London after Sir George, and found him at my Lord Admiral's. "What, Master Winchcombe," quoth he, "you are heartily welcome to London, and I thank you for my good cheer. I pray you how doth your good wife, and all our friends in Berkshire?"

"All well and merry, I thank you good Sir George," quoth he: "I left them in health, and I hope they do so continue. And trust me sir," quoth he, "having earnest occasion to come up to talk with a bad debtor, in my journey it was my chance to light in company of a gallant widow: a gentlewoman she is, of wondrous good wealth, whom grisly death hath bereft of a kind husband, making her a widow, ere she had been half a year a wife: her land, Sir George, is as well worth a hundred pound a year as one penny, being as fair and comely a creature, as any of her degree in our whole country: Now sir, this is the worst, by the reason that she doubts herself to be with child, she hath vowed not to marry these twelve months: but because I wish you well, and the gentlewoman no hurt, I came of purpose from my business to tell you thereof: Now Sir George, if you think her a fit wife for you, ride to her, woo her, win her, and wed her."

"I thank you good Master Winchcombe," quoth he, "for your favour ever toward me, and gladly would I see this young widow if I wist where."

"She dwelleth not half a mile from my house," quoth Master Winchcombe, "and I can send for her at any time if you please."

Sir George hearing this, thought it was not best to come there, fearing Joan would father a child upon him, and therefore answered, he had no leisure to come from my lord: "But," quoth he, "would I might see her in London, on the condition it cost me twenty nobles."

"Tush Sir George," quoth Master Winchcombe, "delays in love are dangerous, and he that will woo a widow, must take time by the forelock, and suffer none other to step before him, lest he leap without the widow's love. Notwithstanding, seeing now I have told you of it, I will take my gelding and get me home: if I hear of her coming to London, will send you word, or perhaps come myself: till when adieu good Sir George."

Thus parted Master Winchcombe from the knight: and being come home, in short time he got a fair taffeta gown, and a French hood for his maid, saying: "Come ye drab, I must be fain to cover a foul fault with a fair garment, yet all will not hide your great belly: but if I find means to make you a lady, what will you say then?"

"O master," quoth she, "I shall be bound while I live to pray for you."

"Come then minion," quoth her mistress, "and put you on this gown and French hood: for seeing you have lain with a knight, you must needs be a gentlewoman."

The maid did so: and being thus attired, she was set on a fair gelding, and a couple of men sent with her up to London: and being well instructed by her master and dame what she should do, she took her journey to the city in the [low court] term time, and lodged at the Bell in the Strand: and Mistress Loveless must be her name, for so her master had warned her to call herself: neither did the men that waited on her, know the contrary; for Master Winchcombe had borrowed them of their master, to wait upon a friend of his to London, because he could not spare any of his own servants at that time: notwithstanding, they were appointed for the gentlewoman's credit, to say they were her own men. This being done, Master Winchcombe sent Sir George a letter, that the gentlewoman which he told him of, was now in London, lying at the Bell in the Strand, having great business at the term.

With which news Sir George's heart was on fire, till such time as he might speak with her: three or four times went he thither, and still she would not be spoken withal, the which close keeping of herself, made him the more earnest in his suit.

At length he watched her so narrowly, that finding her going forth in an evening, he followed her, she having one man before, and another behind: carrying a very stately gate in the street, it drove him into the greater liking of her, being the more urged to utter his mind. And suddenly stepping before her, he thus saluted her, "Gentlewoman, God save you, I have often been at your lodging, and could never find you at leisure."

"Why sir," quoth she (counterfeiting her natural speech), "have you any business with me?"

"Yes fair widow," quoth he, "as you are a client to the law, so am I a suitor for your love: and may I find you so favourable to let me plead my own case at the bar of your beauty, I doubt not but to unfold so true a tale, as I trust will cause you to give sentence on my side."

"You are a merry gentleman" quoth she, "but for my own part, I know you not; nevertheless, in a case of love, I will be no let to your suit, though perhaps I help you little therein. And therefore sir, if it please you to give attendance at my lodging, upon my return from the Temple, you shall know more of my mind," and so they parted.

Sir George receiving hereby some hope of good hap, stayed for his dear at her lodging door: whom at her coming she friendly greeted, saying, "Surely sir, your diligence is more than the profit you shall get thereby: but I pray you how shall I call your name?"

"George Rigley," quoth he, "I am called, and for some small deserts I was knighted in France."

"Why then Sir George," quoth she, "I have done you too much wrong to make you thus dance attendance on my worthless person. But let me be so bold to request you to tell me, how you came to know me: for my own part I cannot remember that ever I saw you before."

"Mistress Loveless," said Sir George, "I am well acquainted with a good neighbour of yours, called Master Winchcombe, who is my very good friend, and to say the truth, you were commended unto me by him."

"Truly Sir George," said she, "you are so much the better welcome: Nevertheless, I have made a vow not to love any man for this twelve months' space. And therefore sir, till then I would wish you to trouble yourself no further in this matter till that time be expired: and then if I find you be not entangled to any other, and that by trial I find out the truth of your love, for Master Winchcombe's sake your welcome shall be as good as any other gentleman's whatsoever."

Sir George having received this answer, was wondrous woe cursing the day that ever be meddled with Joan, whose time of deliverance would come long before a twelve month were expired to his utter shame, and overthrow of his good fortune: for by that means should he have Master Winchcombe his enemy, and therewithal the loss of this fair gentlewoman. Wherefore to prevent this mischief, he sent a letter in all haste to Master Winchcombe, requesting him most earnestly to come up to London, by whose persuasion he hoped straight to finish the marriage. Master Winchcombe fulfilled his request, and then presently was the marriage solemnized at the Tower of London, in presence of many gentlemen of Sir George's friends. But when he found it was Joan whom he had gotten with child, he fretted and fumed, stamped, and stared like a devil.

"Why," quoth M. Winchcombe, "what needs all this? Came you to my table to make my maid your strumpet? had you no man's house to dishonour but mine? Sir, I would you should well know, that I account the poorest wench in my house too good to be your whore, were you ten knights: and seeing you took pleasure to make her your wanton, take it no scorn to make her your wife: and use her well too, or you shall hear of it. And hold thee, Joan," quoth he, "there is a hundred pounds for thee: And let him not say thou camest to him a beggar."

Sir George seeing this, and withal casting in his mind what friend Master Winchcombe might be to him, taking his wife by the hand, gave her a loving kiss, and Master Winchcombe great thanks. Whereupon he willed him for two years space to take his diet and his lady's at his house: which the knight accepting, rode straight with his wife to Newbury.

Then did the mistress make curtsy to the maid, saying: "You are welcome madam," giving her the upper hand in all places. And thus they lived afterward in great joy: and our king hearing how Jack had matched Sir George, laughing heartily thereat, gave him a living forever, the better to maintain my lady his wife.

A sample of the pamphlet rhetoric of the Martin Marprelate controversy when what Shakespeare would call paper bullets of the brain were fired off in all directions:

By the time I think Goodman Puritan, that thou art persuaded, that I know as well as thy own conscience thee, namely Martin Makebate of England, to be a most scurvy and beggarly benefactor to obedience, and *per consequens,* to fear neither men, nor that God Who can cast both body and soul into unquenchable fire. In which respect I neither account you of the Church, nor esteem of your blood, otherwise than the blood of Infidels. Talk as long as you will of the joys of heaven, or pains of hell, and turn from yourselves the terror of that judgment how you will, which shall bereave blushing iniquity of the fig leaves of hypocrisy, yet will the eye of immortality discern of your painted pollutions, as the ever-living food of perdition. The humours of my eyes are the habitations of fountains, and the circumference of my heart the enclosure of fearful contrition, when I think how many souls at that moment shall carry the name of Martin on their foreheads to the vale of confusion, in whose innocent blood thou swimming to hell, shalt have the torments of ten thousand sinners at once, inflicted upon thee. There will envy, malice, and dissimulation be ever calling for vengeance against thee, and incite whole legions of devils to thy deathless lamentation. Mercy will say unto thee, I know thee not, and Repentance, what have I to do with thee? All hopes shall shake the head at thee, and say: there goes the poison of purity, the perfection of impiety, the serpentine seducer of simplicity. Zeal herself will cry out upon thee, and curse the time that ever she was mashed by thy malice, who like a blind leader of the blind, sufferedst her to stumble at every step in Religion, and madest her seek in the dimness of her sight, to murder her mother the Church, from whose paps thou like an envious dog but yesterday pluckedst her. However, proud scorner, thy whorish impudency may happen hereafter to insist in the derision of these fearful denunciations, and sport thy jester's pen at the speech of my soul, yet take heed least despair be predominant in the day of thy death, and thou instead of calling for mercy to thy Jesus, repeat more oftener to thyself, *Sie morior damnatus ut Judas!* And thus much, Martin, in the way of compassion, have I spoke for thy edification, moved thereto by a brotherly commiseration, which if thou be not too desperate in thy devilish attempts, may reform thy heart to remorse, and thy pamphlets to some more profitable theme of repentance.

Narrative poetry had more of a market in Elizabethan England than it has anywhere now; even commercial writers such as the talented Michael Drayton provided it to the public in great quantities. Here is an excerpt from the sixth canto of The Barons' Wars *that describes Queen Isabella and Mortimer at Nottingham Castle in a scene worthy of Keats'* St. Agnes Eve:

The night waxed old (not dreaming of these things),
And to her chamber is the Queen withdrawn,
To whom a choice musician plays and sings
While she sat under an estate of lawn,
In night-attire, more god-like glittering
Than any eye had seen the cheerful dawn,
   Leaning upon her most-loved Mortimer,
   Whose voice, more than the music, pleased her ear.

Where her fair breasts at liberty were let,
Whose violet veins in branchéd riverets flow,
And Venus' swans, and milky doves were set
Upon those swelling mounts of driven snow;
Whereon whilst Love to sport himself doth get,
He lost his way, nor back again could go,
   But with those banks of beauty set about,
   He wand'red still, yet never could get out.

Her loose hair looked like gold (Oh word too base!
Nay, more than sin, but so to name her hair)
Declining as to kiss her fairer face;
No word is fair enough for thing so fair,
Nor never was there epithet could grace
That, by much praising, which we much impair;
   And where the pen fails, pencils cannot show it,
   Only the soul may be supposed to know it.

She laid her fingers on his manly cheek,
That God's pure sceptres, and the darts of Love,
That with their touch might make a tiger meek,
Or might great Atlas from his seat remove;
So white, so soft, so delicate, so sleek,
As she had worn a lily for a glove,
   As might beget life, where was never none
   And put a spirit into the hardest stone.

The fire of precious wood; the light, perfume,
Which left a sweetness on each thing it shone,
As ev'ry thing did to itself assume
The scent from them, and made the same their own;
So that the painted flowers within the room
Were sweet, as if they naturally had grown;
  The light gave colours, which upon them fell,
  And to the colours the perfume gave a smell.

When on those sundry pictures they devise
And from one piece they to another run,
Commend that face, that arm, that hand, those eyes,
Show how that bird, how well that flower was done,
How this part shadowed, and how that did rise,
This top was clouded, and that trail was spun,
  The landskip, mixture and delineatings,
  And in that art a thousand curious things.

Looking upon proud Phaethon, wrapped in fire,
The gentle Queen did much bewail his fall;
But Mortimer commended his desire,
To lose one poor life or to govern all:
What though (quoth he) he madly did aspire
And his great mind made him proud Fortune's thrall?
  Yet, in despite when she her worst had done,
  He perished in the chariot of the Sun.

Shakespeare took no trouble to publish plays, though some of them appeared in quarto in his lifetime in good or bad texts, with or without his name on them. He did take care, however, to see that his poetry, of which Venus and Adonis *(1593) is an example, reached the public in correct form. Ordinarily, I have omitted Shakespeare's work as being too well known and easily available, but I shall include a part of* Venus and Adonis *as a sample of the erotic literature of the period and as something from The Bard with which even some of his greatest admirers may not have read. As we join the pair, Venus has got Adonis off his horse but not onto herself. She embraces him, links her fingers behind his back, and addresses him in very suggestive language.*

This time we shall need something else I have tried to do without: footnotes: *(see p. 103).*

'Fondling,' she saith, 'since I have hemmed thee here
Within the circuit of this ivory pale.
I'll be a park, and thou shalt be my deer:[1]
Feed where thou wilt, on mountain or in dale;
  Graze on my lips, and if those hills be dry,

Stray lower, where the pleasant fountains lie.

'Within this limit is relief enough,[2]
Sweet bottom grass and high delightful plain,
Round rising hillocks, brakes obscure and rough,[3]
To shelter thee from tempest and from rain:
Then be my deer, since I am such a park,
No dog shall rouse thee,[4] though a thousand bark.'

At this Adonis smiles as in disdain,
That in each cheek appears a pretty dimple;
Love made those hollows, if himself were slain,
He might be buried in a tomb so simple,
Foreknowing well, if there he came to lie,
Why there love lived, and there he could not die.

These lovely caves, these round enchanting pits,
Opened their mouths to swallow Venus' liking:[5]
Being mad before, how doth she now for wits?
Struck dead before, what needs a second striking?
Poor queen of love, in thine own law forlorn,[6]
To love a cheek that smiles at thee in scorn!

Now which way shall she turn? what shall she say?
Her words are done, her woes the more increasing;
The time is spent, her object will away,
And from her twining arms doth urge releasing.
'Pity,' she cries, 'some favour, some remorse!'
Away he springs, and hasteth to his horse.

But lo from forth a copse that neighbours by,
A breeding jennet,[7] lusty, young and proud,
Adonis' trampling courser doth espy,
And forth she rushes, snorts and neighs aloud:
The strong-necked steed being tied unto a tree,
Breaketh his rein, and to her straight goes he.

Imperiously he leaps, he neighs, he bounds,
And now his woven girths he breaks asunder;
The bearing earth with his hard hoof he wounds
Whose hollow womb resounds like heaven's thunder;
The iron bit he crusheth 'tween his teeth,
Controlling what he was controlléd with.

His ears up-pricked, his braided hanging mane
Upon his compassed[8] crest now stand on end;

His nostrils drink the air, and forth again
As from a furnace, vapours doth he send;
His eye which scornfully glisters like fire,
Shows his hot courage and his high desire.

Sometimes he trots, as if he told[10] the steps,
With gentle majesty and modest pride;
Anon he rears upright, curvets and leaps,
As who should say 'Lo thus my strength is tried:
And this I do to captivate the eye
Of the fair breeder that is standing by.'

What recketh[12] he his rider's angry stir,
His flattering 'holla' or his 'Stand, I say'?
What cares he now for curb or pricking spur,
For rich caparisons or trappings gay?
He sees his love, and nothing else he sees,
For nothing else with his proud sight agrees.

Look when a painter would surpass the life
In limning out a well-proportioned steed,
His art with nature's workmanship at strife,
As if the dead the living should exceed:
So did this horse excel a common one,
In shape, in courage, colour, pace and bone.

Round-hoofed, short-jointed, fetlocks shag and long,
Broad breast, full eye, small head, and nostril wide,
High crest, short ears, straight legs, and passing strong,
Thin mane, thick tail, broad buttock, tender hide:
Look what a horse should have he did not lack,
Save a proud rider on so proud a back.

Sometimes he scuds far off, and there he stares;
Anon he starts at stirring of a feather.
To bid the wind a base he now prepares,[11]
And where he run or fly, they know not whether[12]
For through his mane and tail the high wind sings,
Fanning the hairs, who wave like feathered wings.

He looks upon his love, and neighs unto her:
She answers him, as if she knew his mind,
Being proud, as females are, to see him woo her,
She puts on outward strangeness,[13] seems unkind,
Spurns at his love, and scorns the heat he feels,
Beating his kind embracements with her heels.

Then like a melancholy malcontent,
He vails[14] his tail that like a falling plume
Cool shadow to his melting buttock lent;
He stamps, and bites the poor flies in his fume.[15]
  His love perceiving how he was enraged,
  Grew kinder, and his fury was assuaged.

His testy master goeth about to take him,
When lo the unbacked[16] breeder, full of fear,
Jealous of catching,[17] swiftly doth forsake him;
With her the horse, and left Adonis there:
  As they were mad unto the wood they hie them,
  Outstripping crows that strive to overfly them.

[1]pun on *dear*.
[2]This area offers ample pasture
[3]breasts and *mons Veneris*
[4]drive you from cover
[5]Venus' desire
[6]deprived in a thing which you are supposed to control
[7]small Spanish mare
[8]curved
[9]lust
[10]counted
[11]What does he care about his rider's angry agitation
[12]To challenge the wind to a race and whether to run or fly he knew not which
[13]show of indifference
[14]droops
[15]anger
[16]untamed
[17]anxious not to be caught

The Unfortunate Traveler, or The Life of Jack Wilton *(1594) is a novel noted above as a picaresque story (part autobiography and part anatomy, part romance and part satire). Here is Nashe's section on the hero in Rome which gives us another angle on the narrative's popularity and the narrator's scene-setting and the deep-dyed villain's vile, almost pornographic viciousness:*

What adventures happened him after we parted I am ignorant, but Florence we both forsook. And I, having a wonderful ardent inclination to see Rome (the queen of the world and metropolitan mistress of all other cities) made thither with my bag and baggage as fast as I could.

Attained thither, I was lodged at the house of one Johannes de Imola, a Roman cavaliero. Who, being acquainted with my courtesan's deceased, doting husband, for his sake used us with all the familiarity that might be. He showed us all the monuments that were to be seen, which are as many as there have been emperors, consuls, orators, conquerors, famous painters, or players in thought these *cimices* [bedbugs], like the Cimbrians, had been some strange nation he had brought under, and they were no more but things like sheep lice which, alive, have the venonmost sting that may be and, being dead, do stink out of measure. St. Austen [Augustine] compareth heretics unto them.

The chiefest thing that my eyes delighted in was the Church of the Seven Sibyls, which is a most miraculous thing. All their prophecies and oracles being there enrolled, as also the beginning and ending of their whole catalogue of the heathen gods, with their manner of worship. There are a number of other shrines and statues also dedicated to their emperors, and withal some statues of idolatry reserved for detestation. I was at Pontius Pilate's house and pissed against it. [Add in second edition: The name of the place I remember not, but it is as one goes to St. Paul's Church, not far from the iemmes (Jews?) plaza.]

There is the prison yet packed up together (an old rotten thing) where the man that was condemned to death, and could have nobody come to him and succor him but was searched, was kept alive a long space by sucking his daughter's breasts.

These are but the shop dust of the sights that I saw, and in truth I did not behold with any care hereafter to report but contented my eye for the present. And so let them pass. Should I memorize half the miracles which they were told me had been done about martyrs' tombs, or the operations of the earth of the sepulcher, and other relics brought from Jerusalem, I should be counted the monstrost liar that ever came in print.

The ruins of Pompey's theater, reputed one of the nine wonders of the world; Gregory the Sixth's tomb; Priscilla's gate; or the thousands of pillars arreared amongst the razed foundations of old Rome—it were here frivolous to specify since he that hath but once drunk with a traveler talks of them. Let me be a historiographer of my own misfortunes and not meddle with the continued trophies of so old a triumphing city.

At my first coming to Rome, I being a youth of the English cut, wore my hair long, went appareled in light colors, and imitated four or five sundry nations in my attire at once. Which no sooner was noted, but I had all the boys of the city in a swarm wondering about me. I had not gone a little farther but certain officers crossed the way of me and demanded to see my rapier, which when they found (as also my dagger) with his point unblunted, they would have haled me headlong to the strappado but that with money I appeased them. And my fault was more pardonable in that I was a stranger, altogether ignorant of their customs.

Note, by the way, that it is the use in Rome for all men whatsoever to wear their hair short; which they do not so much for conscience's sake, or any religion they place in it, if they should not do so, they should not have a hair left on their heads to stand upright when they were scared with sprites. And he is counted no gentleman amongst them that goes not in black; they dress their jesters and fools only in fresh colors, and say variable garments do argue unstayedness and unconstancy of affection.

The reason of their strait ordinance for carrying weapons without points is this: the bandettos, which are certain outlaws that lie betwixt Rome and Naples and besiege the passage, that none can travel that way without robbing. Now and then, hired for some few crowns, they will steal to Rome and do a murder and betake them to their heels again. Disguised as they go, they are not known from strangers; sometimes they will shroud themselves under the habit of grave citizens. In this consideration neither citizen nor stranger, gentleman, knight, marquis, or any, may wear any weapon endamageable upon pain of the strappado. I bought it out; let others buy experience of me better cheap.

To tell you of the rare pleasure of their gardens, their baths, their vineyards, their galleries were to write a second part of the *Gorgeous Gallery of Gallant Devices* [by Thomas Proctor, 1578]. Why, you should not come into any man's house of account but he had fishponds and little orchards on the top of his leads [roof]. If by rain or any other means those ponds were so full they need to be sluiced or let out, even of their superfluities they made melodious use; for they had great wind instruments, instead of leaden spouts, that went duly in consort, only with this water's rumbling descent.

I saw a summer banqueting house, belonging to a merchant, that was the marvel of the world and could not be matched except God should make another paradise. It was built round of green marble, like a theater without; within, there was a heaven and earth comprehended both under one roof. The heaven was a clear, overhanging vault of crystal, wherein the sun and moon and each visible star had his true similitude, shine, situation, and motion; and, by what enwrapped art I cannot conceive, these spheres in their proper orbs observed their circular wheelings and turnings, making a certain kind of soft, angelical, murmuring music in their often windings and going about. Which music the philosophers say in the true heaven, by reason of the grossness of our senses, we are not capable of.

For the earth, it was counterfeited in that likeness that Adam lorded it out before his fall. A wide, vast spacious room it was, such as we would conceit prince Arthur's hall to be, where he feasted all his knights of the Round Table together every Pentecost. The floor was painted with the beautifullest flowers that ever man's eye admired, which so lineally were delineated that he that viewed them afar off, and had not directly stood poringly over them would have sworn they had lived indeed. The walls round about were hedged with olives and palm trees, and all other odoriferous, fruit-bearing plants, which at any solemn entertainment dropped myrrh and frankinsence. Other trees, that bare no fruit, were set in just order one against another and divided the room into a number of shady lanes, leaving but one overspreading pine tree arbor, where we sat and banqueted.

On the well-clothed boughs of this conspiracy of pine trees against the resembled sunbeams were perched as many sorts of shrill-breasted birds as the summer hath allowed for singing men in her sylvan chapels. Who, though there were bodies without souls, and sweet-resembled substances without sense, yet by the mathematical experiments of long silver pipes secretly inrinded in the entrails of the boughs whereon they sat, and undiscernibly conveyed unto their bellies into their small throats' sloping, they whistled and freely caroled their natural field note. Neither went those silver pipes straight, but, by many-edged, unsundered writhings, and crankled wanderings aside, strayed from bough to bough into an hundred throats. But into this silver pipe so writhed and wandering aside, if any demand how the wind was breathed, forsooth the tail of the silver pipe stretched itself into the mouth of a great pair of bellows, where it was close soldered and baled about with iron; it could not stir or have any vent betwixt. Those bellows, with the rising and falling of leaden plummets wound up on a wheel, did beat up and down incessantly, and so gathered in wind, serving with one blast all the snarled pipes to and fro of one tree at once. But so closely were all those organizing implements obscured in the corpulent trunks of the trees that every man there present renounced conjectures of art and said it was done by enchantment.

One tree for his fruit bare nothing but enchained, chirruping birds, whose throats being conduit piped with squared, narrow shells, and charged syringe-wise with searching sweet water, driven in by a little wheel for the nonce that fed it afar off, made a spiriting sound, such as chirping is, in bubbling upwards through the rough crannies of their closed bills.

Under tuition of the shade of every tree that I have signified to be in this round hedge, on delightful leafy cloisters, lay a wild, tyrannous beast asleep, all prostrate; under some, two together—as the dog nuzzling his nose under the neck of the deer, the wolf glad to let the lamb lie upon him to keep warm, the lion suffering the ass to cast his leg over him (preferring one honest, unmannerly friend before a number of crouching pickthanks). No poisonous beast there reposed (poison was not before our parent Adam transgressed). There were no sweet-breathing panthers that would hide their terrifying heads to betray, no men imitating hyenas that changed their sex to seek after blood. Wolves as now when they are hungry eat earth, so then did they feed on earth only and abstained from innocent flesh. The unicorn did not put his horn into the stream to chase away venom before he drunk, for there was no such thing as venom extant in the water or on the earth. Serpents were as harmless to mankind as they are still one to another. The rose had no cankers, the leaves no caterpillars, the sea no sirens, the earth no usurers. Goats then bare wool as it is recorded in Sicily they do yet. The torrid zone was habitable. Only jays loved to steal gold and silver to build their nests withal, and none cared for covetous clientry or running to the Indies. As the elephant understands his country speech, so every beast understood what men spoke. The ant did not hoard up against winter, for there was no winter but a perpetual spring, as Ovid saith. No frosts to make the green almond tree counted rash and improvident, in budding soonest of all other; or the mulberry tree a strange politician, in blooming late and ripening early. The peach tree at the first planting was fruitful and wholesome, whereas now, till it be transplanted, it is poisonous and hateful. Young plants for their sap had balm; for their yellow gum, glistering amber. The evening dewed not water on flowers, but honey. Such a golden age, such a good age, such an honest age was set forth in this banqueting house.

* * *

For the pope and his pontificalibus, I will not deal with; only I will dilate unto you what happened whiles I was in Rome.

So it fell out that, it being a vehement hot summer when I was a sojourner there, there entered such a hotspurred plague as hath not been heard of. Why, it was but a word and a blow, Lord have mercy upon us, and he was gone. Within three quarters of a year in that one city there died of it a hundred thousand. Look in Lanquet's chronicle and you shall find it [under the year 1522]. To smell of a nosegay that was poisoned, and turn your nose to a house that had the plague—it was all one. The clouds, like a number of cormorants that keep their corn till it stink and is musty, kept in their stinking exhalations till they had almost stifled all Rome's inhabitants. Physicians' greediness of gold made them greedy of their destiny. They would come to visit those with whose infirmities their art had no affinity; and even as a man with a fee should be hired to hang himself, so would they quietly go home and die presently after they had been with their patients. All day and all night long cart men did nothing but go up and down the streets with their carts and cry, "Have you any dead to bury? Have you any dead to bury?" and had many times out of one house their whole loading. One grave was the sepulcher of seven score; one bed was the altar whereon whole families were offered.

The walls were hoared and furred with the moist, scorching steam of their desolation. Even as before a gun is shot off, a stinking smoke funnels out and prepares the way for him; so before any gave up the ghost, death (arrayed in a stinking smoke) stopped his nostrils and crammed itself full into his mouth that closed up his fellow's eyes, to give him warning to prepare for his funeral. Some died sitting at their meat, others as they were asking counsel of the physician for their friends. I saw, at the house where I was hosted, a maid bring her master warm broth for to comfort him and she sink down dead herself ere he had self eat it up.

During this time of visitation, there was a Spaniard, one Esdras of Granada, a notable bandetto authorized by the pope because he assisted him in some murders. This villain, colleagued with one Bartol, a desperate Italian, practiced to break into those rich men's houses in the night where the plague had most rained; and if there were none but the mistress and maid left alive, to ravish them both and bring away all the wealth they could fasten on. In a hundred chief citizens' houses where the hand of God had been, they put this outrage *in ure.* Though the women so ravished cried out, none durst come near them for fear of catching their deaths by them; and some thought they cried out only with the tyranny of the malady.

Amongst the rest, the house where I lay he invaded; where, all being snatched up by the sickness but the good wife of the house, a noble and chaste matron called Heraclide, and her zany, and I and my courtesan, he, knocking at the door late in the night, ran into the matron and left me and my love to the mercy of his companion. He charged with his rapier, thinking I would resist him; but as good luck was, I escaped him and betook me to my pistol in the window uncharged. He, fearing it had been charged, threatened to run her through if I once offered but to aim at him. Forth the chamber he dragged her, holding his rapier at her heart, whilst I still cried out, "Save her, kill me, and I'll ransom her with a thousand ducats." But lust prevailed; no prayers would be heard. Into my chamber I was locked, and watchmen charged (as he made semblance when there was none there) to knock me down with their halberds if I stirred but a foot down the stairs. So threw I myself pensive again on my pallet and dared all the devils in hell, now I was alone, to come and fight with me one after another in defense of that detestable rape. I beat my head against the walls and called them bawds, because they would see such a wrong committed and not fall upon him.

To return to Heraclide below, whom the ugliest of all bloodsuckers, Esdras of Granada, had under shrift. First he assailed her with rough means, and slew her zany at her foot that stepped before her in rescue. Then when all armed resist was put to flight, he assayed her with honey speech and promised her more jewels and gifts than he was able to pilfer in an hundred years after. He discoursed unto her how he was countenanced and borne out by the pope, and how many execrable murders with impunity he had executed on them that displeased him.

"This is the eighth-score house," quoth he, "that hath done homage unto me; and here I will prevail, or I will be torn in pieces."

"Ah," quoth Heraclide with a heart-rendering sigh, "art thou ordained *to be* a worse plague to me than the plague itself? Have I escaped the hands of God to fall into the hands of man? Hear me, Jehovah, and be merciful in ending my misery. Dispatch me incontinent, dissolute homicide, death's usurper. Here lies my husband stone cold on the dewy floor. If thou beest of more power than God to strike me speedily, strike home. Strike deep. Send me to heaven with my husband. Aye me, it is the spoil of my honor thou seekest in my soul's troubled departure; thou art some devil sent to tempt in my soul's troubled departure; thou art some devil sent to tempt me. Avoid from me. Satan: my soul is my Savior's. To him I have bequeathed it; from him can no man take it. Jesu, Jesu spare me undefiled for thy spouse. Jesu, Jesu never fail those that put their trust in thee."

With that she fell in a swoon; and her eyes in their closing seemed to spawn forth in their outward sharp corners new created seed pearl, which the world before never set eye on. Soon he rigorously revived her and told her that he had a charter above Scripture. She must yield; she should yield. See who durst remove her out of his hands. Twixt life and death thus she faintly replied:

"How thinkest thou? Is there a power above thy power? If there be, he is here present in punishment; and on thee will take present punishment if thou persistest in thy enterprise. In the time of security every man sinneth. But when death substitutes one friend his special baily to arrest another by infection, and disperseth his quiver into ten thousand hands at once, who is it but looks about him? A man that hath an inevitable huge stone hanging only by a hair over his head, which he looks every paternoster-while to fall and pash him in pieces, will not he be submissively sorrowful for his transgressions, refrain himself from the lest thought of folly, and purify his spirit with contrition and pentinence? God's hand, like a huge stone, hangs inevitably over thy head. What is the plague but death playing the provost marshal, to execute all those that will not be called home by any other means? This my dear knight's body is a quiver of his arrows, which already are shot into thee invisible.

"If thou ever camest of a woman, or hopest to be saved by the seed of a woman, spare a woman. Deers oppressed with dogs, when they cannot take soil, run to men for succor. To whom should women in their disconsolate and desperate estate run but to men, like the deer, for succor and sanctuary? If thou be a man, thou wilt succor me; but if thou be a dog and a brute beast, thou wilt spoil me, defile me, and tear me. Either renounce God's image or renounce the wicked mind that thou bearest."

These words might have moved a compound heart of iron and adamant. But in his heart they obtained no impression; for he sitting in his chair of state against the door all the while that she pleaded, leaning his overhanging, gloomy eyebrows on the pommel of his unsheathed sword, he never looked up or gave her a word. But when he perceived she expected his answer of grace or utter perdition, he started up and took her currishly by the neck, and asked her how long he should stay for her ladyship.

"Thou tellest me," quoth he, "of the plague, and the heavy hand of God, and thy hundred infected breaths in one. I tell thee I have cast the dice an hundred times for the galleys in Spain and yet still missed the ill chance. Our order of casting is this: if there be a general or captain new come home from the wars, and hath some four or five hundred crowns overplus of the king's in his hand, and his soldiers all paid, he makes proclamation that whatsoever two resolute men will go to dice for it, and win the bridle or lose the saddle, to such a place let them repair and it shall be ready for them. Thither go I and find another such needy squire resident. The dice run, I win, he is undone I, winning, have the crowns; he, losing, is carried to the galleys. This is our custom, which a hundred times and more hath paid me custom of crowns, when the poor fellows who have gone to Gehenna [prison as Hell] had coarse bread and whipping cheer all their life after.

"Now thinkest thou that I, who so oft have escaped such a number of hellish dangers (only depending on the turning of a few pricks), can be scare-bugged with the plague? What plague canst thou name worse than I have had? Whether diseases, imprisonment, poverty, banishment—I have passed through them all. My own mother gave I a box of the ear, and broke her neck down a pair of stairs, because she would not go into a gentleman when I bade her. My sister I sold to an old leno [pimp] to make his best of her. Any kinswoman that I have, knew I she were not a whore, myself would make her one. Thou art a whore; thou shalt be a whore in spite of religion or precise ceremonies."

Therewith he flew upon her and threatened her with his sword, but it was not *that* he meant to wound her with. He grasped her by the ivory throat and shook her as a mastiff would shake a young bear, swearing and staring he would tear out her weasand if she refused. Not content with that savage constraint, he slipped his sacrilegious hand from her lily lawn-skinned neck and enscarfed it in her long silver locks, which was struggling were unrolled. Backward he dragged her even as a man backward would pluck a tree down by the twigs. And then, like a traitor that is drawn to execution on a hurdle, he traileth her up and down the chamber by those tender, untwisted braids; and, setting his barbarous foot on her bare, snowy breast, bade her yield or have her wind stamped out.

She cried, "Stamp! Stifle me in my hair, hang me up by it on a beam, and so let me die rather than I should go to heaven with a beam in my eye."

"No," quoth he, "nor stamped, nor stifled, nor hanged, nor to heaven shalt thou go till I have had my will of thee. Thy busy arms in these silken fetters I'll enfold."

Dismissing her hair from his fingers and pinioning her elbows therewithal, she struggled, she wrested, but all was in vain. So struggling and so resisting, her jewels did sweat, signifying there was poison coming towards her. On the hard boards he threw her and used his knee as an iron ram to beat open the two-leaved gate of her chastity. Her husband's dead body he made a pillow to his abomination.

Conjecture the rest. My words stick fast in the mire and are clean tired; would I had never undertook this tragical tale. Whatsoever is born is born to have end. Thus endeth my tale: his boorish lust was glutted, his beastly desire satisfied; what in the house of any worth was carriageable, he put up and went his way.

Let not your sorrow die, you that have read the proem and narration of this elegiacal history. Show you have quick wits in sharp conceit of compassion. A woman that hath viewed all her children sacrificed before her eyes, and after the first was slain wiped the sword with her apron to prepare it for the cleanly murder of the second, and so on forward till it came to the empiercing of the seventeenth of her loins—will you not give her great allowance of anguish? This woman, this matron, this forsaken Heraclide, having buried fourteen children in five days, whose eyes she howlingly closed and caught many wrinkles with funeral kisses. Besides having her husband within a day after laid forth as a comfortless corpse, a carrionly block that could neither eat with her, speak with her, nor weep with her, is she not to be borne withal though her body swells with a tympany of tears, though her speech be as impatient as unhappy Hecuba's, though her head raves and her brain dotes? Devise with yourselves that you see a corpse rising from his bier after he is carried to church, and such another suppose Heraclide to be, rising from the couch of enforced adultery.

Her eyes were dim, her cheeks bloodless, her breath smelled earthy, her countenance was ghastly. Up she rose after she was deflowered; but loath she arose, as a reprobate soul rising to the day of judgment. Looking on the one side as she rose, she spied her husband's body lying under her head. Ah, then she bewailed as Cephalus when he had killed Procris unwittingly, or Oedipus when ignorant he had slain his own father and known his mother incestuously. This was her subdued reason's discourse:

"Have I lived to make my husband's body the bier to carry me to hell? Had filthy pleasure no other pillow to lean upon but his spreaded limbs? On thy flesh my fault shall be imprinted at the day of resurrection. Oh, beauty, the bait ordained to ensnare the irreligious! Rich men are robbed for their wealth; women are dishonested for being too fair. No blessing is beauty, but a curse. Curst be the time that ever I was begotten; curst be the time that my mother brought me forth to tempt. The serpent in paradise did no more; the serpent in paradise is damned sempiternally. Why should not I hold myself damned (if predestination's opinions be true) that am predestinate to this horrible abuse? The hog dieth presently if he loseth an eye; with the hog have I wallowed in the mire. I have lost my eye of honesty, it is clean plucked out with a strong hand of unchastity. What remaineth but I die? Die I will, though life be unwilling. No recompense is there for me to redeem my compelled offense, but with a rigorous, compelled death. Husband, I'll be thy wife in heaven; let not thy pure, deceasing spirit despise me when we meet because I am tyrannously polluted. The devil, the belier of our frailty and common accuser of mankind, cannot accuse me though he would of unconstrained submitting. If any guilt be mind, this is my fault—that I did not deform my face ere it should so impiously allure."

Having passioned thus a while, she hastily ran and looked herself in her glass to see if here sin were not written on her forehead. With looking she blushed though none looked upon her but her own reflected image.

Then began she again: "*Heu quam difficile est crimen non prodere vultu:* How hard is it not to bewray a man's fault by his forehead. Myself do but behold myself, and yet I blush. Then God beholding me, shall not I be ten times more ashamed? The angels shall hiss at me, the saints and martyrs fly from me; yea, God himself shall add to the devil's damnation because he suffered such a wicked creature to come before him. Agamemnon, thou wert an infidel; yet when thou wentest to the Trojan war thou leftest a musician at home with thy wife who, by playing the foot spondaeus till thy return, might keep her in chastity. My husband, going to war with the devil and his enticements, when he surrendered, left no musician with me but mourning and melancholy. Had he left any, as Aegisthus killed Agamemnon's musician ere he could be successful, so surely would he have been killed ere this Aegisthus surceased."

"My distressed heart, as the hart when he loseth his horns is astonied and sorrowfully runneth to hide himself, so be thou afflicted and distressed; hide thyself under the Almighty's wings of mercy. Sue, plead, entreat; grace is never denied to them that ask. It may be denied; I may be a vessel ordained to dishonor. The only repeal we have from God's undefinite chastisement is to chastise ourselves in this world. And so I will. Nought but death be my penance; gracious and acceptable may it be. My hand and my knife shall manumit me out of the horror of mind I endure. Farewell life hast more weeds than flowers, more woes than joys. Point pierce, edge enwiden; I patiently afford thee a sheath. Spur forth my soul to mount post to heaven. Jesu forgive me; Jesu receive me."

So, thoroughly stabbed, fell she down and knocked her head against her husband's body; wherewith, he not having been aired his full four and twenty hours, started as out of a dream (whiles I, through a cranny of my upper chamber unsealed, had beheld all this sad spectacle). Awaking, he rubbed his head to and fro and, wiping his eyes with his hand, began to look about him. Feeling something lie heavy on his breast, he turned it off and, getting upon his legs, lighted a candle.

Here beginneth my purgatory. For he, good man, coming into the hall with the candle and spying his wife with her hair about her ears, defiled and massacred, and his simple zany Capestrano run through, took a halberd in his hand and, running from chamber to chamber to search who in his house was likely to do it, at length found me lying on my bed, the door locked to me on the outside and my rapier unsheathed on the window. Wherewith he straight conjectured it was I. And calling the neighbors hard by, said I had caused myself to be locked into my chamber after that sort, sent away my courtesan whom I called my wife, and made clean my rapier, because I would not be suspected. Upon this was I laid in prison, should have been hanged, was brought to the ladder, had made a ballad for my farewell in a readiness called "Wilton's Wantonness"—and yet, for all that, scaped dancing in a hempen circle. He that hath gone through many perils and returned safe from them makes but a merriment to dilate them.

I had the knot under my ear; there was fair play; the hangman had one halter, and another about my neck which was fastened to the gallows; the riding device [slip knot] was almost thrust home, and his foot on my shoulder to press me down, when I made my faint-like confession, as you have heard before, that such and such men at such an hour brake into the house, slew the zany, took my courtesan, locked me into my chamber, ravished Heraclide, and, finally, how she slew herself.

Present at the execution was there a banished English earl who, hearing that a countryman of his was to suffer for such a notable murder, came to hear his confession and see if he knew him. He had not heard me tell half of that I have recited but he craved audience and desired the execution might be stayed.

"Not two days since it is, gentlemen and noble Romans," said he, "since going to be let blood in a barber's shop against the infection, all on a sudden in a great tumult and uproar was there brought in one Bartol, an Italian, grievously wounded and bloody. I seeming to commiserate his harms, courteously questioned him with what ill debtors he had met, or how or by what casualty he came to be so arrayed."

" 'Oh,' quoth he, long I have lived sworn brothers in sensuality with one Esdras of Grenada. Five hundred rapes and murders have we committed betwixt us. When our iniquities were grown to the height, and God had determined to countercheck our amity, we came to the house of Johannes de Imola (whom this young gentleman hath named); there did he justify all those rapes in manner and form as the prisoner here hath confessed."

"But lo, an accident, after, which neither he nor his audience is privy to. Esdras of Granada, not content to have ravished the matron Heraclide and robbed her, after he had betook him from thence to his heels lighted on his companion Bartol with his courtesan; whose pleasing face he had scarce winkingly glanced on but he picked a quarrel with Bartol to have her from him. On this quarrel they fought. Bartol was wounded to the death, Esdras fled, and the fair dame left to go whither she would. This Bartol in the barber's shop freely acknowledged (as both the barber and his man and other here present can amply depose)." Deposed as they were; their oaths went for current; I was quit by proclamation. To the banished earl I came to render thanks.

* * *

A famous passage from Thomas Dekker's The Seven Deadly Sins:

O Candle-light! and art thou one of the cursed crew? hast thou been set at the table of Princes and Nobelmen? have all sorts of people done reverence unto thee, and stood bare so soon as ever they have seen thee? have thieves, traitors, and murderers been afraid to come in thy presence, because they knew thee just, and that thou wouldest discover them? And art thou now a harbourer of all kinds of vices? nay, dost thou play the capital Vice thyself? Hast thou had so many learned Lectures read before thee, and is the light of thy understanding now clean put out, and have so many profound scholars profited by thee? hast thou done such good to Universities, been such a guide to the lame, and seen the doing of so many good works, yet dost thou now look dimly, and with a dull eye, upon all goodness? What comfort have sick men taken (in weary and ikrsome nights) but only in thee? thou hast been their physician and apothecary, and when the relish of nothing could please them, the very shadow of thee hath been to them a restorative consolation. The nurse hath stilled her wayward infant, shewing it but to thee: What gladness hast thou put into mariners' bosoms when thou hast met them on the sea! What joy into the faint and benighted traveller when he has met thee on the land! How many poor handicraftsmen by thee have earned the best part of their living! And art thou now become a companion for drunkards, for leaders, and for prodigals? Art thou turned reprobate? thou wilt burn for it in hell. And so odious is this thy apostasy, and hiding thyself from the light of the truth, that at thy death and going out of the world, even they that love thee best will tread thee under their feet: yea, I that have thus played the herald, and proclaimed thy good parts, will now play the crier and call thee into open court, to arraign thee for thy misdemeanours.

Anthony Munday (1560-1633) wrote many popular, varied things such as ballads, plays about Robin Hood, entertainments for the Lord Mayor's Show, and translated romances such as Amadis of Gaul *and* Palmedin of England. *He is the "A.M." of a book whose titlepage of 1580 read in full (for the titlepage was the advertisement for the contents in those days:*

Zelauto: The Fountain of Fame. Erected in an Orchard of Amorius Adventures. Containing a Delicate Disputation, gallantly discoursed between two noble Gentlemen of Italy. Given for a friendly entertainment to Euphues, on his late arrival into England. By A.M. Servant to the Right Honorable the Earl of Oxenford. Honos alit Artes. Imprinted at London by John Charlewood. 1580.

Here is a bit of that romantic fiction:

Most magnificent Judge, time was (quoth Truculento) when firm affection, and pure zeal of friendship, moved me to mind the destitute estate of these two gentlemen, when as either they had not money to their contentment: or wanted such necessaries, as then was to them needful. At which time (as the lamb endangered by the ravenous wolf, flyeth for safeguard to his fold, or as the ship abiding the hazard of Fortune, and fearing the imminent danger, posteth to some port, or hasteth to some haven in hope of succour): Even so these twin repaired to me, who being sufficiently stored of that which they wanted, and besides, willing to pleasure them, to their greater profit: committed to their custody, a certain sum of money, which amounteth unto four thousand crowns. Now their necessity indifferently satisfied, and they being bound to deliver the sum at a certain day: they have broken their promise, which is open perjury, and falsified their faiths, in not restoring the money. Wherefore, that all gentlemen may be warned by such wilful offenders, and that God may be glorified in putting them to punishment: I have thus determined how the debt shall be discharged. The rendering of the money I do not account of, nor will I be pleased with twice as much restored: the breach of the Law I mean to exact, and to use rigor, where it is so required.

The forfeiture of their lands, is the one part of the penalty, the loss of their right eyes the whole in general, now remembering the woeful estate of their solitary wives, how in depriving their substance, they might be pinched by penury: I let their lands remain unto them in full possession, whereon hereafter they may live more honestly. I claim their right eyes for falsifying their faith: to move others regard how they make like reckless promises. So shall justice be ministered without partiality, they rightly served for infringing their fidelity: and myself not thought to deal with cruelty. . . .

From "The Lamentable History of Titus Andronicus," a ballad (I, 392 in *Roxburghe Ballads*) entered in The Stationers' Register the same day as a play of this title. Note the people are in Elizabethan dress.

Hey nonny nonny

Shepherd and Bagpipe.
From the Engraved titlepage to the first Folio of Drayton's Poems

The authorship of this song is unknown and its date rather uncertain, but it is Elizabethan in feeling, as is the much more familiar Greensleeves, *which follows it.*

Both subjects walked the streets, Tom as a mad beggar and Greensleeves as a whore.

Tom o'Bedlam's Song

From the hagg and hungrie goblin
That into raggs would rend ye,
And the spirit that stands by the naked man
In the Book of Moones defend yee!
That of your five sounde sences
You never be forsaken
Nor wander from your selves with Tom
Abroad to begg your bacon.

While I doe sing "any foode, any feeding,
Feedinge, drinke or clothing,"
Come dame or maid, be not afraid,
Poor Tom will injure nothing.

Of thirty bare years have I
Twice twenty bin enragèd,
And of forty bin three tymes fifteene
In durance soundlie cagèd.
On the lordlie loftes of Bedlam,
With stubble softe and dainty,
Brave braceletts strong, sweet whips ding-dong,
With wholsome hunger plenty.

And nowe I sing, etc.

With a thought I tooke for Maudlin,
And a cruse of cockle pottage,
With a thing thus tall, skie blesse you all,
I befell into this dotage.
I slept not since the Conquest,
Till then I never wakèd,
Till the rogysh boy of love where I lay
Mee found and strip't mee naked.

And nowe I sing, etc.

When I short have shorne my sowre face
And swigg'd my horny barrel,
In an oaken inne I pound my skin
As a suite of guilt apparell.
The moon's my constant Mistrisse,
And the lowlie owle my morrowe,
The flaming Drake and the Nightcrowe make
Mee musicke to my sorrowe.

While I doe sing, etc.

The palsie plagues my pulses
When I prigg your pigs or pullen,
Your culvers take, or matchles make
Your Chanticleare, or sullen.
When I want provant, with Humfrie
I sup, and when benighted,
I repose in Powles with waking soules
Yet nevere am affrighted.

But I doe sing, etc.

I knowe more then Apollo,
For oft, when hee ly's sleeping,
I see the starres att bloudie warres
In the wounded welkin weeping;
The moone embrace her shepheard,
And the quene of Love her warryor,
While the first doth borne the star of morne,
And the next the heavenly Farrier.

While I doe sing, etc.

The Gipsie Snap and Pedro
Are none of Tom's comradoes.
The punk I skorne and the cut purse sworn
And the roaring boyes bravadoe.
The meeke, the white, the gentle,
Me handle touch and spare not
But those that crosse Tom Rynosseros
Doe what the panther dare not.

Although I sing, etc.

With an host of furious fancies,
Whereof I am commander,
With a burning speare, and a horse of aire,
To the wildernesse I wander.
By a knight of ghostes and shadowes
I summon'd am to tourney
Ten leagues beyond the wide world's end.
Me thinke it is noe journey.

Yet will I sing, etc.

Elizabeth's father, Henry VIII, an accomplished musician, is often mentioned as the composer of the tune, but the words of A New Courtly Sonnet of the Lady Greensleeves; to the Tune of Greensleeves *were not published until 1584 and probably date from that decade. The word* sonnet *in this title is in the old sense of an amatory lyric; this is, of course, a ballad. Shakespeare knew and mentioned it. You should note these few words:* kerchers *(handkerchiefs or scarves),* sendal *(silk),* pincase *(a container for pins, which were then rather expensive),* aglets *(metal tags of little lover's gifts). Sleeves in those days were often elaborately embroidered and so detachable from the bodice or doublet, which could be stained with wear or wear out. In Droeshout's famous picture of Shakespeare in the First Folio (1623), we see The Bard's sleeves are laced onto his ruffed doublet. But green sleeves, some say, were a sign of a prostitute.*

Greensleeves was all my joy,
  Greensleeves was my delight;
Greensleeves was my heart of gold,
  And who but Lady Greensleeves?

Alas, my love, ye do me wrong
  To cast me off discourteously;
And I have lovèd you so long,
  Delighting in your company.

Greensleeves was all my joy, &c.

I have been ready at your hand
  To grant whatever you would crave;
I have both wagèd life and land,
  Your love and good will for to have.

Greensleeves was all my joy, &c.

I bought thee kerchiefs to thy head,
  That were wrought fine and gallantly;

I kept thee both at board and bed,
  Which cost my purse well favouredly.

Greensleeves was all my joy, &c.

I bought thee petticoats of the best,
  The cloth so fine as fine might be;
I gave thee jewels for thy chest,
  And all this cost I spent on thee.

Greensleeves was all my joy, &c.

Thy smock of silk both fair and white,
  With gold embroidered gorgeously;
Thy petticoat of sendal right,
  And thus I bought thee gladly.

Greensleeves was all my joy, &c.

Thy girdle of gold so red,
  With pearls bedeckèd sumptuously,
The like no other lasses had,
  And yet thou wouldst not love me.

Greensleeves was all my joy, &c.

Thy purse and eke thy gay gilt knives,
  Thy pin-case, gallant to the eye,
No better wore the burgess' wives,
  And yet thou wouldst not love me.

Greensleeves was all my joy, &c.

Thy crimson stockings all of silk,
  With gold all wrought above the knee,
Thy pumps as white as was the milk,
  And yet thou wouldst not love me.

Greensleeves was all my joy, &c.

Thy gown was of the grassy green,
  Thy sleeves of satin hanging by,
Which made thee be our harvest queen,
  And yet thou wouldst not love me.

Greensleeves was all my joy, &c.

My gayest gelding I thee gave,
  To ride wherever likèd thee;
No lady ever was so brave,
  And yet thou wouldst not love me.

Greensleeves was all my joy, &c.

My men were clothèd all in green,
  And they did ever wait on thee;
All this was gallant to be seen,
  And yet thou wouldst not love me.

Greensleeves was all my joy, &c.

They set thee up, they took thee down,
  They served thee with humility;
Thy foot might not once touch the ground,
  And yet thou wouldst not love me.

Greensleeves was all my joy, &c.

For every morning when thou rose
  I sent thee dainties orderly,
To cheer thy stomach from all woes,
  And yet thou wouldst not love me.

Greensleeves was all my joy, &c.

Thou couldst desire no earthly thing,
  But still thou hadst it readily;
Thy music still to play and sing,
  And yet thou wouldst not love me.

Greensleeves was all my joy, &c.

And who did pay for all this gear
  That thou didst spend when pleasèd thee?
Even I that am rejected here,
  And thou disdain'st to love me.

Greensleeves was all my joy, &c.

Well, I will pray to God on high
  That thou my constancy mayest see;
And that yet once before I die

Thou wilt vouchsafe to love me.

Greensleeves was all my joy, &c.

Greensleeves, now farewell, adieu,
God I pray to prosper thee;
For I am still thy lover true,
Come once again and love me.

Greensleeves was all my joy, &c.

This poem incorporates some folklore of flowers and you may recall a reference to it in Hamlet.

A Nosegay, lacking flowers fresh,
To you now I do send;
Desiring you to look thereon,
When that you may intend:
For flowers fresh begin to fade,
And Boreas in the field
Even with his hard congealèd frost
No better flowers doth yield.

But if that winter could have sprung
A sweeter flower than this,
I would have sent it presently
To you withouten miss:
Accept this then as time doth serve,
Be thankful for the same,
Despite it not, but keep it well,
And mark each flower his name.

Lavender is for lovers true,
Which evermore be fain,
Desiring always for to have
Some pleasure for their pain;
And when that they obtainèd have
The love that they require,
Then have they all their perfect joy,
And quenchèd is the fire.

Rosemary is for remembrance
Between us day and night;
Wishing that I might always have
You present in my sight.
And when I cannot have

As I have said before,
Then Cupid with his deadly dart
Doth wound my heart full sore.

Sage is for sustenance,
That should man's life sustain;
For I do still lie languishing
Continually in pain,
And shall do still until I die,
Except thou favour show
My pain and all my grievous smart
Full well you do it know.

Fennel is for flatterers,
An evil thing it is sure:
But I have always meant truly,
With constant heart most pure;
And will continue in the same
As long as life doth last,
Still hoping for a joyful day
When all our pains be past.

Violet is for faithfulness
Which in me shall abide;
Hoping likewise that from your heart
You will not let it slide;
And will continue in the same
As you have now begun,
And then for ever to abide,
Then you my heart have won.

Thyme is to try me,
As each be trièd must,
Letting you know while life doth last
I will not be unjust;
And if I should I would to God
To hell my soul should bear,
And eke also that Belzebub
With teeth he should me tear.

Roses is to rule me
With reason as you will,
For to be still obedient
Your mind for to fulfil;
And thereto will not disagree
In nothing that you say,

But will content your mind truly
  In all things that I may.

Gillyflowers is for gentleness,
  Which in me shall remain,
Hoping that no sedition shall
  Depart our hearts in twain.
As soon the sun shall lose his course,
  The moon against her kind
Shall have no light, if that I do
  Once put you from my mind.

Carnations is for graciousness,
  Mark that now by the way,
Have no regard to flatterers,
  Nor pass not what they say:
For they will come with lying tales
  Your ears for to fulfil:
In any case do you consent
  Nothing unto their will.

Marigolds is for marriage,
  That would our minds suffice,
Lest that suspicion of us twain
  By any means should rise:
As for my part, I do not care,
  Myself I will still use
That all the women of the world
  For you I will refuse.

Pennyroyal is to print your love
  So deep within my heart,
That when you look this Nosegay on
  My pain you may impart;
And when that you have read the same,
  Consider well my woe,
Think ye then how to recompense
  Even him that loves you so.

Cowslips is for counsel,
  For secrets us between,
That none but you and I alone
  Should know the thing we mean:
And if you will thus wisely do,
  As I think to be best,

Then have you surely won the field
And set my heart at rest.

I pray you keep this Nosegay well,
And set by it some store:
And thus farewell! the gods thee guide
Both now and evermore!
Not as the common sort do use,
To set it in your breast,
That when the smell is gone away,
On the ground he takes his rest.

Henry Chettle in Kind-Heart's Dream *(1592) says ballad-mongering in the streets could make a man a pound a day if he was very lucky and notes that many young men turned to it, that*

a company of idle youths, loathing honest labor, and despising, lawful trades, betake themselves to a vagrant and vicious life, in every corner of cities and market towns of the realm, singing and selling ballads.... There is many a tradesman, of a worshipful trade yet no stationer, who after a little bringing up apprentices to singing brokery, takes into his shop some fresh men, and trusts his servants of two months standing with a dozen gross of ballads. In which if they prove thrifty he makes them petty chapmen.

Sir William Cornwallis (d. 1631) published essays at the end of Elizabeth's reign and the beginning of James' and in one writes of ballads:

I have not been ashamed to adventure mine ears with a ballad singer, and they have come home loaden to my liking, doubly satisfied, with profit and with recreation. The profit to see earthlings satisfied with such coarse stuff, to hear vice rebuked, and to see the power of virtue that pierceth the head of such a base historian and vile auditory. The recreation, to see how thoroughly the standers by are affected, what strange gestures come from them, what strained stuff from their poet, what shift they make to stand to hear, what extremities he is driven to for rime, how they adventure their purses, he his wits, how well both their pains are recompensed, they with a filthy noise, he with a base reward.

A bit of Scottish history of the 16th century is preserved in the ballad of "the Bonnie Earl of Murray," who also fell afoul of flames. In his case (in 1592) the Earl of Huntly and his men attacked the Castle of Donibristle, where Murray was staying with his mother, setting it on fire. Murray escaped through the cordon of Huntly's men but, unfortunately, he could not disappear into the dark by the craggy shore: the tip of his helmet was afire and so he was captured and "unmercifully slain." The death of Murray was much lamented by the common folk and was still going strong in 1750 when a miscellany published this, the earliest text of the ballad I can find. It's a braw *(brave, fine) one.*

Ye Highlands, and ye Lawlands,
Oh where have you been?
They have slain the Earl of Murray,
And they layd him on the green.

"Now wae be to thee, Huntly!
And wherefore did you sae?
I bade you bring him wi' you,
But forbade you him to slay."

He was a braw gallant,
And he rid at the ring;
And the bonny Earl of Murray,
Oh he might have been a king!

He was a braw gallant,
And he play'd at the ba';
And the bonny Earl of Murray
Was the flower among them a'.

He was a braw gallant,
And he play'd at the glove;
And the bonny Earl of Murray,
Oh he was the Queen's love!

Oh lang will his lady
Look o'er the castle Down,
Ere she see the Earl of Murray
Come sounding thro the town!

Sensational events, especially murders, caused ballads to be hurriedly composed, printed, and sung and sold in the street. This one (by Thomas Deloney) is based on the true story of Ulalia Glandfield, who fell in love with her father's manager, George Strangwidge. Her parents moved to Plymouth and her father forced her to marry a Plymouth man, a rich widower named Page. The new Mrs. Page hated him and had him strangled by one of her servants and one of George Strangwidge's. She, Strangwidge, and the two servants were all hanged for the crime, and at least two other ballads, a pamphlet, and a play (by Ben Jonson and Thomas Dekker, now lost, dated 1599) were devoted to exploiting public interest in forced marriage and premeditated murder.

The Lamentation of Mr. Page's Wife
Of Plymouth, who, being forced to wed him, consented to his
Murder, for the love of G. Strangwidge: for
which they suffered at Barnstable
in Devonshire

The tune is *Fortune My Foe, &c.*

Unhappy she whom Fortune hath forlorn
Despis'd of grace that proffered grace did scorn,
My lawless love hath luckless wrought my woe,
My discontent content did overthrow.

My loathèd life too late I do lament,
My woeful deeds in heart I do repent:
A wife I was that wilful went awry,
And for that fault am here prepared to die.

In blooming years my father's greedy mind,
Against my will, a match for me did find:
Great wealth there was, yea, gold and silver store,
But yet my heart had chosen one before.

Mine eyes disliked my father's liking quite,
My heart did loathe my parent's fond delight:
My childish mind and fancy told to me,
That with his age my youth could not agree.

On knees I prayed they would not me constrain;
With tears I cried their purpose to refrain;
With signs and sobs I did them often move,
I might not wed whereas I could not love.

But all in vain my speeches still I spent:
My mother's will my wishes did prevent,
Though wealthy Page possessed the outward part,
George Strangwidge still was lodgèd in my heart.

I weddèd was, and wrappèd all in woe;
Great discontent within my heart did grow;
I loathed to live, yet lived in in deadly strife,
Because perforce I was made Page's wife.

My closen eyes could not his sight abide;
My tender youth did loathe his agèd side:
Scant could I taste the meat whereon he fed;

My legs did loathe to lodge within his bed.

Cause knew I none I should despise him so,
That such disdain within my heart should grow,
Save only this, that fancy did me move,
And told me still, George Strangwidge was my love.

Lo I here began my downfall and decay.
In mind I mused to make him straight away:
I that became his discontented wife,
Contented was he should be rid of life.

Methinks the heavens cry vengeance for my fact,
Methinks the world condemns my monstrous act,
Methinks within my conscience tells me true,
That for that deed hell fire is my due.

My pensive soul doth sorrow for my sin,
For which offence my soul doth bleed within;
But never could I wish, of low or high,
A longer life than see sweet Strangwidge die.

O woe is me I that had no greater grace
To stay till he had run out Nature's race.
My deeds I rue, but I do repent
That to the same my Strangwidge gave consent.

You parents fond, that greedy-minded be,
And seek to graft upon the golden tree,
Consider well and rightful judges be,
And give you doom 'twixt parents' love and me.

I was their child, and bound for to obey,
Yet not to love where I no love could lay.
I married was to muck and endless strife;
But faith before had made me Strangwidge' wife.

O wretched world I who cankered rust doth bind,
And cursèd men who bear a greedy mind;
And hapless I, whom parents did force so
To end my days in sorrow, shame and woe.

You Devonshire dames, and courteous Cornwall knights,
That here are come to visit woeful wights,
Regard my grief, and mark my woeful end,
But to your children be a better friend.

And thou, my dear, that for my fault must die,
Be not afraid the sting of death to try:
Like as we lived and loved together true,
So both at once we'll bid the world adieu.

Ulalia, thy friend, doth take her last farewell,
Whose soul with thee in heaven shall ever dwell.
Sweet Saviour Christ do Thou my soul receive:
The world I do with all my heart forgive.

And parents now, whose greedy minds do show
Your hearts' desire and inward heavy woe,
Mourn you no more, for now my heart doth tell,
Ere day be done my soul shall be full well.

And Plymouth proud, I bid thee now farewell.
Take heed, you wives, let not your hands rebel;
And farewell, life, wherein such sorrow shows,
And welcome, death, that doth my corpse enclose.

And now, sweet Lord forgive me my misdeeds.
Repentance cries for soul that inward bleeds:
My soul and body I commend to Thee,
That with Thy blood from death redeemèd me.

Lord bless our Queen with long and happy life,
And send true peace betwixt each man and wife;
And give all parents wisdom to foresee,
The match is marred where minds do not agree.

Madrigal singing was a family and friendly pastime. Some of the anonymous poets provided excellent texts to be set by William Byrd:

Come, woeful Orpheus, with the charming lyre,
And tune my voice unto thy skilful wire;
Some strange chromatic notes do you devise,
That best with mournful accents sympathise;
Of sourest sharps and uncouth flats make choice,
And I'll thereto compassionate my voice.

or by Orlando Gibbons:

The silver swan, who living had no note,
When death approached unlocked her silent throat;
Leaning her breast against the reedy shore,

Thus sung her first and last, and sung no more:
Farewell, all joys; O death, come close mine eyes;
More geese than swans now live, more fools than wise.

or by Thomas Morley:

Sing we and chant it
While love doth grant it.
Not long youth lasteth,
And old age hasteth.
Now is best leisure
To take our pleasure.

All things invite us
Now to delight us.
Hence, care, be packing!
No mirth be lacking!
Let spare no treasure
To live in pleasure.

or by the lesser-known Thomas Vautor:

Sweet Suffolk owl, so trimly dight
With feathers like a lady bright,
Thou singest alone, sitting by night,
Te whit, te whoo, te whit, te whit.
Thy note, that forth so freely rolls,
With shrill command the mouse controls,
And sings a dirge for dying souls,
Te whit, te whoo, te whit, te whit.

or by Robert Jones:

My love is neither young nor old,
Not fiery hot, nor frozen cold;
But fresh and fair as springing briar,
Blooming the fruit of love's desire.

Not snowy white nor rosy red,
But fair enough for shepherd's bed;
And such a love was never seen
On hill or dale or country green.

Where I live there is a radio station that advertizes that it plays, "Love Songs, Nothing But Love Songs." The moon-June type of song has always been popular, love and its pains and pleasures the principal topic of song. Here are two Elizabethan examples.

Come away, come sweet Love,
The golden morning breaks:
All the earth, all the air,
Of love and pleasure speaks.
Teach thine arms then to embrace,
And sweet rosy lips to kiss:
And mix our souls in mutual bliss.
Eyes were made for beauty's grace,
Viewing, ruing Love's long pain:
Procur'd by beauty's rude disdain.

Come away, come sweet Love,
The golden morning wasts:
While the Sun from his Sphere
His fiery arrows casts,
Making all the shadows fly,
Playing, staying in the Grove:
To entertain the stealth of love.
Thither sweet Love let us hie
Flying, dying in desire:
Wing'd with sweet hopes and heavenly fire.

Come away, come sweet Love,
Do not in vain adorn
Beauty's grace that should rise
Like to the naked morn.
Lillies on the River's side,
And fair Cyprian flowers new blown,
Desire no beauties but their own.
Ornament is Nurse of pride,
Pleasure, measure, Loves delight:
Haste then sweet Love our wished flight.

A love song from A Poetical Rhapsody *(1602) by "A.W.," which may represent someone's initials or just "Anonymous Writer."*

The night, say all, was made for rest;
  And so say I, but not for all:
To them the darkest nights are best
  Which give them leave asleep to fall;
  But I that seek my rest by light
  Hate sleep, and praise the clearest night.

Bright was the moon, as bright as day,
  And Venus glistered in the west,
Whose light did lead the ready way,
  That brought me to my wishèd rest:
  Then each of them increased their light
  While I enjoyed her heavenly sight.

Say, gentle dames, what moved your mind
  To shine so fair above your wont?
Would Phoebe fair Endymion find?
  Would Venus see Adonis hunt?
  No, no, you fearèd by her sight
  To lose the praise of beauty bright.

At last for shame you shrunk away,
  And thought to reave the world of light;
Then shone my dame with brighter ray,
  Than that which comes from Phoebus' sight:
  None other light but hers I praise,
  Whose nights are clearer than the days.

From the Roxburghe Ballads, a risqué song from the 1570s about how not to be a mome, *or simpleton.*

An Amorous Dialogue Between John and His Mistress

Being a complete and true relation of some merry passages between the Mistress and her Apprentice; who pleased her so well that she rewarded him with fifty broad pieces for his pains.

Here by this dialogue you may discern,
While old cats nibble cheese, the young ones learn.

[*to the tune of* Packington's Pound; or, What Should a Young Woman, etc.; or, Captain Digby.]

"Come, John, sit thee down, I have somewhat to say,
In my mind I have kept it this many a day.
Your master you know is a fool, and a sot,
And minds nothing else but the pipe and the pot.
Till twelve or till one he will never come home,
And then he's so drunk that he lies like a mome:
  Such usage as this would make any one mad,
  But a woman will have it if 'tis to be had."

" 'Tis true forsooth, mistress, the case is but hard,

That a woman should be of her pleasure debarred:
But 'tis the sad fate of a thousand beside,
Or else the whole city is foully belied:
There is not a man amoung twenty that thrives,
Not ten in fifteen that do lie with their wives:
    Yet still you had better be merry than sad,
    And take it wherever it is to be had."

"But John, 'tis a difficult matter to find,
A man that is trusty and constantly kind:
An Inns-of-Court gallant he cringes and bows,
He's presently known by his oaths and his vows,
And though both his clothes and his speeches be gay,
Yet he loves you but only a night and away:
    Such usage as this would make any one mad,
    Yet a woman will have it, if 'tis to be had."

"What think you of one that belongs to the court,
They say they are youthful, and given to sport:
He'll present you with bracelets, and jewels, and rings,
With stones that are precious and twenty fine things;
Or if you are not for the court nor the town,
What think you forsooth of a man with a gown?
    You must have a gallant, a good or a bad,
    And take it wherever it is to be had."

The Second Part [to the same tune]

"No, John, I confess that not any of these,
Had ever the power my fancy to please;
I like no such blades for a trick that I know,
For as soon as they've trod they are given to crow;
Plain dealing is best, and I like a man well,
That when he has kissed will be hanged ere he'll tell:
    My meaning is honest, and thou art the lad,
    Then give it and take it where 'tis to be had."

"Alas! my dear mistress, it never can be,
That you can affect such a fellow as me:
Yet heaven forbid, since I am but your man,
I should ever refuse to do all that I can;
But then if my master should know what we've done,
We both should be blown up as sure as a gun:
    For after our joys, he would make us both sad,
    For taking it where it ought not to be had."

"But how should he know it, thou scrupulous elf,
Do'st think I'm so silly to tell him myself?
If we are but so wise our own counsel to keep,
We may laugh and lie down while the sot is asleep:
Some hundreds I know in the city that use
To give to their men what their masters refuse;
 The man is the master, the 'prentice the dad,
 For women must take it where 'tis to be had."

"Some 'prentices use it, forsooth, I allow,
But I am a novice and cannot tell how:
However, I hope that I shall not be blamed,
For to tell you the truth I am somewhat asham'd;
I know how to carry your Bible to church,
But to play with my mistress I'm left in the lurch:
 Yet if you can shew me the way good or bad,
 I'll promise you all that there is to be had."

"Alas, pretty mistress, the pleasure is such,
We never can give one another too much:
If this be the business the way is so plain,
I think I can easily find it again:
Twas thus we began; and...Thus we lie down,
And thus...Oh thus! that we fell in a swoon:
 Such sport to refuse who was ever so mad,
 I'll take it where ever it is to be had.":

"Now, Johnny, you talk like an ignorant mome,
You can have such pleasures no where but at home,
Here's fifty broad pieces for what you have done,
But see that you never a-gadding do run:
For no new employment than trouble your brains,
For here when you work you'll be paid for your pains:
 But should you deceive me no woman so sad,
 To lose all the pleasure that once she had had."

"A mistress so noble I never will leave,
'Twere a sin and a shame such a friend to deceive;
For my master's shop no more will I care,
'Tis pleasanter handing my mistress' ware:
A fig for indentures, for now I am made
Free of a gentler and pleasanter trade:
 I know when I'm well, I was never so mad,
 To forsake a good thing when 'tis to be had."

To conclude our selection of anonymous songs, two from Percy's Folio MSS, volume 4, which are of uncertain date but pre-1600. The first compares the maidenhead not to a cherry but a damascene plum and the second makes a joke of putting in at the last moment an unexpected word, the rhyme suggesting the real (bleeped) word intended. This technique is imitated in at least one modern "barrack-room ballad" or "rugby song" and the reason is that we like to

Banish the use of the four-letter words
Whose meanings are never obscure.
The Angles and Saxons, those hardy old birds,
Were vulgar, obscene, and impure.

Today we have "cleaned up our act," more or less, but Elizabethan English was more direct. Even the Queen used the four-letter words. However, do not try such vibrant English everywhere today, for (if you will permit a whole stanza from the modern song of which I have already quoted a bit, before we move on to the Elizabethan ones):

When Nature is calling, plain speaking is out,
When ladies (God bless 'em) are milling about.
You may piddle, make water, or empty the glass.
You can powder your nose. Even Johnny can pass.
Shake the dew off the lily. See man about dog.
When everyone's soused, it's condensing the fog.
But please to remember, if your would know bliss,
That only in Shakespeare do characters piss.

A Maidenhead

Come, sit thee down by these cool streams
Never yet warmed by Titan's beams!
My tender youth thy waist shall clip,
And fix upon the cherry lip;
And lay thee down on this green bed,
Where thou shalt lose thy maidenhead.

See how the little Phillip Sparrow,
Whose joints do overflow with marrow,
On yonder bough how he doth prove
With his mate the joys of love,
And doth instruct thee, as he doth tread,
How thou shalt lose thy maidenhead.

O you younglings, be not nice!
Coyness in maids is such a vice,
That if in youth you do not marry,

In age young men will let you tarry.
By my persuasion then be led,
And lose in time thy maidenhead.

Clothes that embroidered be with gold,
If never worn, will quickly mold;
If in time you do not pluck
The damisine or the apricot,
In pinching autumn thee'll be dead;
Then lose in time thy maidenhead!

A Friend of Mine

A friend of mine not long ago
desired at my hand
Some pretty toy to move delight
to those that hearers stand.
The which I mean to gratify
by all the means I may,
And move delight in every wight
that with affection stay.

Some thought to prove wherein I should
these several humours please,
The which to do, reason forbids,
but I should some displease;
But since my muse doth pleasure choose,
and thereon bends her skill,
Whereby I may drive time away,
and sorrows quite beguile.

It was my chance, not long ago,
by a pleasant wood to walk,
Where I unseen of any one
did hear two lovers talk;
And as these lovers forth did pass,
hard by a pleasant shade,
Hard by a mighty Pine tree there,
their resting place they made.

"Insooth," then did this young man say,
"I think this fragrant place
Was only made for lovers true
each other to embrace."
He took her by the middle small,—
good sooth I do not mock,—
Not meaning to do any thing

but to pull up her [smock] block.
Whereon she sat, poor silly soul,
to rest her weary bones.
This maid she was no whit afraid,
but she caught him fast by the [stones] thumbs;
Whereat he vext and grieved was,
'so that his flesh did wrinkle;
This maid she was no whit afraid,
but caught him fast hold by the [pintle] pimple.

Which he had on his chin likewise;—
but let that pimple pass;—
There is no man here but he may suppose
she were a merry lass.
He boldly ventured, being tall,
yet in his speech but blunt,
He never ceast, but took up all,
and caught her by the[—]: plumpe.

And red rose lips he kissed full sweet;
quote she, "I crave no succour."
Which made him to have a mighty mind
to clip, kiss, and to[—]pluck her
Into his arms. "Nay! soft!" quoth she,
"what needeth all this doing?
For if you will be ruled by me,
you shall use small time in wooing."

"For I will lay me down," quoth she,
"upon the slippery segs,
And all my clothes I'll truss up round.
And spread abroad my [legs] eggs.
Which I have in my apron here
under my girdle tucked;
So shall I be most fine and brave,
most ready to be[—]ducked.

A street cry of London is in integral part of this charming song by Thomas Campion:

There is a garden in her face,
Where roses and white lilies grow,
A heavenly paradise is that place,
Wherein all pleasant fruits do flow.
There cherries grow, which none may buy

Till "Cherry ripe!" themselves do cry.

Those cherries fairly do enclose
Of orient pearl a double row;
Which when her lovely laughter shows,
They look like rosebuds filled with snow.
Yet them nor peer nor prince can buy,
Till "Cherry ripe!" themselves to cry.

Her eyes like angels watch them still;
Her brows like bended bows do stand,
Threatening with piercing frowns to kill
All that attempt with eye or hand
Those sacred cherries to come nigh,
Till "Cherry ripe!" themselves do cry.

Here is a kind of combination of the street cry of the peddler with the sort of song Autolycus sings in The Winter's Tale. *Sung to music by John Dowland, it combined grace with the erotic connotations of the contents of the peddler's sack. Once again by that prolific poet, Anonymous.*

A Peddler's Song

Fine knacks for ladies, cheap, choice, brace and new!
Good pennyworths, but money cannot move.
I keep a fair but for the fair to view;
  A beggar may be liberal of love.
Though all my wares be trash, the heart is true,
  The heart is true.
  The heart is true.

Great gifts are guiles and look for gifts again;
  My trifles come as treasures from my mind.
It is a precious jewel to be plain;
  Sometimes in shell the orient pearls we find.
Of others take a sheaf, of me a grain,
  Of me a grain,
  Of me a grain.

Within this pack pins, points, laces, and gloves,
  And divers toys fitting a country fair.
But in my heart, where duty serves and loves,
  Turtles and twins, court's brood, a heavenly pair.
Happy the heart that thinks of no removes,
  Of no removes,
  Of no removes.

Popular song forms were used for a number of literary purposes, including religious verse. Here is a lullaby supposed to be sung to the Christ Child by the Blessed Virgin Mary. The author was Richard Rowlands who, forced out of England as a Catholic, went to Antwerp, adopted the surname of his Dutch grandfather, and (as Richard Verstegan) disseminated Roman Catholic propaganda in England. In 1587 the English ambassador in Paris, on Elizabeth's instructions, succeeded in getting him jailed there for a book about how badly Elizabeth treated the Catholics in her domains. He lived at least until 1620, when he was last heard of back in Antwerp.

Upon my lap my sovereign sits
   And sucks upon my breast,
Meanwhile his love sustains my life,
   And gives my body rest.
   Sing lullaby, my little boy,
   Sing lullaby, my only joy.

When thou hast taken thy repast,
   Repose, my babe, on me;
So may thy mother and thy nurse
   Thy cradle also be.
   Sing lullaby, my little boy,
   Sing lullaby, my only joy.

I grieve that duty doth not work
   All what my wishing would,
Because I would not be to thee
   But in the best I should.
   Sing lullaby, my little boy,
   Sing lullaby, my only joy. . . .

Elizabethans liked tricky verses whose initial letters spelled (say) ELIZABETHA REGINA. This "honeysuckle" from William Hunnis gives you the message "If thou desire to live in rest, give ear and see but say the best" if you read the first iamb (two-syllable foot) of each line. This goes a step beyond acrostic verse, don't you think?

If thou delight in quietness of life,
Desire to shun from broils, debate, and strife,
To live in love with God, with friend and foe,
In rest shalt sleep when others cannot so.
Give ear to all, yet do not all believe,
And see the end, and then do sentence give;
But say, for truth, of happy lives assigned
The best hath he that quiet is in mind.

More wordplay, this rhetorical, in Nicholas Breton's Melancholic Humours *(1600), full of "odd conceit":*

Lovely kind, and kindly loving
Such a mind were worth the moving;
Truly fair, and fairly true—
Where are all these, but in you?
Wisely kind, and kindly wise;
Blessèd life, where such love lies!
Wise, and kind, and fair, and true—
Lovely live all these in you.
Sweetly dear, and dearly sweet;
Blessèd, where these blessing meet!
Sweet, fair, wise, kind, blessed, true—
Blessèd be all these in you!

William Webbe flourished about the end of the 16th century and, having gone to college with Edmund Spenser, took an interest in poetry and undertook to judge the poets of his time. His views on individual poets do not concern us here; however, he makes points about the lively literary market of his day and the popularity of works in verse:

Among the innumerable sorts of English books, and infinite fardels of printed pamphlets, wherewith this country is pestered, all shops stuffed, and every study furnished; the greater part, I think, in any one kind, are such as are either mere poetical, or which tend in some respects (as either in matter or form) to poetry. Of such books, therefore, sith I have been one that have had a desire to read not the fewest, and because it is an argument which men of great learning have no leisure to handle, or at least having to do with more serious matters do least regard. If I write something, concerning what I think of our English poets, or adventure to set down my simple judgment of English poetry, I trust the learned poets will give me leave, and vouchsafe my book passage, as being for the rudeness thereof no prejudice to their noble studies, but even (as my intent is) an *instar cotis* to stir up some other of meet ability to bestow travail in this matter; whereby, I think, we may not only get the means which we yet want, to discern between good writers and bad, but perhaps also challenge from the rude multitude of rustical rhymers, who will be called poets, the right practice and orderly course of true poetry.

The Elizabethan age was one not only of piracy and colonization but also of translation, imitation and adaption in literature. Edward Fairfax translated in 1600 the Gerusalemme Liberata *of Tasso as* Tasso's Godfrey of Bulloigne *and this is a steamy scene from Book 16 that the public liked:*

Her breasts were naked, for the day was hot,

Her locks unbound waved in the wanton wind,
Somedeal she sweat (tired with the game you wot);
Her sweat drops bright, white, round, like pearls of Ind,
Her humid eyes a fiery smile forth shot,
That like sun-beams in silver fountains shined,
  O'er him her looks she hung, and her soft breast
  The pillow was, here he and love took rest.

His hungry eyes upon her face he fed,
And feeding them so pined himself away;
And she, declining often down her head,
His lips, his cheeks, his eyes kissed, as he lay,
Wherewith he sighed, as if his soul had fled
From his frail breast to hers, and there would stay
  With her belovèd sprite: the armèd pair
  These follies all beheld and this hot fare.

Down by the lovers' side there pendant was
A crystal mirror, bright, pure, smooth and neat;
He rose and to his mistress held the glass
(A noble page, graced with that service great);
She with glad looks, he with inflamed (alas!)
Beauty and love beheld, both in one seat;
  Yet them in sundry objects each espies,
  She, in the glass; he saw them in her eyes.

Her, to command; to serve, it pleased the knight;
Her proud of bondage; of her empire, she;
My dear (she said) that blessest with thy sight
Even blessed angels, turn thine eyes to me,
For painted in my heart and portrayed right
Thy worth, thy beauties, and perfections be,
  Of which the form, the shape, and fashion best,
  Not in this glass is seen, but in my breast.

And if thou me disdain, yet be content
At least so to behold thy lovely hue,
That while thereon thy looks are fixed and bent,
Thy happy eyes themselves may see and view;
So rare a shape, no crystal can present,
No glass contain that heav'n of beauties true;
  Oh let the skies thy worthy mirror be,
  And in clear stars thy shape and image see!

And with that word she smiled, and ne'ertheless
Her love-toys still she used, and pleasures bold:

Her hair that done she twisted up in tress,
And looser locks in silken laces rolled,
Her curles garland-wise she did updress,
Wherein (like rich enamel laid on gold)
The twisted flow'rets smiled, and her white breast
The lilies (there that spring) and roses dressed.

Another narrative poem with sex appeal was Marlowe's erotic Hero and Leander, *a poem Shakespeare read, admired, and quoted, referring to the author as "dead Shepherd," for by then Marlowe's all too brief career was over, his last pastoral or poem or play written, his life abruptly ended in a tavern brawl in Deptford. He was stabbed in the eye by Ingram Frizer, over a tavern bill (some said), or over some matter connected with his working for the Elizabethan equivalent of the CIA (whose connections had got him his master's degree from Cambridge).*

On his feast day, Oh cursèd day and hour,
Went Hero through Sestos, from her tower
To Venus' temple, where unhappily,
As after chanced, they did each other spy.
So fair a church as this, had Venus none:
The walls were of discoloured jasper stone,
Wherein was Proteus carvèd, and o'erhead
A lively vine of green sea-agate spread;
Where by one hand, light-headed Bacchus hung,
And with the other, wine from grapes outwrung.
Of crystal shining fair the pavement was;
The town of Sestos called it Venus' glass.
There might you see the gods in sundry shapes,
Committing heady riots, incest, rapes:
For know, that underneath this radiant floor
Was Dana's statue in a brazen tower,
Jove slily stealing from his sister's bed,
To dally with Idalian Ganymed;
And for his love, Europa, bellowing loud,
And tumbling with the Rainbow in a cloud:
Blood-quaffing Mars heaving the iron net
Which limping Vulcan and his Cyclops set:
Love kindling fire, to burn such towns as Troy,
Sylvanus weeping for the lovely boy
That now is turned into a cypress tree,
Under whose shade the wood-gods love to be.
And in the midst a silver altar stood;
There Hero sacrificing turtles' blood,
Vailed to the ground, vailing her eyelids close,
And modestly they opened as she rose:

Thence flew Love's arrow with the golden head,
And thus Leander was enamourèd.
Stone still he stood, and evermore he gazed,
Till with the fire that from his count'nance blazed,
Relenting Hero's gentle heart was strook:
Such force and virtue hath an amorous look.
It lies not in our power to love, or hate,
For will in us is overruled by fate.
When two are stript, long ere the course begin,
We wish that one should lose, the other win;
And one especially do we affect
Of two gold ingots, like in each respect.
The reason no man knows; let it suffice,
What we behold is censured by our eyes.
Where both deliberate, the love is slight;
Who ever loved, that loved not at first sight?

Here is the lover's authentic voice in one of Drayton's famous sonnets, a far cry from the old-fashioned and even artificial language of the previous poem:

Since there's no help, come let us kiss and part;
Nay, I have done, you get no more of me,
And I am glad, yea glad with all my heart
That thus so cleanly I myself can free;
Shake hands forever, cancel all our vows,
And when we meet at any time again,
Be it not seen in either of our brows
That we one jot of former love retain.
Now at the last gasp of love's latest breath,
When, his pulse failing, passion speechless lies,
When faith is kneeling by his bed of death,
And innocence is closing up his eyes,
  Now if thou wouldst, when all have given him over,
  From death to life thou mightst him yet recover.

From the Plays: An Age of Song

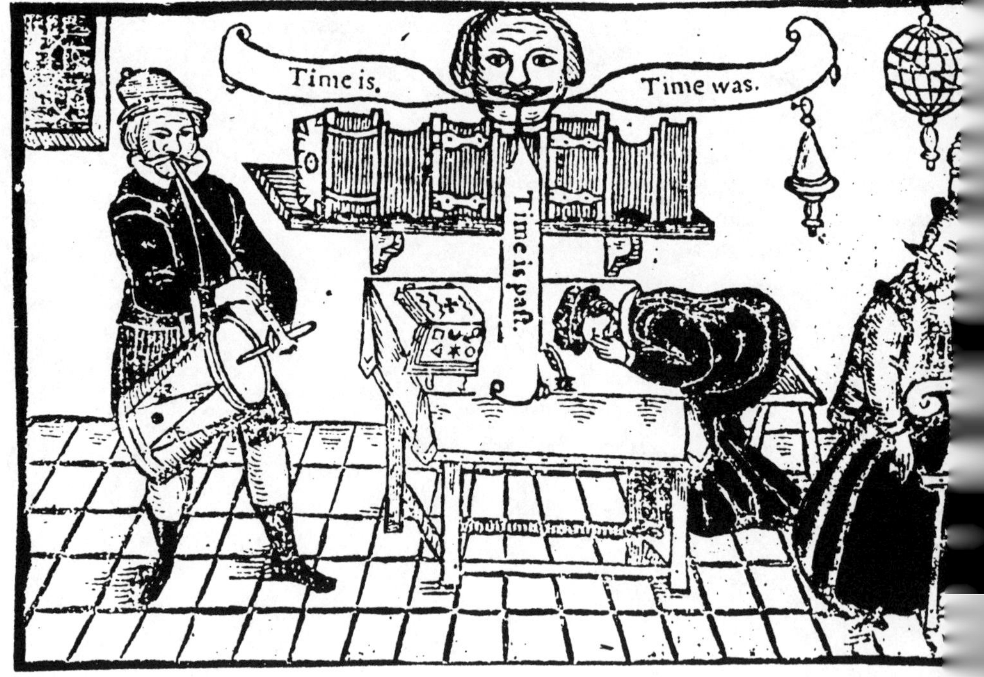

A scene from Robert Greene's hit play *Friar Bacon and Friar Bungay* (with the marvelous brazen head said to have been created by Roger Bacon, who lived 1214-1294) can remind us of the influence plays, and the songs they contained so often in that tuneful age, had on popular culture.

Sometimes the songs in plays advanced the dramatic action (not so new an idea as you might imagine unless you believe the hyped histories of modern musicals). Sometimes they just set a mood or provided a break. We have omitted quoting from plays (selecting songs because these are briefer and also because the public might well extract a song from a play and make it popular).

An old Scottish poem tells of the power of music:

He'd harpit a fish out o' saut water,
  Or water out o' a stane,
Or milk out o' a maiden's breast,
  That bairn had never nane.

When combined with memorable words in ballads, songs had an effect that was almost magical. The age of Elizabeth was an age of song. Songs were a recreation and, in some narrative ballads, an education for the common people.

Thomas Lodge, who may have been born the very year that Elizabeth became Queen, was the son of a Lord Mayor of London. He traveled widely, even to South America, and on a voyage to the Canary Islands wrote his best-known romance, Rosalynde *(1590). Here is a madrigal from it, with three other songs:*

Love in my bosom like a bee
  Doth suck his sweet;
Now with his wings he plays with me,
  Now with his feet.
Within mine eyes he makes his nest,
His bed amidst my tender breast,
My kisses are his daily feast,
And yet he robs me of my rest—
  Ah, wanton, will ye?

And if I sleep, then percheth he
  With pretty flight,
And makes his pillow of my knee
  The livelong night.
Strike I my lute, he tunes the string,
He music plays if so I sing,

He lends me every lovely thing,
Yet cruel he my heart doth sting—
   Whist, wanton, still ye!

Else I with roses every day
   Will whip you hence,
And bind you, when you long to play,
   For your offence.
I'll shut mine eyes to keep you in,
I'll make you fast it for your sin,
I'll count your power not worth a pin;
Alas! what hereby shall I win
   If he gainsay me?

What if I beat the wanton boy
   With many a rod?
He will repay me with annoy,
   Because a god.
Then sit thou safely on my knee,
And let thy bower my bosom be,
Lurk in mine eyes, I like of thee.
O Cupid, so thou pity me,
   Spare not, but play thee!

. . .

My mistress when she goes
To pull the pink and rose
Along the river bounds,
And trippeth on the grounds,
And runs from rocks to rocks
With lovely scattered locks,
Whilst amorous wind doth play
With hairs so golden gay;
The water waxeth clear,
The fishes draw her near,
The sirens sing her praise,
Sweet flowers perfume her ways,
And Neptune, glad and fain,
Yields up to her his reign.

. . .

My Phillis hath the morning sun
   At first to look upon her,
And Phillis hath morn-waking birds

Her risings for to honour.
My Phillis hath prime-feathered flowers
That smile when she treads on them,
And Phillis hath a gallant flock
That leaps since she doth own them.
But Phillis hath so hard a heart
(Alas, that she should have it!)
As yields no mercy to desert
No grace to those that crave it.
Sweet sun, when thou lookest on,
Pray her regard my moan;
Sweet birds, when you sing to her,
To yield some pity woo her;
Sweet flowers, whenas she treads on.
Tell her, her beauty deads one;
And if in life her love she nill agree me,
Pray her, before I die she will come see
me.

I'll teach thee, lovely Phillis, what love is:
It is a vision, seeming such as thou,
That flies as fast as it assaults mine eyes;
It is affection that doth reason miss;
It is a shape of pleasure like to you,
Which meets the eye, and seen on sudden dies;
It is a doubled grief, a spark of pleasure
Begot by vain desire. And this is love,
Whom in our youth we count our chiefest treasure,
In age, for want of power, we do reprove.
Yea, such a power is love, whose loss is pain,
And having got him, we repent our gain.

Robert Greene was really what he seems to have accused Shakespeare of being, a factotum of the literary world of Elizabethan London. Among his many talents was writing songs for his own plays:

Sephestia's Song

Weep not, my wanton, smile upon my knee,
When thou art old there's grief enough for thee.
Mother's wag, pretty boy,
Father's sorrow, father's joy,
When thy father first did see
Such a boy by him and me,
He was glad, I was woe;
Fortune changèd made him so,
When he left his pretty boy,

  Last his sorrow, first his joy.

Weep not, my wanton, smile upon my knee,
When thou art old there's grief enough for thee.
  The wanton smiled, father wept,
  Mother cried, baby leapt;
  More he crowed, more we cried,
  Nature could not sorrow hide.
  He must go, he must kiss
  Child and mother, baby bliss,
  For he left his pretty boy,
  Father's sorrow, father's joy.

Weep not, my wanton, smile upon my knee,
When thou art old there's grief enough for thee.

The Shepherd's Wife's Song

Ah, what is love? It is pretty thing,
As sweet unto a shepherd as a king—
    And sweeter too,
For kings have cares that wait upon a crown,
And cares can make the sweetest love to frown.
  Ah then, ah then,
If country loves such sweet desires do gain,
What lady would not love a shepherd swain?

His flocks once folded, he comes home at night
As merry as a king in his delight—
    And merrier too,
For kings bethink them what the state require,
Where shepherds careless carol by the fire.
  Ah then, ah then,
If country loves such sweet desires gain,
What lady would not love a shepherd swain?

He kisseth first, then sits as blithe to eat
His cream and curds as doth the king his meat—
  And blither too,
For kings have often fears when they do sup,
Where shepherds dread no poison in their cup.
  Ah then, ah then,
If country loves such sweet desires gain,
What lady would not love a shepherd swain?

To bed he goes, as wanton then, I ween,

As is a king in dalliance with a queen—
   More wanton too,
For kings have many griefs, affects to move,
Where shepherds have no greater grief than love.
   Ah then, ah then,
If country loves such sweet desires gain,
What lady would not love a shepherd swain?

Upon his couch of straw he sleeps as sound
As doth the king upon his beds of down—
   More sounder too,
For cares cause kings full oft their sleep to spill,
Where weary shepherds lie and snort their fill.
   Ah then, ah then,
If country loves such sweet desires gain,
What lady would not love a shepherd swain?

Thus with his wife he spends the year, as blithe
As doth the king, at every tide or sithe—
   And blither too,
For kings have wars and broils to take in hand,
Where shepherds laugh and love upon the land.
   Ah then, ah then,
If country loves such sweet desires gain,
What lady would not love a shepherd swain?

Sweet are the Thoughts that Savor of Content

Sweet are the thoughts that savor of content,
   The quiet mind is richer than a crown;
Sweet are the nights in careless slumber spent,
   The poor estate scorns fortune's angry frown:
Such sweet content, such minds, such sleep, such bliss,
Beggars enjoy, when princes oft do miss.

The homely house that harbors quiet rest,
   The cottage that affords no pride nor care,
The mean that grees with country music best,
   The sweet consort of mirth and music's fare,
Obscurèd life sets down a type of bliss;
A mind content both crown and kingdom is.

At Christmas 1564-1565 a "tragical comedy," Damon and Pythias, *was acted before the Queen at Whitehall (Cardinal Wolsey's York Place) by the Children of the Chapel. It was by Richard Edwards (1523?-1566), Master of the Chapel Royal singers. He likewise staged for Elizabeth's court a* Palamon and Arcite *at Oxford. Such court entertainments were not without effect on the plays the public was to see, and in fact* Damon and Pythias *was eventually published (1582); therefore, we have this one play by Edwards and can quote the song with which it ended:*

The strongest guard that kings can have,
Are constant friends their state to save:
True friends are constant both in word and deed,
True friends are present, and help at each need;
True friends talk truly, they gloss for no gain;
When treasure consumeth, true friends will remain:
True friends for their true prince refuse not their death:
The Lord grant her such friends, most noble Queen
Elizabeth!

Long may she govern in honor and wealth,
Void of all sickness, in most perfect health:
Which health to prolong, as true friends require,
God grant she may have her own heart's desire:
Which friends will defend with most steadfast faith,
The Lord grant her such friends, most noble Queen
Elizabeth!

Thomas Dekker or one of his collaborators at turning a fairy tale into the play Patient Grissil *(1603) wrote this song:*

Art thou poor, yet hast thou golden slumbers?
  Oh sweet content!
Art thou rich, yet is thy mind perplexed?
  Oh punishment!
Dost thou laugh to see how fools are vexed
To add to golden numbers, golden numbers?
Oh sweet content! Oh sweet content!
  Work apace, apace, apace, apace;
  Honest labour bears a lovely face;
  Then hey nonny nonny, hey nonny nonny!

Canst drink the waters of the crispèd spring?
  Oh sweet content!
Swim'st thou in wealth, yet sink'st in thine own tears?
  Oh punishment!
Then he that patiently want's burden bears
No burden bears, but is a king, a king!
Oh sweet content! Oh sweet content!
  Work apace, apace, apace, apace;

Honest labour bears a lovely face;
Then hey nonny nonny, hey nonny nonny!

Three songs from Thomas Middleton's Blurt, Master Constable *of about 1601-1602:*

Love for such a cherry lip
Would be glad to pawn his arrows;
Venus here to take a sip
Would sell her doves and team of sparrows.
But they shall not so;
Hey nonny, nonny no!
None but I this lip must owe,
Hey nonny, nonny no!

Did Jove see this wanton eye,
Ganymede must wait no longer;
Phoebe here one night did lie,
Would change her face and look much younger.
But they shall not so;
Hey nonny, nonny no!
None but I this lip must owe;
Hey nonny, nonny, no!

. . .

Pity, pity, pity,
Pity, pity, pity,
That word begins that ends a true love ditty.
Your blessed eyes, like a pair of suns,
Shine in the sphere of smiling;
Your pretty lips, like a pair of doves,
Are kisses still compiling.
Mercy hangs upon your brow, like a precious jewel;
Oh, let not then,
Most lovely maid, best to be loved of men,
Marble lie upon your heart, that will make you cruel.
Pity, pity, pity,
Pity, pity, pity,
That word begins that ends a true love ditty.

. . .

Midnight's bell goes ting, ting, ting, ting, ting,
Then dogs do howl, and not a bird does sing
But the nightingale, and she cries twit, twit, twit:

Owls then on every bough do sit;
Ravens croak on chimney's tops;
The cricket in the chamber hops,
  And the cats cry mew, mew, mew.
The nibbling mouse is not asleep,
But he goes peep, peep, peep, peep, peep,
  And the cats cry mew, mew, mew,
  And still the cats cry mew, mew, mew.

By Nicholas Breton from his Honorable Entertainment Given to the Queen's Majesty in Progress at Elvetham *(1591):*

In the merry month of May,
In a morn by break of day,
Forth I walked by the woodside,
Whenas May was in his pride.
There I spied all alone
Phyllida and Corydon.
Much ado there was, God wot,
He would love and she would not.
She said, never man was true:
He said, none was false to you.
He said, he had loved her long;
She said, love should have no wrong.
Corydon would kiss her then;
She said, maids must kiss no men
Till they did for good and all.
Then she made the shepherd call
All the heavens to witness truth,
Never loved a truer youth.
Thus with many a pretty oath.
Yea and nay, and faith and troth,
Such as silly shepherds use
When they will not love abuse;
Love, which had been long deluded,
Was with kisses sweet concluded.
And Phyllida with garlands gay
Was made the Lady of the May.

And by Thomas Watson from the same entertainment:

With fragrant flowers we strew the way,
And make this our chief holiday:
For though this clime were blessed of yore,
Yet was it never proud before.
  O beauteous Queen of second Troy,

Accept of our unfeignèd joy!

Now th' air is sweeter than sweet balm,
And satyrs dance about the palm;
Now earth, with verdure newly dight,
Gives perfect sign of her delight.
O beauteous Queen of second Troy,
Accept of our unfeignèd joy!

Now birds record new harmony,
And trees do whistle melody;
Now every thing that nature breeds
Doth clad itself in pleasant weeds.
O beauteous Queen of second Troy,
Accept of our unfeignèd joy!

Two of the songs from Cynthia's Revels, *acted 1601, by Ben Jonson, whose plays for the public theatre were as masterful as his extravagant masques for the court. In both, songs were a favorite feature.*

Slow, slow, fresh fount, keep time with my salt tears:
Yet slower, yet; oh, faintly, gentle springs,
List to the heavy part the music bears,
Woe weeps out her division when she sings.
Droop herbs and flowers;
Fall grief in showers,
Our beauties are not ours;
Oh, I could still,
Like melting snow upon some craggy hill,
Drop, drop, drop, drop,
Since nature's pride is now a withered daffodil.

. . .

Queen and huntress, chaste and fair,
Now the sun is laid to sleep,
Seated in thy silver chair,
State in wonted manner keep:
Hesperus entreats thy light,
Goddess excellently bright.

Earth, let not thy envious shade
Dare itself to interpose;
Cynthia's shining orb was made
Heaven to clear when day did close:

Bless us then with wishèd sight,
Goddess excellently bright.

Lay thy bow of pearl apart,
And thy crystal shining quiver;
Give unto the flying hart
Space to breathe, how short soever:
Thou that mak'st day of night,
Goddess excellently bright.

. . .

From Jonson's The Poetaster, *acted 1601:*

If I freely may discover
What would please me in my lover,
I would have her fair and witty,
Savouring more of court than city;
A little proud, but full of pity;
Light and humorous in her toying;
Oft building hopes, and soon destroying;
Long, but sweet in the enjoying;
Neither too easy nor too hard:
All extremes I would have barred.

She should be allowed her passions,
So they were but used as fashions;
Sometimes froward, and then frowning,
Sometimes sickish, and then swowning,
Every fit with change still crowning.
Purely jealous I would have her,
Then only constant when I crave her;
'Tis a virtue should not save her.
Thus, nor her delicates would cloy me,
Neither her peevishness annoy me.

Written at about the end of Elizabeth's reign, Thomas Heywood's The Fair Maid of The Exchange *contained this song:*

Ye little birds that sit and sing
Amidst the shady valleys,
And see how Phyllis sweetly walks
Within her garden-alleys;
Go, pretty birds, about her bower;
Sing, pretty birds, she may not lour;
Ah, me! methinks I see her frown;

Ye pretty wantons, warble!

Go, tell her through your chirping bills,
As you by me are bidden,
To her is only known my love,
Which from the world is hidden.
Go, pretty birds, and tell her so;
See that your notes strain not too low,
For still, methinks, I see her frown;
Ye pretty wantons, warble!

Go, tune your voices' harmony,
And sing, I am her lover;
Strain loud and sweet, that every note
With sweet content may move her:
And she that hath the sweetest voice,
Tell her I will not change my choice;
Yet still, methinks, I see her frown;
Ye pretty wantons, warble!

Oh, fly! make haste! see, see, she falls
Into a pretty slumber!
Sing round about her rosy bed
That, waking, she may wonder:
Say to her, 'tis her lover true
That sendeth love to you, to you!
And when you hear her kind reply,
Return with pleasant warblings.

This is by Thomas Dekker from Old Fortunatus *(acted in 1599):*

Virtue's branches wither, virtue pines,
O pity, pity, and alack the time
Vice doth flourish, vice in glory shines,
Her gilded boughs above the cedar climb.
Vice hath golden cheeks, O pity, pity!
She in every land doth monarchize:
Virtue is exiled from every city,
Virtue is a fool, vice only wise.
O pity, pity! virtue weeping dies,
Vice laughs to see her faint, alack the time!
This sinks; with painted wings the other flies:
Alack, that best should fall, and bad should climb!
O pity, pity, pity! mourn, not sing!
Vice is a saint, virtue an underling.
Vice doth flourish, vice in glory shines,

Virtue's branches wither, virtue pines.

From Dekker's play full of folk humor, The Shoemaker's Holiday *(1600), something about the folk celebrations of May:*

Oh, the month of May, the merry month of May,
So frolic, so gay, and so green, so green, so green!
Oh, and then did I unto my true Love say,
Sweet Peg, thou shalt be my Summer's Queen.
Now the nightingale, the pretty nightingale,
The sweetest singer in all the forest's quite,
Entreats thee, sweet Peggy, to hear thy true Love's tale:
Lo, yonder the sitteth, her breast against a brier.
But oh, I spy the cuckoo, the cuckoo, the cuckoo;
See where she sitteth; come away, my joy:
Come away, I prithee, I do not like the cuckoo
Should sing where my Peggy and I kiss and toy.
Oh, the month of May, the merry month of May,
So frolic, so gay, and so green, so green, so green;
And then did I unto my true Love say,
Sweet Peg, thou shalt be my Summer's Queen.

In Peele's The Arraignment of Paris, *Paris asks Oenone to "begin some toy that I can play upon this pipe of mine" and she suggests* Cupid's Curse, *so she sings this "pretty sonnet," or song, and he sings and pipes, too.*

En. Fair and fair, and twice so fair,
As fair as any may be;
The fairest shepherd on our green,
A love for any lady.
Par. Fair and fair, and twice so fair,
As fair as any may be;
Thy love is fair for thee alone,
And for no other lady.
En. My love is fair, my love is gay,
As fresh as bin the flowers in May,
And of my love my roundelay,
My merry, merry, merry roundelay,
Concludes with Cupid's curse,—
They that do change old love for new,
Pray gods they change for worse!
Both. They that do change, &c.
En. Fair and fair, &c.
Par. Fair and fair, &c.
Thy love is fair, &c.
En. My love can pipe, my love can sing,

My love can many a pretty thing,
And of his lovely praises ring
My merry, merry, roundelay,
Amen to Cupid's curse,—
Par. They that do change, &c.
Both. Fair and fair, and twice so fair,
As fair as any may be;
Thy love is fair for thee alone;
And for no other lady.

A notable biblical play was Peele's The Love of King David and Fair Bethsabe *(1594). Its power lies mostly in the trumpet-call speeches of the bold Absalom but it also has the sweeter music of Bethsabe at her bath.*

Hot sun, cool fire, tempered with sweet air,
Black shade, fair nurse, shadow my white hair:
Shine, sun; burn, fire; breathe, air, and ease me;
Shadow, my sweet nurse, keep me from burning,
Make not my glad cause cause of mourning.
Let not my beauty's fire
Inflame unstaid desire,
Nor pierce any bright eye
That wand'reth lightly.

Peele's The Old Wives' Tale *combines fantasy and folklore, romance and satire. Three songs from the play:*

When as the rye reach to the chin,
And chopcherry, chopcherry ripe within,
Strawberries swimming in the cream,
And schoolboys playing in the stream;
Then Oh, then Oh, then Oh, my true-love said,
Till that time come again
She could not live a maid.

. . .

Be not afraid of every stranger;
Start not aside for every danger;
Things that seem are not the same;
Blow a blast at every flame;
For when one flame of fire goes out,
Then come your wishes well about:
If any ask who told you this good,
Say, the white bear of England's wood.

. . .

Spread, table spread,
Meat, drink and bread,
Ever may I have
What I ever crave,
When I am spread,
Meat for my black cock,
And meat for my red.

Elizabethan actors struck stylized poses, according to this alphabet of gestures published in *Chirologia* (1644), by John Bulwer.

The Playhouse and the Bearbaiting Pit

From a sketch made of The Swan Theatre about 1596 by the Dutch traveler, Johannes de W

Laurence, Lord Oliver has said acting, even in films, is respectable in America because Americans have a healthy respect for anything that makes good money. It is therefore necessary to translate a passage from medieval Latin (found in Sir Edmund K. Chambers' The Medieval Stage*) so that Americans can appreciate the long tradition of disrepute against which Shakespeare and his fellows struggled. The words of Bishop Thomas de Cobham (d.* 1313*), often echoed in Elizabethan England:*

There are three kinds of play-actors. Some transform and distort their own bodies by base contortions and base gestures, or by basely stripping themselves, or by wearing horrible masks; and all such are to be damned unless they abandon their calling. Others, again, do no work, but commit criminal deeds, having no fixed abode, but haunting the courts of great men and backbiting the absent opprobriously and ignominiously in order to please others. Such men also are to be damned; for the Apostle bids us take no food with such men as this; and such men are called wandering buffoons, for they are good for nothing but gluttony and backbiting. There is also a third kind of actors who have musical instruments for men's delight; and such are of two kinds. Some haunt public drinkings and wanton assemblies, where they sing various songs to move men to wantonness; and such are to be damned like the rest. But there are others called jougleurs, who sing the deeds of princes and the lives of the saints, and solace men in their sickness or in their anguish, and do not those innumerable base deeds which are done by dancing-men and dancing-women and others who play in indecent figures, and make men see a certain show of phantasms by enchantment or in any other way. If therefore these do no such thing, but sing to their instruments of the deeds of princes and other such profitable things, for the solace of their even-Christians, as is aforesaid, then such may well be borne with, as was said by Pope Alexander. For, when a jougleur asked of him whether he could save his soul in that calling, the Pope asked him whether he knew any other work for his livelihood; and he answered that he knew none. Then the Pope permitted him to live by that calling, so long as he abstained from the aforesaid base and wanton practices. And it must be noted that all commit mortal sin who give any of their goods to buffoons or jesters or the aforesaid play-actors; for to give to play-actors is no other than to throw our money away.

To prove that Puritan opposition to the playhouse as drawing the congregation away from church was part of an old rivalry between devotions and divertisements, we need only look at a sermon Bishop Latimer preached before Elizabeth's brother, little Edward VI, on 12 April 1549. The Protestant bishop wants more sermons and less folk celebration:

I came once myself to a place, riding on a journey homeward from London, and I sent word over night into the town that I would preach there in the morning because it was holy day, and methought it was an holy day's work. The church stood in my way, and I took my horse, and my company, and went thither. I thought I should have found a great company in the church, and when I came there, the church door was fast locked.

I tarried there half an hour and more, at last the key was found, and one of the parish comes to me and says: 'Sir this is a busy day with us, we cannot hear you, it is Robin Hood's day. I pray you let [hinder] them not.' I was fain there to give place to Robin Hood; I thought my rocket [symbol of ecclesiastical authority] should have been regarded, though I were not, but it would not serve, it was fain to give place to Robin Hood's men.

It is no laughing matter my friends, it is a weeping matter, a heavy matter, under the pretense for gathering for Robin Hood, a traitor, and a thief, to put out a preacher, to have his office less esteemed, to prefer Robin Hood before the ministration of God's word, and all this hath come of unpreaching prelates. This realm hath been ill provided for, that it hath had such corrupt judgments in it, to prefer Robin Hood to God's word.

Peter Fryer in Mrs. Grundy *(1963), his learned study of English prudery, tells the story of Sunday observance (or the lack of it) in the Age of Elizabeth.*

Thomas Becon (he was chaplain to Archbishop Cranmer) wrote in his Catechism that to observe the Sabbath was not to "pass over that day idly in lewd pastimes, in banqueting, in dicing and carding, in dancing and bear-baiting, in bowling and shooting, in laughing and whoring, and in such like beastly and filthy pleasures of the flesh; nor yet in bargaining, buying and selling...."

Under Queen Mary, breaking the Sabbath was first made a penal offense (Canterbury, 1554-1555) and when Elizabeth came to the throne (more to enforce Protestantism than Puritanism, however) she instituted a fine of 12 pence (which Fryer identifies as a carpenter's day's pay) for any adult who did not attend church on Sunday. But the Queen would not absent herself from Sunday revels: the Earl of Leicester's lavish entertainment for her at Kenilworth featured Sunday fireworks and fun; Robert Laneham reports that a week after the Kenilworth festivities she attended a wedding with "an ambrosial banquet," Morris dancing, sports and a play; and Henry Machyn's diary records that at Lord Arundel's one Sunday evening very early in her reign—1559, she having become Queen about mid-November of 1558—she was regaled with "supper, banquet, and masque, with drums and flutes, and all the music that could be, till midnight; and as for cheer [the like] has not been seen nor heard." The official church view deplored this. An Homily of the Place and Time of Prayer *(1574) described it as "ungodliness and filthiness, prancing in their pride, pranking and pricking, pointing and painting themselves, to be gorgeous and gay" and alleged sabbath-*

breakers "rest in excess and superfluity. In gluttonnerss and drunkenness, like rats and swine...in wantonness, in toyish talking, in filthy fleshliness."

But the Queen, who worked on Sunday (even Parliament met on Sunday in part of her reign), also celebrated on the Lord's Day, along with the common people who had no other day off from their labors, while Puritans complained that "Hell breaks loose [when] we permit our youth to have their swing."

Chief Puritan targets were Sunday sports and Sunday playgoing. Henry Brinkelow (a former Franciscan who wrote satires in the reign of Mary under the name "Roderigo Mors") said that after Latin Mass the congregation

> depart the church as empty of all spiritual knowledge as they came thether. And the rest of the day they spend in all wanton and unlawful games, as dice, cards, dallying with women, dancing and such like. But if any man do any bodily work...he shall be punished, and called heretic, too.

St. Thomas More quoted a joker who noted that, while many people were watching bearbaiting at Beverley, the local church fell down on the congregation at evensong: "Now may you see what it is to be a evensong when you should be at the bear-bating." This was just a reversal of the situation, which continued past St. Thomas More's time into the reign of Henry VIII's daughter Elizabeth, of disasters being blamed on sabbath-breakers. At Ely in 1595 they made sabbath-breakers stand up in church and confess they were "very heartily sorry." Not to do so, some Sabbatarians felt, was to call down the wrath of God at the breaking of the Holy Commandment to keep the Sabbath.

Not only did the court stage plays and masques on holy days; the common playhouses were open, too. The clergy was especially annoyed that these "sinks of sin" were doing better box-office business—the collections taken at the theatres were ample, and stored in a box locked up in the office of the tiring house—than the churches were, while on the public stages there were boys dressed as women, and the "lies" of fiction, and other abominations specifically condemned in the Old Testament. Puritan preachers inveighed and Sunday plays were banned in Canterbury (1575), Norwich (1579), London (1580), and elsewhere.

The plays triumphed and the only major result of all the condemnation was the portrayal of Puritans on the stage as spoilsports who wanted no more "cakes and ale."

The ale flowed freely, too, as usual; moreso than usual, for men and apprentices had no work on the Day of Rest. Some Elizabethans thought it might be better not to give workmen a day off for wantonness and idleness and drinking. They agreed with this epigram of 1550, from Marian times:

> How hallow they the Sabbath
> that do the time spend
> In drinking and idleness
> till the day be at an end?
> Not so well as he doeth

that goeth to the plough
Or pitcheth up the sheaves
from the cart to the mow.

Thomas White, born about the year 1550, in a sermon preached at St. Paul's Cross in 1578, attributed his belief that London was going to hell in a handcart due to Sunday sports and entertainments, idleness and drinking:

The wealthiest citizens have fine houses for the nonce; they that have none, make shift with alehouses, Taverns, and Inns, some rowing on the water, some roving in the field, some idle at home.... Is this the Lord's day or no? If it be, how intolerable, nay how accused & most condemnable are these outrageous *Bachanalia, Lupanaria,* I cannot tell what to call them, such as Heathe[n] men were ever ashamed of (I am sure), and therefore practised better matters, although profane exercises; but ours savors so of *Venus'* Court and *Bacchus'* kitchen, that it may rightly be entitled an abhominable and filthy City.

The accession of James I saw a proclamation against Sunday bearbaiting, bullbaiting, and plays. But the public still rejoiced and resisted, the Court continued to have Sunday plays and masques throughout James I's reign, and there is a record that one Sunday night in 1631 the Bishop of London had a play acted in his house, probably that play about putting on a play and other festivities, A Midsummer Night's Dream.

Stephen Gosson (1554-1624) wrote some plays (which are all lost) and some vituperative attacks on the theatre (which still exist). Responding to Thomas Lodge and The Play of Plays *he authored* Plays Confuted in Five Actions *(1582). That contains this complaint that plays were not serious, that this extremely popular form of popular entertainment offered no "schooling" or moral message at all.*

The argument of tragedies is wrath, cruelty, incest, injury, murder, either violent by sword or voluntary by poison; the persons, gods, goddesses, furies, fiends, kings, queens and mighty men. The ground-work of comedies is love, cozenage, flattery, bawdry, sly conveyance of whoredom; the persons, cooks, queans, knaves, bawds, parasites, courtezans, lecherous old men, amorous young men. Therefore Plautus in his prologue before the comedy of *The Captives,* desiring to curry favour with his auditors, exhorteth them earnestly to mark that play, because it shall cast no such stench of impurity into their noses as others do. There is in it (saith he) neither forsworn bawd, nor harlot, nor bragging soldier. Why could he not give this commendation to all the rest? Because it was the practice of the devil, to weave in a thread of his own spinning. Why is this rather purged of filthiness than the rest? Because it is the juggling of the devil, to turn himself sometimes to an angel of light, to deceive us the sooner. The best play you can pick out, is but a mixture of good and evil, how can it be then the schoolmistress of life? The beholding of troubles and miserable slaughters that are in tragedies drive us to immoderate sorrow, heaviness, womanish weeping and mourning, whereby we become lovers of dumps and lamentation, both enemies to fortitude. Comedies so tickle our senses with a pleasanter vein, that they make us lovers of laughter and pleasure, without any mean, both foes to temperance. What schooling is this? Sometime you shall see nothing but the adventures of an amorous knight, passing from country to country for the love of his lady, encountering many a terrible monster made of brown paper, and at his return is so wonderfully changed, that he cannot be known but by some posy in his tablet, or by a broken ring, or a handketcher, or a piece of a cockle shell. What learn you by that? When the soul of your plays is either mere trifles, or Italian bawdry, or wooing of gentlewomen, what are ye taught? Peradventure you will say, that by these kind of plays the authors instruct us how to love with constancy, to sue with modesty, and to loath whatsoever is contrary unto us. In my opinion, the discipline we get by plays is like to the justice that a certain schoolmaster taught in Persia, which taught his scholars to lie and not to lie, to deceive and not to deceive, with a distinction how they might do it to their friends, and how to their enemies; to their friends, for exercise; to their foes, in earnest. Wherein many of his scholars became so skillful by practice, by custom so bold, that their dearest friends paid more for their learning than their enemies. I would wish the players to beware of this kind of schooling, lest that whilst they teach youthful gentlemen how to love and not to love, how to woo and not to woo, their scholars grow as cunning as the Persians.

Another clergyman, this one John Stockwood and in a sermon of 1578, also criticized the theatre-going public:

Will not a filthy play, with the blast of a trumpet, sooner call thither a thousand, than an hour's tolling of a bell bring to the sermon a hundred? Nay even here in the city, without it be at this place and some other certain ordinary audience, where shall you find a reasonable company? Whereas if you resort to the Theater, the Curtain, and other places of plays in the city, you shall on the Lord's day have those places, with many other that I cannot reckon, so full as possible they can throng, besides a great number of other lets to pull from the hearing of the word of which I will speak hereafter.... What should I speak of beastly plays, against which out of this place every man crieth out? Have we not houses of purpose built with great charges for the maintenance of them; and that without the liberties, as who would say: 'There, let them say what they will, we will play'. I know not how I might with the godly learned especially more discommend the gorgeous playing-place erected in the fields than to term it, as they plese to have it called, a Theater.... For reckoning with the least, the gain that is reaped of eight ordinary places in the city, which I know, by playing but once a week (whereas many times they play twice or sometimes thrice) it amounteth to two thousand pounds by the year.

On 28 July 1597 the Lord Mayor and Aldermen thought that things had become so bad in London that they wrote this to the Privy Council:

To the Lords against Stage-Plays

Our humble duties remembered to your good Lords and the rest. We have signified to your Honours many times heretofore the great inconvenience which we find to grow by the common exercise of stage-plays. We presumed to do [so], as well in respect of the duty we bear towards her Highness for the good government of this her city, as for conscience sake, being persuaded (under correction of your Honours' judgment) that neither in polity nor in religion they are to be suffered in a Christian commonwealth, specially being of that frame and matter as usually they are, containing nothing but profane fables, lascivious matters, cozening devices, and scurrilous behaviours, which are so set forth as that they move wholly to imitation and not to the avoiding of those faults and vices which they represent. Among other inconveniences it is not the least that they give opportunity to the refuse sort of evil-disposed and ungodly people that are within and about this city to assemble themselves and to make their matches for all their lewd and ungodly practices; being as heretofore we have found by the examination of divers apprentices and other servants who have confessed unto us that the said stage-plays were the very places of their rendezvous, appointed by them to meet with such other as were to join with them in their designs and mutinous attempts, being also the ordinary places for masterless men to come together and to recreate themselves. For avoiding whereof we are now again most humble and earnest suitors to your Honours to direct your letters as well to ourselves as to the justices of peace of Surrey and Middlesex for the present stay and final suppressing of the said stage-plays, as well at the Theater, Curtain and Bankside as in all other places in and about the city; whereby we doubt not but the opportunity and the very cause of many disorders being taken away, we shall be more able to keep the worse sort of such evil and disordered people in better order than hertofore we have been. And so most humbly we take our leaves. From London the 28th of July 1597.

The inconveniences that grow by stageplays about the city of London.

1. They are a special cause of corrupting their youth, containing nothing but unchaste matters, lascivious devices, shifts of cozenage, and other lewd and ungodly practices, being so as that they impress the very quality and corruption of manners which they represent, contrary to the rules and art prescribed for the making of comedies even among the heathen, who used them seldom and at certain set times, and not all the year long as our manner is. Whereby such as frequent them, being of the base and refuse sort of people or such young gentlemen as have small regard of credit or conscience, draw the same into imitation and not to the avoiding the like vices which they represent.

2. They are the ordinary places for vagrant persons, masterless men, thieves, horse-stealers, whoremongers, cozeners, coney-catchers, contrivers of treason and other idle and dangerous persons to meet together and to make their matches to the great displeasure of Almighty God and the hurt and annoyance of her Majesty's people; which cannot be prevented nor discovered by the governors of the city for that they are out of the city's jurisdiction.

3. They maintain idleness in such persons as have no vocation, and draw apprentices and other servants from their ordinary works and all sorts of people from the resort unto sermons and other Christian exercises to the great hindrance of trades and profanation of religion established by her Highness within this realm.

4. In the time of sickness it is found by experience that many, having sores and yet not heart-sick, take occasion hereby to walk abroad and to recreat themselves by hearing a play. Whereby others are infected, and themselves also many things miscarry.

In his classic study of Shakespeare's Audience *(1941), Alfred Harbage quotes three different Lords Mayor of London on the state of the public theatres. There's a formula for decrying it!*

When Marlowe's Tamburlaine *and* Dr. Faustus *were revived, one wrote on 3 November 1594 that:*

lascivious devices, shifts of cozenage & matters of like sort, which are so framed & represented by them that such as resort to see & hear the same. . .draw the same into example of imitation & not avoiding the said lewd offenses.

When Shakespeare's Romeo and Juliet *and* Richard II *were the theatrical fare, another wrote on 13 September 1595 of:*

nothing but profane fables, lascivious matters, cozening devices, & other unseemly & scurrilous behaviors, which are so set forth; as that they move wholy to imitation & not to the avoiding of those vices which they represent.

When Shakespeare's Henry VI *and George Chapman's* A Humorous Day's Mirth *were the plays presented nearest the date cited, another wrote on 28 July 1597 about:*

nothing but profane fables, lascivious matters, cozening devices & scurrilous behaviors, which are so set forth as that they move wholly to imitation & not to avoiding of those faults & vices which they represent.

At the end of Elizabeth's reign things were much the same. Henry Crosse in 1603:

Now the common haunters [of theatres] are the most part of the lewdest persons in the land, apt for pilfery, forgery, or any rogueries, the very scum, rascality, and baggage of the people, thieves, cutpurses, shifters, cozeners; briefly, an unclean generation, a spawn of vipers; must not here be a good rule, where is such a brood of hellbent creatures? For a play is like a sink in a Town, whereunto all the filth doth run, or a boil in the body, that draweth all the ill humours into it.

Admitting the general public to Merchant Taylors Hall to see entertainments had to be abandoned, according to the Memorials of the Merchant Taylors, *a livery company that benefitted the public a great deal by setting up a London school for poor boys. But admitting the populace for plays The Worshipful Company invited riot:*

Whereas at our Common Plays and such like Exercises which be commonly exposed to be seen for money, every lewd person thinketh himself (for his penny) worthy of the chief and most commodious place without respect of any other, either for age or estimation in the commonweal, which bringeth the youth to such an impudent familiarity with their betters that often times great contempt of Masters, Parents, and Magistrates followeth thereof.

Harbage's study of the Shakespearian audience confirms that even the playwright Thomas Dekker, whose heart was with the artisan, not the aristocrat, agreed with his "betters":

Sithence then the place is so free in entertainment, allowing a stool as well to the Farmer's son as to your Templer [law student]: that your Stinkard had the self-same liberty to be there in his Tobacco-Fumes which your sweet [-smelling] Courtier hath: and that your Carman and Tinker claim as strong a voice in their suffrage and sit to give judgement on the play's life and death as well as the proudest Momus among the tribe of Critic.

The public theatre was a dangerous leveler of society, took people away from work and prayer (much to the annoyance of employers and clergy), and even incensed businessmen of the City who saw pennies being spent across The Thames in Surrey. Thomas Nashe in Pierce Penniless, His Supplication to the Devil *(1592):*

As for the hindrance of Trades and Traders in the City by them, that is an Article foisted in by the Vintners, Alewives, and Victualers, who surmise if there were no Plays they should have all the company that resort to them lie boozing and beer-bathing in their public houses every afternoon.

And Crosse in Virtue's Commonwealth *says the poor waste their few pence on playgoing:*

Nay many more poor, pinched, needy creatures, that live of alms, and have scarce neither cloth to their back nor food for the belly, yet will make hard shift but they will see a Play, let wife & children beg. . . .

To the English, London has long been the City and everywhere else is the Provinces. Jokes about country bumpkins appealed even to newly-arrived Londoners in Elizabeth's day. Here is playwright and chronicler of London life Thomas Nashe (in Pierce Penniless, *1595) laughing at how when The Queen's Men carried her livery into the country as players on tour, bringing along the famous clown Richard Tarlton (who had a brief but acclaimed career 1583-1588 after the Earl of Leicester found him and introduced him to the Queen, who made him one of her players). Tarlton mugged and danced and "Tarltonized" (ad-libbing jokes in doggerel) and the public joked back and forth with him and adored him, even when he disrupted whatever action of the play the dramatist had "then to be considered." To a provincial representative of law and order he might well have seemed to be out of line.*

Amongst other choletic wise justices he was one, that having a play presented before him and his township by Tarlton and the rest of his fellows, her Majesty's servants, and they were now entering into their first merriment (as they call it), the people began exceedingly to laugh when Tarlton first peeped out his head. Whereat the justice, not a little moved, and seeing with his becks and nods he could not make them cease, he went with his staff, and beat them round about unmercifully on the bare pates, in that they, being but farmers and poor country hinds, would presume to laugh at the Queen's men, and make no more account of her cloth in his presence.

The first professional London theatre was The Theatre (1576), erected in Finnsbury Fields. When it became popular and the landlord tried to raise the rent excessively, the Burbages and their associates dismantled it and re-erected it across London Bridge on the Surrey side. Some other theatres were also erected on the Bankside and used both for plays and bearbaiting. Shakespeare in Henry V *refers to The Globe as a cockpit. One of the buildings used for bearbaiting and plays, a large building in Paris Garden, had a rotten old gallery collapse during a Sunday performance of a play on 13 June 1583. Several people were killed and others injured; the Puritans took that as God's judgment on sabbath-breaking players. The City of London and then the Privy Council banned Sunday performances, but the Sabbatarian and Puritan opposition to plays and players was still strong and getting stronger when Shakespeare arrived on the London theatrical scene a few years later.*

Nonetheless the public clamored for what a Tudor academic had called "toying plays" and what Marlowe dismissed as

jigging veins of rhyming mother wits
And such conceits as clownage keeps in pay. . . .

The Puritans could rise to great heights of denunciation of the theatre:

Do they not maintain bawdry, insinuate foolery, and renew the remembrance of heathen idolatry? Do they not induce whoredom and uncleanness? Nay, are they not rather plain devourers of maidenly virginity and chastity? For proof whereof but mark the flocking and running to Theaters and Curtains, daily and hourly, night and day, time and tide, to see plays and interludes, where such wanton gestures, such bawdy speeches, such laughing and fleering, such kissing and bussing, such clipping and culling, such winking and glancing of wanton eyes, and the like is used, as is wonderful to behold. Then these goodly pageants being ended, every mate sorts to his mate, every one brings another homeward of their way very friendly, and in their secret conclaves (covertly) they play the sodomites, or worse. And these be the fruits of plays and interludes, for the most part. And whereas, you say, there are good examples to be learnt in them: truly so there are; if you will learn falsehood; if you will learn cozenage; if you will learn to deceive; if you will learn to play the hypocrite, to cog, to lie and falsify; if you will learn to jest, laugh and fleer, to grin, to nod and mow; if you will learn to play the Vice, to swear, tear and blaspheme both heaven and earth; if you will learn to become a bawd, unclean, and to devirginate maids, to deflower honest wives; if you will learn to murder, flay, kill, pick, steal, rob and rove; if you will learn to rebel against princes, to commit treasons, to consume treasures, to practise idleness, to sing and talk of bawdy love and venery; if you will learn to deride, scoff, mock and flout, to flatter and smooth; if you will learn to play the whore-master, the glutton, drunkard, or incestuous person; if you will learn to become proud, haughty and arrogant; and finally, if you will learn to contemn God and all His laws, to care neither for Heaven nor Hell, and to commit all kinds of sin and mischief, you need to go to no other school, for all these good examples may you see painted before your eyes in interludes and plays.

That is from Philip Stubbes, The Anatomy of Abuses *(1583).*

The Rev. Thomas White preached at Paul's Cross in 1578 that "the cause of plagues is sin. . .and the cause of sin are plays: therefore the cause of plagues are plays."

Gabriel Harvey was a bitter and vituperative man who took a perverse pleasure in the fact that his enemy, Robert Greene, as so many playwrights did in that time, died penniless.

He never envied me so much as I pitied him from my heart, especially when his hostess Isam, with tears in her eyes and sighs from a deeper fountain (for she loved him dearly) told me of his lamentable begging of a penny pot of Malmesy, and sir reverence, how lowsy he and the mother of Infortunatus were (I would her surgeon found her no worse than lowsy) and how he was fain, poor soul, to borrow her husband's shirt whiles his own was a-washing, and how his doublet and hose and sword were sold for three shillings; and beside the charges of his winding sheet, which was four shillings, and the charges of his burial yesterday in the new churchyard near Bedlam, which was six shillings and fourpence, how deeply he was indebted to her poor husband, as appeared by his own bond of ten pounds, which the good woman kindly showed me, and beseeched me to read the writing beneath, which was a letter to his abandoned wife, in the behalf of his gentle host, not so short as persuasible in the beginning and pitiful in the ending.

"Doll, I charge thee by the love of our youth and by my soul's rest, that thou wilt see this man paid; for if he and his wife had not succoured me, I had died in the streets. —Robert Greene."

The low esteem in which dramatists were held does much to explain why their names are more likely to be found in obscure legal files than in literary criticism and why their personal papers and even their most popular plays have been lost to posterity in almost all cases.

Though his work was published the year Shakespeare died (1616), whoever "T.G." of Rich Cabinet *was he was probably echoing the Elizabethan genius' idea of what an actor ought to be when he wrote:*

Player hath many times many excellent qualities: as dancing, activity, music, song, elocution, ability of body, memory, vigilancy, skill of weapon, pregnancy of wit, and such like: in all of which he resembleth an excellent spring of water, which grows the more sweeter and the more plentiful by the often drawing out of it: so are all these the more perfect and plausible by the more often practice.

Sir Francis Bacon's view of players was more severe, and more common.

You shall now see them on the stage play a king, or an emperor, or a duke; but they are no sooner off the stage but they are base rascals, vagabond abjects, and porterly hirelings, which is their natural and original condition.

Working in what Bernard Shaw called the "romantic commercial style," and with great speed, Shakespeare wrote nearly 40 plays. His great friend Ben Jonson in his Discoveries *remembered the Warwickshire man but was not afraid to be frank about him.*

I remember the players have often mentioned it as an honour to Shakespeare, that in his writing (whatsoever he penn'd) he never blotted out line. My answer hath been, would he had blotted a thousand which they thought a malevolent speech. I had not told posterity this, but for their ignorance, who choose that circumstance to commend their friend by, wherein he most faulted. And to justify mine own candour, for I lov'd the man, and do honour his memory, on this side Idolatry, as much as any. He was indeed, honest, and of an open and free nature, had an excellent fantasy, brave notions and gentle expressions, wherein he flowed with that facility, that sometime it was necessary he should be stopp'd: *Sufflaminandus erat* ["he was to be checked"], as Augustus said of Haterius. His wit was in his own power; would the rule of it had been so too. Many times he fell into those things could not escape laughter, as when he said in the person of Caesar, one speaking to him, "Caesar, thou dost me wrong." He replied, "Caesar did never wrong, but with just case"; and such-like, which were ridiculous. But he redeemed his vices with his virtues. There was ever more in him to be praised, than to be pardoned.

Thomas Dekker (1570-1641?)'s The Gull's Hornbook, *one critic writes, "although not printed until 1609...should be at least sampled for a flavor of the theater of the time." So here is the satirical and famous passage,*

How a Gallant Should Behave Himself in a Playhouse

Present not yourself on the stage (especially at a new play) until the quaking prologue hath (by rubbing) got colour into his cheeks, and is ready to give the trumpets their cue that he's upon point to enter: for then it is time, as though you were one of the properties, or that you dropped out of the hangings, to creep from behind the arras [tapestry curtain] with your tripos or three-footed stool in one hand, and a teston [sixpence] mounted between a forefinger and a thumb in the other: for if you should bestow your person upon the vulgar, when the belly of the house is but half full, your apparel is quite eaten up, the fashion lost, and the proportion of your body in more danger to be devoured than if it were served up in the Counter amongst the Poultry [a prison in that section where poultry was sold in Cheapside]: avoid that as you would the bastome [baton, cudgel]. It shall crown you with rich commendation to laugh aloud in the midst of the most serious and saddest scene of the terriblest tragedy: and to let that clapper (your tongue) be tossed so high, that all the house may ring of it: your lords use it; your knights are apes of the lords, and do so too: your Inne-a-court-man is zany to the knights, and (marry very scurvily) comes likewise limping after it: be thou a beagle to them all, and never lin [leave off] snuffing till you have sented them: for by talking and laughing (like a ploughman in a morris) you heap Pelion upon Ossa, glory upon glory: As first, all the eyes in the galleries will leave walking after the players, and only follow you: the simplest dolt in the house snatches up your name, and when he meets you in the streets, or that you fall into his hands in the middle of a watch, his word shall be taken for you, he'll cry, He's such a gallant, and you pass. Secondly, you publish your temperance to the world, in that you seem not to resort thither to taste vain pleasures with a hungry appetite, but only as a gentleman, to spend a foolish hour or two, because you can do nothing else. Thirdly you mightily disrelish the audience, and disgrace the author: marry, you take up (though it be at the worst hand) a strong opinion of your own judgment and enforce the poet to take pity of your weakness, and, by some dedicated sonnet, to bring you into a better paradise, only to stop your mouth.... Now Sir, if the writer be a fellow that hath either epigrammed you or hath had a flirt at your mistress, or hath brought either your feather or your red beard, or your little legs, etc. on the stage, you shall disgrace him worse than by tossing him in a blanket, or giving him the bastinado in a tavern, if in the middle of his play (be it Pastoral or Comedy, Moral or Tragedy), you rise with a screwed and discontented face from your stool to be gone: no matter whether the scenes be good or no, the better they are the worse do you distaste them: and, being on your feet, sneak not away like a coward, but salute all your gentle acquaintance, that are spread either on the rushes, or on stools about you, and draw what troop you can from the stage after you: the mimics are beholden to you, for allowing them elbow room: their poet cries, perhaps, a pox go with you, but care not for that, there's no music without frets.

Marry if either the company or indisposition of the weather bind you to sit it out, my counsel is then that you turn plain ape, take up a rush, and tickle the earnest ears of your fellow gallants, to make other fools fall a laughing: mew at passionate speeches, blare at merry, find fault with the music, where at the childrens' [boy actors'] action, whistle at the songs: and above all, curse the sharers, that whereas the same day you had bestowed forty shillings on an embroidered felt and feather (Scotch-fashion), for your mistress in the Court, or your punk [whore] in the City, within two hours after, you encounter with the very same block on the stage, when the habedasher swore to you the impression was extant but that morning.

Elizabethan plays had a terrific effect upon their impressionable audiences. There were no grand scenic or lighting effects to transport spectators—the Chorus in Shakespeare's Henry V *encourages "on your imaginary forces work"—but the incantation of the verse was powerful magic. There are some few literary references to lines and characters in plays—one preserves for us a "punchline" from the lost* Ur-Hamlet, *Shakespeare's source—but few poems that refer, as this one does, to the effect of watching a real play. The author of this poem is "R.T., Gentleman" and it occurs in the obscure* Alba: The Month's Mind of a Melancholy Lover *(1598). If the "R. T." was Robert Tofte, he died in 1620.*

Love's Labour Lost, I once did see a play
Ycleped so, so called to my pain,
Which I to hear to my small joy did stay,
Giving attendance on my froward dame;
  My misgiving mind presaging to me ill,
  Yet was I drawn to see it 'gainst my will.

This play, no play but plague was unto me,
For there I lost the Love I likèd most:
And what to others seemed a jest to be,
I, that, in earnest, found unto my cost:
  To every one save me 'twas comical,
  Whilst tragic-like to me it did befall.

Each actor plays in cunning-wise his part,
But chiefly those entrapped in Cupid's snare:
Yet all was feignèd, 'twas not from the heart,
They seemed to grieve, but yet they felt no care;
   'Twas I that grief indeed did bear in breast,
   The others did but make a show in jest.

Yet neither feigning theirs, nor my mere truth,
Could make her once so much as for to smile:
Whiles she, despite of pity mild and ruth,
Did sit as scorning of my woes the while.
   Thus did she sit to see Love lose his Love,
   Like hardened rock that force nor power can move.

We omit Shakespeare's magnificent plays but may notice what they have contributed to folk speech in the way of expressions that seem to be not famous quotations (such as "To be, or not to be") but the product not of an author but the people themselves. Here is just one example from each of the plays:

All's Well that Ends Well: Poor but honest
Antony and Cleopatra: It beggared all description
As You Like It: Answer me in one word
Comedy of Errors, The: There is something in the wind
Coriolanus: Death by inches
Cymbeline: The game is up
Hamlet: It smells to heaven
Henry IV, Part I: I'll be hanged
Henry IV, Part II: Eaten me out of house and home
Henry V: As cold as any stone
Henry VI, Part I: Fight till the last gasp
Henry VI, Part II: Thrice is he armed that hath his quarrel just
Henry VI, Part III: Tiger's heart wrapped in a woman's hide
Henry VIII: Fling away ambition
Julius Caesar: Though last, not least
King John: Bell, book and candle
King Lear: More sinned against than sinning
Macbeth: What's done is done
Measure for Measure: I'll tell the world
Merchant of Venice, The: Love is blind
Merry Wives of Windsor, The: What the dickens
Midsummer Night's Dream, A: Every mother's son
Much Ado about Nothing: As merry as the day is long
Othello: Foregone conclusion
Pericles, Prince of Tyre: The great ones eat up the little ones
Richard II: Spotless reputation

Richard III: A tower of strength
Romeo and Juliet: What's in a name?
Taming of the Shrew, The: Small choice in rotten apples
Tempest, The: I shall laugh myself to death
Timon of Athens: We have seen better days
Titus Andronicus: Sleep in peace
Troilus and Cressida: The end crowns all
Twelfth Night: Laugh yourself into stitches
Two Gentlemen of Verona: The uncertain glory of an April day
Winter's Tale, The: What's past help should be past grief

Whenever Elizabeth deigned to visit the great country house of a courtier, it cost him a fortune to entertain her. (Lord Burghley spent twice as much as it would take to support an average peer for a year each and every time she came, and she arrived over and over, with her vast retinue.) Robert Laneham wrote about the festivities at Kenilworth, where one of her favorites entertained Elizabeth in 1575 with feasts, masques, dancing, and (among other things) bear-baiting:

It was a sport very pleasant to see the bear with his pink eyes leering after his enemies' approach, the nimbleness and wait of the dog to take his advantage, and the force and experience of the bear to avoid the assaults. If he were bitten in one place, how he would pinch in another to get free: that if he were taken once, then what shift, with biting, with clawing, with roaring, tossing and tumbling he would work to wind himself from them: and when he was loose to shake his ears twice or thrice with the blood and the slaver about his physiognomy was a matter of goodly relief.

Bearbaiting had survived from medieval times and Elizabeth's father was fond of it: he made the mastership of the bears and dogs, etc., a court office in 1526 and supported the creation of the Paris Garden on the Bankside. There such cruel Sunday sports as bearbaiting and cockfighting could go on without the interference of the Puritans of the City. Up to half a dozen mastiffs were set loose on a bear chained to a stake and as many dog replacements were used as was necessary to "defeat" the bear. (Bears were valuable and seldom killed.) Bulls or a horse with an ape on his back might also be baited by dogs.

Bearbaiting pits such as Paris Garden (and The Hope, which succeeded it) and cockfight rings (such as that at St. James' Park) were also used for plays. In Shakespeare's Henry VIII *a servant reprooves a noisy crowd who are restless as they await the procession for the christening of the Princess Elizabeth: "Do you take the court for the Paris Garden?" But the court could turn to the same rough entertainments as the Paris Garden. For Elizabeth were staged both plays and bearbaiting, tumbling and tournaments, clowning and concerts, for she had very much the taste of her common subjects, which endeared her to them. She was, she boasted, "mere English."*

What kind of people went to see bearbaiting? Some hint comes from a group of persons mentioned as present at Paris Garden one Sunday in 1583 when there was a serious accident and some were killed, some miraculously saved. At the bearbaiting that day were 1000 people, among them according to the preacher John Field's Exhortation:

Adam Spencer, a felmonger of Southwark; William Cockram, a baker of Shoreditch; John Burton, a clerk of St. Marie Wolmers in Lombard Street; Mathew Mason, a servant with Master Garland of Southwark; Thomas Peace, a servant with Rob. Tasker of Clerkenwell; Alice White, a servant to a pursemaker without Cripplegate; Marie Harrison, daughter to John, a water-bearer of Lombard St.; Mrs. Webb, wife of a pewterer of Limestreet; and an unidentified woman and her small child.

Foreign visitors were also entertained with bearbaiting. The Queen had a Keeper of The Bears and a Keeper of The Mastiffs as court officials and bearbaiting was put on at Whitehall with foreign dignitaries and the court watching from a gallery of the royal palace. The common people might also look on here, or visit the bears at Paris Garden on the other side of The Thames.

From the diary of Henry Machyn for October 28, 1561 we learn that he

was at Whitehall great baiting of the bull and bear for the ambassadors of France...the which the Queen's grace was there, and her council and many noblemen.

George Stone, Harry Hunks, Sackerson, Tom of Lincoln, Ned of Canterbury, Don Jon, and Blind Robin were Elizabethan popular idols. Never heard of them? They were fighting bears of the professional bearbaiting pit. Bearbaiting had much of the appeal of modern boxing and was described by its many fans as "a sweet and comfortable recreation fitted for the solace and comfort of a peaceable people," good for any day when there was not a public execution at Tyburn.

*Edward Hake (*News out of Paul's Churchyard, *1579):*

What else but gain and money got
Maintains each Sabbath day
The baiting of the Bear and the Bull?
What brings this brutish play?

Days when the workingclass elements were at large (such as Sundays) recommended themselves to violent public sports such as bearbaiting; it kept the lower classes from other violence. Bearbaiting served a useful political purpose and was so favored by Elizabeth that when 7 people were killed at the collapse of some seats in the Paris Garden, and the Puritans declared it was the judgment of God on the place, the bearbaiting was permitted to go on. When plays began to threaten the attendance at bearbaitings, the theatres were officially ordered closed on Thursdays to encourage "the game of bear-baiting and like pastimes which are maintained by Her Majesty's pleasure and were suffering neglect."

Ralph Aggas' drawing (*c.* 1560) shows bearbaiting ampitheatres existed on the South Bank of The Thames before public theatres were erected there. "The Beare bayting" one on the right looks *somewhat* like the later Globe.

Festivals and Celebrations

A water pageant for Elizabeth at Elvetham (Hampshire) in 1591 featured a Snail Mount other constructions in a crescent-shaped pond.

Richard Burton in The Anatomy of Melancholy:

The country hath his recreations, the city his several gym[nast]icks, exercises, feasts, and merry meetings—What so pleasant as to see some pageant as at Coronations, wedding, and suchlike solemnities, to see an Ambassador or a Prince met, received, and entertained with masques, Shows, Fireworks, &c.

Some religious people looked on the age-old rural recreations, pastimes and festivities as pagan, and one wrote:

Against May, Whitsunday, or some other time of the year, every parish, town and village assemble themselves together, both men, women and children, old and young, even all indifferently; and either going all together or dividing themselves into companies, they go some to the woods and groves, some to the hills and mountains, some to one place and some to another, where they spend all the night in pleasant pastimes; and in the morning they return, bringing with them birch boughs and branches of trees, to deck their assemblies withal. And no marvel, for there is a great lord present amongst them, as superintendent and lord over their pastimes and sports, namely Sathan, prince of hell. But their chiefest jewel they bring from thence is their May-pole, which they bring home with great veneration. . . .

The Maypole and other things of the Old Religion survived in a number of customs the full and original meaning of which many or most people may well have completely forgotten. The May Day celebrations were just one folk custom that still flourished in Elizabeth's time. Though a Virgin Queen, and far too old to go into the greenwood and come back with a "green gown" from being "tumbled" on the grass, as late as 1602 Elizabeth, like so many of her subjects, went to the woods and brought back the flowering branches of May. It was an ancient rite of spring, deeply English.

The Roxburghe Ballads record that the old Christmas festivities still were honored, though more in the country than among the citizens of London who grew from 100,000 at the beginning of Elizabeth's reign to twice that number at the end of it:

The Court in all state, now opens her gate,
  And bids a free welcome to most;
The City likewise, though somewhat precise,

Doth willingly part with her cost;
And yet by report, from City and Court,
The Country gets the day;
More liquor is spent, and better content,
To drive the cold winter away.

At court a Master of the Revels organized two weeks of Christmas celebrations, banquets, music and masques far into the night and the Queen was a great one for receiving presents at New Year's, though less apt to give ones, though she did part with silver plate, or an orange. The Earl of Leicester once presented her with "a very fair jewel of gold, being a clock fully furnished with small diamonds and rubies: about the same are six bigger diamonds pointed, and a pendant of gold, diamonds, and rubies, very small; and upon each side a lozenge diamond and an apple of gold enamelled green and russet."

Shakespeare's England *gives a convenient summary of the Christmas festivities of the court:*

Christmas, unless plague rendered the neighbourhood of a populous city undesirable, was generally spent by the court at Whitehall. On New Year's Day, it was customary, as it had been customary since the Roman emperors took their *strenae,* to give presents to the sovereign, who rewarded the donors with orders upon the Master of the Jewel House for plate of a value proportionate to their degree. Several rolls setting out these New Year gifts are in existence. The cupidity of Elizabeth was not offended by the offer of twenty 'dimy soveraignes' in a silken purse; but many courtiers went to the trouble of thinking out costly and appropriate jewels, while the ladies brought finery and 'sweet bags', and the humbler household servants prepared with anxious pains symbolical masterpieces of their offices. Thus the apothecary would bring 'one pott of grene gynger, and a pott of orenge flowers', or the Serjeant of the Pastry 'a greate pye of guynses and wardyns guilte'. Another joust often enlivened the Christmas holidays, which was also the especial period for indoor festivities such as plays and masques. These were generally given in the evening, after supper, on one of the three saint's-days immediately following Christmas, or on New year's Day or Twelfth Night. They were the charge of a special department of the Household under the control of the Lord Chamberlain, known as the Office of the Revels, and consisting of a Master with a Clerk, a Clerk Comptroller, and a yeoman as his subordinate staff. The post of the Master was held by Sir Thomas Benger from 1559 to 1572, by Edmund Tilney from 1578 to 1610, and by Sir George Buck from 1610 to 1622. John Lyly, the dramatist, was an unsuccessful candidate for the succession to Tilney, and at a later date Ben Jonson had a reversion of the office, which he did not live to enjoy. Both plays and masques were sometimes brought to court, at their own expense, by amateurs, such as the gentlemen of the Inns of Court. As examples may be taken the performance of Norton and Sackville's *Gorboduc* or *Rock Adamantine* presented by Gray's Inn on March 3, 1595. Ordinarily, however, the Revels office was responsible for providing the entertainment. During the weeks preceding Christmas the officers called in the companies of men and boys then playing publicly in London, made them rehearse their new pieces, and appointed them days on which to produce those selected at the court. Properties and costumes were supplied, when necessary, from the wardrobe of the Revels, and the players received a reward, generally amounting to £10, for which the Privy Council signed a warrant payable by the Treasury of the Chamber.

In the country, Yuletide collections were traditional and elaborate. Sir William Holles, according to Gervase Holles (who wrote Memorials *of his family),*

began his Christmas at All-Hallow tide [with November] and continued it to Candlemas [in early January]; during which time any man was permitted freely to stay three days without being asked from whence he came or who he was.... And I have heard that his proportion which he allowed during the twelve days of Christmas was a fat ox every day with sheep and other provision answerable.... This liberal hospitality of his caused the first Earl of Clare to let fall an unbecoming word, that his grandfather sent all his revenewes down the privy house.

Christmas was celebrated without the Christmas tree that German Albert brought in in the 19th century. Christmas in the Old English tradition, in Elizabeth's time, involved the Druids' holly and ivy and miseltoe. An Elizabethan Christmas had the yule log and the spiced wine of medieval days, even into the 17th century, when Nicholas Breton eloquently wrote this (1626):

It is now Christmas, and not a cup of drink must pass without a carol; the beasts, fowl, and fish, come to a general execution; and the corn is ground to dust for the bakehouse, and the pastry. Cards and dice purge many a purse, and the youth shew their agility in shoeing of the wild mare. Now 'Good cheer' and 'Welcome,' and 'God be with you,' and 'I thank you.' and 'Against the new year,' provide for the presents. The Lord of Misrule is no mean man for his time, and the guests of the high table must lack no wine. The lusty bloods must look about them like men, and piping and dancing puts away much melancholy. Stolen venison is sweet, and a fat coney is worth money. Pit-falls are now set for small birds, and a woodcock hangs himself in a gin. A good fire heats all the house, and a full alms-basket makes the beggars prayers. The masquers and mummers make the merry sport; but if they lose their money, their drum goes dead. Swearers and swaggerers are sent away to the ale-house, and unruly wenches go in danger of judgment. Musicians now make their instruments speak out, and a good song is worth the hearing. In sum, it is a holy time, a duty in Christians for the remembrance of Christ, and custom among friends for the maintenance of good fellowship. In brief, I thus conclude of it: I hold it a memory of the Heaven's love and the world's peace, the mirth of the honest, and the meeting of the friendly.

And, from the same writer, Eastertide:

It is now Easter, and Jack of Lent is turned out of doors. The fishermen now hang up their nets to dry, while the calf and the lamb walk toward the kitchen and the pantry. The velvet heads of the forests fall at the loose of the cross-bow. The salmon-trout plays with the fly, and the March rabbit runs dead into the dish. The Indian commodities pay the merchant's adventure: and Barbary sugar puts honey out of countenance. The holy feast is kept for the faithful, and a known Jew hath no place among Christians. The earth now begins to paint her upper garment, and the trees put out their young buds. The little kids chew their cuds, and the swallow feeds on the flies in the air. The stork cleanseth the brooks of the frogs, and the spar-hawk prepares her wing for the partridge. The little fawn is stolen from the doe, and the male deer begin to herd. The spirit of youth is inclined to mirth, and the conscionable scholar will not break a holy day. The minstrel calls the maid from her dinner, and the lover's eyes do troll like tennis balls. There is mirth and joy, when there is health and liberty: and he that hath money will be no mean man in his mansion. The air is wholesome and the sky comfortable, the flowers odoriferous and the fruits pleasant. I conclude, it is a day of much delightfulness: the sun's dancing day, and the earth's holy-day.

The Merchant Adventurers of Bristol are on record forbidding apprentices to "dance, dice, [play] card[s], mum [as in 'mummers'], or use any music either by day or night in the streets."

Nonetheless, people sang and danced. Here is an anonymous May song:

Since Bonny-boots was dead, that so divinely
Could toot and foot it, (O he did it finely!)
  We ne'er went more a-Maying
  Nor had that sweet fa-laing.

And this is obviously a spring ditty:

Every bush new springing,
Every bird now singing,
Merrily sat poor Nicho,
Chanting troli lo loli lo,
Till her he had espied
On whom his hope relied,
Down a down, with a frown,
O she pulled him down.

Still another May song, by Thomas Nashe (1595):

Trip and go, heave and ho!
Up and down, to and fro!
From the town to the grove,
Two and two, let us rove
A-maying, a-playing:
Love hath no gainsaying,
So merrily trip and go!

The strict heirarchies of feudal England had weakened and by Elizabeth's century most of the serfs were gone, but the old traditions of overturning the heirarchy and celebrating riotously at festivals remained, nowhere more noticeably than in the Lord of Misrule and Boy Bishop reversals of order that delighted the common folk and outraged the Puritans. Here is one of the latter (Stubbes) in a furious outburst (1598) about the Lord of Misrule:

The name, indeed, is odious both to God and good men, and such as the very heathen people would have blushed at, once to have named amongst them. And if the name importeth some evil, then what may the thing itself be, judge you? But because you desire to know the manner of them, I will show you as I have seen them practised myself. First, all the wildheads of the parish, conventing together, choose them a Grand-Captain (of all mischief) whom they ennoble with the title of my Lord of Misrule, and him they crown with great solemnity and, adopt for their king. This king anointed, chooseth forth twenty, forty, threescore or a hundred lusty guts, like to himself, to wait upon his lordly majesty, and to guard his noble person. Then, every one of these his men, he investeth with his liveries of green, yellow, or some other light wanton colour; and as though they were not bawdy—gaudy enough I should say, they bedeck themselves with scarfs, ribbons and laces hanged all over with gold rings, precious stones, and other jewels: this done, they tie about either leg twenty or forty bells, with rich handkerchiefs in their hands, and sometimes laid across their shoulders and necks, borrowed for the most part of their pretty Mopsies and loving Bessies, for bussing them in the dark. Thus all things set in order, then have they their hobby-horses, dragons and other antics, together with their bawdy pipers and thundering drummers to strike up the devil's dance withal. Then march these heathen company towards the church and church-yard, their pipers piping, their drummers thundering, their stumps dancing, their bells jingling, their handkerchiefs swinging about their heads like madmen, their hobby-horses and other monsters of skirmishing amongst the throng; and in this sort they go to the church (I say) and into the church (though the minister be at prayer or preaching), dancing, and swinging their handkerchiefs, over their heads in the church, like devils incarnate, with such a confused noise, that no man can hear his own voice. Then, the foolish people they look, they stare, they laugh, they fleer, and mount upon forms and pews to see these goodly pageants solemnized in this sort.

Then, after this, about the church they go again and again, and so forth into the church-yard, where they have commonly their summer-halls, their bowers, arbours, and banquetting houses set up, wherein they feast, banquet and dance all that day and (peradventure) all the night too. and thus these terrestrial furies spend the Sabbath day.

They have also certain papers, wherein is painted some babblery or other of imagery work, and these they call 'my Lord of Misrule's badges': these they give to every one that will give money for them to maintain them in their heathenry, devilry, whoredom, drunkenness, pride, and what not. And who will not show himself buxom to them and give them money for these the devil's cognizances, they shall be mocked and flouted at shamefully. And so assotted are some, that they not only give them money to maintain their abomination withal, but also wear their badges and cognizances in their hats or caps openly. But let them take heed; for these are the badges, seals, brands, and cognizances of the devil, whereby he knoweth his servants and clients from the children of God, and so long as they wear them, *Sub vexillo diaboli militant contra Dominum et legem suam:* they fight under the banner and standard of the devil against Christ Jesus and all his laws. Another sort of fantastical fools bring to these hell-hounds (the Lord of Misrule and his complices) some bread, some good ale, some new cheese, some old cheese, some custards and cakes, some flawns, some tarts, some cream, some meat, some one thing, some another; but if they knew that as often as they bring anything to the maintenance of these execrable pastimes, they offer sacrifice to the devil and Sathanas, they would repent and withdraw their hands; which God grant they may!

At least the Lord of Misrule festivities were, as far as anyone knew, not pagan in origin, but the maypole was an even greater outrage to the Puritans, a phallic symbol and "stinking idol."

Once a year the citizens of London enjoyed the Lord Mayor's Show, with a barge on The Thames beautifully decorated, the new Lord Mayor (elected from their number by members of the livery companies, or guilds) in his glorious carriage in a parade to the Mansion House, and a pageant with "floats" and song and speeches honoring the trade and the person of the man who would lead the aldermen of The City for the coming year.

The pageant for Sir Thomas Offley (1554) was written by a "Mr. Grimbald," according to Henry Machyn, perhaps Nicholas Grimald (1519-1562). In Elizabeth's reign others were penned by Richard Mulcaster (1530-1611), James Peele, and his son George Peele. George Peele's "Device of the Pageant Borne before Sir Woolstone Dixi" (1585) is the earliest extant and complete Lord Mayor's entertainment. Here is how I have summarized it in a biography I wrote of George Peele (footnotes omitted):

The title page of the unique copy of the pageant, in the Bodleian Library, reads:

The Device of the Pageant borne before Woolstone Dixi Lord Maior of the Citie of London. An[no]. 1585 October 29. Imprinted at London by Edward Allde. 1585.

The text ends with "Donne by George Peele Maister of artes in Oxford." Joseph Ritson added it to the Peele canon in 1802 and since then it has appeared in all collections of Peele's complete works and elsewhere. It has even been produced in modern times.

The pageant for Wolstan Dixi begins with "A Speech spoken by him that rid on a Luzarne before the Pageant [wagon] apparelled like a Moore," with an "Emblem...in showe significant":

Loe lovely London riche and fortunate,
Famed through the Worlde for peace and happiness:
Is heer advaunct and set in Highest seat,
Beawtified thoroughly as her state requires.
First, over her a Princely Trophey standes,
Of beaten golde: a riche and Royall Armes:
Wher-too this London ever more bequeathes,
Service of Honour and of Loyaltie.
Her props are well advisèd Majestrates,
That carefully attend her person still.
The honest Franklin and the Husband-man,
Layes downe his sackes of Corne at Londons feet,
And bringes such presents as the Countrie yeeldes.
The pleasaunt Thames a sweet and daintye Nymphe,
For Londons good convayes with gentle streame,
And safe and easie passage what shee can,
And keepes her leaping Fishes in her lappe.
The souldier and the Sayler franckly bothe,
For Londons ayde are all in readines,
To Venture and to fight by Land and Sea.
And this thrise reverend honorable Dame,
Science the sap of every common wealth.
Surnam's Mechanicall or Liberall
Is vowed to honour London with her skill,
And London by these friends so happy made.

(lines 9-13)

The tournament remained even in Elizabeth's time a form of entertainment and display of pomp and power. While it was chiefly the upper classes, of course, who enjoyed these entertainments, the ordinary man and woman were at least aware that they were held and may have on occasion been able to watch their "betters" at chivalric play. In any case, the common man knew of the continuation of medieval tradition and it gave him a sense of England's glorious past, just as did the ceremonial processions, coronations, royal progresses and such did.

From my book George Peele: The Man and His Work *(1968) a few paragraphs about a 1590 tournament and the work Peele published about it (footnotes omitted):*

The next year (1590)...Richard Jones printed a longer work by Peele called *Polyhymnia.* Since November 17, 1559, Sir Henry Lee (1530-1610), the nephew of Sir Thomas Wyatt, had been the Queen's Champion and he and 26 knights met annually to celebrate the anniversary of Elizabeth's accession (1558) with a tilt or tournament. Tournaments had often been the subject of descriptive poetry (Poliziano's *Stanze per il giostra* are deservedly famous) and Peele's *Polyhymnia* describes the 1590 festivities and the thirteen "couples" who "ran" against each other. (In the fifth tilt, for example "The Earle of Essex" was pitted against "M[aster]. Foulke Greevill".) Then comes a description of the resignation of the Champion's office by the sixty-year-old Lee, subsequently made master of the ordnance. The lines 275-309 (end of the poem) describe this ceremony. Of most interest, however, is this lyric, appended to *Polyhymnia:*

A Sonnet

His Golden lockes, Time hath to Silver turn'd,
O Time too swift, o Swiftnesse never ceasing:
His Youth gainst Time and Age hath ever spurn'd
But spurn'd in vain, Youth waineth by increasing.
  Beauty [,] Strength, Youth, are flowers, but fading seen,
  Dutie, Faith, Love are roots, and ever greene.
His Helmet now, shall make a hive for Bees,
And Lovers Sonets, turn'd to holy Psalmes:
A man at Armes must now serve on his knees.
And feede on praiers, which are Age his almes.
  But through from Court to Cottage he depart,
  His Saint is sure of his unspotted heart.
And when he saddest sits in homely Cell,
Heele teach his Swaines this Carroll for a Song.
Blest be the heartes that wish my Soveraigne well,
Curst be the soules that thinke her any wrong.
  Goddesse, allow this agèd man his right,
  To be your Beads-man now, that was your Knight.

A Lady Lee is buried in the parish church at Aylesbury in Buckinghamshire with this inscription of 1584:

Good friend, stick not to strew with crimson flowers,
This marble tomb wherein her cinders rest.

Margaret Gascoigne in Discovering English Customs and Traditions *(1969) writes: "Ever since Lady Lee's death in 1584 a fresh red flower has been kept on her memorial in the vestry of Aylesbury parish church."*

Ms. Gascoigne also tells us of old customs and practices which date from Elizabeth's time. Here are 10 still honored:

An annual pilgrimage is made on the Thursday and Sunday nearest July 12th to Padley Chapel near Grindleford [Derbyshire], in remembrance of two Roman Catholic priests who were discovered hiding in Padley in 1588, and taken to nearby Derby to be hanged, drawn and quartered.

*

The curiously named Fyshinge Feast, held annually at Plymouth on a convenient date in June or July, commemorates the bringing of water to the town in 1590 from the river Meavy by Sir Francis Drake and the annual "Survey of the Works and the Head Weir" which used to be very necessary to ensure that the tinners were not diverting the town's water supply for their own uses. The Council and guests meet on the lawn by the Head Weir and toast the memory of Drake in river water, and his descendants in mulled ale that they may "never want wine"....

*

A Rush Sermon is preached on a Sunday near the feast of St. Peter (June 29th) in the church of St. Giles the Abbot, Farnborough [Kent] under a sixteenth-century bequest. One George Dalton was saved from drowning and left the legacy for the sermon and for the strewing of the church porch with reeds as a thanksgiving.

*

Every twentieth year since 1562 the Preston Guild Merchant [festivity] has been held for a week in early September [Lancashire].

*

An annual sermon is preached in Leicester on a Sunday in July or August to commemorate the Armada. The churches do this by rota.

*

On December 10th each year [in Boston, Lincolnshire] the Beast Mart is proclaimed under a charter granted to the Corporation in 1573 by Elizabeth I. The proclamation takes place at noon in the playground of the local grammar school where the Mart [cattle fair] was formerly held. It is read by the Town Clerk in the presence of the Mayor and the boys are granted a half-holiday, symbolic of the times when the school had to be closed during the Mart.

*

April 5th [London]:—A Memorial service to John Stow [London's historian], attended by the Lord Mayor and Aldermen, is held in the church of St. Andrew Undershaft on or near the anniversary of his death. A new quill is placed in the hand of Stow's statue during the service.

*

The Hymn of Thanksgiving—the *Te Deum Patrem Colimus* written about 1600—is always included in the May Day Carols which are sung from the top of Magdalen College [Oxford] Tower at 6 a.m. on May 1st. After the singing the College bells ring out and there is Morris dancing in the High [Street].

*

The first time a Peer of the Realm passes through Oakham [in what used to be Rutland] he is required to present a horseshoe, or the money to have one made, to the Lord of the Manor. There is a remarkable collection of these shoes in the castle, including one purporting to have been left by Elizabeth I....

Will Kempe is shown here on his famous dance from London to Norwich. An immensely popular clown and creator of such roles as Sir John Falstaff, his loss when he quit the company was deeply felt at Shakespeare's theatre even though in *Hamlet* the dramatist complains about the tomfoolery the clowns put in to please the groundlings often held up the progress of the plays.

From 'A most excellent Ditty of the Lovers promises' and 'The Ladies prudent answer to her Love' (*Roxburghe Ballads* I. 205).

Love and Marriage

An Elizabethan couple from a broadside in the Roxburghe Ballads, *Great little Cupid said, "Take thy Desire."*

Nora Epton in Love and the English *(1960) pieces together useful information about wives in the Elizabethan period so expertly that perhaps we may be excused if we let her offer several items in our anthology, on the subject of love and marriage. She draws on the same sources we should have chosen and is able to hint at riches there she has not space to show more extensively. If I quote much of her work, she quotes much of others'.*

Sir Edward Coke, the Lord Chief Justice, a terror to the world at large, suffered much from his domineering wife Lady Russell, who pleaded her own cause in the Star Chamber at the age of seventy-eight and was rebuked by the judges for her "pryde and willfulness." Many of these ladies had a keen business acumen. They were as mercenary as their husbands. When Anne Savage, wife of the sixth Earl of Berkeley, was left a widow in 1534, Henry VII suggested she should marry Edward Dudley, but he had no money and she frowned on the proposal. And yet, as her suitor complained in a letter to Wriothesley, "She entertained me after the most loving sort at my first cummings to her as I could desire; for when she was in her chamber, sewing, she would suffer me to lie in her lap, with many other as familiar fashions as I could desire. But at my cumming with the King's letters [recommending the marriage] I was nothing so well welcomed."

When Lady Compton's husband came into money, she set down her wishes very clearly in writing to her "Sweet Life," as she called her lord: "Now I have declared to you my mind for the settling of your estate, I suppose that that were best for me to bethink or consider with myself what allowance were meetest for me." Her demands follow: a yearly sum of £1,600, to be paid quarterly; a dress allowance of £600; three horses for her own saddle; two gentlewomen; six or eight gentlemen; two coaches, one lined with velvet with four very fair horses and a coach for her women "lined with sweet cloth," one laced with gold the other with scarlet and lined with watched lace and silver with four good horses; two footmen; £6,000 for jewels and £4,000 for a pearl chain; a house delicately furnished with hangings, couch, glass, carpet, chairs, cushions." She ends by urging her husband to purchase land and "lend no money as you love God to the Lord Chamberlain."

Many wives, however, must have been of the patient Griselda type like Lady Southampton, who dared not make a move without first asking permission of her lord and master. Lady Rich must have waited with scornful impatience while the friend whose company she desired in London wrote off submissively to her husband in Ireland: "My deare Lord and only joy of my life, beseech you love me ever and be pleased to know that my lady Rich will nedes have me send word how important it is she go to London. She is most desirous to have me with her. I protest unto you that your wil, either in this or anything else, shale be most pleasing to me.... Let me, I pray you, know your pleasure what I shall do, which no earthly power shall make me disobey.... Your faithful and obedient wife."

Of course there were scores of horrid husbands. Lady Anne Clifford wrote sorrowfully: "I must confess...that tho'... I was born a happy creature in Mind, body, and fortune, and that those two lords of mine, to whom I was afterwards by the Divine Providence marryed, were in their several kinds worthy noblemen as any then were in this kingdom, yet was it my misfortune to have contradictions and crosses with them both...so as in both their lifetimes, the Marble Pillars of Knowle in Kent, and Wilton in Wiltshire, were to me oftentimes but the gay arbour of anguish."

Relatives sometimes intervened when domestic strife became acute. In 1534, Lord Berkeley's sister, who was married to the Earl of Ormonde, in Ireland, complained to him of her husband's ill-usage, so he addressed a supplicatory note to Thomas Radcliffe, Earl of Sussex, then Lord Deputy of Ireland: "Whereas I am informed by such as of late are come out of Ireland that my lady Ormonde, my sister, is not so well-used by my Lord her husband, as I would wish her to be.... I am so bold at this present to desire your Lordship that it may please you by your letters to signify unto me whether you understand there be any such sulking between them or not and the causes thereof, that I may travel therein accordingly."

Lower down the social scale, we find a gay burlesque of domestic life by that realistic painter of *petite bourgeois* life, Thomas Deloney: " 'Wherefore then do you not marry?' quoth Margaret. 'In my opinion, it is the most pleasing life that may be, when a woman shall have her husband come home and speake in this sort unto her: 'How now, wife? How dost thou, my sweetheart? What wilt thou have, or what dost thou lacke?' And therewithal kindly embracing her gives her a gentle kiss, saying: 'Speake, my prettie mouse, wilt thou have a cup of claret wine, white wine, or sacke to supper?' And then perhaps he carves unto her the leg of a capon or the wing of a chicken, and if there be one bit better than the other, shee hath the choice of it; and if she chance to long for anything by and by, it is sent for with all possible speed, and nothing is thought too deare to do her good. At last, having well refresht themselves, she sets her silver whistle to her mouth and calles the maid to clear the board. Then going to the fire, he sets her on his knee and wantonly stroking her cheeke, amorously he chocks her under the chin, fetching many stealing touches at her rubie lips; and so soone he hears the bell ring eight a clocke, he calles her to go to bed with him. Oh, how sweet these words sound in a woman's ears! But when they are once close betweene a paire of sheets, O Gillian, then, then...' 'Why, what of that?' quoth she. 'Nay, nothing,' saith Margaret, 'but they sleep soundly all night.' 'Truly' quoth Gillian, 'there be many wives, but few that meete with such kind husbands.' "

One suspects that most bourgeois wives were like *The Merry Wives of Windsor:* capable, healthy, affectionately disposed towards their husbands and with a keenly developed sense of humour. They must have enjoyed sex without any Owlish complexes, and they were fundamentally honest. Opportunities for infidelity may have been more frequent in the wicked cities, but even there one feels that few wives would have replied to an accusing husband in the language of a Robert Greene character: "O sweet husband, we see the strongest tower at length fallen down by the canon's force, though the Bullets be but iron: then how can the weake Bulwarke of a Woman's breast make resistance, when the hot canons of deepe persuading words are shotte off with golden bullets, and every one as big as a Portigue?"—particularly since the double standard of morality was well in force and stoutly defended by most men with exceptions like Robert Vaughan, in his *Dyalogue of Defense for Women* (1542). As for the average lady of the manor, "It fortuned," wrote the author of a popular book of husbandry, "that she has so many things to do that she does not know where to begin." Her duties included: "skill in physics, surgerie, extraction of oils, banqueting stuffe, ordering of great feasts, distillations, perfumes, ordering of wool, hemp, flax, making cloth, dyeing, office of malting, oats, brewing, baking and all other things belonging to a household." These were bound to keep her well out of mischief's way.

Elizabethan chronicler William Harrison says of the covered dishes (as we might call food brought by guests today) at the weddings of farmers:

In feasting the husbandmen do exceed after their manner, especially at bridals, purifications of women [after childbirth], and such odd meetings, where it is incredible to tell what meat is consumed and spent, each one bringing such a dish, or so many, as his wife and he do consult upon.

Shakespeare's England *cites a description which I modernize of the wedding of the daughter of the keeper of London Bridge in July 1562:*

At the celebration whereof were present my Lord Mayor and all the Aldermen with many Ladies etc. and Mr. [Thomas] Becon [1512-1567], an eminent Divine, preached a Wedding sermon. Then all the Company went home to the Bridge House to dinner, where was as good cheer as ever was known, with all manner of Music and Dancing all the remainder of the day, and at night a goodly supper, and then followed a Masque till midnight. The next day the wedding was kept at the Bridge House with great cheer, and after Supper came in Masquers. One was in cloth of gold.

Clearly the Elizabethan bourgeois entertained at weddings with as much feasting and entertainment as he could afford of the sort that had for a long time been traditional in the houses of the nobility. Food was in liberal supply, whether the parents of the bride were wealthy enough to lay it on or guests brought dishes as one today might bring food to a party or church supper.

Marriages were avoided in Lent and popular in spring and fall, especially April and November. The June bride was a later development. So was white as the only color for bridal gowns. In fact, white was the color of mourning according to some old customs and the English considered it unlucky. A white wedding dress did not bring much luck to the Princess Elizabeth (daughter of King James, lived 1596-1662, sometime Queen of Bohemia) and when Charles I wore white for his coronation it was regarded as a dire omen by many.

Nicholas Udall (1505-1556) died before the reign of Elizabeth but his Ralph Roister-Doister *was not printed until 1566 and throughout her reign exercised an influence on English comedy, of which it was the model. Dismissed because of a scandal at Eton (where his schoolboys performed his comedy), he wound up as headmaster at Westminster School, nonetheless. A song from* Ralph Roister-Doister:

I mun be married a Sunday;
I mun be married a Sunday;
Whosoever shall come that way,
I mun be married a Sunday.

Roister Doister is my name;
Roister Doister is my name;
A lusty brute I am the same;
I mun be married a Sunday.

Christian Custance have I found;
Christian Custance have I found;
A widow worth a thousand pound;
I mun be married a Sunday.

Custance is as sweet as honey;
Custance is as sweet as honey;
I her lamb, and she my coney;
I mun be married a Sunday.

When we shall make our wedding feast,
When we shall make our wedding feast,
There shall be cheer for man and beast,
I mun be married a Sunday.
I mun be married a Sunday, &c.

John Parker and Thomas Bright, yeomen of Derbyshire (1600) contracted that John Parker, eldest son of him the said John Parker, shall and will marry and take to his wife Dyonise, daughter of the said Thomas, if she will consent thereto, *according to* Derbyshire Archeological Society Publications, *v.*

An anonymous ballad of about the time of Elizabeth's accession, though in a manuscript of James I's reign:

If ever I marry, I'll marry a maid;
To marry a widow, I am sore afraid:
For maids they are simple, and never will grutch,
But widows full oft, as they say, know too much.

A maid is so sweet, and so gentle of mind,
That a maid is the wife I will choose to my mind:
A widow is froward, and never will yield;
Or if such there be, you will meet them but seeld.

A maid ne'er complaineth, do what so you will;
But what you mean well, a widow takes ill:
A widow will make you a drudge and a slave,
And, cost ne'er so much, she will ever go brave.

A maid is so modest, she seemeth a rose
When it first beginneth the bud to unclose;
But a widow full-blowen full often deceives,
And the next wind that bloweth shakes down all
her leaves.

The widows be lovely, I never gainsay,
But too well all their beauty they know to display;
But a maid hath so great hidden beauty in store,
She can spare to a widow, yet never be poor.

Then, if ever I marry, give me a fresh maid,
If to marry with any I be not afraid;
But to marry with any, it asketh much care;
And some bachelors hold they are best as they are.

The old-fashioned idea that a daughter was her father's property and must do as he said, marry whom he dictated, was not universally popular in Elizabethan England, much as Shakespeare (who seems to have had some difficulties with his own daughters) made sure that daughters who disobeyed their fathers (with the exception of Shylock's daughter, Jessica) came to no good. Enlightened Elizabethans saw reason in verses such as these which we had occasion to quote earlier:

Lord! Give all parents wisdom to foresee
The match is marred where minds do not agree.

George Whetstone in A Heptameron *(1582) wrote:*

I cry out upon forcement in Marriage, as the extremest bondage there is:. . . the father thinks he hath a happy purchase, if he get a rich young Ward to match with his daughter: but God He knows, and the unfortunate couple often feel that he buyeth sorrow to his Child, slander to himself and perchance the ruin of an ancient gentleman's house by the riot of the son in Law not loving his wife.

Translated by Rye from van Meteren's Dutch history of 1575:

Wives in England are entirely in the power of their husbands, their lives only excepted. Therefore, when they marry, they give up the surname of their father and of the family from which they are descended, and take the surname of their husbands, except in the case of duchesses, countesses and baronesses, who, when they marry gentlemen of inferior degree, retain their first name and title, which, for the ambition of the said ladies, is rather allowed than commended. But although the women there are entirely in the power of their husbands, except for their lives, yet they are not kept so strictly as they are in Spain or elsewhere. Nor are they shut up: but they have the free management of the house or housekeeping, after the fashion of those of the Netherlands, and others their neighbours. They go to market to buy what they like best to eat. They are well dressed, fond of taking it easy, and commonly leave the care of household matters and drudgery to their servants. They sit before their doors, decked out in fine clothes, in order to see and be seen by the passers-by. In all banquets and feasts they are shown the greatest honour; they are placed at the upper end of the table, where they are the first served; at the lower end they help the men. All the rest of their time they employ in walking and riding, in playing at cards or otherwise, in visiting their friends and keeping company, conversing with their equals (whom they term gossips) and their neighbours, and making merry with them at child-births, christenings, churchings and funerals; and all this with the permission and knowledge of their husbands, as such is the custom. Although the husbands often recommend to them the pains, industry and care of the German or Dutch women, who do what the men ought to do both in the house and in the shops, for which services in England men are employed, nevertheless the women usually persist in retaining their customs. This is why England is called the Paradise of married women. The girls who are not yet married are kept much more rigorously and strictly than in the Low Countries.

The women are beautiful, fair, well-dressed and modest, which is seen there more than elsewhere, as they go about the streets without any covering either of huke or mantle, hood, veil, or the like. Married women only wear a hat both in the street and in the house; those unmarried go without a hat, although ladies of distinction have lately learnt to cover their faces with silken masks or vizards, and feathers—for indeed they change very easily, and that every year, to the astonishment of many.

J. Cordy Jeaffreson in Brides and Bridals *(1872) describes one of the most unusual marriages in Elizabeth's reign.* The Book of Common Prayer *prescribed that marriage vows be exchanged in spoken words, and the groom, Thomas Filsby, was deaf and dumb. The Bishop of London (John Chippendale) devised a ceremony that was duly carried out in Leicester as Ursula Bridget was wed to Filsby:*

First he embraced Ursula with his arms, took her by the hand and put the ring on her finger. Then he laid his right hand significantly upon his heart and after putting their palms together, he extended both his hands to heaven. Having thus sued for divine blessing, he declared his purpose to dwell with Ursula till death should separate them by closing his eyelids with his fingers, digging the earth with his feet as though he wished to make a hole in the ground and then moving his arms and body as if he were tolling a funeral bell.

F.J. Furnivall edited papers of Child Marriages, Divorces, Etc. in the Diocese of Chester *(1897) and records that one groom was only 11 and unwilling, his bride (age 13) testifying that*

he wept to go home with his father but by his father's entreating and by the persuasion of the priest, the said John did come to bed to his Respondent far into the night; and there lay still, till in the morning, in such sort as this deponent might take unkindness with him; for he lay with his back toward her all night and the boy says he never touched her bare skin.

When Gilbert Gerrard (aged 5) was married to Emma Talbot (nearly 6, but you know of the occasional attractiveness of an Older Woman) the boy's uncle spoke the groom's part in the ceremony for him, but the little girl had her part by heart. A clergyman held John Rigmarden in his arms for a wedding to a bride aged 5. The boy was only 3 and the clergyman "coaxed him to repeat the words of matrimony; before he got through the lesson, the child said he would learn no more that day, but the priest told him: 'You must speak a little more, then go play you.' "

Some explanation of these Elizabethan child marriages is needed. Nina Epton in Love and the English *writes:*

But the main reason for child marriages was a materialistic one: the desire of grasping parents to increase their proportion and also the desire to evade the feudal law of the sovereign's guardianship of all infants. When a father died, the crown had the right to hold the person and estate of the propertied orphan until it came of age and could be sold in marriage for the benefit of the crown or its grantee. If the orphan refused, he had to pay his guardian a heavy fine for refusing his choice. It was all very well for Shakespeare to declare that "Marriage is a matter of more worth than to be dealt in by attorneyship," but attorneys intervened for many years to come.

An old warning:

Marry in May,
Rue for aye.

Another went:

Marry in Lent,
Live to repent.

June has long been the best month for weddings, according to folklore, and as for the day of the week:

Monday for wealth,
Tuesday for health,
Wednesday the best day of all.
Thursday for losses,
Friday for crosses,
And Saturday no luck at all.

Elizabeth liked pearls, though some people thought they were unlucky. Men such as Ralegh wore a single pearl earring in the African fashion—Shakespeare in Othello *refers to the pearl in an Ethiopian's ear—but women did not wear earrings then. (Female headdresses concealed the ears.) The male wearing of earrings may have come from the old sailor's habit of wearing one gold earring, to cover the expense of a funeral (it was said) should the body be washed ashore or the sailor die destitute in some far-off place.*

Probably the commonest pieces of jewelry were the brooches used to hold a feather in the hats of both men and women and the rings that lovers exchanged or that were worn as symbols of authority by bishops and other officials.

A lover's or marriage ring was worn on the third finger of the left hand because it was thought that a vein ran from there directly to the heart, then considered to be the seat of the emotions. But seal rings could be worn on the little finger or the thumb.

This song of 1591 by Thomas Campion refers to unmarried women having to "lead apes in hell," an idea Shakespeare also has in The Taming of the Shrew. It was an old folk belief:

Hark, all you ladies that do sleep;
The fairy queen Proserpina
Bids you awake and pity them that weep.
   You may do in the dark

What the day doth forbid;
  Fear not the dogs that bark,
  Night will have all hid.
But if you let your lovers moan,
  The fairy queen Proserpina
Will send abroad her fairies ev'ry one,
  That shall pinch black and blue
Your white hands and fair arms
  That did not kindly rue
  Your paramours' harms.
In myrtle arbours on the downs
  The fairy queen Proserpina,
This night by moonshine leading merry rounds
  Holds a watch with sweet love,
Down the dale, up the hill;
  No plaints or groans may move
  Their holy vigil.
All you that will hold watch with love,
  The fairy queen Proserpina
Will make you fairer than Dione's dove;
  Roses red, lilies white,
And the clear damask hue,
  Shall on your cheeks alight:
  Love will adorn you.
All you that love, or loved before,
  The fairy queen Proserpina
Bids you increase that loving humour more:
  They that yet have not fed
On delight amorous,
  She vows that they shall lead
  Apes in Avernus.

Popular Belief and Reform in Religion

The fecundity of sacrifice: the cross bears fruit

A Convocation of the clergy meeting to consider Articles of Faith in 1562 defeated by a vote of 59 to 58 these propositions against popery:

1. That Sundays and the principal feasts of Christ be kept holy days, and all other holy days abrogated.
2. That the minister in common prayer turn his face to the people.
3. That making the cross on the child's head in baptism be omitted as tending to superstition.
4. That kneeling in [taking] Communion be left to the minister's discretion.
5. That it is sufficient for the minister to use a surplice [and not a cope, etc.].
6. That the use of organs cease.

Ten years later the Puritans were still fighting about vestments which in an Admonition *to Parliament (1572) they said were alleged to be*

for order and decency commanded, yet we know and have proved that there is neither order nor comeliness nor obedience in using it. There is no order in it, but confusion; no comeliness, but deformity; no obedience, but disobedience to God and to the prince...copes, caps, surplices, tippets and such like baggage, the preaching signs of popish priesthood...garments of the Idol...garments of the Balamites [idolators], of popish priests, enemies to God and all Christians.

They were determined to serve God without Romish reminders and warned:

...we will by God's grace address ourselves to defend His truth by our suffering, and willingly lay our heads to the block, and this shall be our peace, to have quiet consciences with our God, whom we will abide for, with all patience, until He work our full deliverance.

For such issues Elizabethans went to the cudgels, the courts, the prisons and the gallows and the stake.

Released from captivity by the Ottoman Turks, an unfortunate English Protestant fell into the hands of His Most Catholic Majesty of Spain, which was something like going from the frying pan into the fire.

Then I asked him why he kept me so long in prison, which never committed offence to them, knowing very well that I had been captive in Algiers nearly five years space, saying, that when God, by His merciful providence had, through many great dangers, set me in a Christian country, and delivered me from the cruelty of the Turk, when I thought to find such favour as one Christian oweth to another, I found them now more cruel than the Turks, not knowing any cause why. "The cause," said he, "is because the King hath wars with the Queen of England." For at that instant, there was their army prepared ready to go to England. Whereupon they would divers times give me reproachful words, saying that I should hear shortly of their arrival in England, with innumerable vain brags, which I omit for brevity. Then did I demand, "If there were not peace between the King and the Queen's Majesty, whether they would keep me still?" "Yea," said he, "unless thou wilt submit thyself to the faith of the Romish Church." So he commanded me away. I asked wherefore he sent for me, and to send me away, not alleging any matter against me. He said I should have no other matter alleged but that which I had spoken with mine own mouth. Then I demanded why they would have the Romish Church to have the supremacy? Whereto he would make no answer. Then I asked if they took me to be a Christian? "Yes," said he, "in some respects; but you are out of the faith of the true Church." Then the keeper took me to prison again.

And after for the space of three weeks I was brought forth to answer three several times every week. At which times they did sometimes threaten me with death, somewhile with punishment; and many times they attempted to seduce me with fair words and promises of great preferment; but when they saw nothing would draw me from the truth, they called me "shameless Lutheran," saying many times, "See, he is of the very blood of Luther! He hath his very countenance!" with many other frivolous speeches.

After all this, he commanded to put me in the dungeon within the Castle, five fathoms under ground; giving me, once a day, a little bread and water. There remained I one whole year, lying on the bare ground, seeing neither sun nor moon; no, not hearing man, woman nor child speak, but only the keeper which brought my small victual.

Stories of this sort, many of them true, were a popular type of reading and contributed considerably to anti-Catholic feeling in England, where foreign spies and native recusants were always feared.

It might be argued that the profoundest change in divine services in England in the Renaissance was the Protestant stress on hymn singing by the congregation. Many people rendered the psalms into verse. Here we see Thomas Sternhold (d. 1549) and John Hopkins (d. 1570) struggling with (for example) the word organum, *rendering it as "harps and instruments," which straddles the translations of The Geneva Bible (1560, "We hanged our harps upon the willows") and the Roman Catholic or Douai-Rheims version (1582-1610, "On the willows...we hung up our instruments"). Sternhold used the meter of "Chevy Chase" for a number of his psalms.*

His versions and Hopkins' were reprinted in the 1560s and popular in Elizabeth's reign.

Whenas we sat in Babylon,
the rivers round about,
And in remembrance of Zion
the tears for grief burst out.
We hanged our harps and instruments
the willow trees upon,
For in that place men for their use
had planted many one.

Then they to whom we prisoners were
said to us tauntingly:
Now let us hear your Hebrew songs
and pleasant melody.
Alas, said we, who can once frame
his sorrowful heart to sing
The praises of our loving God,
thus under the strange king.

But yet if I Jerusalem
out of my heart let slide,
Then let my fingers quite forget
the warbling harp to guide;
And let my tongue within my mouth
be tied for ever fast,
If that I joy before I see
thy full deliverance past.

These are two of the prayers from The Book of Common Prayer *that Elizabethans said in the morning and at night:*

A Prayer at the Putting on of Our Clothes

Most gracious and merciful Saviour, Jesus Christ, thou knowest how we be born, clothed and clogged with the grievous and heavy burthen of the first man, who fell away unto fleshliness thorough disobedience. Vouchsafe, therefore, I beseech thee, to strip me out of the old corrupt Adam, which, being soaked in sin, transformeth himself into all incumbrances and diseases of the mind, that may lead away from Thee.

Rid me also quite and clean of that his tempter, the deceitful Eve, which turneth us away from the obedience of Thy Father. Clothe me with Thyself, O my redeemer and sanctifier, clothe me with Thyself, which art the second man, and hast yielded Thyself obedient in all things to God Thy Father, to rid away all lusts of the flesh, and to destroy the kingdom thereof through righteousness.

Be Thou our clothing and apparel, to keep us warm from the cold of this world. For, if thou be away, by and by all things become numb, weak, and stark dead: whereas, if thou be present, they be lively, sound, strong, and lusty. And, therefore, like as I wrap my body in these clothes, so clothe Thou me all over, but specially my soul, with Thine own self. Amen.

A Prayer to be Said at the Setting of the Sun

Wretched are they, O Lord, to whom Thy day-sun goeth down,—I mean that sun of Thine, which never setteth to Thy saints, but is always at the noon-point with them ever bright, and ever shining. A droopy night ever deepeth the minds of them, even at high noontide, which depart from Thee. But unto them, that are conversant with Thee, it is continually clear day-light. This day-sun, that shineth in the sky, goeth and cometh by turns: but Thou (if we love Thee in deed) dost never go away from us. O that Thou wouldest remove away this impediment of sin from us, that it might always be day-light in our hearts! Amen.

Annibale Romei spoke of Renaissance man in the highest terms and what he wrote in 1547 was translated thus in Courtier's Academy *(1598):*

This heavenly creature whom we call man was compounded of soul and body, the which body, having to be the harbor of a most fair and immortal soul, was created...most exquisite, with his eyes toward heaven, and was placed in the midst of the world to the end that, as in an ample theatre, he might behold and contemplate the works of the great God, and the beauty of the whole world: as also there was granted unto him a perfect tongue and speech, that, enflamed with love divine and replenished with admiration, he might praise, and with words extol divine beauty.

The Elizabethans were fully aware of the greatness of man, which Alexander Pope was later to call "the glory, jest, and riddle of the world," but they also thought of how small a cog they were in the great scheme of things that reached from the smallest fragment of inanimate nature (which had mere existence), up through plant life (exists and grows), animal life (exists and grows and feels), to man (exists and grows and feels and thinks). Sir John Davies in what Theodore Spencer called "one of the finest of all the accounts of traditional psychology," a poem of 1599:

I know my body's of so frail a kind,
As force without, fevers within can kill;
I know the heavenly nature of my mind,
But 'tis corrupted both in wit and will.

I know my Soul hath power to know all things,
Yet she is blind and ignorant in all;

I know I am one of Nature's little kings,
Yet to the least and vilest things am thrall.

I know my life's a pain and but a span,
I know my Sense is mock'd with everything:
And to conclude, I know myself a MAN,
Which is a proud, and yet a wretched thing.

The physical churches of Elizabeth's time were greatly altered by Protestants ready to destroy as many vestiges of Roman Catholic beliefs as possible. Stained glass windows, memorials, anything that smacked of what they thought of as superstition—a great deal was destroyed forever. A.L. Rowse found in Home Counties Magazine, *X:181 something about tearing down the rood screen in the church at Throwley (Kent) in 1561:*

Richard Gotely was warned by name, by Mr. Sonds and the most part of the ancients of the parish, to be at the pulling down of the rood-loft, as well as others, for that he was an accuser in Queen Mary's time. Then Gotely, thus admonished, did not only stubbornly absent himself, but spake these words of Robert Upton, being churchwarden, because he said that the rood-loft must come down: 'Let him take heed that his authority be good before it be pulled down, for we know what we have had, but we know not what we shall have.'...Richard Gotely said unto George Overy, 'I will see the Queen's broad seal [forbidding its destruction] or I will see it down.'

The outrageous destruction of cathedrals, stained glass, statuary, etc., belongs to a later period, one in which the Roundheads flourished, but "nasty people" (as A.L. Rowse puts it) defaced the gilt cross in Cheapside as early as 1581. In 1599 the Queen ordered repair of the cross, which had survived the breaking of the lower images on the monument but was then in decay. Then

about twelve nights following, the image of our Lady was again defaced, by plucking off her crown and almost her head, taking from her her naked child and stabbing her in the breast, etc. Thus much for the Cross in West Cheap.

Rowland Taylor was a rural vicar in Hadleigh (Essex), martyred in the reign of "Bloody Mary", whose story John Foxe in Acts and Monuments *(usually called "Foxe's* Book of Martyrs"*) held up as a model for Elizabethans. Here is the tale of a man who looked upon the steps to the scaffold as a short ladder to Heaven and went bravely to his death in 1555:*

Now when the Sheriff and his company came against St. Botolph's Church, Elizabeth cried, saying, "O my dear Father! Mother! mother! here is my father led away." Then cried his wife, "Rowland, Rowland, where art thou?"—for it was a very dark morning, that the one could not well see the other. Dr. Taylor answered, "Dear wife, I am here," and stayed. The Sheriff's men would have led him forth, but the Sheriff said, "Stay a little, masters, I pray you, and let him speak with his wife," and so they stayed. Then came she to him, and he took his daughter Mary in his arms, and he, his wife and Elizabeth knelt down and said the Lord's Prayer. At which sight the Sheriff wept apace, and so did divers other of the company. After they had prayed he rose up and kissed his wife and shook her by the hand, and said, "Farewell, my dear wife, be of good comfort, for I am quiet in my conscience. God shall stir up a father for my children."... Then said his wife, "God be with thee, dear Rowland. I will with God's grace meet thee at Hadleigh."...All the way Dr. Taylor was joyful and merry as one that accounted himself going to a most pleasant banquet or bridal.... Coming within a two mile of Hadleigh he desired to light off his horse, which done he leaped and set a frisk or twain, as men commonly do in dancing. "Why, master Doctor," quoth the Sheriff, "how do you now?" He answered, "Well, God be praised, good master Sheriff, never better; for now I know I am almost at home. I lack not past two stiles to go over, and I am even at my Father's house."

A Confession of Faith mostly the work of John Knox and adopted 1 August 1560 is still the creed of the Presbyterian Church of Scotland. It includes such beliefs as these:

I. We confess and acknowledge one only God...in three persons.

II. We confess and acknowledge this our God to have created man (to wit, our first father Adam), of whom also God formed the woman in His own image...so that in the whole nature of man could be noted no imperfection. From which honor and perfection man and woman did both fall, the woman being deceived by the serpent, and man obeying to the voice of the woman....

III. By which transgression, commonly called Original Sin, was the image of God utterly defiled in man; and he and his posterity of nature became enemies to God, slaves to Satan, and servants to sin, in samekill that death everlasting has had, and shall have, power and dominion over all that has not been, are not, or shall not be regenerate from above; which regeneration is wrought by the Holy Ghost, working in the hearts of the elect of God an assured faith in the promise of God...by which faith they apprehend Christ Jesus....

VIII. That same eternal God and Father...of mere mercy elected us in Christ Jesus...before the foundation of the world....

XVI. We most earnestly believe that from the beginning there has been, now is, and to the end of the world shall be, a Church, that is to say, a company and multitude of men chosen by God, who rightly worship and embrace Him by true faith in Christ Jesus.... out of which Church there is neither life nor eternal felicity. And therefore we utterly abhor the blasphemy of those that affirm that men which live accordingly to equity and justice shall be saved, what religion soever they have professed....

XXI. ...We acknowledge...two chief sacraments only...Baptism and the Supper.... Not that we imagine any transubstantiation of bread into God's natural body...but, by the operation of the Holy Ghost...we believe that the Faithful, in the right use of the Lord's Table, so do eat the body, and drink the blood, of the Lord Jesus....

XXIV. We confess and acknowledge empires, kingdoms, dominions, and cities to be...ordained by God.... To kings, princes and magistrates...chiefly and most principally the conservation and purgation of the Religion appertains; so that not only are they appointed for civil policy, but also for maintenance of the true Religion, and for suppressing of idolatry and superstition whatsoever....

This act of the Reformation Parliament in Scotland was to have far-reaching effects on Britain for the rest of the 16th century and later.

Martin Luther grapples with Predestination:

Common sense and natural reason are highly offended that God by His mere will deserts, hardens, and damns, as if He delighted in sin and in such eternal torments, He Who is said to be of such mercy and goodness. Such a concept of God seems wicked, cruel, and intolerable, and by it many men have been revolted in all ages. I myself was once offended to the very depth of the abyss of desperation, so that I wished that I had never been created. There is no use trying to get away from this by ingenious distinctions. Natural reason, however much as it is offended, must admit the consequences of the omniscience and omnipotence of God.... If it is difficult to believe in God's mercy and goodness when He damns those who do not deserve it, we must recall that if God's justice could be recognized as just by human comprehension, it would not be divine.

In one of the very many publications that poured from him and engulfed Europe, De servo arbitrio *(1525), Luther put the idea of Predestination squarely, with his famed obstinacy ("Here I stand. I can do no other"):*

The human will is like a beast of burden. If God mounts it, it wishes and goes as God wills; if Satan mounts it, it wishes and goes as Satan wills. Nor can it choose its rider.... The riders contend for its possession.... God foresees, foreordains, and accomplishes all things by an unchanging, eternal, and efficacious will. By this thunderbolt free will sinks shattered in the dust.

In Scotland, John Knox (1505-1572) announced that

by idolatry we understand the Mass, invocation of saints adoration of images, and the keeping and retaining of the same, and all honoring of God not contained in His Holy Word.

His Appellation to the Nobility and Estates of Scotland *just months before Elizabeth assumed the English throne declared war to the death on Roman Catholics:*

None provoking the people to idolatry ought to be exempted from the punishment of death.... The same ought to be done wheresoever Christ Jesus and His Evangel is so received...that the magistrates and people have solemnly avowed and promised to defend the same; as under King Edward of late days was done in England. In such place, I say, it is not only lawful to punish to the death such as labor to subvert the true religion, but the magistrates and people are bound to do so unless they will provoke the wrath of God against themselves.... I fear not to affirm that it had been the duty of the nobility, judges, rulers, and people of England not only to have resisted and againstanded Mary, that Jezebel...but also to have punished her to the death.

Pope Paul III reinstituted The Inquisition (1542) and Giovanni Cardinal Caraffa (one of the men he put in charge of it) immediately adopted a stringent policy:

1. When the faith is in question, there must be no delay, but on the slightest suspicion rigorous measures must be taken with all speed.
2. No consideration is to be shown to any prince of prelate, however high his station.
3. Extreme severity is rather to be exercised against those who attempt to shield themselves under the protection of any potentate. Only he who makes plenary confession should be treated with gentleness and fatherly compassion.
4. No man must debase himself by showing toleration toward heretics of any kind, above all toward Calvinists.

In 1539 Henry VIII published 6 articles of religion. In 1552 Mary published 42 but without the consent of Parliament. In Elizabeth's reign (1563) the Articles of Religion were reduced to 39 and were ratified by Parliament (1571). These are still in effect as the Thirty-Nine Articles of the Church of England. The Irish got 104 articles from Archbishop Ussher (1614, established 1634) but with the union of the established churches Irish members accepted the Thirty-Nine Articles. The Roman Catholics called them "Forty Stripes save One."

Walter Travers (1548?-1635), according to Izaak Walton, took "orders with the Presbytry in Antwerp—and with them some opinions that could never be eradicated" and was instrumental in setting up the first Presbyterian congregation in England (Wandsworth, 1572). In August of the next year, Edwin Sandys (1516?-1588), later to be Archbishop of York and at that time Bishop of London, wrote to Henry Bullinger about the alarming rise of Presbyterianism:

New orators are rising up among us: foolish young men who despise authority and admit of no superior. They are seeking the complete overthrow and uprooting of the whole of our ecclesiastical polity, and striving to shape out for us I know not what platform of a church.

But the "platform" was all too clear, and the bishop was able to summarize it pretty well thus:

i. The civil magistrate has no authority in ecclesiastical matters. He is only a member of the Church, the government of which ought to be committed to the clergy.
ii. The Church of Christ admits of no other government than that by the Presbyteries: *viz.*, by the Minister, Elders, and Deacons.
iii. The names and authority of Archbishops, Archdeacons, Deans, Chancellors, Commissaries, and other titles and dignitaries of the kind, should be altogether removed from the Church of Christ.
iv. Each parish should have its own Presbytry.
v. The choice of Ministers of necessity belongs to the people.
vi. The goods, possessions, lands, revenues, tithes, honours, authorities, and all other things relating either to Bishops or Cathedrals, and which now of right belong to them, should be taken away forthwith and forever.
vii. No one should be allowed to preach who is not a pastor of some Congregation; and he ought to preach to his own flock exclusively, and nowhere else.
viii. Infants of Papists are not to be baptised [in the Anglican Communion].
ix. The judicial laws of Moses are binding upon Christian Princes, and they ought not in the slightest degree to depart from them.

St. Edmund Campion (1540-1581, canonized 1970), like many Elizabethans of the old faith, studied at Douai. He became a Jesuit preacher in England, was arrested, tortured, and executed. His views on martyrdom for the Roman Catholic faith:

It is not our death that ever we feared. But we knew that we were not lords of our own lives, and therefore for want of answer would not be guilty of our own deaths. The only thing that we have now to say is that if our religion do make us traitors we are worthy to be condemned; but otherwise are and have been true subjects as ever the queen had. In condemning us you condemn all your own ancestors—all the ancient priests, bishops, and kings—all that was once the glory of England, the island of saints and the most devoted child of the see of Peter. For what have we taught, however you may qualify it with the odious name of treason, that they did not uniformly teach? To be condemned with these old lights—not of England only, but of the world—by their degenerate descendants is both gladness and glory to us. God lives;

posterity will live; their judgment is not so liable to corruption as that of those who are now going to sentence us to death.

There are only two million Britons today of the 45 million adults in that country who regularly practice their religion, though half of them were baptized in the Church of England and religion is Established and influential far beyond proportion to the participation of the public in it. That the British have long been more practical than pious is shown by this Elizabethan tale from a jestbook about the fact that the wheat in the field is more to be heeded than the chaff from the pulpit.

There was on a time a priest in the country that preached upon a holiday in his parish church; and as he stood in the pulpit, he perceived through a hole in the glass window that other men's swine were in his corn.

"What the mischief," said he, "stand I here fading [wasting] the time to the devil and see yonder swine are spoiling my corn?" And then he leapt out of the pulpit and ran as if he had been mad and left all the people to stand there like a company of fools.

In Machiavelli's The Prince *Englishmen found a hint about the susceptibility to frauds, especially but not exclusively in religion, of that many-headed monster the populace. It affected some of Elizabethan England's attitude toward religion. Machiavelli noted that*

untutored and ignorant men are more easily persuaded to adopt new laws or new opinions, yet that does not make it impossible to persuade civilized men who claim to be enlightened. The people of Florence are far from considering themselves ignorant and benighted, and yet Fra Girolamo Savonarola succeeded in persuading them that he communicated with God. I will not pretend to judge whether it was true or not, for we must speak with all respect of so great a man; but I may well say that an immense number believed it without having seen any extraordinary manifestations that should have compelled them to believe it; but it was the purity of his life, the doctrines that he preached, and the subjects he selected for his sermons, that were enough to make the people have faith in him. Let nobody, then, fear he cannot accomplish what others have accomplished, for all men. . .are born to live and die in the same way; therefore they resemble each other.

Dissension tore at the Christian community as old and new religious ideas clashed in Renaissance England. In the following Advertisement Touching the Controversies of the Church of England *are examined in some detail many of the battles that produced both learned arguments and polemical and popular pamphlets throughout the 16th century, and beyond. This piece cannot be said to be "popular" in itself, but it does throw light on the source of much popular literature and sub-literature of the period, "curious controversies and profane scoffing," so I believe it is worth the space and the necessarily close attention of the patient reader. Many Latin quotations are translated in the original; the others I shall translate in brackets. Note their frequency!*

It is but ignorance if any man find it strange that the state of Religion (especially in the days of peace) should be exercised and troubled with controversies. For as it is the condition of the Church Militant to be ever under trials, so it cometh to pass that when the fiery trial of persecution ceaseth there succeedeth another trial, which as it were by contrary blasts of doctrine doth sift and winnow men's faith, and proveth them whether they know God aright, even as that other of afflictions discovereth whether they love Him better than the World. Accordingly was it foretold by Christ, saying, That in the latter times it should be said, Lo here, lo there is Christ: which is to be understood, not as if the very person of Christ should be assumed and counterfeited, but his authority and pre-eminence (which is to be Truth itself) that should be challenged and pretended. Thus have we read and seen to be fulfilled that which followeth, *Ecce in deserto, ecce in penetralibus* ["Behold he is in the desert, behold he is in the secret chambers."—*Mathew* XXIV:26]; while some have sought the truth in the conventicles and conciliables of heretics and sectaries, and others in the extern face and representation of the Church, and both sorts been seduced. Were it then that the controversies of the Church of England were such as did divide the unity of the spirit, and not such as only do unswathe her of her bonds (the bonds of peace), yet could it be no occasion for any pretended Catholic to judge us, or for any irreligious person to despise us. Or if it be, it shall but happen to us all as it hath used to do; to them to be hardened, and to us to endure the good pleasure of God. But now that our contentions are such, as we need not so much that general canon and sentence of Christ pronounced against heretics, *Erratis, nescientes Scripturas, nec potestatem Dei* ["You err, not knowing Scriptures, not the power of God."—*Mathew* XXII:29], as we need the admonition of St. James, "let every man be swift to hear, slow to speak, slow to wrath;" and that the wound is no way dangerous, except we poison it with our remedies; as the former sort of men have less reason to make themselves music in our discord, so I have good hope that nothing shall displease ourselves which shall be sincerely and modestly propounded for the appeasing of these dissensions. For if any shall be offended at this voice, *Vos estis fratres* (ye are brethren, why strive ye?), he shall give a great presumption against himself, that he is the party that doth his brother wrong.

The controversies themselves I will not enter into, as judging that the disease requireth rather rest than any other cure. Thus much we all know and confess, that they be not of the highest nature; for they are not touching the high mysteries of faith, such as detained the churches after their first peace for many years; what time the heretics moved curious questions, and made strange anatomies of the natures and person of Christ; and the Catholic fathers were compelled to follow them with all subtility of decisions and determinations, to exclude them from their evasions and to take them in their labyrinths; so as it is rightly said, *illis temporibus inveniosa res fuit esse Christianum* (in those days it was an ingenious and subtle matter to be a Christian). Neither are they concerning the great parts of the worship of God, of which it is true that *non servatur unitas in credendo, nisi eadem adsit in colendo* (there will be kept no unity in believing, except it be entertained in worshipping); such as were the controversies of the east and west churches touching images; and such as are many of those between the Church of Rome and us; as about the adoration of the Sacrament and the like. But we contend about ceremonies and things indifferent; about the extern policy and government of the Church. In which kind, if we would but remember that the ancient and true bonds of unity are one faith, one baptism, and not one ceremony, one policy; if we would observe the league amongst Christians that is penned by our Saviour, "He that is not against us is with us:" if we could but comprehend that saying, *differentia rituum commendat unitatem doctrina* (the diversity of ceremonies doth set forth the unity of doctrine); and that *habet religio qua sunt aeternitatis, habet qua sunt temporis* (Religion hath parts which belong to eternity, and parts which pertain to time): and if we did but know the virtue of silence and slowness to speak, commended by St. James; our controversies of themselves would close up and grow together. But most especially, if we would leave the over-weening and turbulent humours of these times, and revive the blessed proceeding of the Apostles and Fathers of the primitive Church, which was, in the like and greater cases, not to enter into assertions and positions, but to deliver counsels and advices, we should need no other remedy at all. *Si eadem consulis, frater, qua affirmas, debetur consulenti reverentia, cum non debeatur fides affirmanti* (Brother, if that which you set down as an assertion, you would deliver by way of advice, there were reverence due to your counsel, whereas faith is not due to your affirmation). St. Paul was content to speak thus, *Ego, non Dominus* (I, and not the Lord); *Et, secundum consilium meum* (according to my counsel). But now men do too lightly say, *Non ego, sed Dominus* (not I, but the Lord): yea, and bind it with heavy denunciations of His judgments, to terrify the simple, which have not sufficiently understood out of Salomon, that the causeless curse shall not come.

Therefore seeing the accidents are they which breed the peril, and not the things themselves in their own nature, it is meet the remedies be applied unto them, by opening what it is on either part that keepeth the wound green, and formalizeth both sides to a further opposition, and worketh an indisposition in men's minds to be reunited. Wherein no accusation is pretended; but I find in reason, that peace is best built upon a repetition of wrongs: and in example, that the speeches which have been made by the wisest men *de concordia ordinum* [regarding concord of arrangements] have not abstained from reducing to memory the extremities used on both parts. So as it is true which is said, *Qui pacem tractat non repetitis conditionibus dissidii, is magis animos hominum dulcedine pacis fallit, quam aquitate componit.* "Whosoever seeks treaty of peace without restating the causes of dissension rather beguiles men's minds with the sweetness of peace than brings them into accord by equity."

And first of all, it is more than time that there were an end and surseance made of this immodest and deformed manner of writing lately entertained, whereby matters of Religion are handled in the style of the stage. Indeed, bitter and earnest writing may not hastily be condemned; for men cannot contend coldly and without affection about things which they hold dear and precious. A politic man may write from his brain, without touch and sense of his heart, as in a speculation that pertaineth not unto him; but a feeling Christian will express in his words a character either of zeal or love. The latter of which as I could wish rather embraced, being more fit for these times, yet is the former warranted also by great examples. But to leave all reverent and religious compassion towards evils, or indignation towards faults, and to turn religion into a comedy or satire; to search and rip up wounds with a laughing countenance; to intermix Scripture and scurrility sometime in one sentence; is a thing far from the devout reverence of a Christian, and scant beseeming the honest regard of a sober man. *Non est major confusio, quam serii et joci* (there is no greater confusion, than the confounding of jest and earnest). The majesty of religion, and the contempt and deformity of things ridiculous, are things as distant as things may be. Two principal causes have I ever known of Atheism: curious controversies, and profane scoffing. Now that these two are joined in one, no doubt that sect will make no small progression.

And here I do much esteem the wisdom and religion of that bishop which replied to the first pamphlet of this kind, who remembered that "a fool was to be answered, but not by becoming like unto him"; and considered the matter that he handled, and not the person with whom he dealt. Job, speaking of the majesty and gravity of a judge in himself, saith, "If I did smile, they believed it not:" as if he should have said, If I diverted, or glanced unto conceit of mirth, yet men's minds were so possessed with a reverence of the action in hand, as they could not receive it. Much more ought this to be amongst bishops and divines disputing about holy things. And therefore as much do I dislike the invention of him who (as it seemeth) pleased himself in it as in no mean policy, that these men are to be dealt withal at their own weapons, and pledged in their own cup. This seemed to him as profound a device, as when the Cardinal Sansovino counselled Julius II. to encounter the Council of Pisa with the Council Lateran; or as lawful a challenge as Mr. [John] Jewel made to confute the pretended Catholics by the Fathers. But these things will not excuse the imitation of evil in another. It should be contrariwise with us, as Caesar said, *Nil malo, quam eos similes esse sui, et me mei* ["I desire nothing but that they be like themselves, I like myself," quoted in Cicero's letters to Atticus]. But now, *Dum de bonis contendimus, in malis consentimus* (while we differ about good things, we resemble in evil). Surely, if I were asked of these men who were the more to be blamed, I should percase remember the proverb, "that the second blow maketh the fray," and the saying of an obscure fellow, *Qui replicat, multiplicat* (he that replieth, multiplieth). But I would determine the question with this sentence: *Alter principium malo dedit, alter modum abstulit* (by the one's means we have a beginning, and by the other's we shall have none end). And truly, as I do marvel that some of those preachers which call for reformation (whom I am far from wronging so far as to join them with these scoffers) do not publish some declaration whereby they may satisfy the world that they dislike their cause should be thus solicited; so I hope assuredly that my lords of the clergy have none intelligence with this other libeller, but do altogether disallow that their credit should be thus defended. For though I observe in him many glosses, whereby the man would insinuate himself into their favours, yet I find it to be ordinary, that many pressing and fawning persons do misconjecture of the humours of men in authority, and many times *Veneri immolant suem* (they seek to gratify them with that which they most dislike). For I have great reason to satisfy myself touching the judgments of my lords the bishops in this matter, by that which was written by one of them, which I mentioned before with honour. Nevertheless I note, there is not an indifferent [impartial] hand carried towards these pamphlets as they deserve. For the one sort flieth in the dark, and the other is uttered openly; wherein I might advise that side out of a wise writer, who hath set it down that *punitis ingeniis gliscit auctoritas* ["when wits are punished their authority grows"]. And indeed we see it ever falleth out that the forbidden writing is thought to be certain sparks of a truth that fly up in the faces of those that seek to choke it and tread it out; whereas a book authorised is thought to be but *temporis voces* (the language of the time). But in plain truth I do find (to my understanding) these pamphlets as meet to be suppressed as the other. First, because as the former sort doth deface the government of the Church in the persons of the bishops and prelates, so the other doth lead into contempt the exercises of religion in the persons of sundry preachers; so as it disgraceth an higher matter, though in the meaner person. Next, I find certain indiscreet and dangerous amplifications, as if the civil government itself of this estate had near lost the force of her sinews, and were ready to enter into some convulsion, all things being full of faction and disorder; which is as unwisely acknowledged as untruly affirmed. I know his meaning is to enforce this unreverent and violent impugning of the government of bishops to be a suspected forerunner of a more general contempt. And I grant there is sympathy between the states, but no such matter in the civil policy as deserveth so dishonourable a taxation. To conclude this point: As it were to be wished that these writings had been abortive, and never seen the sun; so the next is, since they be comen abroad, that they be censured [considered] (by all that have understanding and conscience) as the intemperate extravagancies of some light persons. Yea further, that men beware (except they mean to adventure to deprive themselves of all sense of religion, and to pave their own hearts, and make them as the highway) how they be conversant in them, and much more how they delight in that vein; but rather to turn their laughing into blushing, and to be ashamed, as of a short madness, that they have in matters of religion taken their disport and solace. But this perchance is of those faults which will be soonest acknowledged; though I perceive nevertheless that there want not some who seek to blanch and excuse it.

But to descend to a sincere view and consideration of the accidents and circumstances of these controversies, wherein either part deserveth blame or imputation; I find generally, in causes of church controversies, that men do offend in some or all of these five points.

1. The first is, the giving of occasion unto the controversies: and also the inconsiderate and ungrounded taking of occasion.

2. The next is, the extending and multiplying the controversies to a more general opposition or contradiction than appeareth at the first propounding of them, when men's judgments are less partial.

3. The third is, the passionate and unbrotherly practices and proceedings of both parts towards the person each of others, for their discredit and suppression.

4. The fourth is, the courses holden and entertained on either side, for the drawing of their partisans to a more strait union within themselves, which ever importeth a further distraction of the entire body.

5. The last is, the undue and inconvenient propounding, publishing, and debating of the controversies. In which point the most palpable error hath been already spoken of; as that which, through the strangeness and freshness of the abuse, first offereth itself to the conceits of all men.

1. Now concerning the occasion of controversies, it cannot be denied but that the imperfections in the conversation and government of those which have chief place in the Church have ever been principal causes and motives of schisms and divisions. For whilst the bishops and governors of the Church continue full of knowledge and good works; whilst they feed the flock indeed; whilst they deal with the secular states in all liberty and resolution, according to the majesty of their calling, and the precious care of souls imposed upon them: so long the Church is situate as it were upon an hill; no man maketh question of it, or seeketh to depart from it. But when these virtues in the fathers and leaders of the Church have lost their light, and that they wax worldly, "lovers of themselves, and pleasers of men," then men begin to grope for the Church as in the dark; they are in doubt whether they be the successors of the Apostles, or of the Pharisees; yea, howsoever they sit in Moses' chair, yet they can never speak *tanquam auctoritatem habentes* (as having authority), because they have lost their reputation in the consciences of men, by declining their steps from the way which they trace out to others. So as men had need continually have sounding in their ears this saying, *Nolite exire* (go not out); so ready are they to depart from the Church upon every voice. And therefore it is truly noted by one that writeth as a natural man, "that the hypocrisy of freres did for a great time maintain and bear out the irreligion of bishops and prelates." For this is the double policy of the spiritual enemy, either by counterfeit holiness of life to establish and authorise errors; or by corruption of manners to discredit and draw in question truth and things lawful. This concerneth my lords the bishops, unto whom I am witness to myself that I stand affected as I ought. No contradiction hath supplanted in me the reverence I owe to their calling; neither hath any detractation or calumny embased mine opinion of their persons.

I know some of them, whose names are most pierced with these accusations, to be men of great virtues; although the indisposition of the time, and the want of correspondence many ways, is enough to frustrate the best endeavours in the edifying of the Church. And for the rest generally, I can condemn none. I am no judge of them that belong to so high a master; neither have I two witnesses. And I know it is truly said of Fame, *Pariter facta, atque infecta canebat* ["She sang both what was done and what was not done."—Statius, *Thebiad* III:430]. Their taxations arise not all from one coast; they have many and different enemies, ready to invent slander, more ready to amplify it, and most ready to believe it. And *Magnes mendacii credulitas* (credulity is the adamant of lies). But if any be, against whom the supreme bishop hath not a few things but many things; if any have "lost his first love;" if any "be neither hot nor cold"; if any have stumbled too foully at the threshold, in sort that he cannot sit well which entered ill; it is time "they return whence they are fallen, and confirm the things that remain." Great is the weight of this fault; *et eorum causa abhorrebant homines a sacrificio Domini* (and for their cause did men abhor the adoration of God). But howsoever it be, those which have sought to deface them, and cast contempt upon them, are not to be excused.

It is the precept of Salomon, "that the rulers be not reproached; no, not in thought," but that we draw our very conceit into a modest interpretation of their doings. The holy angel would give no sentence of blasphemy against the common slanderer, but said, *Increpet te Dominus* (the Lord rebuke thee). The Apostle St. Paul, though against him that did pollute sacred justice with tyrannous violence he did justly denounce the judgment of God, in saying *Percutiet te Dominus* (the Lord will strike thee); yet in saying *paries dealbate,* ["whitewashed wall"] he thought he had gone too far, and retracted it: whereupon a learned father said, *Ipsum quamvis inane nomen et umbram sacerdotis cogitanus expavit* ["Upon reflection he had dread even for the empty name and shadow of a priest"]. The ancient councils and synods (as is noted by the ecclesiastical story), when they deprived any bishop, never recorded the offence, but buried it in perpetual silence. Only Cham purchased his curse with revealing his father's disgrace. And yet a much greater fault is it to ascend from their person to their calling, and draw that in question. Many good fathers spake rigorously and severely of the unworthiness of bishops, as if presently it did forfeit and cease their office. One said, *Sacerdotes nominamur et non sumus* (we are called priests, but priests we are not). Another saith, *Nisi bonum opus amplectaris, episcopus esse non potes* (except thou undertake the good work, thou canst not be a bishop). Yet they meant nothing less than to make doubt of their calling or ordination.

The second occasion of controversies, is the nature and humour of some men. The Church never wanteth a kind of persons which love "the salutation of Rabbi, master;" not in ceremony or compliment, but in an inward authority which they seek over men's minds, in drawing them to depend upon their opinion, and "to seek knowledge at their lips." These men are the true successors of Diotrephes, the lover of preeminence, and not lords bishops. Such spirits do light upon another sort of natures, which do adhere to them; men *quorum gloria in obsequio* (stiff followers, and such as zeal marvellously for those whom they have chosen for their masters). This latter sort, for the most part, are men of young years and superficial understanding, carried away with partial respect of persons, or with the enticing appearance of goodly names and pretences. *Pauci res ipsas sequuntur, plures nomina rerum, plurimi nomina magistrorum* (few follow the things themselves, more the names of the things, and most the names of their masters). About these general affections are wreathed accidental and private emulations and discontentments, all which together break forth into contentions; such as either violate truth, sobriety, or peace. These generalities apply themselves. The universities are the seat and continent of this disease, whence it hath been and is derived into the rest of the realm. There some will no longer be *e numero* (of the number). There some others side themselves before "they know their right hand from their left." So it is true which is said, *transeunt ab ignorantia and prejudicium* (they leap from ignorance to a prejudicate opinion), and never take a sound judgment in their way. But as it is well noted, *inter juvenile judicium of senile prejudicium, omnis veritas corrumpitu* (when men are indifferent, and not partial, then their judgment is weak and unripe through want of years; and when it groweth to strength and ripeness, by that time it is forestalled with such a number of prejudicate opinions, as it is made unprofitable: so as between these two all truth is corrupted). In the meanwhile, the honourable names of sincerity, reformation, and discipline are put in the foreward: so as contentions and evil zeals cannot be touched, except these holy things be thought first to be violated. But howsoever they shall infer the solicitation for the peace of the Church to proceed from carnal sense, yet I will conclude ever with the Apostle Paul, *Cum sit inter vos zelus et contentio, nonne carnales estis?* (Whilst there is amongst you zeal and contention, are ye not carnal?) And however they esteem the compounding of controversies to savour of man's wisdom and human policy, and think themselves led by the wisdom which is from above, yet I say with St. James. *Non est ista sapientia de sursum descendens, sed terrena, animalis, diabolica: ubi enim zelus et contentio, ibi inconstantia et omne opus pravum* ["This wisdom does not descend from above but is earthly, sensual, devilish. For where envy and strife are, there is confusion and every evil work."—*James* III:15,16]. Of this inconstancy, it is said by a learned father, *Procedere volunt non ad perfectionem, sed ad permutationem* (they seek to go forward still, not to perfection, but to change).

The third occasion of controversies I observe to be, an extreme and unlimited detestation of some former heresy or corruption of the Church already acknowledged and convicted. This was the cause that produced the heresy of Arius, grounded chiefly upon detestation of Gentilism, lest the Christians should seem, by the assertion of the co-equal divinity of our Saviour Christ, to approach unto the acknowledgment of more gods than one. The detestation of the heresy of Arius produced that of Sabellius [error? for Sabellius was Third Century and Arius, Fourth Century], who, holding for execrable the dissimilitude which Arius pretended in the Trinity, fled so far from him, as he fell upon that other extremity, to deny the distinction of persons; and to say they were but only names of several offices and dispensations. Yea, most of the heresies and schisms of the Church have sprung up of this root; while men have made it as it were their scale, by which to measure the bounds of the most perfect religion; taking it by the furthest distance from the error last condemned. These be *posthumi haresium flii* (heresies that arise out of the ashes of other heresies that are extinct and amortized). This manner of apprehension doth in some degree possess many in our times. They think it the true touchstone to try what is good and holy, by measuring what is more or less opposite to the institutions of the Church of Rome; be it ceremony, be it policy or government, yea, be it other institution of greater weight, that is ever most perfect which is removed most degrees from that Church; and that is ever polluted and blemished which participateth in any appearance with it. This is a subtle and dangerous conceit for men to entertain, apt to delude themselves, more apt to seduce the people, and most apt of all to calumniate their adversaries. This surely (but that a notorious condemnation of that position was before our eyes) had long since brought us to the re-baptising of children baptised according to the pretended catholic religion. For I see that which is a matter of much like reason, which is the re-ordaining of priests, is a matter already resolutely maintained. It is very meet that men beware how they be abused by this opinion; and that they know that it is a consideration of much greater wisdom and sobriety to be well advised, whether in the general demolition of the institutions of the Church of Rome there were not (as men's actions are imperfect) some good purged with the bad, rather than to purge the Church, as they pretend, every day anew; which is the way to make a wound in her bowels, as is already begun.

The fourth and last occasion of these controversies (a matter which did also trouble the Church in former times) is the partial affectation and imitation of foreign churches. For many of our men, during the time of persecution and since, having been conversant in churches abroad, and received a great impression of the form of government there ordained, have violently sought to intrude the same upon our Church. But I answer, *Consentiamus in eo quod convenit, non in eo quod receptum est* (let us agree in this, that every church do that which is convenient for the estate of itself, and not in particular customs). Although their churches had received the better form, yet many times it is to be sought, *non quid optimum, sed e bonis quid proximum* (not what is best, but of good things what is next and readiest to be had). Our church is not now to plant; it is settled and established. It may be, in civil states, a republic is a better policy than a kingdom: yet God forbid that lawful kingdoms should be tied to innovate and make alteration. *Qui mala introducit, voluntatem Dei oppugnat revelatam in verbo; qui nova introducit, voluntatem Dei oppugnat revelatam in rebus* (he that bringeth in evil customs, resisteth the will of God revealed in His Word; he that bringeth in new things, resisteth the will of God revealed in the things themselves). *Consule providentiam Dei, cum verbo Dei* (take counsel of the providence of God, as well as of His Word). Neither yet do I admit that their form (though it were possible and convenient) is better than ours, if some abuses were taken away. The parity and equality of ministers is a thing of wonderful great confusion; and so is an ordinary government by synods, which doth necessarily ensue upon the other. It is hard in all causes, but especially in matters of religion, when voices shall be "numbered and not weighted." *Equidem* (saith a wise father) *ut vere quod res est scribam, prorsus decrevi fugere omnem conventum episcoporum; nullius enim concilii bonum exitum unquam vidi; concilia enim non minuunt mala, sed augent potius* (To say the truth, I am utterly determined never to come to any council; for councils abate not ill things, but rather increase them): which is to be understood not so much of general councils, as of synods gathered for the ordinary government of the Church; as for deprivation of bishops, and such-like causes; which mischief hath taught the use of archbishops, patriarchs, and primates; as the abuse of them since hath taught men to mislike them. But it will be said, Look to the fruits of the churches abroad and ours. To which I say, that I beseech the Lord to multiply his blessings and graces upon those churches an hundredfold. But yet it is not good, that we fall on numbering of them. It may be our peace hath made us more wanton: it may be also (though I would be loath to derogate from the honour of those churches, were it not to remove scandals) that their fruits are as torches in the dark, which appear greatest afar off. I know they may have some more strict orders for the repressing of sundry excesses. But when I consider of the censures of some persons, as well upon particular men as upon churches, I think of the saying of a Platonist, who saith, *Certe vitia irascibilis partis anima sunt gradu praviora quam concupiscibilis, tametsi occultiora* ["Certainly the vices of the irascible part of the soul are a degree worse than those of the concupiscible, though more hidden"], a matter that appeared well by the ancient contentions of bishops. God grant that we may contend with other churches, as the vine with the olive, which of us beareth best fruit; and not as the brier with the thistle, which of us is most unprofitable. And thus much touching the occasion of these controversies.

2. Now, briefly to set down the growth and progression of these controversies; whereby will be verified the wise counsel of Salomon, that the course of contentions is to be stopped at the first; being else "as the water," which if they gain a breach, it will hardly be ever recovered. It may be remembered, that on their part which call for reformation, was first propounded some dislike of certain ceremonies supposed to be superstitious; some complaint of dumb ministers who possessed rich benefices; and some invectives against the idle and monastical continuance within the universities, by those who had living to be resident upon; and such-like abuses. Thence they went on to condemn the government of bishops as an hierarchy remaining to us of the corruptions of the Roman Church, and to except to sundry institutions as not sufficiently delivered from the pollutions of the former times. And lastly, they are advanced to define of an only and perpetual form of policy in the Church; which (without consideration of possibility, or foresight of peril and perturbation of the church and state) must be erected and planted by the magistrate. Here they stay. Others (not able to keep footing in so steep a ground) descend further; That the same

must be entered into and accepted of the people, at their peril, without the attending of the establishment of authority: and so in the meantime they refuse to communicate with us, reputing us to have no church. This hath been the progression of that side: I mean of the generality. For I know, some persons (being of the nature, not only to love extremities, but also to fall to them without degrees) were at the highest strain at the first. The other part, which maintaineth the present government of the Church, hath not kept one tenor neither. First, those ceremonies which were pretended to be corrupt they maintained to be things indifferent, and opposed the examples of the good times of the Church to that challenge which was made unto them, because they were used in the later superstitious times. Then were they also content mildly to acknowledge many imperfections in the Church: as tares come up amongst the corn; which yet (according to the wisdom taught by our Saviour) were not with strife to be pulled up, lest it might spoil and supplant the good corn, but to grow on together until the harvest. After, they grew to a more absolute defence and maintenance of all the orders of the Church, and stiffly to hold that nothing was to be innovated; partly because it needed not, partly because it would make a breach upon the rest. Thence (exasperate through contentions) they are fallen to a direct condemnation of the contrary part, as of a sect. Yea, and some indiscreet persons have been bold in open preaching to use dishonourable and derogative speech and censure of the churches abroad; and that so far, as some of our men (as I have heard) ordained in foreign parts have been pronounced to be no lawful ministers. Thus we see the beginnings were modest, but the extremes are violent; so as there is almost as great a distance now of either side from itself, as was at the first of one from the other. And surely, though my meaning and scope be not (as I said before) to enter into the controversies themselves, yet I do admonish the maintainers of the alone discipline to weigh and consider seriously and attentively, how near they are unto those with whom I know they will not join. It is very hard to affirm that the discipline which they say we want is one of the essential parts of the worship of God, and not to affirm withal that the people themselves upon peril of salvation, without staying for the magistrate, are to to gather themselves into it. I demand, if a civil state should receive the preaching of the word and baptism, and interdict and exclude the sacrament of the supper, were not men bound upon danger of their souls to draw themselves to congregations, wherein they might celebrate that mystery, and not to content themselves with that part of the worship of God which the magistrate hath authorised? This I speak, not to draw them into the mislike of others, but into a more deep consideration of themselves: *Fortasse non redeunt, quia suum progression non intelligunt* ["Perhaps they do not return because they do not know how they got to where they are"]. Again, to my lords the bishops I say, that it is hard for them to avoid blame (in the opinion of an indifferent person) in standing so precisely upon altering nothing. *Leges, novis legibus non recreate, acescunt* (laws, not refreshed with new laws, wax sour). *Qui mala non permutat, in bonis non perseverat* (without change of the ill, a man cannot continue the good). To take away abuses supplanteth not good orders, but establisheth them. *Morosa moris retentio res turbulenta est, aeque ac novitas* (a contentious retaining of custom is a turbulent thing, as well as innovation). A good husbandman is ever proyning and stirring in his vineyard or field; not unseasonably, indeed, nor unskilfully. But lightly he findeth ever somewhat to do. We have heard of no offers of the bishops of bills in parliament; which (no doubt) proceeding from them to whom it properly pertaineth, would have everywhere received acceptation. Their own constitutions and orders have reformed little. Is nothing amiss? Can any man defend the use of excommunication as a base process to lackey up and down for duties and fees; it being the greatest judgment next the general judgment of the latter day? Is there no means to train up and nurse ministers (for the yield of the universities will not serve, though they were never so well governed)—to train them, I say, not to preach (for that every man confidently adventureth to do), but to preach soundly, and handle the Scriptures with wisdom and judgment? I know prophesying was subject to great abuse, and would be more abused now; because heat of contentions is increased. But I say the only reason of the abuse was, because there was admitted to it a popular auditory, and it was not contained within a private conference of ministers. Other things might be spoken of. I pray God to inspire the bishops with a fervent love and care of the people; and that they may not so much urge things in controversy as things out of controversy which all men confess to be gracious and good. And thus much for the second point.

3. Now, as to the third point, of unbrotherly proceedings on either part, it is directly contrary to my purpose to amplify wrongs: it is enough to note and number them; which I do also to move compassion and remorse on the offending side, and not to animate challenges and complaints on the other. And this point (as reason is) doth chiefly touch that side which can do most. *Injuria potentiorum sunt* (injuries come from them that have the upper hand).

The wrongs of them which are possessed of the government of the Church towards the other, may hardly be dissembled or excused. They have charged them as though "they denied tribute to Caesar," and withdrew from the civil magistrate their obedience which they have ever performed and taught. They have ever sorted and coupled them with the family of those whose heresies they have laboured to descry and confute. They have been swift of credit to receive accusations against them from those that have quarrelled with them but for speaking against sin and vice. Their examinations and inquisitions have been strait. Swearing men to blanks and generalities (not included within a compass of matter certain, which the party that is to take the oath may comprehend) is a thing captious and strainable. Their urging of subscription to their own articles is but *lacessere et irritare morbos ecclesiae*, which otherwise would spend and exercise themselves. *Non consensum quarit sed dissidium, qui quod factis prastatur in verbis exigit* (he seeketh not unity, but division, which exacteth in words that which men are content to yield in action). And it is true, there are some which (as I am persuaded) will not easily offend by inconformity, who notwithstanding make some conscience to subscribe. For they know this note of inconstancy and defection from that which they have long held shall disable them to do that good which otherwise they would do: for such is the weakness of many that their ministry should be thereby discredited. As for their easy silencing of them, in such great scarcity of preachers, it is to punish the people, and not them. Ought they not (I mean the bishops) to keep one eye open to look upon the good that these men do, but to fix them both upon the hurt that they suppose cometh by them? Indeed, such as are intemperate and incorrigible, God forbid they should be permitted to teach. But shall every inconsiderate word, sometimes captiously watched, and for the most part hardly enforced, be a forfeiture of their voice and gift of teaching? As for sundry particular molestations, I take no pleasure to recite them. If a minister shall be troubled for saying in baptism, "Do you believe?" for, "Dost thou believe?" If another shall be called in question for praying for her Majesty without the addition of her style; whereas the very form of prayer in the Book of Common Prayer hath "Thy servant Elizabeth," and no more: if a third shall be accused, upon these words uttered touching the controversies, *tollatur lex et fiat certamen* (whereby was meant that the prejudice of the law removed, either's reasons should be equally compared) of calling the people to sedition and mutiny, as if he had said, "Away with the law, and try it out by force:" if these and sundry other like particulars be true, which I have but by rumour, and cannot affirm; it is to be lamented that they should labour amongst us with so little comfort. I know "restrained governments are better than remiss;" and I am of his mind that said, "Better is it to live where nothing is lawful, than where all things are lawful." I dislike that laws be contemned, or disturbers be unpunished. But laws are likened to the grape, that being too much pressed yields an hard and unwholesome wine. Of these things I must say, *Ira viri non operatur justitiam Dei* (the wrath of man worketh not the righteousness of God).

As for the injuries of the other part, they be *ictus inermium;* as it were headless arrows; they are fiery and eager invectives, and in some fond men uncivil and unreverent behaviour towards their persons. This last invention also, which exposeth them to derision and obloquy by libels, chargeth not (as I am persuaded) the whole side: neither doth that other, which is yet more odious, practised by the worst sort of them, which is, to call in as it were to their aids certain mercenary bands, which impugn bishops and other ecclesiastical dignities, to have the spoil of their endowments and livings. Of this I cannot speak too hardly. It is an intelligence between incendiaries and robbers—the one to fire the house, the other to rifle it. And thus much touching the third point.

4. The fourth point wholly pertaineth to them which impugn the present ecclesiastical government; who, although they have not cut themselves off from the body and communion of the Church, yet do they affect certain cognizances and differences, wherein they seek to correspond amongst themselves, and to be separated from others. And it is truly said, *tam sunt mores quidam schismatici, quam dogmata schismatica* (there be as well schismatical fashions as opinions). First, they have impropered to themselves the names of zealous, sincere, and reformed; as if all others were cold, minglers of holy things and profane, and

friends of abuses. Yea, be a man endued with great virtues and fruitful in good works, yet if he concur not with them, they term him in derogation a civil and moral man, and compare him to Socrates or some heathen philosopher: whereas the wisdom of the Scriptures teacheth us contrariwise to judge and denominate men religious according to their works of the second table; because they of the first are often counterfeited and practised in hypocrisy. So St. John saith, that "a man doth vainly boast of loving God whom he hath not seen, if he love not his brother whom he hath seen." And St. James saith, "This is true religion, to visit the fatherless and the widow," &c. So as that which is with them but philosophical and moral, is, in the phrase of the Apostle, true religion and Christianity. As in affection they challenge the said virtues of zeal and the rest, so in knowledge they attribute unto themselves light and perfectior. They say, the Church of England in King Edward's time, and in the beginning of her Majesty's reign, was but in the cradle; and the bishops in those times did somewhat for daybreak, but that maturity and fulness of light proceeded from themselves. So Sabinus, Bishop of Heraclea, a Macedonian, said that the fathers in the Council of Nicea were but infants and ignorant men; and that the Church was not so to priest in their decrees as to refuse that further ripeness of knowledge which the time had revealed. And as they censure virtuous men by the names of civil and moral, so do they censure men truly and godly wise who seen into the vanity of their assertions by the name of politiques; saying that their wisdom is but carnal and savouring of man's brain. So likewise if a preacher preach with care and meditation (I speak not of the vain scholastical manner of preaching, but soundly indeed, ordering the matter he handleth distinctly for memory, deducing and drawing it down for direction, and authorising it with strong proofs and warrants), they censure it as a form of speaking not becoming the simplicity of the Gospel, and refer it to the reprehension of St. Paul, speaking of the enticing speech of man's wisdom.

Now for their own manner of teaching, what is it? Surely they exhort well, and work compunction of mind, and bring men well to the question, *Viri, fratres, quid agemus* ["Men, brothers, what shall we do?"]? But that is not enough, except they resolve that question. They handle matters of controversy weakly and *obiter*, and as before a people that will accept of anything. In doctrine of manners there is little but generality and repetition. The Word (the "bread of life") they toss up and down, they break it not. They draw not their directions down *ad casus conscientia* [to a case of conscience] that a man may be warranted in his particular actions whether they be lawful or not. Neither indeed are many of them able to do it, what through want of grounded knowledge, what through want of study and time. It is an easy and compendious thing to call for the observation of the Sabbath-day, or to speak against unlawful gain; but what actions and works may be done upon the Sabbath, and in what cases; and what courses of gain are lawful, and what not; to set this down, and to clear the whole matter with good distinctions and decisions, is a matter of great knowledge and labour, and asketh much mediation and conversation in the Scriptures, and other helps which God hath provided and preserved for instruction. Again, they carry not an equal hand in teaching the people their lawful liberty, as well as their restraints and prohibitions: but they think a man cannot go too far in that that hath a show of a commandment. They forget that there are "sins on the right hand, as well as on the left"; and that "the word is double-edged," and cutteth on both sides, as well the superstitious observances as the profane transgressions. Who doubteth but it is as unlawful to shut where God hath opened, as to open where God hath shut? To bind where God hath loosed, as to loose where God hath bound? Amongst men it is commonly as ill taken as to turn back favours as to disobey commandments. In this kind of zeal (for example) they have pronounced generally, and without difference, all untruths unlawful; notwithstanding that the midwives are directly reported to have been blessed for their excuse; and Rahab is said "by faith" to have concealed the spies; and Salomon's selected judgment proceeded upon a simulation; and our Saviour, the more to touch the hearts of the two disciples with a holy dalliance, made as if he would have passed Emmaus. Further, I have heard some sermons of mortification, which I think (with very good meaning) they have preached out of their own experience and exercise, and things in private counsels not unmeet; but surely no sound conceits; much like to Persons's "Resolution," or not so good; apt to breed in men rather weak opinions and perplexed despairs, than filial and true repentance which is sought. Another point of great inconvenience and peril, is to entitle the people to hear controversies and all points of doctrine. They say no part of the counsel of God must be suppressed, nor the people defrauded: so as the difference which the Apostle maketh between "milk and strong meat" is confounded: and his precept "that the weak be not admitted unto questions and controversies" taketh no place. But most of all is to be suspected, as a seed of further inconvenience, their manner of handling the Scriptures; for whilst they seek express Scripture for everything; and that they have (in manner) deprived themselves and the Church of a special help and support by embasing the authority of the fathers; they resort to naked examples, conceited inferences, and forced allusions, such as do mine into all certainty of Religion. Another extremity is the excessive magnifying of that which, though it be a principal and most holy institution, yet hath it limits as all things else have. We see wheresoever (in manner) they find in the Scriptures the Word spoken of, they expound it of preaching. They have made it almost the essence of the sacrament of the supper, to have a sermon precedent. They have (in sort) annihilated the use of liturgies, and forms of divine service, although the house of God be denominated of the principal, *domus orationis* (a house of prayer), and not a house of preaching. As for the life of the good monks and the hermits in the primitive Church, I know they will condemn a man as half a Papist, if he should maintain them as other than profane, because they heard no sermons. In the meantime, what preaching is, and who may be said to preach, they make no question. But as far as I see, every man that presumeth to speak in chair is accounted a preacher. But I am assured that not a few that call hotly for a preaching ministry deserve to be of the first themselves that should be expelled. These and some other errors and misproceedings they do fortify and entrench by being so greatly addicted to their opinions, and impatient to hear contradiction or argument. Yea, I know some of them that would think it a temptying of God to hear or read what might be said against them; as if there could be a *quod bonum est tenete* ["hold fast to what is good"], without an *omnia probate* ["test everything"] going before.

This may suffice to offer unto themselves a view and consideration, whether in these things they do well or no, and to correct and assuage the partiality of their followers and dependants. For as for any man that shall hereby enter into a contempt of their ministry, it is but his own hardness of heart. I know the work of exhortation doth chiefly rest upon these men, and they have zeal and hate of sin. But again, let them take heed that it be not true which one of their adversaries said, "that they have but two small wants, knowledge and love." And so I conclude this fourth point.

5. The last point, touching the due publishing and debating of these controversies, needeth no long speech. This strange abuse of antics and pasquils hath been touched before. So likewise I repeat that which I said before, that a character of love is more proper for debates of this nature than that of zeal. As for all indirect or direct glances or levels at men's persons, they were ever in these cases disallowed. Lastly, whatsoever be pretended, the people is no meet judge nor arbitrator, but rather the quiet, moderate, and private assemblies and conferences of the learned. *Qui apud incapacem loquitur, non disceptat, sed calumniatur.* ["He who speaks with the incapable resolves nothing, only worries."] The press and pulpit would be freed and discharged of these contentions. Neither promotion on the one side, nor glory and heat on the other, ought to continue those challenges and cartels at the Cross and other places. But rather all preachers, especially all such as be of good temper, and have wisdom with conscience, ought to inculcate and beat upon a peace, silence, and surseance. Neither let them fear Solon's law, which compelled in factions every particular person to range himself on the one side; nor yet the fond calumny of neutrality; but let them know that is true which is said by a wise man, that "neuters in contentions are either better or worse than either side."

These things have I in all sincerity and simplicity set down, touching the controversies which now trouble the Church of England; and that without all art and insinuation, and therefore not like to be grateful to either part. Notwithstanding, I trust what hath been said shall find a correspondence in their minds which are not embarked in partiality, and which love the whole better than a part. Whereby I am not out of hope that it may do good. At the least I shall not repent myself of the meditation.

That was written as An Advertisement touching the Controversies of the Church of England *by Francis Bacon then a lawyer aged 29, at the time that the Martin Marprelate pamphlet war "pistled the Bishops" and caught up the public in a violent quarrel in print between Puritans (one of whom was hanged and another left to die in prison when a hearing was denied him because his evidence was expected to be against the Establishment) and the clergy they attacked in unlicensed publications (one of those who answered vehemently was Thomas Cooper, Bishop of Winchester). It was a time when the Catholic poet and martyr Robert Southwell* (d. 1595) *and others were hanged or protestant heretics like Matthew Hawmont, Francis Ket, and others were burned at the stake for their beliefs. The partianship is seen even in Spenser's* The Faerie Queene, *a masterpiece of bigotry. It was more than half a century since Henry VIII had made himself ruler of the English Church and still the prayer that William Tyndale uttered as he was put to death had not been answered. "Lord," said Tyndale at the stake for burning in 1536, "open the King of England's eyes."*

Papists confront Protestants as God looks on (with some concern?) in this old print. Notic that the peasant with his flail and other common people are with the Protestants, on th right.

The works of Phillipus Aureolus Paracelsus (1493?-1541) were among many Continental influences on English thought in Elizabeth's time and *One Hundred and Fourteen Experiments and Cures* were published in English translation in 1596. He was "beyond Celsus" (the Greek Physician), interested in zinc (which he discovered), gnomes (which he named), the mines of the earth and the planets in the sky—everything, in Renaissance fashion—and very much respected and debated. Like many thinkers of his time, he combined both science and superstition.

Superstition

A Detection
of damnable driftes, practi-
zed by three VVitches arraigned at
Chelmisforde in Essex, at the
laste Assises there holden, whiche
were executed in Aprill.
1579.

Set forthe to discouer the Ambushementes of
Sathan, whereby he would surprise vs
lulled in securitie, and hardened
with contempte of Gods
vengeance threatened
for our offences.

Imprinted at London for Edward White,
at the little North-dore of Paules.

Probably the earliest English picture of a witch's familiar, the title page of the anonymous *A Detection of Damnable Drifts* (1579).

The Elizabethans were fascinated by all kinds of magic, black and white, and ready to believe that Vergil had been a magician, Mohammed a charlatan.

Their search for power encouraged some to attempt (in the words of Marlowe's magnificent Tragical History of Dr. Faustus, *based on the legends that had grown up around a real German student of the occult), "more than heavenly power permits."*

Here is what Sir Walter Ralegh in his unfinished History of the World *says about the black arts, arts in which he himself, and others who were said to be connected with a School of Night, the public suspected of dabbling.*

It is true that there are many arts, if we may so call them, which are covered with the name of magic, and esteemed abusively to be as branches of that tree on whose root they never grew. The first of these hath the name of necromancy or *goetia;* and of this again there are divers kinds. The one is an invocation at the graves of the dead, to whom the Devil himself gives answer instead of those that seem to appear. For certain it is, that the immortal souls of men do not inhabit the dust and dead bodies, but they give motion and understanding to the living; death being nothing else but a separation of the body and soul; and therefore the soul is not to be found in the graves.

A second practice of those men who pay tribute, or are in league with Satan, is that of conjuring or of raising up devils, of whom they hope to learn what they list. These men are distract, as they believe that by terrible words they make the Devil to tremble; that being once impaled in a circle (a circle which cannot keep out a mouse) they therein, as they suppose, ensconce themselves against the great monster. Doubtless they forget that the Devil is not terrified from doing ill, and all that is contrary to God and goodness; no, but by the fearful word of the Almighty; and that he feared not to offer to sit in God's seat; that he made no scruple to tempt our Saviour Christ, whom himself called the Son of God. So, forgetting these proud parts of his, an unworthy wretch will yet resolve himself, that he can draw the Devil out of hell, and terrify him with a phrase; whereas in very truth, the obedience which devils seem to use, is but thereby to possess themselves of the bodies and souls of those which raise them up; as his majesty [James I] in his book aforenamed hath excellently taught, That the Devils obedience is only *secundum quid, scilicet, ex pacto;* "respective, that is, upon bargain."

"Superstition," someone wrote, "is the religion of the ignorant." Bishop John Hall said it was

godlesse religion, devout impietie. The superstitious is fond [foolish] in observation, servile in feare.... This man dares not stirre forth till his breast be crossed, and his face sprinkled: if but an hare crosse him the way, he returnes; or if his journey began unawares on the dismall day; or if he stumble at the threshold. If he see a snake unkilled, he feares a mischiefe; if the salt fall towards him, he lookes pale and red, and is not quiet till one of the waiters have powred wine on his lappe; and when he sneezeth, thinks them not his friends that uncover not [do not take off their hats]. In the morning he listens whether the Crow crieth even or odd, and by that token pressages of the weather. If he heare but a Raven croke from the next roofe, he makes his will, or if a Bittour flie over his head by night: but if his troubled fancie shall second his thoughts with the dreame of a fairie garden, or greene rushes, or the salutation of a dead friend, he takes leave of the world, and sayes he cannot live. He will never set to sea but on a Sunday; neither ever goes without an Erra Pater [almanac with lucky days, &c., marked] in his pocket. Saint Paul's day and Saint Swithune's with the Twelve, are his Oracles; which he dares believe against the Almanacke.... Old wives and starres are his counsellors; his night-spell is his guard, and charmes his Physicians. He weares Paracelsian Characters for the toothach, and a little hallowed waxe is his Antidote for all evils.... Some wayes he will not goe, and some he dares not; either there are bugges [frightful creatures], or he faineth them; every lantern is a ghost, and every noise is of chaines. He knowes not why, but his custome is to goe a little about, and to leave the Crosse still on the right hand.

Reginald Scot on the old wives' tales that (as Sidney said) kept children from their play and old men from the chimney corner:

In our childhood [he writes in *The Discovery of Witchcraft*, 1595, and for once let us retain the charming Elizabethan spellings] our mothers maides have so terrified us with an oughlie [ugly] divell having hornes on his head, fier in his mouth, and a taile in his breech, eies like a bason, fanges like a dog, clawes like a beare, a skin like a Niger, and a voice roaring like a lion, whereby we start and are afraid when we heare one cry Bough ["Boo"]: and they have so fraied us with bull beggers, spirits, witches, urchens, elves, hags, fairies, satyrs, pans, faunes, sylens, kit with the cansticke, tritons, centaurs, dwarfes, giants, imps, calcars, conjurors, nymphes, changlings, Incubus, Robin goodfellowe, the spoorne, the mare, the man in the oke, the hellwaine, the fierdrake, the puckle, Tom Thombe, hob gobblin, Tom tumbler, boneles, and such other bugs, that we are afraid of our own shadows: in so much as some never feare the divell, but in a dark night; and then a polled sheepe is a perilous beast, and manie times is taken for our fathers soule, speciallie in a churchyard, where a right hardie man heretofore scant durst passe by night, but his haire would stand upright.

Anne Boleyn (famous in Music Hall as the ghost "with her head tucked underneath her arm") probably holds some sort of record, for she is said to haunt: Hampton Court Palace, Hever Castle, Blickling Hall, Salle Church, Rochford Hall, Bollin Hall, Marwell Hall, the undercroft of Lambeth Palace, and The Tower of London.

Another ghost still walking since Elizabethan times can have its story told here in summary rather than through quotation.

Wicked Will Darrell of Littlecote, a Tudor mansion west of Hungerford (Berkshire), indulged in incest with his sister and got her pregnant. When her time for delivery came, Will sent a couple of his servants to bring the midwife, Mother Barnes, to him secretly. They blindfolded her and brought her to the mansion from her own home in Great Shefford.

Mother Barnes found Wicked Will's sister in labor, delivered the baby, and wrapped the newborn boy in her apron to take him to his father. Wicked Will was standing by the fire when she met him in a room downstairs. He threw the infant into the fire and held it there with his boot until it perished.

The horrified Mother Barnes was kept under close guard until nightfall and then, once again blindfolded, taken back to her home. She took the precaution, however, of collecting evidence: she snipped a piece out of the bed curtains to prove she had been in the bedroom and counted the steps down to the room where she met Wicked Will to prove she had been there.

With this evidence she succeeded in bringing Wicked Will to trial before Sir John Popham (1531?-1607), but by the time the trial took place she was dead. Wicked Will went free. He died some time later in a riding accident, the locals saying that his horse had been startled by the appearance of the murdered infant on the road. People still point to Will's or Darrell's Stile as the place where Wicked Will saw the ghost and died.

In the bedroom at Littlecote the ghosts of the baby and its mother are still haunting, some believe, and Mother Barnes (with the infant in her apron) is claimed to have been seen on the stairs of the infamous house—a house, by the way, which was acquired in 1589 by Sir John Popham, none other than the judge who was forced to acquit Wicked Will for lack of Mother Barnes' testimony, after the sudden death of Wicked Will.

Sympathetic magic was at work in a number of Elizabethan recipes for food and medicine. Thomas Dawson in The Good Housewife's Jewel *(expanded 1596) has "a tart to provoke courage in either man or woman" that includes the "brains of three or four cock sparrows." Gervase Markham's* The English Housewife *(1615) starts the recipe for "a water for the stone" (by which he means gall stones) with "take a new milk of a red cow," the red being significant, just as is the warning in his recipe for gout medicine calling for "a pint or better of new milk of a cow which is all of one entire color" to be mixed with "as much of the urine of a man that is fasting" and other ingredients.*

Color is important in Markham's recipe for hepititis cure:

For the yellow jaundice, take two pennyworth of the best English saffron, dry it and grind it to an exceeding fine powder, then mix it with the pap of a roasted apple, and give it to the diseased party to swallow down in the manner of a pill; and this do divers mornings together, and without doubt it is the most present cure that can be for the same, as hath often times been proved.

Flowers and herbs were thought to bear "signatures" that told us of their medicinal uses: saxifrage's very name showed that it broke stones, so it would be good for kidney stones and gall stones. Heart-shaped leaves on digitalis signaled that it was a heart medicine. Euphrasy had a spot which looked like the pupil of an eye and so was eyebright and used in recipes such as this (from Markham) for "a precious water for the eyes":

Take of red rose leaves, of smallage, of maidenhair, euphrasy, endive, succory, red fennel, hillwort, and celandine, of each half a quarter of a pound, wash them clean and lay them in steep in white wine a whole day, then [di]still them in an ordinary still, and the first water will be like gold, the second like silver, and the third like balm; any of these is most precious for sore eyes, and hath recovered sight lost for the space of ten years, having been used but four days.

Radish or other plants hot to the taste were supposed to warm you up sexually, as were any resembling human genitals. Melted snow obviously produced water that was more cooling *than ordinary water and was to be used in treating burns, scalds, high temperatures, and "great heat and inflammation" (especially of the liver). The colors of flowers were important: red for the blood, for example.*

Literature offers precious little documentation of one very important aspect of popular culture in Elizabeth England, namely rural superstition. In every little hamlet people clung to old, irrational beliefs. The local wise woman dealt in amulets and talismans and curses as well as herbs and folk medicine and cures. Wandering vagabonds and gypsies arrived from time to time to read palms or otherwise tell fortunes, and those too poor to "cross their palms with silver" paid their penny or half-penny and believed. Something of what the confidence trickster could do with such a gullible public is suggested in this passage from Henry Chettle's Kind-Heart's Dream.

It happened within these few years about Hampshire, there wandered a walking Mort [beggar woman] that went about the country selling of tape; she had a good voice, and would sing sometime to serve the turn; she would often be a leech, another time a fortune-teller. In this last occupation we will now take her, for therefore was she taken, having first overtaken an honest simple farmer and his wife in this manner. On a summer's evening, by the edge of the forest, she chanced to meet the forenamed farmer's wife, to whom, when she had offered some of her tape, she began quickly with her to fall in talk, and at the first, staring her in the face, assures her she shall have such fortune as never had any of her kin, and if her husband were no more unlucky than she, they should be possessed of so infinite a sum of hidden treasure as no man in England had ever seen the like. The plain woman, tickled with her soothing, entreated her to go home, which she at first making somewhat strange, was at last content. There had she such cheer as farmers' houses afford, who fare not with the meanest. Shortly the good man comes in, to whom his wife relates her rare fortune and what a wise woman she had met with. Though the man were very simple, yet made he some question what learning she had, and how she came by knowledge of such things.

"O sir," said she, "my father was the cunningest juggler in all the country, my mother a gipsy; and I have more cunning than any of them both."

"Where lies the treasure thou talkest on?" said the farmer.

"Within this three miles," quoth she.

"I wonder thou thyself gettest it not," said the man, "but livest, as it seems, in so poor estate."

"My poverty", answered this cozener, "is my chiefest pride: for such as we cannot ourselves be rich, though we make others rich. Beside, hidden treasure is by spirits posssessed and they keep it only for them to whom it is destined. And more," said she, "if I have a several room to myself, hanged round about with white linen, with other instruments, I will by morning tell yet whether it be destined to you."

The goodman and wife giving credit to her words, fetched forth their finest sheets and garnished a chamber as she appointed; seven candles she must have lighted, and an angel she would have laid in every candlestick. Thus furnished, she locks herself into the room, and appoints them two only to watch, without making any of their servants privy. Where, using sundry mumbling fallacies, at last she called the man unto her, whom she saddled and bridled, and having seven times rid him about the room, caused him to arise and call his wife, for to her belonged the treasure. Both man and wife being come, in very sober manner she told them that they alone must attend in that place, whilst she forced the spirits to release the treasure and lay it in some convenient place for them to fetch, but in any wise they must not reveal about what she went, neither touch bread nor drink till her return. So, taking up the seven angels, away she went, laughing to herself how she had left them waiting.

All night sat the man and his wife attending her coming, but she was wise enough. Morning came, the servants mused what their master and dame meant, that were wont with the lark to be the earliest risers, yet sith they heard them talk, they attempted not to disturb them. Noon drawing on, the farmer feeling by the chimes in his belly 'twas time to dine, was by his wife counselled to stay till the wise woman's return; which he patiently intending, on a sudden the scent of the ploughswains' meat so pierced his sense, that had all India been the meed of his abstinence, eat he will, or die he must. His wife, more money wise, intended rather to starve than lose the treasure, till about evening one of their neighbours brought them news of a woman cozener that by a Justice was sent to Winchester for many lewd pranks. The man would needs see if it were the same, and coming thither, found it to be no other; where, thinking at least to have good words, she impudently derided him, especially before the Bench, who asked her what reason she had to bridle and saddle him. "Faith," said she, "only to see how like an ass he looked."

In Sussex on New Year's Eve the country people went out to wassail the apple trees. They sang:

Stand fast root, bear well top,
Pray that God send us a good howling crop,
Even twig, apples big,
Every bough, apples enow,
Hats full, caps full,
Full quarter sacks full.

In my books The Wonderful World of Superstition, Prophecy, and Luck *(1984) and* The Wonderful World of Magic and Witchcraft *(1986) I discuss many old English (as well as other) beliefs, some of which were very widely held in Elizabethan England. Elizabethans did not have Christmas trees; they had the ancient Scandinavian yule log, of which Robert Herrick wrote:*

Kindle the Christmas brand, and then
  Till sunset let it burn,
Which quenched, then lay it up again,
  Till Christmas next return.

Holly, ivy, and mistletoe from the ancient Druidic ceremonies of the winter solstice still played their part in Elizabethan Christmases, and the "first footing" ceremonies of New Year go back farther. Farmers even then believed that if the sun shines through an apple tree on Christmas day it will be heavy with fruit the next season. Also: light Christmas, light wheatsheaves to follow; dark Christmas, heavy wheatsheaves to follow. An overcast Christmas was believed to promise an abundant harvest.

Some old beliefs the British brought to America were altered. For instance, slaves here were permitted to feast as long as the yule log burned, so it was thoroughly soaked before being lighted and they tried to keep it smouldering for days. No "Till sunset let it burn" for them! We did not change the old beliefs for these holidays (among others):

Epiphany: *Make a cake containing a ring and a button. Whoever gets the ring will be married during the year; whoever gets the button will not.*

Shrove Tuesday: *Make pancakes for the family and throw one to the chickens. If the rooster eats most of it, expect bad luck; if the hens eat most of it, expect good luck.*

St. Swithin's Day: *If it rains on the feast (July 15) of this Bishop of Winchester* (d. *832) who requested that he be buried outside the church under "the sweet rain of heaven," it will rain for 40 days thereafter.*

All Hallows Eve: *Our Halloween, with bobbing for apples (once a way of finding out whom one would marry), jack-o'-lanterns (formerly skulls), goblins and ghosts.*

All Souls' Day: *At the beginning of November are the feast of all souls and the feast of all saints and at this time expect ghosts; for 24 hours the souls in Purgatory are given a holiday. People used to believe that if at midnight two people were to walk around a room in opposite directions in total darkness they would never meet, for one would be spirited away.*

Christmas Eve: *The animals remember the birth of Christ in the manger and kneel at the appropriate time to do Him honor.* Hamlet *has a reference to superstition about the rooster crowing all night long on Christmas Eve, Thomas Hardy a poem expressing his wish he could believe that the animals kneel....*

From Robert Herrick's Hesperides, *an old superstition:*

Let the superstitious wife
Near the child's heart lay a knife;
Point be up and haft be down,
(While she gossips in the town):
This, 'mongst other mystic Charms,
Keeps the sleeping Child from harms.

Robert Ashley (1565-1641) was a lawyer and miscellaneous writer, a linguist who knew a number of languages. Translating from the French of Louis LeRoy, in Of the Interchangeable Course or Variety of Things in the Whole World *(1594) he echoed the public fear that the Elizabethan period of expansion and prosperity was about to end soon. As it turned out, 1604 was indeed the year that James I came to London—he had been afraid to arrive for about a year after he gained the throne—and the beginning of a darker period, the Jacobean era so full of "dark November days, when Englishmen hang themselves."*

There are certain periods appointed for the world, which while they endure, all things do come to their vigour; and which being ended, they do all perish: but all of them end their course within the revolution of the Great Year. And...when the one cometh to end, and the other is ready to begin, there are many strange signs seen both in earth and in heaven. Wherefore many are of opinion that some great alteration doth approach, considering the signs which within these few years have appeared in heaven, in the stars, in the elements, and in all nature.... [Some authorities believe] that there have already been seven Great Years in the space of five thousand, five hundred and thirty years...and that the eighth shall be in the year of Christ 1604.

Edmund, in King Lear, *is an outsider in many ways, not least in his rejection of popular Elizabethan belief in astrology in which we "make guilty of our disasters the sun, the moon, and the stars: as if we were villains by necessity; fools by heavenly compulsion; knaves, thieves, and treachers by spherical predominance; drunkards, liars, and adulterers, by an enforced obedience of planetary influence. . . ."* Most Elizabethans put faith in astrology.

*John Maplet (*d. *1592) in* The Dial of Destiny *(1581) explains something that modern proponents of astrology almost never address: just how do the stars exercise their influence over us?*

In the head of man there are seven Pores or holes, allotted to diverse and sundry offices, as of the which every one of them is subject to a sundry Planet. As that Pore or hole which is the right Ear appurtaineth to Saturn; that in the left, to Jupiter. Mars also hath the government of that which is in the right side of the nose; Venus of the contrary [nostril]; Sol is master over that which holdeth the strings of the right Eye; Luna over the other in the left Eye; and all the whole workmanship is proper alone to Mercury.

For those of you who believe implicitly in astrology: you have holes in your heads!

The Folio of Michael Drayton's collected poems (1627) recalled the baleful influence of John Lyly's euphuism on the speech of the court and on fashionable writers, Shakespeare included, until he, too, mocked the flowery style of

Talking of Stones, Stars, Plants, of Fishes, Flies,
Playing with words and idle Similies,
As th' English, Apes and Zanies be
Of everything that they do hear and see
So imitating his ridiculous tricks
They spoke and wrote, all like mere lunatics.

Lord Burghley cast the horoscope of Queen Elizabeth for her but her semi-official consultant on the occult was Dr. John Dee, mathematician, astronomer and astrologer and alchemist, necromancer and spy. (He used the pseudonym "007," in fact!)

An alchemist, employed by the Queen (though the laws forbade alchemy) was committed to The Tower of London in January 1567, according to Cecil's diary, "for abusing the Queen's Majesty in Somerset House in promising to make the elixir." On February 10 of that year Cecil records that the alchemist "abused many in promising to convert any metal into gold" and on March 13 the alchemist wrote to Cecil saying, that if he were released from imprisonment and given financial support, he could make for Cecil an unlimited amount of gold and gems.

Ben Jonson, author of The Alchemist, *a riotous comedy about two confidence men (Subtle and Face), about how little alchemy brought its practitioners who prey on popular belief in alchemy and astrology, writes in an epigram:*

If all you boast of your great art be true,
Sure, willing poverty lives most in you.

However, the Queen deeply believed in the powers of that extraordinary Dr. John Dee (1527-1608). His magic glass (an Aztec mirror, now in The British Museum) fascinated her and his occult knowledge impressed her as it did it emperors and princes around Europe.

C.F. Smith's John Dee (1527-1608) *(1909) deserves a modern successor.*

*Few people understood the search for perfection represented by the Philosopher's Stone but many wanted to get rich by the transmutation of base metals into gold. The main result, says Thomas Nashe in his attack on Gabriel Harvey (*Have with you to Saffron Walden) *was to fire the imagination of the greedy and*

whether you call his fire Purgatory or no, the fire of Alchemy hath wrought such a purgation or purgatory in a great number of men's purses in England that it has cleaned fired them out of all they have.

An alchemist also is the baker who bakes bread, and the vintner who makes wine; what comes of nature that is of use to man, he who brings it to the end ordained by nature, he is the alchemist.

—Philipp Theophrastus Bombastus von Hohenheim, alias Paracelsus (1493?-1541):

Philip Henslowe (d. *1617) was a hard-headed man who settled in Southwark in 1577, made money as a dyer, lent it at interest, got rich, managed theatres, married his daughter to the leading actor Edward Alleyn, and so on. What a diary he could have kept with all the playwrights and actors he employed! What diary he did keep (preserved in son-in-law Alleyn's foundation, The College of God's Gift at Dulwich) is mostly an account book, a usurer's notes, a businessman's books, but in it we also find this, which also he found practical. In exactly his own words:*

To know where a thinge is that is stolen.

Take vergine waxe and write upon yt "Jasper + Melchisor + Balthasar +," and put yt under his head to whome the good partayneth, and he shall knowe in his sleape wher the thinge is become.

Sir John Harington describes his first interview with James I and how it got around to the subject of witchcraft, which James had long been interested in in Scotland. Witches had convinced King James of their power by telling him "the very words which had passed between him and his Queen at Upsala in Norway the first night of their marriage." (The secret was probably the fact that James was gay.) What James did want to talk about with Harington was this:

His Majesty did much press for my opinion touching the power of Satan in matter of witchcraft; and asked me, with much gravity, if I did truly understand why the Devil did work more with ancient women than others? . . . His Highness told me [the Queen his mother's death] was visible in Scotland before it did really happen, being, as he said, spoken of in secret by those whose power of sight presented to them a bloody head dancing in the air. He then did remark much on this gift and said, he had sought out of certain books a sure way to attain knowledge of future chances.

Coral, Shakespeare alleges The Tempest, *is made of drowned men's bones. George Sandys (1578-1644) reported in his translation of Ovid's* Metamorphoses *(1632) the old belief that "coral sympathizes with the wearer, and waxeth pale with his sickness." It was given to babies to teeth on and worn as an amulet. In Sandys' report on his travels to Italy, Turkey, Egypt, and Palestine, we find coral described as*

a soft shrub, green when under the water, and bearing a white berry:
Hardness assuming from touched air alone,
Under the sea a twig, above a stone.
And changeth unto red [when taken out of water].

Gerard(e)'s famous Herbal *(1597) is full of superstitions and folklore about such plants as the mandrake. He says it tends to grow chiefly under gibbets and that some "simple and unlearned" people believe that one will go crazy if one hears its human-like scream as it is pulled out of the earth. For that reason, Elizabethans used to pull up mandrakes by tying its leaves to a dog's tail and then running out of hearing.*

Moonrakers of the West Country were supposed to be able to rake the image of the moon out of standing water and thus to produce the dark night needed for smuggling and other nefarious deeds.

Probably the most powerful belief of Elizabethan England that we would reject today has to do with the four elements, the four humours (liquids) associated with them, and the psychology that arose from a system derived from these. So we end this section with a bit of the psychological rather than the religious. New ways of looking at the personality of man created new ways of looking at his relationship of God, and led to many superstitions, too.

As the ancient believed with Galen that everything was made of Four Elements (Fire, Water, Earth, Air), so the Elizabethan psychology was based on Four Humours (Yellow Bile, Blood, the products of the spleen, the products of the liver) creating four temperaments (Choleric, Phelgmatic, Melancholy, Sanguine) related to four planets (Mars, Moon, Saturn, Jupiter) and the Zodiac (Aries, Leo, Sagittarius; Taurus, Virgo, Capricorn; Cancer, Scorpio, Pisces; Gemini, Libra, Aquarius), four seasons (summer, autumn, winter, spring), four winds (west, east, north, south), gems, plants, etc., etc. The earth had four ages (Gold, Silver, Bronze, Iron). Marlowe wrote of

Nature that framed us of four elements
Striving within our breasts for regiment.

These are the four personalities in Renaissance terms:

Choleric Man hath nature of Fire, hot and dry, naturally is lean and slender, covetous, ireful, hasty, brainless, foolish, malicious. He hath wine of the Lion: he chideth, fighteth and commonly he loveth to be clad in black.

Sanguine Man hath nature of Air. Hot and moist. He is large, plenteous, attempered, amiable, abundant in nature, merry, singing, laughing, liking, ruddy and gracious. He hath his wine of the Ape: more he drinketh the merrier he is and draweth to women, and naturally loveth high coloured cloth.

Phlegmatic Man hath nature of Water, cold and moist. He is heavy, slow, sleepy, ingenious, commonly he spitteth when he is moved, and hath his wine of the Sheep, for when he is drunken he accounteth himself wisest, and loveth most green colour.

Melancholic Man hath nature of Earth, cold and dry. He is heavy, covetous, backbiter, malicious and slow. His wine is of the Hog, for when he is drunken he desireth sleep. And he loveth black colour.

Education

In the sixteenth-century hierarchy shown here from the *Liber de Sapiente* of Bovillus, minerals exist, plants exist and grow, animals exist and grow and feel, and man adds to all this the ability to think. Of men, the scholar is ranked highest. He has the "discourse of reason" in the highest degree.

Sir Thomas Elyot (1499?-1546)'s Book of The Governor *remained influential throughout Elizabeth's reign. What he said about children includes (in the English of his first edition, 1531):*

By a cruell and irous maister the wittes of children be dulled; and that thinge for the whiche children, be often tymes beaten is to them ever after fastidious; whereof we nede no better autor for witnes than daily experience.

The seconde occasion wherefor gentylmens children seldome have sufficient lernynge is avarice; for where theyr parentes wyll nat adventure to send them farre out of theyr propre countrayes, partely for feare of dethe, whiche perchance dare nat approche them at home with theyre father; partely for expence of money, whiche they suppose wolde be lesse in theyre owne houses, or in a village with some of theyr tenantes or frendes; havyng seldome any regarde to the teacher, whether he be well lerned or ignorant. For if they hiare a schole maister to teche in theyr house, they chiefely enquire with howe small a salary he will be contented, and never do inserche howe moche good lernynge he hath, and howe amonge well lerned men he is therin estemed, usinge therin lasse diligence than in takynge servantes, whose service is of moche lasse importance, and to a good schole maister is nat in profite to be compared. A gentil man er he take a cooke in to his service, he wyll firste diligently examine hymn, howe many sortes of meates, potages, and sauces, he can perfectly make, and howe well he can season them, that they may be bothe pleasant and nourishynge; yea and if it be but a fauconer, he wyll scrupulously enquire what skyll he hath in feedyng, called diete, and kepyng of his hauke from all sickenes, also how he can reclaime her and prepare her to flyght. And to suche a cooke or fauconer, whom he findeth expert, he spareth nat to gyve moche wages with other bounteous rewardes. But of a schole maister, to whom he will committe his childe, to be fedde with lernynge and instructed in vertue, whose lyfe shall be the principall monument of his name and honour, he never maketh further enquirie but where he may have a schole maister, and with howe litel charge; and if one be perchance founden, well lerned, but he will nat take paynes to teache without he may have a great salary, he than speketh nothing more, or els saith, What? shall so moche wages he gyven to a schole maister whiche wolde kepe me two servantes? To whom maye be saide these wordes, that by his sonne being wel lerned he shall receive more commoditie and also worship than by the service of a hundred cokes and fauconers [who are traditionally paid more than a tutor].

Lord God! howe many good and clene wittes of children be nowe a dayes perisshed by ignorant scholemaisters! Howe litle substantial doctrine is apprehended, by the fewenesse of good gramariens!... I call nat them gramariens, whiche onely can teache or make rules, whereby a childe shall onely lerne to speake congrue latine, or to make sixe versis standyng in one fote, wherein perchance shal be neither sentence nor eloquence.... Undoubtedly ther be in this realme many well lerned, whiche (if the name of a schole maister were nat so moche had in contempte, and also if theyr labours with abundant salaries mought be requited), were righte suffycient and able to induce their herers to excellent lernynge, so they be nat plucked away grene, and er they begin doctrine sufficiently rooted. But nowe a dayes, if to a bachelar or maister of arte studie of philosophie waxeth tedious, if he have a spone full of latine, he wyll shewe forth a hoggesheed without any lernyng, and offre to teache grammer and expoune noble writers, and to be in the roome of a maister: he wyll, for a small salrie, sette a false colour of lernyng on propre wittes, whiche wyll be wasshed away with one shoure of raine. For if the children be absent from schole by the space of one moneth, the best lerned of them will uneth [scarcely] tell wheder *Fato*, wherby Eneas was brought in to Itali, were other [either] a man, a horse, a shyppe, or a wylde goose. Al though their maister wyll perchance avaunte hymn selfe to be a good philosopher.

The Elizabethan schoolboy was still set to study the trivium *of medieval scholars, here described by Thomas Wilson (*c. *1525-1581) in his* The Rule of Reason *(1551), a book on rhetoric which, like his* The Art of Rhetoric *(first published 1553), was influential all through Elizabeth's reign:*

GRAMMAR doth teach to utter words,
To speak both apt and plain.
LOGIC by art sets forth the truth
And tells us what is vain.
RHETORIC at large paints well the cause,
And makes that seem right gay
Which LOGIC spake but as a word
And taught as by the way.

To this was added the quadrivium *at university:*

MUSIC with tunes delights the ear
And makes us think of Heaven.
ARITHMETIC by number can make
Reckonings to be even.
GEOMETRY things thick and broad
Measures by line and square.
ASTRONOMY by stars doth tell
Of foul and eke of fair.

Elizabethans treated children the same way they portrayed them in pictures: as little adults. They did this all through the 16th century and beyond. Here (translated) is what an Italian visitor to England wrote home in 1500:

The want of affection in the English is strongly manifested toward their children; for after having kept them at home till they arrive at the age of 7 or 9 years at the utmost, they put them out, both males and females, to hard service in the houses of other people, binding them generally for another 7 to 9 years. And these are called apprentices, and during that time they perform all the most menial offices; and few are born who are exempted from this fate, for every one, however rich he may be, sends away his children into the houses of others, whilst he, in return, receives those of strangers into his own. And on being asked their reason for this severity, they answered that they did it in order that their children might learn better manners. But I, for my part, believe that they do it because they like to enjoy all their comforts themselves, and that they are better served by strangers than they would be by their own children. Besides which the English being great epicures, and very avaricious by nature, indulge in the most delicate food themselves and give their household the coarsest bread, and beer, and cold meat baked on Sunday for the week, which, however, they allow them in great abundance. That if they had their own children at home, they would be obliged to give them the same food they made use of for themselves. That if the English sent their children away from home to learn virtue and good manners, and took them back again when their apprenticeship was over, they might, perhaps, be excused; but they never return, for the girls are settled by their patrons, and the boys make the best marriages they can, and, assisted by their patrons, not by their fathers, they also open a house and strive diligently by this means to make some fortune for themselves, whence it proceeds that, having no hope of their paternal inheritance, they all become so greedy of gain that they feel no shame in asking, almost "for the love of God," for the smallest sums of money; and to this it may be attributed, that there is no injury that can be committed against the lower orders of the English that may not be atoned for by money.

(That Italian Relation of England *lies outside the time-frame of this book, but I should like to recommend scholars study the 1847 edition of it from The Camden Society).*

Elizabeth's father had enriched both universities (as well as many noblemen) by the Dissolution of the Monasteries, but that led to the decay of the colleges. Thomas Le(a)ver (1521-1577) fled England during Mary's reign and returned on Elizabeth's succession to be in time Canon of Durham and hold other offices. This is what he preached before Elizabeth's young brother, Edward VI, in 1550, a sermon—let us keep the strange spelling of that early time—that hints at how bad a higher educational system Elizabethan England started with.

If ye hadde anye eyes ye shoulde se and be ashamed that in the great aboundance of landes and goods taken from Abbeis, Colleges and Chauntryes for to serve the kynge in all necessaryes, and charges (especially in provision of relyefe for the pore, and for mayntenaunce of learnynge), the kynge is so dysapoynted that bothe the pore be spoyled, all mayntenance of learnyng decayed, and you only enryched. But, for because ye have no eyes to se wyth, I wyll declare that you may heare wyth youre eares, and so perceyve and knowe, that w[h]ere as God and the kynge hathe bene moste liberall to gyve and bestowe, there you have been moste unfayethfull to dyspose and delyver. For accordying unto gods word and the k[y]nges pleasure, the universities, which be the scholes of all godlynes and vertue, should have bene nothyng decayed, but much increased and amended by thys [the] reformacion of religion....

For before that you did beginne to be the disposers of the kinges liberalitye towardes learnyng and poverty, there was in houses belongynge unto the unyversyte of Cambryge, two hundred studentes of dyvynytye, manye verye learned, whyche been nowe all clene gone, house and manne, young towarde scholers, and old fatherlye Doctors, not one of them lefte: one hundred also of an other sorte, that havyng rych frendes or beyng benefyced men dyd lyve of theym selves in Ostles and Innes, be eyther gon awaye or elles fayne to crepe into Colleges and put poore men from bare lyvynges. Those bothe be all gone, and a small number of poore godly dylygent studentes now remaynynge only in Colleges be not able to tary and contynue theyr studye in the universitye, for lacke of exibicion [scholarships] and healpe. There be dyvers ther whych ryse dayly betwixte foure and fyve of the clocke in the mornynge; and, from fyve untyll syxe of the clocke, use common prayer wyth an exhortacion of gods worde in a commune chappell; and from sixe unto ten of the clocke use ever eyther pryvate study or commune lectures. At ten of the clocke they go to dynner, whereas they be contente wyth a penye pyece of byefe amonsgest iiij, havyng a fewe porage made of the brothe of the same byefe wyth salte and otemell, and nothynge els. After thys slender dinner they be either teachynge or learnynge untyll v. of the clocke in the evenyng, when as they have a supper not much better then theyr dyner. Immedyatelye after the whyche, they go eyther to reasonyng in problemes or unto some other studye, untyll it be nyne or tenne of the clocke; and there, beyng wythout fyre, are fayne to walk or runne up and downe halfe an houre to gette a heate on their feete whan they go to bed.

William Turner (d. 1568), whose published works made him "The Father of English Botany," complained that at Cambridge no one else knew anything of the subject:

Being yet a student of Pembroke Hall, whereas I could learn never one, Greek, neither Latin nor English name, even amongst the physicians of any herbs or tree: such was the ignorance at that time.

In his books he recorded much that he had learned from the common people whose knowledge of plants often made the difference between wealth and starvation for them. Turner's New Herbal *was printed at Cologne in the year of his death with a dedication to Queen Elizabeth (whom he complimented on her Latin). Henry Lyte's* New Herbal *of ten years later was not original, being only a translation of the French version of the great Dutch herbal by Dodoens (1554). Lyte's book was printed in Antwerp. It was also dedicated to the Queen, but it was designed, he said, for the common man:*

that even the meanest of my Countrymen (whose skill is not so profound that they can fetch this knowledge out of strange tongues, nor their ability so wealthy, as to entertain a learned physician) may yet in time of their necessity have some helps in their own or their neighbours' fields and gardens at home.

The average man of Elizabethan England spakes through Nicholas Breton in The Courtier and the Countryman:

Now for learning, what your need is thereof I know not, but with us, this is all we go to school for: to read Common Prayers at church, and set down common prices at Markets; write a letter and make a Bond; set down the day of our Birth, our Marriage day, and make our Wills when we are sick for the disposing of our goods when we are dead; these are the chief matters that we meddle with.

Clark's Register of the University of Oxford *(1887) tells us of the comparatively small numbers who went on to higher education then. At Oxford between 1567 and 1622 (which takes us well beyond the reign of Elizabeth) there were*

Sons of Noblemen (Earls, Lords, Barons)	84
Sons of Knights	590
Sons of Esquires	902
Sons of Gentlemen	3615
Sons of plebians	6635
Sons of the clergy	985
Those whose status is not given	754

The medieval origins of the Elizabethan universities still were obvious, even to foreigners such as Paul Hentzner (who visited in 1598), not only in their older buildings, which dominated despite generous new Tudor foundations, but in the regulation of life and even of the academic gowns (which went all the way back to Arab gowns Roger Bacon had brought back to England after his studies in Toledo, where Moors, Jews, and Christians all met to exchange knowledge—and, some whispered, the secrets of the black arts).

The students lead a life almost monastic; for as the monks had nothing in the world to do but, when they had said their prayers at stated hours, to employ themselves in instructive studies, no more have these. They are divided into three tables. The first is called the fellows' table, to which are admitted earls, barons, gentlemen, doctors and masters of arts, but very few of the latter; this is more plentifully and expensively served than the other. The second is for masters of arts, bachelors, some gentlemen and eminent citizens. The third for people of low condition. While the rest are at dinner or supper in a great hall, where they are all assembled, one of the students reads aloud the Bible, which is placed on a desk in the middle of the hall, and this office everyone of them takes upon himself in his turn. As soon as grace is said after each meal, everyone is at liberty, either to retire to his own chambers, or to walk in the college garden, there being none that has not a delightful one. Their habit is almost the same as that of the Jesuits, their gowns reaching down to their ankles, sometimes lined with fur; they wear square caps; doctors, masters of arts and professors have another kind of gown that distinguishes them: every student of any considerable standing has a key to the college library, for no college is without one.

And, from a native, John Lyly of Euphues *fame:*

There are also in this Island two famous Universities, the one Oxford, the other Cambridge, both for the profession of all sciences, for Divinity, Physic, Law, and all kind of learning, excelling all the Universities in Christendom.

I was myself in either of them, and like them both so well that I mean not in the way of controversy to prefer any for the better in England, but both for the best in the world, saving this, that Colleges in Oxenford are much more stately for the building, and Cambridge much more sumptuous for the houses in the town; but the learning neither lieth in the free stones of the one, nor the fine streets of the other, for out of them both do daily proceed men of great wisdom to rule in the commonwealth, of learning to instruct the common people, of all singular kind of professions to do good at all. And let this suffice, not to inquire which of them is the superior, but that neither of them have their equal; neither to ask which of them is the most ancient, but whether any other be so famous.

The plain Yorkshireman Roger Ascham (1515-1568) had a very sensible plan for education in The Schoolmaster *(1570) and a strong, sensible prose style to go with it. Here he inveighs against Italy as "Circe's Court," which brutalizes Englishmen who visit it and fills their heads with foolish Italianate fads:*

But I am afraid that over-many of our travelers into Italy do not eschew the way to Circe's Court, but go, and ride, and run, and fly thither; they make great haste to come to her; they make great suit to serve her; yea, I could point out some with my finger, that never had gone out of England but only to serve Circe in Italy. Vanity and vice and any license to ill living in England was counted stale and rude unto them. And so, being mules and horses before they went, returned very swine and asses home again; yet everywhere very foxes with subtle and busy heads; and where they may, very wolves with cruel malicious hearts. A marvelous monster, which, for filthiness of loving, for dullness to learning himself, for wiliness in dealing with others, for malice in hurting without cause, should carry at once, in one body, the belly of a swine, the head of an ass, the brain of a fox, the womb of a wolf. If you think we judge amiss and write too sore against you, hear what the Italian saith of the Englishman, what the master reporteth of the scholar; who uttereth plainly what is taught by him, and what is learned by you, saying *"Inglese Italianato e un diabolo incarnato,"* that is to say, you remain men in shape and fashion, but become devils in life and condition.

This is not the opinion of one for some private spite, but the judgment of all in a common proverb, which riseth of that learning and those manners which you gather in Italy: a good schoolhouse of wholesome doctrine, and worthy masters of commendable scholars, where the master had rather defame himself for his teaching, than not shame his scholar for his learning. A good nature of the master, and fair conditions of the scholars. And now choose you, you Italian Englishmen, whether you will be angry with us for calling you monsters, or with the Italians for calling you devils, or else with your own selves that take so much pains and go so far to make yourselves both. If some yet do not well understand what is an Englishman Italianated, I will plainly tell him. He that by living and traveling in Italy bringeth home into England out of Italy the religion, the learning, the policy, the experience, the manners of Italy. That is to say, for religion, papistry, or worse; for learning, less, commonly, than they carried out with them; for policy, a factious heart, a discoursing head, a mind to meddle in all men's matters; for experience, plenty of new mischiefs never known in England before; for manners, variety of vanities, and change of filthy living.

These be the enchantments of Circe, brought out of Italy to mar men's manners in England; much by example of ill life, but more by precepts of fond books of late translated out of Italian into English, sold in every shop in London, commended by honest titles, the sooner to corrupt honest manners; dedicated over-boldly to virtuous and honorable personages, the easier to beguile simple and innocent wits. It is pity that those which have authority and charge to allow and disallow books to be printed, be no more circumspect herein than they are. Ten sermons at Paul's Cross do not so much good for moving men to true doctrine, as one of those books do harm with enticing men to ill living. Yea, I say farther, those books tend not so much to corrupt honest living, as they do to subvert true religion. More papists be made by your merry books of Italy than by your earnest books of Louvain. And because our great physicians do wink at the matter, and make no account of this sore, I, though not admitted one of their fellowship, yet having been many years a prentice to God's true religion, and trust to continue a poor journeyman therein all days of my life, for the duty I owe and love I bear both to true doctrine and honest living, though I have no authority to amend the sore myself, yet I will declare my good-will to discover the sore to others.

St. Paul saith that sects and ill opinions be the works of the flesh and fruits of sin. This is spoken no more truly for the doctrine than sensible for the reason. And why? For ill doings breed ill thinkings. And of corrupted manners spring perverted judgments. And how? There be in man two special things: man's will, man's mind. Where will inclineth to goodness, the mind is bent to truth. Where will is carried from goodness to vanity, the mind is soon drawn from truth to false opinion. And so the readiest way to entangle the mind with false doctrine is first to entice the will to wanton living. Therefore, when the busy and open papists abroad could not by their contentious books turn men in England fast enough from truth and right judgment in doctrine, then the subtle and secret papists at home procured bawdy books to be translated out of the Italian tongue, whereby over-many young wills and wits, allured to wantonness, do now boldly contemn all severe books that sound to honesty and godliness.

In our forefathers' time, when papistry, as a standing pool, covered and overflowed all England, few books were read in our tongue, saving certain books of chivalry, as they said, for pastime and pleasure, which, as some say, were made in monasteries by idle monks or wanton canons: as one, for example, *Morte Arthur,* the whole pleasure of which book standeth in two special points—in open manslaughter and bold bawdry. In which book those be counted the noblest knights that do kill most men without any quarrel, and commit foulest adulteries by subtlest shifts: as Sir Launcelot with the wife of King Arthur, his master; Sir Tristram with the wife of King Mark, his uncle; Sir Lamerock with the wife of King Lot, that was his own aunt. This is good stuff for wise men to laugh at, or honest men to take pleasure at! Yet I know when God's Bible was banished the court, and *Morte Arthur* received into the prince's chamber. What toys the daily reading of such a book may work in the will of a young gentleman or a young maid that liveth wealthily and idly, wise men can judge and honest men do pity. And yet ten *Morte Arthurs* do not the tenth part so much harm as one of these books made in Italy and translated in England. They open not fond and common ways to vice, but such subtle, cunning, new, and diverse shifts to carry young wills to vanity and young wits to mischief, to teach old bawds new schoolpoints, as the simple head of an Englishman is not able to invent, nor never was heard of in England before, yea, when papistry overflowed all. Suffer these books to be read, and they shall soon displace all books of godly learning. For they, carrying the will to vanity and marring good manners, shall easily corrupt the mind with ill opinions and false judgment in doctrine; first, to think ill of all true religion, and at last to think nothing of God himself—one special point that is to be learned in Italy and Italian books. And that which is most to be lamented, and therefore more needful to be looked to, there be more of these ungracious books set out in print within these few months than have been seen in England many score years before. And because our Englishmen made Italians cannot hurt but certain persons and in certain places, therefore these Italian books are made English to bring mischief enough openly and boldly to all states, great and mean, young and old, everywhere.

And thus you see how will enticed to wantonness doth easily allure the mind to false opinions; and how corrupt manners in living breed false judgment in doctrine; how sin and fleshliness bring forth sects and heresies. And, therefore, suffer not vain books to breed vanity in men's wills, if you would have God's truth take root in men's minds.

That Italian that first invented the Italian proverb against our Englishmen Italianated, meant no more their vanity in living than their lewd opinion in religion. For in calling them devils, he carrieth them clean from God; and yet he carrieth them no farther than they willingly go themselves, that is, where they may freely say their minds, to the open contempt of God and all godliness, both in living and doctrine.

And how? I will express how, not by a fable of Homer, nor by the philosophy of Plato, but by a plain truth of God's Word, sensibly uttered by David [in the Pslams] thus: "These men, *abominabiles facti in studiis suis,* think verily and sing gladly the verse before, *Dixit insipiens in corde suo, non est Deus,"* that is to say, they giving themselves up to vanity, shaking off the motions of grace, driving from them the fear of God, and running headlong into all sin, first lustily contemn God, then scornfully mock his Word, and also spitefully hate and hurt all well-willers thereof. Then they have in more reverence the *Triumphs* of Petrarch than the *Genesis* of Moses. They make more account of Tully's *Offices* than St. Paul's *Epistles;* of a tale in Boccaccio than a story of the Bible. Then they count as fables the holy mysteries of Christian religion. They make Christ and his Gospel only serve civil policy. Then neither religion cometh amiss to them. In time they be promoters of both openly; in place, again, mockers of both privily, as I wrote once in a rude of rime:

> Now new, now old, now both, now neither,
> To serve the world's course, they care not with whether.

For where they dare, in company where they like, they boldly laugh to scorn both protestant and papist. They care for no Scripture; they make no account of general councils; they contemn the consent of the church; they pass for no doctors; they mock the Pope; they rail on Luther; they allow neither side; they like none, but only themselves. The mark they shoot at, the end they look for, the heaven they desire, is only their own present pleasure and private profit; whereby they plainly declare of whose school, of what religion they be, that is, epicures in living and aoeoi [atheists] in doctrine. This last word is no more unknown now to plain Englishmen than the person was unknown some time in England, until some Englishman took pains to fetch that devilish opinion out of Italy. These men thus Italianated abroad cannot abide our godly Italian church at home; they be not of that parish; they be not of that fellowship; they like not that preacher; they hear not his sermons, except sometimes for company they come thither to hear the Italian tongue naturally spoken, not to hear God's doctrine truly preached.

And yet these men in matters of divinity openly pretend a great knowledge, and I have privately to themselves a very compendious understanding of all, which, nevertheless, they will utter when and where they list. And that is this: all the mysteries of Moses, the whole law and ceremonies, the Psalms and prophets, Christ and his Gospel, God and the devil, heaven and hell, faith, conscience, sin, death, and all they shortly wrap up, they quickly expound with this one half verse of Horace: *Credat Judaeus Apella.* [Let the Jew Apella believe it.]

Yet though in Italy they may freely be of no religion, as they are in England in very deed too, nevertheless, returning home in to England, they must countenance the profession of the one or the other, however inwardly they laugh to scorn both. And though for their private matters they can follow, fawn, and flatter noble personages contrary to them in all respects, yet commonly they ally themselves with the worst papists, to whom they be wedded, and do well agree together in three proper opinions: in open contempt of God's Word; in a secret security of sin; and in a bloody desire to have all taken away by sword or burning that be not of their faction. They that do read with an indifferent judgment Pighius and Machiavelli, two indifferent patriarchs of these two religions, do know full well what I say true.

Ye see what manners and doctrine our Englishmen fetch out of Italy. For, finding no other there, they can bring no other hither. And, therefore, many godly and excellent learned Englishmen, not many years ago, did make a better choice, when open cruelty drove them out of this country, to place themselves there where Christ's doctrine, the fear of God, punishment of sin, and discipline of honesty were had in special regard.

I was once in Italy myself; but I thank God my abode there was but nine days. And yet I saw in that little time, in one city, more liberty to sin than ever I heard tell of in our noble city of London in nine years. I saw it was there as free to sin not only without all punishment, but also without any man's marking, as it is free in the city of London to choose without all blame whether a man lust to wear shoe or pantocle. And good cause why; for, being unlike in truth of religion, they must needs be unlike in honesty of living. For blessed be Christ, in our city of London commonly the commandments of God be more diligently taught, and the service of God more reverently used, and that daily in many private men's houses, than they be in Italy once a week in their common churches; where making ceremonies to delight the eye, and vain sounds to please the ear, do quite thrust out of the churches all service of God in spirit and truth. Yea, the Lord Mayor of London, being but a civil officer, is commonly, for his time, more diligent in punishing sin, the bent enemy against God and good order, than all the bloody inquisitors in Italy be in seven years. For their care and charge is not to punish sin, not to amend manners, not to purge doctrine, but only to watch and oversee that Christ's true religion set no sure footing where the Pope hath any jurisdiction.

I learned, when I was at Venice, that there it is counted good policy, when there be four or five brethren of one family, one only to marry, and all the rest to welter with as little shame in open lechery as swine do here in the common mire. Yea, there be as fair houses of religion, as great provision, as diligent officers to keep up this misorder, as Bridewell is and all the masters there to keep down misorder. And, therefore, if the Pope himself do not only grant pardons to further these wicked purposes abroad in Italy, but also (although this present Pope [Pius V, 1566-1572] in the beginning made some show of misliking thereof) assign both meed and merit to the maintenance of stews and brothel-houses at home in Rome, then let wise men think Italy a safe place for wholesome doctrine and godly manners, and a fit school for young gentlemen of England to be brought up in.

Our Italians bring home with them other faults from Italy, though not so great as this of religion, yet a great deal greater than many good men can well bear. For commonly they come home common contemners of marriage and ready persuaders of all others to the same; not because they love virginity, nor yet because they hate pretty young virgins, but, being free in Italy to go whithersoever lust will carry them, they do not like that law and honesty should be such a bar to their like liberty at home in England. And yet they be the greatest makers of love, the daily dalliers, with such pleasant words, with such smiling and secret countenances, with such signs, tokens, wagers, purposed to be lost before they were purposed to be made, with bargains of wearing colors, flowers, and herbs, to breed occasion of often meeting of him and her, and bolder talking of this and that, etc. And although I have seen some innocent of all ill and staid in all honesty, that have used these things without all harm, without all suspicion of harm, yet these [knick] knacks were brought first into England by them that learned them before in Italy in Circe's Court; and how courtly courtesies soever they be counted now, yet, if the meaning and manners of some that do use them were somewhat amended, it were no great hurt neither to themselves nor to others.

Another property of these our English Italians is to be marvelous singular in all their matters; singular in knowledge, ignorant of nothing; so singular in wisdom (in their own opinion) as scarce they count the best counselor the prince hath comparable with them; common discoursers of all matters; busy searchers of most secret affairs; open flatterers of great men; privy mislikers of good men; fair speakers, with smiling countenances and much courtesy openly to all men; ready backbiters, sore nippers, and spiteful reporters privily of good men. And being brought up in Italy in some free city, as all cities be there, where a man may freely discourse against what he will, against whom he lust, against any prince, against any government, yea, against God himself and his whole religion; where he must be either Guelph or Ghibelline, either French or Spanish, and always compelled to be of some party, of some faction, he shall never be compelled to be of any religion; and if he meddle not over much with Christ's true religion, he shall have free liberty to embrace all religions, and become, if he lust, at once, without any let or punishment, Jewish, Turkish, papish, and devilish.

A young gentleman thus bred up in this goodly school, to learn the next and ready way to sin, to have a busy head, a factious heart, a talkative tongue, fed with discoursing of factions, led to contemn God and his religion, shall come home into England but very ill taught, either to be an honest man himself, a quiet subject to his prince, or willing to serve God under the obedience of true doctrine, or within the order of honest living.

I know none will be offended with this my general writing, but only such as find themselves guilty privately therein; who shall have good leave to be offended with me, until they begin to amend themselves. I touch not them that be good; and I say too little of them that be not; and so, though not enough for their deserving, yet sufficiently for this time, and more else when if occasion so require.

* * *

Learning teacheth more in one year, than experience in twenty; and learning teacheth safely, when experience maketh more miserable than wise. He hazardeth sore, that waxeth wise by experience. An unhappy master is he, that is made cunning by many shipwrecks; a miserable merchant, that is neither rich nor wise, but after some bankrupts. It is costly wisdom that is bought by experience. We know by experience itself, that it is a marvelous pain, to find out but a short way by long wandering. And surely, he that would prove wise by experience, he may be witty indeed, but even like a swift runner, that runneth fast out of the way, and upon the night, he knoweth not wither. And verily they be fewest in number, that be happy or wise by unlearned experience. And look well upon the former life of those few, whether your example be old or young, who without learning have gathered by long experience a little wisdom, and some happiness; and when you do consider, what mischief they have committed, what dangers they have escaped (and yet twenty for one do perish in the adventure), then think well with yourself, whether ye would, that your own son should come to wisdom and happiness by the way of such experience, or no.

* * *

Erasmus, the honor of learning of all our time, said wisely, "That experience is the common schoolhouse of fools, and ill men. Men of wit, and honesty be otherwise instructed. For there be, that keep them out of fire, and yet was never burned; that beware of water, and yet was never nigh drowning; that hate harlots, and was never at the stews; that abhor falsehood, and never brake promise themselves."

But will ye see a fit stimilitude of this adventured experience. A father that doth let loose his son to all experiences, is most like a fond hunter, that letteth slip a whelp to the whole herd; twenty to one, he shall fall upon a rascal, and let go the fair game. Men that hunt so be either ignorant persons, privy stealers, or night-walkers.

Learning therefore, ye wise fathers, and good bringing up, and not blind and dangerous experience, is the next and readiest way that must lead your children, first to wisdom, and then to worthiness, if ever ye purpose they shall come there.

And to say all in short, though I lack authority to give counsel, yet I lack not good will to wish that the youth in England, specially gentlemen, and namely nobility, should be by good bringing up so grounded in judgment of learning, so founded in love of honesty, as when they should be called forth to the execution of great affairs, in service of their Prince and country, they might be able to use, and to order all experiences, were they good, were they bad, and that according to the square, rule, and line, of wisdom, learning, and virtue.

And I do not mean by all this my talk that young gentlemen should always be poring on a book, and by using good studies, should lose honest pleasure, and haunt no good pastime; I mean nothing less. For it is well known that I both like and love, and have always, and do yet still use all exercises and pastimes, that befit for my nature and ability. And beside natural disposition, in judgment also I was never, either stoic in doctrine, or Anabaptist in religion to mislike a merry, pleasant, and playful nature, if no outrage be committed against law, measure, and good order.

Therefore I would wish, that beside some good time fitly appointed, and constantly kept, to increase by reading the knowledge of the tongues, and learning; young gentlemen should use, and delight in all courtly exercises, and gentlemanlike pastimes. And good cause why: For the self same noble city of Athens, justly commended of me before, did wisedly, and upon great consideration, appoint the Muses, Apollo, and Pallas, to be patrons of learning to their youth. For the Muses, besides learning, were also ladies of dancing, mirth, and minstrelsy: Apollo was god of shooting, and author of cunning playing upon instruments; Pallas also was lady mistress in wars. Whereby was nothing else meant, but that learning should be always mingled with honest mirth, and comely exercises; and that war also should be governed by learning, and moderated by wisdom; as did well appear in those captains of Athens named by me before, and also in Scipio and Caesar, the two diamonds of Rome. And Pallas was no more feared in wearing Aegida [breastplate] than she was praised for choosing Olivam [the olive branch of peace]; whereby shineth the glory of learning, which thus was governor and mistress in the noble city of Athens, both of war and peace.

Therefore to ride comely, to run fair at the tilt, or ring; to play at all weapons, to shoot fair in bow, or surely in gun; to vault lustily, to run, to leap, to wrestle, to swim; to dance comely, to sing, and to play on instruments cunningly; to hawk, to hunt; to play at tennis, and all pastimes generally, which be joined with labor, used in open place, and on the daylight, containing either some fit exercise for war, or some pleasant pastime for peace, be not only comely and decent, but also very necessary for a courtly gentleman to use.

* * *

Present examples of this present time I list not to touch; yet there is one example for all the gentlemen of this court to follow, that may well satisfy them, or nothing will serve them, nor no example move them to goodness and learning.

It is your shame (I speak to you all, you young gentlemen of England) that one maid [the Queen] should go beyond you all in excellency of learning, and knowledge of divers tongues. Point forth six of the best given gentlemen of this court, and all they together show not so much good will, spend not so much time, bestow not so many hours daily, orderly, and constantly, for the increase of learning and knowledge, as doth the Queen's Majesty herself. Yea I believe, that beside her perfect readiness in Latin, Italian, French and Spanish, she readeth here now at Windsor more Greek every day, than some prebendary of this Church doth read Latin in a whole week. And that which is most praiseworthy of all, within the walls of her privy chamber, she hath obtained that excellency of learning to understand, speak, and write both wittily with head, and fair with hand, as scarce one or two rare wits in both the universities have in many years reached unto. Amongst all the benefits that God has blessed me withal, next the knowledge of Christ's true religion, I count this the greatest, that it pleased God to call me to be one poor minister in setting forward these excellent gifts of learning in this most excellent prince; whose only example if the rest of our nobility would follow, then might England be for learning and wisdom in nobility, a spectacle to all the world beside. But see the mishap of men; the best examples have never such force to move to any goodness, as the bad, vain, light, and fond have to all illness.

Sir Francis Bacon (1561-1626) is quintessentially Elizabethan in his meteoric rise (to Lord Chancellor, Baron Verulam and Viscount St. Albans) and fall for bribery (or "corruption and neglect," as he admitted) and in his Renaissance variety of talents. Of his writings, the major part was philosophy. So a selection follows from the first book of The Advancement of Learning *(though not published until after Elizabeth's death). His legal writings and histories, such as a life of Henry VII, are less known than his terse and thoughtful essays, but they alone gained him acclaim, at least with the average man and woman, unable to read his* Novum Organum *or his abstruse studies in English. The effect of* The Advancement of Learning's *philosophy, however, was important in the life of the common people of his period. Bacon's ideas reached non-readers as those of Freud or Einstein did in our century, informing the public mind. This time, like most modern readers, ignore the Latin quotations used for authority or ornament.*

Now I proceed to those errors and vanities which have intervened amongst the studies themselves of the learned, which is that which is principal and proper to the present argument; wherein my purpose is not to make a justification of the errors, but by a censure and separation of the errors to make a justification of that which is good and sound, and to deliver that from the aspersion of the other. For we see that it is the manner of men to scandalize and deprave that which retaineth the state and virtue, by taking advantage upon that which is corrupt and degenerate: as the heathens in the primitive church used to blemish and taint the Christians with the faults and corruptions of heretics. But nevertheless I have no meaning at this time to make any exact animadversion of the errors and impediments in matters of learning, which are more secret and remote from vulgar opinion, but only to speak unto such as do fall under or near unto a popular observation.

There be therefore chiefly three vanities in studies, whereby learning hath been most traduced. For those things we do esteem vain, which are either false or frivolous, those which either have no truth or no use: and those persons we esteem vain, which are either credulous or curious; and curiosity is either in matter or words: so that in reason as well as in experience there fall out to be these three distempers (as I may term them) of learning: the first, fantastical learning; the second, contentious learning; and the last, delicate learning; vain imaginations, vain altercations, and vain affectations; and with the last I will begin. Martin Luther, conducted (no doubt) by an higher Providence, but in discourse of reason, finding what a province he had undertaken against the bishop of Rome and the degenerate traditions of the church, and finding his own solitude, being no ways aided by the opinions of his own time, was enforced to awake all antiquity, and to call former times to his succours to make a party against the present time: so that the ancient authors, both in divinity and in humanity, which had long time slept in libraries, began generally to be read and revolved. This by consequence did draw on a necessity of a more exquisite travail in the languages original, wherein those authors did write, for the better understanding of those authors, and the better advantage of pressing and applying their words. And thereof grew again a delight in their manner of style and phrase, and an admiration of that kind of writing; which was much furthered and precipitated by the enmity and opposition that the propounders of those primitive but seeming new opinions had against the Schoolmen; who were generally of the contrary part, and whose writings were altogether in a different style and form; taking liberty to coin and frame new terms of art to express their own sense, and to avoid circuit of speech, without regard to the pureness, pleasantness, and (as I may call it) lawfulness of the phrase or word. And again, because the great labour then was with the people (of whom the Pharisees were wont to say, *"Execrabilis ista turba, quae non novit legem"*), for the winning and persuading of them, there grew of necessity in chief price and request eloquence and variety of discourse, as the fittest and forciblest access into the capacity of the vulgar sort: so that these four causes concurring, the admiration of ancient authors, the hate of the Schoolmen, the exact study of languages, and the efficacy of preaching, did bring in an affectionate study of eloquence and copie of speech, which then began to flourish.

This grew steadily to an excess; for men began to hunt more after words than matter; more after the choiceness of the phrase, and the round and clean composition of the sentence, and the sweet falling of the clauses, and the varying and illustration of their works with tropes and figures, than after the weight of matter, worth of subject, soundness of argument, life of invention, or depth of judgement. Then grew the flowing and watery vein of Osorious, the Portugal bishop, to be in price. Then did Sturmius spend such infinite and curious pains upon Cicero the Orator, and Hermogenes the Rhetorician, besides his own books of periods and Imitations, and the like. Then did Car of Cambridge and Ascham with their lectures and writings almost deify Cicero and Demosthenes, and allure all young men that were studious unto that delicate and polished kind of learning. Then did Erasmus take occasion to make the scoffing echo, "*Decem annos consumpsi in legendo Cicerone*"; and the echo answered in Greek One, Asine. Then grew the learning of the Schoolmen to be utterly despised as barbarous. In sum, the whole inclination and bent of those times was rather towards copie than weight.

Here therefore is the first distemper of learning, when men study words and not matter; whereof, though I have represented an example of late times, yet it hath been and will be *secundum majus et minus* in all time. And how is it possible but this should have an operation to discredit learning, even with vulgar capacities, when they see learned men's works like the first letter of a patent, or limned book; which though it hath large flourishes, yet it is but a letter? It seems to me that Pygmalion's frenzy is a good emblem or portraiture of this vanity: for words are but the images of matter; and except they have life of reason and invention, to fall in love with them is all one as to fall in love with a picture.

But yet notwithstanding it is a thing not hastily to be condemned, to clothe and adorn the obscurity even of philosophy itself with sensible and plausible elocution. For hereof we have great examples in Xenophon, Cicero, Seneca, Plutarch, and of Plato also in some degree; and hereof likewise there is great use: for surely, to the severe inquisition of truth and the deep progress into philosophy, it is some hindrance; because it is too early satisfactory to the mind of man, and quencheth the desire of further search, before we come to a just period. But then if a man be to have any use of such knowledge in civil occasions, of conference, counsel, persuasion, discourse, or the like, then shall he find it prepared to his hands in those authors which write in that manner. But the excess of this is so justly contemptible, that as Hercules, when he saw the image of Adonis, Venus' minion, in a temple, said in disdain, "*Nil sacri es*"; so there is none of Hercules' followers in learning, that is, the more severe and laborious sort of inquirers into truth, but will despise those delicacies and affectations, as indeed capable of no divineness. And thus much of the first disease or distemper of learning.

The second which followeth is in nature worse than the former: for as substance of matter is better than beauty of words, so contrariwise vain matter is worse than vain words: wherein it seemeth the reprehension of St. Paul was not only proper for those times, but prophetical for the times following; and not only respective to divinity, but extensive to all knowledge: "*Devita profanas vocum novitates, et oppositiones falsi nominis scientiae.*" For he assigneth two marks and badges of suspected and falsified science: the one, the novelty and strangeness of terms; the other, the strictness of positions, which of necessity doth induce oppositions, and so questions and altercations. Surely, like as many substances in nature which are solid do putrify and corrupt into worms; so it is the property of good and sound knowledge to putrify and dissolve into a number of subtle, idle, unwholesome, and (as I may term them) vermiculate questions, which have indeed a kind of quickness and life of spirit, but no soundness of matter or goodness of quality. This kind of degenerate learning did chiefly reign amongst the Schoolmen: who having sharp and strong wits, and abundance of leisure, and small variety of reading, but their wits being shut up in the cells of a few authors (chiefly Aristotle their dictator) as their persons were shut up in the cells of monasteries and colleges, and knowing little history, either of nature or time, did out of no great quantity of matter and infinite agitation of wit spin out unto us those laborious webs of learning which are extant in their books. For the wit and mind of man, if it work upon matter, which is the contemplation of the creatures of God, worketh according to the stuff and is limited thereby; but if it work upon itself, as the spider worketh his web, then it is endless, and brings forth indeed cobwebs of learning, admirable for the fineness of thread and work, but of no substance or profit.

This same unprofitable subtility or curiosity is of two sorts; either in the subject itself that they handle, when it is a fruitless speculation or controversy (whereof there are no small number both in divinity and philosophy), or in the manner or method of handling of a knowledge, which amongst them was this: upon every particular position or assertion to frame objections, and to those objections, solutions; which solutions were for the most part not confutations, but distinctions: whereas indeed the strength of all sciences, is as the strength of the old man's faggot, in the bond. For the harmony of a science, supporting each part the other, is and ought to be the true and brief confutation and suppression of all the smaller sort of objections. But, on the other side, if you take out every axiom, as the sticks of the faggot, one by one, you may quarrel with them and bend them and break them at your pleasure: so that as was said of Seneca, "*Verborum minutiis rerum frangit pondera,*" so a man may truly say of the Schoolmen, "*Quaestionum minutiis scientiarum frangunt soliditatem.*" For were it not better for a man in a fair room to set up one great light, or branching candlestick of lights, than to go about with a small watch candle into every corner? And such is their method, that rests not so much upon evidence of truth proved by arguments, authorities, similitudes, examples, as upon particular confutations and solutions of every scruple, cavillation, and objection; breeding for the most part one question as fast as it solveth another; even as in the former resemblance, when you carry the light into one corner, you darken the rest; so that the fable and fiction of Scylla seemeth to be a lively image of this kind of philosophy or knowledge; which was transformed into a comely virgin for the upper parts; but then "*Candida succinctam latrantibus inquina monstris*": so the generalities of the Schoolmen are for a while good and proportionable; but then when you descend into their distinctions and decisions, instead of a fruitful womb for the use and benefit of man's life, they end in monstrous altercations and barking questions. So as it is not possible but this quality of knowledge must fall under popular contempt, the people being apt to contemn truth upon occasion of controversies and altercations, and to think they are all out of their way which never meet. And when they see such digladiation about subtilties, and matter of no use or moment, they easily fall upon that judgement of Dionysius of Syracusa, " *Verba ista sunt senum otiosorum.*"

Notwithstanding, certain it is that if those Schoolmen to their great thirst of truth and unwearied travail of wit had joined variety and universality of reading and contemplation, they had proved excellent lights, to the great advancement of all learning and knowledge; but as they are, they are great undertakers indeed, and fierce with dark keeping. But as in the inquiry of the divine truth, their pride inclined to leave the oracle of God's word, and to vanish in the mixture of their own inventions; so in the inquisition of nature, they ever left the oracle of God's works, and adored the deceiving and deformed images which the unequal mirror of their own minds, or a few received authors or principles, did represent unto them. And thus much for the second disease of learning.

For the third vice or disease of learning, which concerneth deceit or untruth, it is of all the rest the foulest; as that which doth destroy the essential form of knowledge, which is nothing but a representation of truth: for the truth of being and the truth of knowing are one, differing no more than the direct beam and the beam reflected. This vice therefore brancheth itself into two sorts: delight in deceiving and aptness to be deceived, imposture and credulity; which, although they appear to be of a diverse nature, the one seeming to proceed of cunning and the other of simplicity, yet certainly they do for the most part concur: for, as the verse noteth, *Percontatorem fugiot, nam garrulus idem est,* an inquisitive man is a prattler; so upon the like reason a credulous man is a deceiver: as we see it in fame, that he that will easily believe rumours, will as easily augment rumours and add somewhat to them of his own; which Tacitus wisely noteth, when he saith "*Fingunt simul creduntque*": so great an affinity hath fiction and belief.

This facility of credit and accepting or admitting things weakly authorized or warranted, is of two kinds according to the subject: for it is either a belief of history, or, as the lawyers speak, matter of fact; or else of matter of art and opinion. As to the former, we see the experience and inconvenience of this error in ecclesiastical history; which hath too easily received and registered reports and narrations of miracles wrought by martyrs, hermits, or monks of the desert, and other holy men, and their relics, shrines, chapels, and images: which though they had a passage for a time by the ignorance of the people, the superstitious simplicity of some, and the politic toleration of others, holding them but as divine poesies; yet after a period of time, when the mist began to clear up, they grew to be esteemed but as old wives' fables, impostures of the clergy, illusions of spirits, and badges of Antichrist, to the great scandal and detriment of religion.

So in natural history, we see there hath not been that choice and judgement used as ought to have been; as may appear in the writings of Plinius, Cardanus, Albertus, and diverse of the Arabians, being fraught with much fabulous matter, a great part not only untried, but notoriously untrue, to the great derogation of the credit of natural philosophy with the grave and sober kind of wits: wherein the wisdom and integrity of Aristotle is worthy to be observed; that, having made so diligent and exquisite a history of living creatures, hath mingled it sparingly with any vain or feigned matter: and yet on the other side hath cast all prodigious narrations, which he thought worthy the recording, into one book: excellently discerning that matter of manifest truth, such whereupon observation and rule was to be built, was not to be mingled or weakened with matter of doubtful credit; and yet again, that rarities and reports that seem uncredible are not to be suppressed or denied to the memory of men.

And as for the facility of credit which is yielded to arts and opinions, it is likewise of two kinds; either when too much belief is attributed to the arts themselves, or to certain authors in any art. The sciences themselves, which have had better intelligence and confederacy with the imagination of man than with his reason, are three in number; astrology, natural magic, and alchemy: of which sciences, nevertheless, the ends or pretences are noble. For astrology pretendeth to discover that correspondence or concatenation which is between the superior globe and the inferior; natural magic pretendeth to call and reduce natural philosophy from variety of speculations to the magnitude of works: and alchemy pretendeth to make separation of all the unlike parts of bodies which in mixtures of nature are incorporate. But the derivations and prosecutions of these ends, both in the theories and in the practices, are full of error and vanity; which the great professors themselves have sought to veil over and conceal by enigmatical writings, and referring themselves to auricular traditions and such other devices, to save the credit of impostures. And yet surely to alchemy this right is due, that it may be compared to the husbandman whereof Aesop makes the fable; that, when he died, told his sons that he had left unto them gold buried underground in his vineyard; and they digged over all the ground, and gold they found none; but by reason of their stirring and digging the mould about the roots of their vines, they had a great vintage the year following: so assuredly the search and stir to make gold hath brought to light a great number of good and fruitful inventions and experiments, as well for the disclosing of nature as for the use of man's life.

And as for the overmuch credit that hath been given unto authors in sciences, in making them dictators, that their words should stand, and not consuls to give advice; the damage is infinite that sciences have received thereby, as the principal cause that hath kept them low at a stay without growth or advancement. For hence it hath cometh, that in arts mechanical the first deviser comes shortest, and time addeth and perfecteth; but in sciences the first author goeth furthest, and time lesseth and corrupteth. So we see, artillery, sailing, printing, and the like, were grossly managed at the first, and by time accommodated and refined: but contrariwise, the philosophies and sciences of Aristotle, Plato, Democritus, Hippocrates, Euclides, Archimedes, of most vigour at the first and by time degenerate and imbase; whereof the reason is no other, but that in the former many wits and industries have contributed in one; and in the latter many wits and industries have been spent about the wit of some one, whom many times they have rather depraved than illustrated. For as water will not ascend higher than the level of the first springhead from whence it descendeth, so knowledge derived from Aristotle and exempted from liberty of examination, will not rise again higher than the knowledge of Aristotle. And therefore although the position be good, "*Oportet discentem credere,*" yet it must be coupled with this,"*Oportet edoctum judicare*"; for disciples do owe unto masters only a temporary belief and a suspension of their own judgement till they be fully instructed, and not an absolute resignation or perpetual captivity: and therefore, to conclude this point, I will say no more, but so let great authors have their due, as time, which is the author of authors, be not deprived of his due, which is, further and further to discover truth. Thus have I gone over these three diseases of learning; besides the which there are some other rather peccant humours than formed diseases, which nevertheless are not so secret and intrinsic but that they fall under a popular observation and traducement, and therefore are not to be passed over.

The first of these is the extreme affecting of two extremities: the one antiquity, the other novelty; wherein it seemeth the children of time do take after the nature and malice of the father. For as he devoureth his children, so one of them seeketh to devour and suppress the other; while antiquity envieth there should be new additions, and novelty cannot be content to add but it must deface: surely the advice of the prophet is the true direction in this matter,"*State super vias antiquas, et videte quaenam sit via recta et bona et ambulate in ea.*" Antiquity deserveth that reverence, that men should make a stand thereupon and discover what is the best way; but when the discovery is well taken, then to make progression. And to speak truly, "*Antiquitas saeculi juventus mundi.*" These times are the ancient times, when the world is ancient, and not those which we account ancient *ordine retrogrado,* by a computation backward from ourselves.

Another error induced by the former is a distrust that anything should be now to be found out, which the world should have missed and passed over so long time; as if the same objection were to be made to time, that Lucian maketh to Jupiter and other the heathen gods; of which he wondereth that they begot so many children in old time, and begot none in his time; and asketh whether they were become septuagenary, or whether the law *Papia,* made against old men's marriages, had restrained them. So it seemeth men doubt lest time is become past children and generation; wherein contrariwise we see commonly the levity and unconstancy of men's judgements, which till a matter be done, wonder that it can be done; and as soon as it is done, wonder again that it was no sooner done: as we see in the expedition of Alexander into Asia, which at first was pre-judged as a vast and impossible enterprise; and yet afterwards it pleaseth Livy to make no more of it than this, "*Nil aliud quam bene ausus vana contemnere.*" And the same happened to Columbus in the western navigation. But in intellectual matters it is much more common; as may be seen in most of the propositions of Euclid; which till they be demonstrate, they seem strange to our assent; but being demonstrate, our mind accepteth of them by a kind of relation (as the lawyers speak) as if we had known them before.

Another error, that hath also some affinity with the former, is a conceit that of former opinions or sects after variety and examination the best hath still prevailed and suppressed the rest; so as if a man should begin the labour of a new search, he were but like to light upon somewhat formerly rejected, and by rejection brought into oblivion: as if the multitude, or the wisest for the multitude's sake, were not ready to give passage rather to that which is popular and superficial, than to that which is substantial and profound; for the truth is, that time seemeth to be of the nature of a river or stream, which carrieth down to us that which is light and blown up, and sinketh and drowneth that which is weighty and solid.

Another error, of a diverse nature from all the former, is the over-early and peremptory reduction of knowledge into arts and methods; from which time commonly sciences receive small or no augmentation. But as young men, when they knit and shape perfectly, do seldom grow to a further stature; so knowledge, while it is in aphorisms and observations, it is in growth but when it once is comprehended in exact methods, it may perchance be further polished and illustrate and accommodate for use and practice; but it increaseth no more in bulk and substance.

Another error which doth succeed that which we last mentioned, is, that after the distribution of particular arts and sciences, men have abandoned universality, or *philosophia prima*: which cannot but cease and stop all progression. For no perfect discovery can be made upon a flat or a level: neither is it possible to discover the more remote and deeper parts of any science, if you stand but upon the level of the same science, and ascend not to a higher science.

Another error hath proceeded from too great a reverence, and a kind of adoration of the mind and understanding of man; by means whereof, men have withdrawn themselves too much from the contemplation of nature, and the observations of experience, and have tumbled up and down in their own reason and conceits. Upon these intellectualists, which are notwithstanding commonly taken for the most sublime and divine philosophers, Heraclitus gave a just censure, saying, "Men sought truth in their own little worlds, and not in the great and common world"; for they disdain to spell, and so by degrees to read in the volume of God's works: and contrariwise by continual meditation and agitation of wit do urge and as it were invocate their own spirits to divine and give oracles unto them, whereby they are deservedly deluded.

Another error that hath some connexion with this latter is, that men have used to infect their meditations, opinions, and doctrines, with some conceits which they have most admired, or some sciences which they have most admired, or some sciences which they have most applied; and given all things else a tincture according to them, utterly untrue and unproper. So hath Plato intermingled his philosophy with theology, and Aristotle with logic; and the second school of Plato, Proclus and the rest, with the mathematics. For these were the arts which had a kind of primogeniture with them severally. So have the alchemists made a philosophy out of a few experiments of the furnace; and Gilbertus our countryman hath made a philosophy out of the observations of a loadstone. So Cicero, when, reciting the several opinions of the nature of the soul, he found a musician that held the soul was but a harmony, saith pleasantly, "*Hic ab arte sua non recessit,*" &c. But of these conceits Aristotle speaketh seriously and wisely when he said, "*Qui respiciunt ad pauca de facili pronunciant.*"

Another error is an impatience of doubt, and haste to assertion without due and mature suspension of judgement. For the two ways of contemplation are not unlike the two ways of action commonly spoken of by the ancients: the one plain and smooth in the beginning, and in the end impassable; the other rough and troublesome in the entrance, but after a while fair and even: so it is in contemplation; if a man will begin with certainties, he shall end in doubts; but if he will be content to begin with doubts, he shall end in certainties.

Another error is in the manner of the tradition and delivery of knowledge, which is for the most part magistral and preemptory, and not ingenuous and faithful; in a sort as may be soonest believed, and not easiliest examined. It is true that in compendious treatises for practice that form is not to be disallowed: but in the true handling of knowledge, men ought not to fall either on the one side into the vein of Velleius the Epicurean, "*Nil tam metuens, quam ne dubitare aliqua de re videretur*"; nor on the other side into Socrates his ironical doubting of all things; but to propound things sincerely with more or less asseveration, as they stand in a man's own judgement proved more or less.

Other errors there are in the scope that men propound to themselves, whereunto they bend their endeavours; for whereas the more constant and devote kind of professors of any science ought to propound to themselves to make some additions to their science, they convert their labours to aspire to certain second prizes: as to be a profound interpreter or commenter, to be a sharp champion or defender, to be a methodical compounder or abridger, and so the patrimony of knowledge cometh to be sometimes improved, but seldom augmented.

But the greatest error of all the rest is the mistaking or misplacing of the last or furthest end of knowledge. For men have entered into a desire of learning and knowledge, sometimes upon a natural curiosity and inquisitive appetite; sometimes to entertain their minds with variety and delight; sometimes for ornament and reputation; and sometimes to enable them to victory of wit and contradiction; and most times for lucre and profession; and seldom sincerely to give a true account of their gift of reason, to the benefit and use of men: as if there were sought in knowledge a couch whereupon to rest a searching and restless spirit; or a terrace for a wandering and variable mind to walk up and down with a fair prospect; or a tower of state for a proud mind to raise itself upon; or a fort or commanding ground for strife and contention; or a shop for profit or sale; and not a rich storehouse for the glory of the Creator and the relief of man's estate. But this is that which will indeed dignify and exalt knowledge, if contemplation and action may be more nearly and straitly conjoined and united together than they have been; a conjunction like unto that of the two highest planets, Saturn, the planet of rest and contemplation, and Jupiter, the planet of civil society and action. Howbeit, I do not mean, when I speak of use and action, that end before-mentioned of the applying of knowledge to lucre and profession; for I am not ignorant how much that diverteth and interrupteth the prosecution and advancement of knowledge, like unto the golden ball thrown before Atalanta, which while she goeth aside and stoopeth to take up, the race is hindered, *Declinat cursus, aurumque volubile tollit.* Neither is my meaning, as was spoken of Socrates, to call philosophy down from heaven to converse upon the earth; that is, to leave natural philosophy aside, and to apply knowledge only to manners and policy. But as both heaven and earth do conspire and contribute to the use and benefit of man; so the end ought to be, from both philosophies to separate and reject vain speculations, and whatsoever is empty and void, and to preserve and augment whatsoever is solid and fruitful: that knowledge may not be as a courtesan, for pleasure and vanity only, or as a bond-woman, to acquire and gain to her master's use; but as a spouse, for generation, fruit, and comfort.

Thus have I described and opened, as by a kind of dissection, those peccant humours (the principal of them) which have not only given impediment to the proficience of learning, but have given also occasion to the traducement thereof: wherein if I have been too plain, it must be remembered, "*fidelia vulnera amantis, sed dolosa oscula malignantis.*" This I think I have gained, that I ought to be the better believed in that which I shall say pertaining to commendation; because I have proceeded so freely in that which concerneth censure. And yet I have no purpose to enter into a laudative of learning, or to make a hymn to the Muses (though I am of opinion that it is long since their rites were duly celebrated), but my intent is, without varnish or amplification justly to weigh the dignity of knowledge in the balance with other things, and to take the true value thereof by testimonies and arguments divine and human.

Sir Philip Sidney (1554-1586) wrote an essay that was published in two versions in 1595, as The Defence of Poesy *and as* An Apology for Poetry. *From the latter version, a few paragraphs of a long discussion, showing at least that Elizabeth's time appreciated some of the literary tradition it had inherited from its countrymen, as well as the classical sources in which the Renaissance revived interest. Sidney writes a good English, even if he must self-consciously pepper it with Latin quotations and at the end fling tags from Horace, Ovid, and Virgil around just to boast his learning (which is not above getting Terence and Aristotle wrong).*

Chaucer, undoubtedly, did excellently in his *Troilus and Cressida;* of whom, truly, I know not whether to marvel more, either that he in that misty time could see so clearly, or that we in this clear age walk so stumblingly after him. Yet had he great wants, fit to be forgiven in so reverent antiquity. I account the *Mirror of Magistrates* meetly furnished of beautiful parts, and in the Earl of Surrey's *Lyrics* many things tasting of a noble birth, and worthy of a noble mind. The *Shepherd's Calendear* hath much poetry in his eclogues, indeed worthy the reading, if I be not deceived. That some framing of his style to an old rustic language I dare not allow, since neither Theocritus in Greek, Virgil in Latin, nor Sannazzaro in Italian did affect it. Besides these, to I not remember to have seen but few (to speak boldly) printed, that have poetical sinews in them: for proof whereof, let but most of the verses be put in prose, and then ask the meaning; and it will be found that one verse did but beget another, without ordering at the first what should be at the last; which becomes a confused mass of words, with a tingling sound of rhyme, barely accompanied with reason.

Our tragedies and comedies (not without cause cried out against), observing rules neither of honest civility nor of skillful poetry, excepting *Gorboduc* (again, I say, of those that I have seen), which not-withstanding, as it is full of stately speeches and well-sounding phrases, climbing to the height of Seneca's style, and as full of notable morality, which it doth most delightfully teach and so obtain the very end of poesy, yet in truth it is very defectious in the circumstances, which grieveth me, because it might not remain as an exact model of all tragedies. For it is faulty both in place and time, the two necessary companions of all corporal actions. For where the stage should always represent but one place, and the uttermost time presupposed in it should be, both by Aristotle's precept and common reason, but one day, there is both many days, and many places, inartificially imagined. But if it be so in *Gorboduc*, how much more in all the rest, where you shall have Asia of the one side, and Afric of the other, and so many other underkingdoms, that the player, when he cometh in, must ever begin with telling where he is, or else that tale will not be conceived? Now yet shall have three ladies walk to gather flowers and then we must believe the stage to be a garden. By and by we hear news of shipwreck in the same place, and then we are to blame if we accept it not for a rock.

Upon the back of that comes out a hideous monster, with fire and smoke, and then the miserable beholders are bound to take it for a cave. While in the meantime two armies fly in, represented with four swords and bucklers, and then what hard heart will not receive it for a pitched field? Now, of time they are much more liberal, for ordinary it is that two young princes fall in love. After many traverses, she is got with child, delivered of a fair boy; he is lost, groweth a man, falls in love, and is ready to get another child; and all this in two hours' space: which, how absurd it is in sense, even sense may imagine, and art hath taught, and all ancient examples justified, and, at this day, the ordinary players in Italy will not err in. Yet will some bring in an example of *Eunuchus* in Terrence [error: he should say *The Self-Tormentor* by Terence], that containeth matter of two days, yet far short of twenty years. True it is, and so was it to be played in two days, and so fitted to the time is set forth. And though Plautus hath in one place done amiss, let us hit with him, and not miss with him. But they will say, How then shall we set forth a story, which containeth both many places and many times? And do they not know that a tragedy is tied to the laws of poesy, and not of history; not bound to follow the story, but, having liberty, either to feign a quite new matter, or to frame the history to the most tragical conveniency? Again, many things may be told which cannot be showed, if they know the difference betwixt reporting and representing. As, for example, I may speak (though I am here) of Peru, and in speech digress from that to the description of Calicut; but in action I cannot represent it without Pacolet's horse. And so was the manner the ancients took, by some nuncius [messenger] to recount things done in former time or other place. Lastly, if they will represent an history, they must not (as Horace saith) begin *ab ovo* [Latin "from the egg," the very beginning] but they must come to the principal point of that one action which they will represent. By example this will be best expressed. I have a story of young Polydorus, delivered for safety's sake, with great riches, by his father Priam to Polymnestor, king of Thrace, in the Trojan war time. He, after same years, hearing the overthrow of Priam, for to make the treasure his own, murdereth the child. The body of the child is taken up by Hecuba. She, the same day, findeth a slight to be revenged most cruelly of the tyrant. Where now would one of our tragedy writers begin, but with the delivery of the child? Then should he sail over into Thrace, and so spend I know not how many years, and travel numbers of places. But where doth Euripides? Even with the finding of the body, leaving the rest to be told by the spirit of Polydorus. This need no further to be enlarged; the dullest wit may conceive it. But besides these gross absurdities, how all their plays be neither right tragedies, nor right comedies, mingling kings and clowns, not because the matter so carrieth it, but thrust in clowns by head and shoulders, to play a part in majestical matters, with neither decency nor discretion, so as neither the admiration and commiseration, nor the right sportfulness, is by their mongrel tragicomedy obtained. I know Apuleius did somewhat so, but that is a thing recounted with space of time, not represented in one moment: and I know the ancients have one or two examples of tragicomedies, as Plautus hath *Amphitrio*. But, if we mark them well, we shall find, that they never, or very daintily, match hornpipes and funerals. So falleth it out that, having indeed no right comedy, in that comical part of our tragedy we have nothing but scurrility, unworthy of any chaste ears, or some extreme show of doltishness, indeed fit to lift up a loud laughter, and nothing else where the whole tract of a comedy should be full of delight, as the tragedy should be still maintained in a well-raised admiration. But our comedians think there is no delight without laughter; which is very wrong, for though laughter may come with delight, yet cometh it not of delight, as though delight should be the cause of laughter; but well may one thing breed both together. Nay, rather in themselves they have, as it were, a kind of contrariety: for delight we scarcely do but in things that have a conveniency to ourselves or to the general nature: laughter almost ever cometh of things most disproportioned to ourselves and nature. Delight hath a joy in it, either permanent or present. laughter hath only a scornful tickling.

For example, we are ravished with delight to see a fair woman, and yet are far from being moved to laughter. We laugh at deformed creatures, wherein certainly we cannot delight. We delight in good chances, we laugh at mischances; we delight to hear the happiness of our friends, or country, at which he were worthy to be laughed at that would laugh. We shall, contrarily, laugh sometimes to find a matter quite mistaken and go down the hill against the bias, in the mouth of some such men, as for the respect of them one shall be heartily sorry, yet he cannot choose but laugh; and so is rather pained than delighted with laughter. Yet deny I not but that they may go well together. For as in Alexander's picture well set out we delight without laughter, and in twenty mad antics we laugh without delight, so in Hercules, painted with his great beard and furious countenance,in woman's attire, spinning at Omphale's commandment, it breedeth both delight and laughter. For the representing of so strange a power in love procureth delight: and the scornfulness of the action stirreth laughter. But I speak to this purpose, that all the end of the comical part be not upon such scornful matters as stirreth laughter only, but, mixed with, that delightful teaching which is the end of poesy. And the great fault even in that point of laughter, and forbidden plainly by Aristotle [error], is that they stir laughter in sinful things, which are rather execrable than ridiculous; or in miserable, which are rather to be pitied than scorned. For what is it to make folks gape at a wretched beggar, or a beggarly clown; or, against the law of hospitality, to jest at strangers, because they speak not English so well as we do? What do we learn, since it is certain *"Nil habet infelix paupertas durius in se, / Quam quod ridiculos homines facit"?* [Juvenal: "Unhappy poverty has nothing worse itself than that it makes men appear ridiculous."] But rather a busy loving courtier, a heartless threatening Thraso, a self-wise-seeming schoolmaster, an awry-transformed traveler—these if we saw walk in stage names, which we play naturally, therein were delightful laughter, and teaching delightfulness: as in the other, the tragedies of Buchanan do justly bring forth a divine admiration. But I have lavished out too many words of this play matter. I do it because, as they are excelling parts of poesy, so is there none so much used in England, and none can be more pitifully abused; which, like an unmannerly daughter showing a bad education, causeth her mother Poesy's honesty to be called in question. Other sorts of poetry almost have we none, but that lyrical kind of songs and sonnets: which, Lord, if he gave us so good minds, how well it might be employed, and with how heavenly fruit, both private and public, in singing the praises of the immortal beauty, the immortal goodness of that God who giveth us hands to write and wits to conceive; of which we might well want words, but never matter; of which we could turn our eyes to nothing, but we should ever have new budding occasions. But truly many of such writings as come under the banner of unresistible love, if I were a mistress, would never persuade me they were in love; so coldly they apply fiery speeches, as men that had rather read lovers' writings, and so caught up certain swelling phrases (which hang together like a man which once told me the wind was at northwest, and by south, because he would be sure to name winds enough), than that in truth they feel those passions, which easily (as I think) may be betrayed by that same forcibleness or *energia* (as the Greeks call it) of the writer. But let this be a sufficient though short note, that we miss the right use of the material point of poesy.

Now, for the outside of it, which is words, or (as I may term it) diction, it is even well worse. So is that honey-flowing matron Eloquence appareled, or rather disguised, in a courtesanlike painted affection: one time with so farfetched words, they may seem monsters, but must seem strangers to any poor Englishman; another time, with coursing of a letter, as if they were bound to follow the method of a dictionary; another time, with figures and flowers, extremely winter-starved. But I would this fault were only peculiar to versifiers, and had not as large possession among prose-printers, and (which is to be marveled) among many scholars, and (which is to be pitied) among some preachers. Truly I could wish, if at least I might be so bold to wish in a thing beyond the reach of my capacity, the diligent immitators of Tully and Demosthenes (most worthy to be imitated) did not so much keep Nizolian paper books of their figures and phrases, as by attentive translation (as it were) devour them whole, and make them wholly theirs. For now they cast sugar and spice upon every dish that is served to the table, like those Indians, not content to wear earrings at the fit and natural place of the ears, but they will thrust jewels through their nose and lips, because they will be sure to be fine.

Tully, when he was to drive out Catiline, as it were with a thunderbolt of eloquence, often used that figure of repetition, *"Vivit. Vivit? Imo in Senatum venit,"* &c. [Cicero: "He lives, he lives? He even comes into the Senate."] Indeed, inflamed with a well-grounded rage, he would have his words (as it were) double out of his mouth, and so do that artificially which we see men do in choler naturally. And we, having noted the grace of those words, hale them in sometime to a familiar epistle, when it were too much choler to be choleric. Now for similitudes in certain printed discourses, I think all herberists, all stories of beasts, fowls, and fishes are rifled up, that they come in multitudes to wait upon any of our conceits; which certainly is as absurd a surfeit to the ears as is possible: for the force of a similitude not being to prove anything to a contrary disputer, but only to explain to a willing hearer; when that is done, the rest is a most tedious prattling, rather overswaying the memory from the purpose whereto they were applied, than any whit informing the judgement, already either satisfied, or by similitudes not to be satisfied. For my part, I do not doubt, when Antonius and Crassus, the great forefathers of Cicero in eloquence, the one (as Cicero testifieth of them) pretended not to know art, the other not to set by it, because with a plain sensibleness they might win credit of popular ears; which credit is the nearest step to persuasion; which persuasion is the chief mark of oratory—I do not doubt (I say) that but they used these knacks very sparingly; which, who doth generally use, any man may see doth dance to his own music; and so be noted by the audience more careful to speak curiously than to speak truly.

Undoubtedly (at least to my opinion undoubtedly) I have found in divers small-learned courtiers a more sound style than in some professors of learning: of which I can guess no other cause, but that the countier, following that which by practice he findeth fittest to nature, therein (though he know it not) doth according to art, though not by art: where the other, using art to show art, and not to hide art (as in these cases he should do), flieth from nature, and indeed abuseth art.

But what? Methinks I deserve to be pounded for straying from poetry to oratory: but both have such an affinity in this wordish consideration, that I think this digression will make my meaning receive the fuller understanding—which is not to take upon me to teach poets how they should do, but only, finding myself sick among the rest, to show some one or two spots of the common infection grown among the most part of writers: that, acknowledging ourselves somewhat awry, we may bend to the right use both of matter and manner; whereto our language giveth us great occasion, being indeed capable of any excellent exercising of it. I know some will say it is a mingled language. And why not so much the better, taking the best of both the other? Another will say it wanteth grammar. Nay truly, it hath that praise, that it wanteth grammar: for grammar it might have, but it needs it not; being so easy of itself, and so void of those cumbersome differences of cases, genders, moods, and tenses, which I think was a piece of the Tower of Babylon's curse, that a man should be put to school to learn his mother tongue. But for the uttering sweetly and properly the conceits of the mind, which is the end of speech, that hath it equally with any other tongue in the world: and is particularly happy in compositions of two or three words together, near the Greek, far beyond the Latin: which is one of the greatest beauties can be in a language.

Now, of versifying there are two sorts, the one ancient, the other modern: the ancient marked the quantity of each syllable, and according to that framed his verse; the modern observing only number (with some regard of the accent), the chief life of it standeth in that like sounding of the words, which we call rhyme. Whether of these be the most excellent, would bear many speeches. The ancient (no doubt) more fit for music, both words and tune observing quantity, and more fit lively to express divers passions, by the low and lofty sound of the well-weighed syllable. The latter likewise, with his rhyme, striketh a certain music to the ear: and, in fine, since it doth delight, though by another way, it obtains the same purpose: there being in either sweetness, and wanting in neither majesty. Truly the English, before any other vulgar language I know, is fit for both sorts: for, for the ancient, the Italian is so full of vowels that it must ever be cumbered with elisions; the Dutch so, of the other side, with consonants, that they cannot yield the sweet sliding fit for a verse; the French, in his whole language, hath not one word that hath his accent in the last syllable saving two, called *antepenultima*; and little more hath the Spanish: and, therefore, very gracelessly may they use dactyls. The English is subject to none of these defects.

Now, for the rhyme, though we do not observe quantity, yet we observe the accent very precisely: which other languages either cannot do, or will not do so absolutely. That *caesura*, or breathing place in the midst of the verse, neither Italian nor Spanish have, the French, and we, never almost fail of. Lastly, even the very rhyme itself the Italian cannot put in the last syllable, by the French named the "masculine rhyme," but still in the next to the last, which the French call the "female," or the next before that, which the Italians term *sdrucciola*. The example of the former is *buono: suono,* of the *sdrucciola, femina: semina*. The French, of the other side, hath both the male, as *bon:son,* and the female, as *plaise:taise,* but the *sdrucciola* he hath not: where the English hath all three, as *due: true, father:rather, motion:potion,* with much more which might be said, but that I find already the triflingness of this discourse is much too much enlarged. So that since the every-praiseworthy poesy is full of virtue-breeding delightfulness, and void of no gift that ought to be in the noble name of learning; since the blames laid against it are either false or feeble; since the cause why it is not esteemed in England is the fault of poet-apes, not poets; since, lastly, our tongue is most fit to honor poesy, and to be honored by poesy; I conjure you all that have had the evil luck to read this ink-wasting toy of mine, even in the name of the nine Muses, no more to scorn the sacred mysteries of poesy, no more to laugh at the name of *poets,* as though they were next inheritors to fools, no more to jest at the reverent title of a *rhymer*; but to believe, with Aristotle, that they were the ancient treasurers of the Grecians' divinity; to believe, with Bembus [Pietro Bembo, 1470-1547], that they were first bringers-in of all civility; to believe, with Scaliger, that no philosopher's precepts can sooner make you an honest man than the reading of Virgil; to believe, with Clauserus, the translator of Cornutus, that it pleased the heavenly Deity, by Hesiod and Homer, under the veil of fables, to give us all knowledge, logic, rhetoric, philosophy, natural and moral, and *Quid non*? ["what not"]; to believe, with me, that there are many mysteries contained in poetry, which of purpose were written darkly, lest by profane wits it should be abused; to believe, with Landino, that they are so beloved of the gods that whatsoever they write proceeds of a divine fury; lastly, to believe themselves, when they tell you they will make you immortal by their verses.

Thus doing, your name shall flourish in the printers' shops; thus doing, you shall be of kin to many a poetical preface; thus doing, you shall be most fair, most rich, most wise, most all; you shall dwell upon superlatives. Thus doing, though you be "*libertino patre natus*" [the son of a free man] you shall suddenly grow *"Herculea proles"* [Herculean offsprings], *"si quid mea carmina possunt"* [of my poems can accomplish anything]. Thus doing, your soul shall be placed with Dante's Beatrix, or Virgil's Anchises. But if (fie of such a but) you be born so near the dull-making cataract of Nilus that you cannot hear the planetlike music of poetry, if you have so earth-creeping a mind that it cannot lift itself up to look to the sky of poetry, or rather, by a certain rustical disdain, will become such a mome as to be a momus of poetry; then, though I will not wish unto you the ass's ears of Midas, nor to be driven by a poet's verses (as Bubonax was) to hang himself, nor to be rhymed to death, as is said to be done in Ireland; yet thus much curse I must send you, in the behalf of all poets, that while you live, you live in love, and never get favor for lacking skill of a sonnet, and, when you die, your memory die from the earth for want of an epitaph.

That a courtier and soldier could write so well (among other things he wrote one of the best sonnet sequences of his time) is extraordinary. Sidney was, indeed,

The courtier's, soldier's, scholar's, eye, tongue, sword,
The expectancy and rose of the fair state,
The glass of fashion and the mold of form,
The observed of all observers.

William Harrison counts the Inns of Court (where law was taught) as a university but Elizabeth's time had really only Oxford and "the other place," Cambridge, even then rivals and accused of being full of mindless noblemen and tuft-hunters (social-climbers who hoped to make connections with the peerage). Poor scholars did, however, get in. Marlowe, for instance, was the son of a shoemaker of Canterbury.

In my time there are three noble universities in England, to wit, one at Oxford, the second at Cambridge and the third in London, of which the first two are the most famous, I mean Cambridge, and Oxford, for that in them the use of the tongues, philosophy and the liberal sciences, beside the profound studies of the civil law, physic and theology are daily taught and had: whereas in the latter the laws of the realm are only read and learned by such as give their minds unto the knowledge of the same. In the first also there are not only divers goodly houses builded four square for the most part of hard freestone or brick, with great numbers of lodgings and chambers in the same for students, after a sumptuous manner, through the exceeding liberality of kings, queens, bishops, noblemen and ladies of the land; but also large livings and great revenues bestowed upon them (the like whereof is not to be seen in any other region, as Peter Martyr did oft affirm) to the maintenance only of such convenient numbers of poor men's sons as the several stipends bestowed upon the said houses are able to support....

The manner to live in these universities is not as in some other of foreign countries we see daily to happen, where the students are enforced for want of such houses to dwell in common inns and taverns, without all order or discipline. But in these our colleges we live in such exact order, and under so precise rules of government, as that the famous learned man Erasmus of Rotterdam, being here among us fifty years past, did not let to compare the trades in living of students in these two places even with the very rules and orders of the ancient monks, affirming moreover, in flat words, our orders to be such as not only came near unto, but rather far exceeded, all the monastical institutions that ever were devised.

In most of our colleges there are also great numbers of students, of which many are found by the revenues of the houses and other by the purveyances and help of their rich friends, whereby in some one college you shall have two hundred scholars, in others an hundred and fifty, in divers a hundred and forty, and in the rest less numbers, as the capacity of the said houses is able to receive: so that at this present, of one sort and other, there are about three thousand students nourished in them both (as by a late survey it manifestly appeared). They were erected by their founders at the first only for poor men's sons, whose parents were not able to bring them up unto learning; but now they have the least benefit of them, by reason the rich do so encroach upon them. And so far hath this inconvenience spread itself that it is in my time an hard matter for a poor man's child to come by a fellowship (though he be never so good a scholar and worthy of that room). Such packing also is used at elections that not be which best deserveth, but he that hath most friends, though he be the worst scholar, is always surest to speed; which will turn in the end to the overthrow of learning. That some gentlemen also, whose friends have been in times past benefactors to certain of those houses, do intrude into the disposition of their estates without all respect of order or statutes devised by the founders, only thereby to place whom they think good (and not without some hope of gain), the case is too too evident: and their attempt would soon take place if their superiors did not provide to bridle their endeavours. In some grammar schools likewise which send scholars to these universities, it is lamentable to see what bribery is used; for, ere the scholar can be preferred, such bribage is made that poor men's children are commonly shut out, and the richer sort received (who in time past thought it dishonour to live as it were upon alms), and yet, being placed, most of them study little other than histories, tables, dice, and trifles, as men that make not living by their study the end of their purposes, which is a lamentable hearing. Besides this, being for the most part either gentlemen or rich men's sons, they oft bring the universities into much slander. For, standing upon their reputation and liberty, they ruffle and roist it out, exceeding in apparel and haunting riotous company (which draweth them from their books unto another trade); and for excuse, when they are charged with breach of all good order, think it sufficient to say that they be gentlemen, which grieveth many not a little.

If you had 13 or 14 pounds a year you could support yourself as a gentleman student at the Inns of Court in London and prepare yourself for a career in law which, like today, also could stand you in good stead in business or politics. You read your law books, ate a certain number of compulsory dinners in Hall, and had a little time and money to gad about in the big city and see the plays or bearbaiting if not the loose women in the streets and low taverns. Sir John Davies describes a young student of the Inns of Court in his epigram In Publiam:

> Publius, student at the Common Law,
> Oft leaves his books, and for his recreation
> To Paris Garden doth himself withdraw,
> Where he is ravished with such delectation,
> As down among the bears and dogs he goes;
> Where, whilst he skipping cries, "To head! to head!"

His satin doublet and his velvet hose
Are all with spittle from above bespread.

Young gentlemen studying the law at the Inns of Court in London were so rowdy (or randy) that Gray's Inn declared in Elizabeth's time that

no laundress, nor women called Victuallers, should henceforth come into the gentlemen's chambers of this society until they are full forty years of age, and not to send their maid-servants of what age soever, into the said gentlemen's chambers, upon penalty for the first offence of him that should admit of any such, to be out of Commons [the dining hall]; and for the second, to be expelled from the House.

Illustration of an archer wearing a shooting glove from *The Art of Archerie* (1634) by Gervase Markham (1568?-1637). Markham was said to have brought the first Arab horse into England and certainly was the leading writer on horsemanship, farriers, etc., in his time. But he also wrote plays and many other books, including *The Art of Archerie*. In 1599 the stores in The Tower of London were inventoried as containing 8185 bows, 6000 bowstaves, 196 gross of bowstrings, 14,000 sheaves of livery arrows (each of two dozen shafts); but by the Seventeenth Century archery was essentially a sport and archers were no longer important for war.

Sports and Games

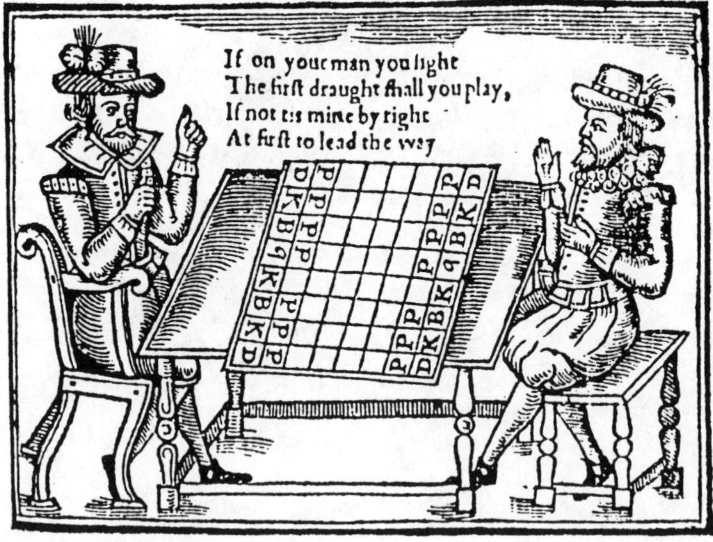

Printed at London for *Roger lackson*, and are to be fould at his shop neere Fleet Street Conduit 1614.

"In these islands sport is not a dissipation for idlers, it is a philosophy of life," wrote Price Collier. "They believe in it as a bulwark against effeminacy and decay." As the sport of archery in medieval times stood England in good stead in time of war and trained the bowmen who won some of the greatest battles abroad, so certain sports in Renaissance England were considered to build the national character as well as the individual's strength and agility. Wrestling matches were a popular event at country fairs.

Shakespeare's England *has a first-rate article on sports and games (to which we are indebted) and asserts thatno better epitome of the popular indoor and outdoor games and pastimes current in Shakespeare's time can be given than is contained in the following verses from* The Letting of Humours Blood in the Head-Vaine, *by Samuel Rowlands (1600):*

Man, I dare challenge thee to throw the sledge,
To jumpe or leape over a ditch or hedge;
To wrastle, play at stooleball, or to runne,
To pitch the barre, or to shoote off a gunne;
To play at loggets, nineholes, or ten pinnes,
To trie it out at foot-ball, by the shinnes;
At Ticktacke, Irish, Noddie, Maw, and Ruffe:
At hot-cockles, leape-frogge, or blindman-buffe.

To drink halfe pots, or deale at the whole canne:
To play at base, or pen-and-ynk-horne sir Ihan [John]:
To daunce the Morris, play at barly-breake,
At all exploytes a man can thinke or speake:
At shove-groate, venter poynt, or crosse and pile,
At 'beshrow him that's last at yonder style';
At leapynge ore a Midsommer bon-fier,
Or at the drawing Dun out of the myer....

Today football still is "a friendly kind of fight," with even amateurs chalking up some 600,000 injuries each year in the United States. It is perhaps not as rough as hockey (the comedians say, "I went to a fight and a hockey game broke out") and some other contact sports. Here is Puritan Philip Stubbes numbering Elizabethan football among "abuses" (1583):

For as concerning football playing, I protest unto you it may rather be called a friendly kind of fight, than a play or recreation; a bloody and murdering practice, than a fellowly sport or pastime. For doth not every one lie in wait for his adversary, seeking to overthrow him and to pick him on his nose, though it be upon hard stones, in ditch or dale, in valley or hill, or what place soever it be he careth not, so he have him down. And he that can serve the most of his fashion, he is counted the only fellow, and who but he? So that by this means, sometimes their necks are broken, sometimes their backs, sometimes their legs, sometime their arms, sometime one part thrust out of joint, sometime another, sometime their noses gush out with blood, sometime their eyes start out, and sometimes hurt in one place, sometimes in another. But whosoever scapeth away the best goeth not scot-free, but is either sore wounded, and bruised, so as he dieth of it, or else scapeth very hardly. And no marvel, for they have sleights to meet one betwixt two, to dash him against the heart with their elbows, to hit him under the short ribs with their gripped fists, and with their knees to catch him upon the hip, and to pick him on his neck, with an hundred such murdering devices. And hereof groweth envy, malice, rancour, choler, hatred, displeasure, enmity and what not else: and sometimes fighting, brawling, contention, quarrel picking, murder, homicide and great effusion of blood, as experience daily teacheth.

John Stow's Survey of London *translates Robert FitzStephen's account of 12th-century sport (still practised in Elizabeth's day, though the word* skate *would not be borrowed from the Dutch for almost a hundred years more):*

When the great fen or moor, which watereth the walls of the City on the north side, is frozen, many young men play upon the ice; some, striding as wide as they may, do slide swiftly: others make themselves seats of ice as great as millstones: one sits down, many hand in hand do draw him, and one slipping on a sudden, all fall together: some tie bones to their feet and under their heels and, shoving themselves by a little picked staff, do slide as swiftly as a bird flyeth in the air or an arrow out of a crossbow.

Sir Thomas Elyot's Book of The Governor *(1531) and Everard Digby's* De arte natandi *(1587) mentioned swimming, the first among useful accomplishments in general and the second recommending that everyone learn to swim. (Many students, Digby noted, were drowning in the Cam at university.) Sir Thomas:*

There is an exercise which is right profitable to extreme danger of wars, but by cause there seemeth to be some peril in the learning thereof, and also it hath not been of long time much used, especially among noblemen, perchance some reader will little esteem it, I mean swimming. But notwithstanding, if they revolve [in their minds] the imbecility of our nature, the hazards and dangers of battle, with the examples which shall hereafter be showed, they will (I doubt not) think it as necessary to a captain or man at arms, as any that I have yet rehearsed.

A Latin record from Oxford University for August 22, 1450 translated reads:

Thomas Blake, currier, William Whyte, barber, John Karyn, glover, husbandemen [householders], appeared before us, Master J. Beek, D.D. and Master Gilbert Kymer, Chancellor of this kindly [*almae*] University of Oxford and Commissary General [of the Bishop of Lincoln], and with their hands on the holy Gospels abjured the game of tennis within the city of Oxford and its precincts.

A century later tennis was a common and acceptable sport, having come first from France (where it was jeu de palmes *and therefore originally played without racquets, giving us also* love *for no score, that being* l'oeuf *or an "egg," zero). Tennis greatly appealed to the English and Scots.*

John Taylor, "The Water Poet," says the inventor of "the unmatchable mystery of Blind-Man['s]-Buff" was Gregorie Dawson. The name is in Samuel Rowlands' The Letting of Humours Blood *(1600). Shakespeare knew the game as Hoodman Blind or Hobman Blind, and mentions it in* Hamlet. *It was also called Harrie-racket and Clignemusset (which suggests it came to England from France, as so many games, including card games, did).*

Hamlet's "Hide fox and all after" may refer to hide and seek. In Romeo and Juliet *Mercutio mentions an old game when Romeo says "I am done":*

If thou art Dun, we'll draw thee from the mire.

Dun (a log representing a cart horse) is pulled out of the supposed mire by opposing teams, with or without ropes. One tries to drop the log on the opponents' toes.

Stephen Gosson's School of Abuse *complains that*

Common Bowling Alleys are privy Moths, that eat up the credit of many idle Citizens, whose gains at home are not able to weigh down their losses abroad [outside the home, at bowling], whose Shops are so far from maintaining their play, that their Wives and Children cry out for bread, and go to bed supperless oft in the year.

John Stow's Survey of London *says that, the commons having been enclosed, there are fewer places for men to practice the approved old sport of archery and they* creep into bowling alleys, and ordinary dicing houses, nearer home, where they have room enough to hazard their money at unlawful games.

Few people recognize that Hamlet's famous, "Ay, there's the rub," refers to bowling: the rub was anything that deflected the bowl from its course. Henry V says the French campaign is well underway and

We doubt not now
But every rub is smoothèd on our way.

Archery had the days of chivalry to glamorize it; bowling was as bad as any other kind of gambling in Elizabethan puritans' eyes. But Roger Ascham in Toxiphilus *(whose title tells you it was for the lover of archery) liked to gamble, that is why he died poor—and he lets the lover of dice and cards argue with his lover of the bow and arrow. Ascham writes:*

A man, no shooter, (not long ago) would defend playing at cards and dice, if it were honestly used, to be as honest a pastime as your shooting: For he laid [out] for him that a man might play for a little at cards and dice, and also a man might shoot away all that he ever had. He said a pair [that is, pack] of cards cost not past ii.d. and that they needed not so much reparation as bow and shafts, they would never hurt a man his hand, nor ever wear his gear. A man should never slay a man with shooting wide at the cards.

*Some people objected to any games that involved gambling; some people objected to any games that took people from more serious business. Fanatic puritans, such as John Northbrook (*A Treatise against Dicing, *1579) argued that playing cards were derived from The Tarot and that "the kings and coat [face] cards that we now use were in old time the images of idols and False Gods," but the fundamental (fundamentalist) objection was that people were irresponsibly enjoying themselves.*

I could find no other strictly Elizabethan quotation that was really useful about bowling, but we must mention it because it was so popular a pastime. (Elsewhere we recall that Sir Francis Drake was bowling when news of the Spanish Armada came.) So here is John Earle in Microcosmography *(1628) with a comment that is apt for an earlier time:*

A bowl-alley is the place where there are three things thrown away besides bowls, to wit, time, money and curses, and the last ten for one. The best sport in it is the gamester's, and he enjoys it that looks on and bets not. it is the school of wrangling, and worse than the schools, for men will cavil here for an hair's breadth, and make a stir where a straw would end the controversy. No antic screws men's bodies into such strange flexures, and you think them here senseless, to speak sense to their bowl, and put their trust in entreaties for a good cast. The bettors are the factious noise of the alley, or the gamesters' beadsmen that pray for them. They are somewhat like those that are cheated by great men, for they lose their money and must say nothing. It is the best discovery of humours; especially in the losers, where you have fine variety of impatience, whilst some fret, some rail, some swear, and others more ridiculously comfort themselves with philosophy. To give you the moral of it: it is the emblem of the world, or the world's ambition; where most are short, or over, or wide, or wrong-biased, and some few jostle in to the 'mistress' fortune. And it is here as in the court, where the nearest are most spited, and all blows aimed at the 'toucher.'

Nichol's Progresses of Queen Elizabeth *seems to describe a handball game (or tennis before racquets were used):*

Ten of my Lord of Hertford's servants, all Somerset men, in a square green court, before Her Majesty's window, did hang up lines, squaring out the form of a tennis-court, and making a cross line in the middle. In this square they (being stripped out of their doubiets) played five to [against] five, with the handball, at "bord and cord," as they call it, to the great liking of Her Highness.

Tennis is but one source of the imagery of this odd poem by a clergyman, Thomas Bastard (1566-1618) who died mad in debtors' prison but before then published the strange Chrestoleros *(1598), which Sir John Harington defended against those who mocked it.*

De Puero Balbutiente

Methinks 'tis pretty sport to hear a child,
Rocking a word in mouth yet undefiled;
The tender racquet rudely plays the sound
Which, weakly bandied, cannot back rebound;
And the soft air the softer roof doth kiss,
With a sweet dying and a pretty miss,
Which hears no answer yet from the white rank
Of teeth, not risen from their coral bank.
The alphabet is searched for letters soft,
To try a word before it can be wrought,
And when it slideth forth, it goes as nice
As when a man does walk upon the ice.

Roger Bacon still had a great reputation as a magician in the 16th century when the popular Famous History of Friar Bacon *was first printed (some time in the 1590s, though the earliest extant edition is 1627) containing this ballad of sport and feasting.*

And did you not hear of a mirth that befell
  The morrow after a wedding day,

At carrying a bride at home to dwell?
And away to Twiver, away, away!

The quintain was set and the garlands were made,
'Tis pity old custom should ever decay;
And woe be to him that was horsed on a jade,
For he carried no credit away, away!

We met a consort of fiddle-de-dees,
We set them a-cock-horse, and made them to play
The *Winning of Bullen* and *Upsie-frees;*
And away to Twiver, away, away!

There was ne'er a lad in all the parish
That would go to the plough that day
But on his fore-horse his wench he carries;
And away to Twiver, away, away!

The butler was quick and the ale he did tap,
The maidens did make the chamber full gay;
The serving-men gave me a fuddling cap,
And I did carry it away, away!

The smith of the town his liquor so took
That he was persuaded the ground looked blue;
And I dare boldly to swear on a book
Such smiths as he there are but a few.

A posset was made and the women did sip
And simpering said they could eat no more;
Full many a maid was laid on the lip:
I'll say no more but so give o'er.

Running at the quintain was a feature of medieval tournaments: the mounted knight ran at a post and tried to strike the shield that hung from it on an arm but miss being hit by the shield (perhaps unhorsed) when the arm swung around. By Elizabethan times this was a country sport sometimes seen at weddings. The ploughboys on farm horses replaced the splendidly bedecked knights in armor.

Shakespeare's plays and other sources are full of references to children's games resembling ring-around-the-rosie, hide and seek, cherry-stone -pit (where cherrystones were rolled into holes like marbles), tops, leapfrog, pushpin (where one player tries to push his pin across his opponent's), varieties of tag, hot cockles ("it" is blindfolded and tries to guess who strikes him—if he succeeds the other person becomes "it"), handy-dandy (guessing the contents of closed hands, full or empty), even drawgloves (simply a race to remove both gloves first). Poins in Henry IV, Part II, *Falstaff says, is loved by Prince Hal because Poins "rides the wild mare with the boys," the wild mare being the see-saw. Sir Philip Sidney in* Arcadia *describes a man making his way along a floating mast in a shipwreck "such as boys are wont...when they ride the wild mare."*

Primero *was a Spanish card game often played for high stakes. Four cards were dealt and the player with all the different suits won the prime; all cards of one suit won with a flush. From* A Manifest Detection of Dice Play:

Primero, now as it hath most use in court, so is there most deceit in it; some play upon the pricks, some pinch the cards privily with their nail—some turn up the corners,—some mark them with fine spots of ink.... At trump, saint, and such other like, cutting at neck is a great vantage, so is cutting by a bum card (finely) under and over, stealing the stock of the discarded cards, if there broad law be forced aforehand.

The Queen's godson, Sir John Harington, in A Treatise on Play *reports that Elizabeth gambled with her courtiers in the Presence Chamber:*

If her Majesty would play at Primero in that proportion to her estate as I have seen some of her mean subjects in their poor callings /do/, she should play a dukedom at a rest /stake/, and a barony stake, and then I know none able to hold a play with her.

Shakespeare refers to primero play in The Comedy of Errors, Henry V, *and* Romeo and Juliet, *so it was known outside the court, too.*

Ruff (a precursor of whist) is contrasted with Ruff (another card game) in Nashe's Martin Marprelate *(1958):*

Leaving the ancient game of England (Trump) where every coat and suit are sorted in their degree. [they] are running to their Ruff where the greatest sort [highest card] of the suit carrieth away the game [wins].

Elizabethans also played card games such as Post and Pair, Noddy, Loadum, and used cards for fortune-telling.

Elizabeth played chequers and chess with her tutor, Roger Ascham, but when James VI of Scotland the future kind called chess (in Basilikon Doron, *1599)*

overfond, because it is over-wise and Philosophic a folly:...it filleth and troubleth men's heads with as many fashious toys of the play, as before it was filled with thoughts of his affairs.

Wise Sayings

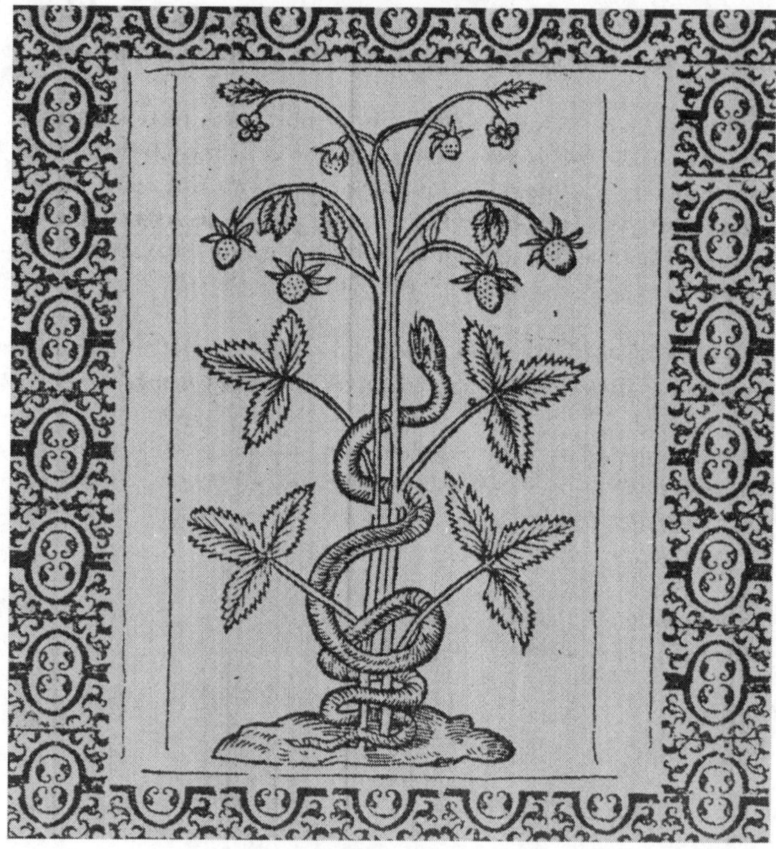

Books of symbolic emblems began a great Renaissance popularity in Italy with Alciato's *Emblematum liber* (1531), which set the pattern of an icon with an explanatory and moral text. Here is an emblem; about the serpent in the grass (an idea that Shakespeare uses in a couple of plays) from Geoffrey Whitney's popular *A Choice of Emblems* (1586). Emblems were everywhere in both high culture and popular culture: Spenser translated some texts in *A Theatre for Worldlings* (1569) but without the original Dutch pictures and emblems appeared in all sorts of literary works, triumphal arches, etc.

The Proverbs *(1546) by John Heywood was the first printed collection of colloquial wisdom in England. It can be included here because it had as great influence on the common people of Elizabeth's time and was, in fact, reprinted in her reign (1562, 1598). Here are 50 of Heywood's proverbs that hit the nail on the head. You may be surprised to learn some of these proverbs go back so far:*

Haste maketh waste.
Look ere ye leap.
When the iron is hot, strike.
Wedding is destiny, and hanging likewise.
Like will to like.
A hard beginning maketh a good ending.
Better to give than to take.
When all candles be out, all cats be grey.
No man ought to look a given horse in the mouth.
Cut my coat after my cloth.
Better is to bow than break.
Two heads are better than one.
All is well that ends well.
Better late than never.
Beggars should be no choosers.
The rolling stone never gathereth moss.
Better one bird in the hand than ten in the wood.
Rome was not built in one day.
Many small make a great.
Better is half a loaf than no bread.
Children and fools cannot lie.
All is fish that cometh to net.
One good turn asketh another.
New broom sweepeth clean.
Burnt child fire dreadeth.
Love me little, love me long.
A woman hath nine lives like a cat.
A penny for your thought.
The grey mare is the better horse.
Three may keep counsel if two be away.
Small pitchers have wide ears.
Many hands make light work.
There is no fire without some smoke.

One swallow maketh not summer.
A cat may look at a king.
He must have a long spoon [who] shall eat with The Devil.
He must needs go whom The Devil doth drive.
The mo[r]e the merrier.
It is better to be an old man's darling than a young man's wearling.
I know on which side my bread is buttered.
It will not [come] out of the flesh that is bred in the bone.
Who is so deaf or so blind as is he that wilfully will neither hear nor see?
Love me, love my dog.
An ill wind that bloweth no man good.
For when I gave you an inch, you took an ell.
Would you both eat your cake and have your cake?
Every man for himself and God for us all.
Though he love not to buy the pig in the poke.
Enough is as good as a feast.
This hitteth the nail on the head.

The Elizabethan period, rich in all aspects of literature, did not lack for wise statements which have become part of the folk heritage. here are some of the aphorisms of the period:

Hope is a good breakfast, but it is a bad supper.—Sir Francis Bacon

He that is thy friend indeed
He will help thee in thy need—Richard Barnfield

The most difficult character in comedy is the fool, and he who plays the part must be no simpleton.—Miguel de Cervantes

Enough's as good as a feast.—George Chapman

A man's house is his castle.—Sir Edward Coke

Nature hath no goal though she hath law.—John Donne

Treason doth never prosper; what's the reason?
Why, if it prosper, none dare call it treason.—Sir John Harington

He is not praised whose praiser deserveth no praise.—Gabriel Harvey

I will like and praise some things in a young writer which yet, if he continue in, I cannot but justly hate him for.—Ben Jonson

In marriage the husband should have two eyes and the wife but one.—John Lyly

Severities should be dealt out all at once, that by their suddenness they may give less offense; benefits should be handed out drop by drop, that they may be relished the more.—Nicolò Machiavelli

Who ever loved that loved not at first sight?—Christopher Marlowe

A man often preaches his beliefs precisely when he has lost them and is looking everywhere for them, and, on such occasions, his preaching is by no means at its worst.—Philip Melancthon

The better day, the better deed.—Thomas Middleton

It is to be noted that children's plays are not sports, and should be regarded as their most serious actions.—Michel de Montaigne

Of wine the middle, of oil the top, and of honey the bottom is best.—Anonymous

The fashion wears out more apparel than the man.—William Shakespeare

What thought can think, another thought can mend.—Robert Southwell

It is as necessary, or rather more necessary, for most men to know how to take mice, than how to take elephants.—Edward Topsell

Except wind stands as never it stood,
If man ill wind turns none to good.—Thomas Tusser

Where to elect there is but one,
'Tis Hobson's choice—take that or none.—Thomas Ward

An ambassador is an honest man sent to lie abroad for the commonwealth.—Sir Henry Wotton

Everyone as he likes, as the goodman said when he kissed his cow.—John Mab(be) (1572-1642?), translation of *Celestina*

It is a blind goose that knoweth not a fox from a fernbush.—John Lyly, *Euphues*

It is as great a pity to see a woman weep as a goose to go barefoot.— *A Hundred Merry Tales*

Fiat justicia et ruat coeli. Let justice be done though the heavens fall.—William Watson (1559-1603)

Fiat justicia, et pereat mundus. Let justice be done though the world perish.—Emperor Ferdinand I (1503-1564)

It is better to be the head of the yeomanry than the tail of the gentry.—Proverb.

Better make a poor match in the country than a worse one in London.—Proverb.

To live by one man's will became the cause of all men's misery.—Richard Hooker (1553-1600)

The coast was clear.—Michael Drayton (1563-1631)

There is no excellent beauty that hath not some strangeness in the proportion.—Sir Francis Bacon (1561-1626)

Though the most be players, some must be spectators.—Ben Jonson (1573?-1637)

Him that makes shoes goes barefoot himself.—Robert Burton (1577-1640)

Laugh and be fat.—John Taylor, "The Water Poet" (1580-1625)

Nor too much wealth or wit come to thee, So much of either may undo thee.—Bishop Richard Corbet (1582-1635)

'Tis not the drinking is to be blamed, but the excess.—John Selden (1584-1654)

Hang sorrow! Care will kill a cat, And therefore let's be merry.

Many old saws were familiar to the Elizabethan and guided him or her in farming and domestic activities, foretelling the weather, etc. Here is one about the month of June and the need for wool raisers to have good weather then:

The man that is to clip his sheep
Must pray for two fair days and one fair week.

The two days were very busy, and shearers worked long days, provided with bread and cheese and a quart of ale at midday and a very big meal when the day's work was done.

A number of catch phrases inevitably entered the language from popular entertainments, such as plays. From one, for instance, we get a line ("Hamlet, revenge!") from The Ghost in what the Germans like to call the Ur-Hamlet, *the lost play by Thomas Kyd on which Shakespeare made a famous improvement. But* Tarlton's Jests *shows us how a catch phrase could arise even from an anecdote.*

There was one Banks, in the time of Tarlton who served the Earl of Essex, and had a horse of strange qualities, and being at Cross Keys in Gracious Street, getting money with him, as he was mightily resorted to. Tarlton then, with his fellows, playing at the Bell by, came into the Cross keys, amongst many people, to see fashions; which Banks perceiving, to make the people laugh, says, 'Signior,' to his horse, 'Go fetch me the veriest fool in the company.' The jade comes immediately, and with his mouth draws Tarlton forth. Tarlton, with merry words, said nothing but 'God a mercy horse.' In the end, Tarlton, seeing the people laugh so, was angry inwardly and said, 'Sir, had I power of your horse, as you have, I would do more than that.' 'Whate'er it be,' said Banks, to please him, 'I will charge him to do it.' Then says Tarlton, 'Charge him to bring me the veriest whoremaster in this company.' The horse leads his master to him. Then 'God a mercy horse, indeed,' says Tarlton. The people had much ado to keep peace; but Banks and Tarlton had like to have squared, and the horse to give aim. But ever after it was a byword through London, 'God a mercy horse,' and is to this day.

A Posy of Gillyflowers *contains a number of once-popular poems typical of their period but of no great merit. Here is about half of another one of them, which will bring us to a line that may sound familiar to you. it's a "most spirited war song," as George Saintsbury said, and I break up the lines more or less as he suggested (but did not do), to stress the rhymes and to downplay what Saintsbury called the "humpty-dumpty measure."*

Ye buds of Brutus' land,
Courageous youths now play your parts,
Unto your tackle stand,
Abide the brunt with valiant hearts,
For news is carried to and fro,
That we must forth to warfare go:
Then muster now in every place,
And soldiers were pressed forth apace.
Faint not, spend blood
To do your Queen and country good:

Fair words, good pay,
Will make men cast all fears away.

The time of war is come,
Prepare your corslet, spear, and shield:
Methinks I hear the drum
Strike doleful marches to the field.
Tantara, tantara the trumpets sound,
Which makes our hearts with joy abound.
The roaring guns are heard afar,
And everything announceth war.
Serve God, stand stout:
Bold courage brings this gear about;
Fear not, forth run:
Faint heart fair lady never won.

This is the second of two panels of Elizabethan emblems from Hardwick Hall. In the empty bands of these emblems were these mottos:

21. *Arsit, crepuit, evanuit* (burning, crackling, vanishing)
22. *Et occulte, et aperte* (both secretly and openly)
23. *Obscure, secure* (hidden, safe)
24. *Fronte nulla fides* (no trustworthiness on his brow)
25. *Sat iniussa calet* (it glows sufficiently in itself)
26. *Ut moreris vives* (when you die you shall live)
27. *Trabit sua quemque* (everyone is drawn by his own pleasures)
28. *O puzzi, o ponga* (each says the other stinks)
29. *Spem fronte* (hope is on her brow)
30. *Descendente adimpleor* (I fill up by going down)
31. *Pie sed temere* (dutiful but rash)
32. *Iam sumus ergo pares* (therefore we are alike in color)
33. *Speravi et perii* (I was hopeful but caught fast)
34. *Pascor, et haud tutus* (supping with danger)
35. *Odi profanum vulgus* (I hate the common herd)
36. *Nusquam tuta fides* (Confidence is nowhere safe)
37. *Nec habet victoria laudem* (victory gains no praise)
38. *Mihi plaudo ipse domi* (praise begins at home)
39. *Desipui sapiendo* ('tis folly to be wise)
40. *Quid ergo fefellit?* (how have we been deceived?)
41. *Haud facile emergit* (it comes up with great difficulty)

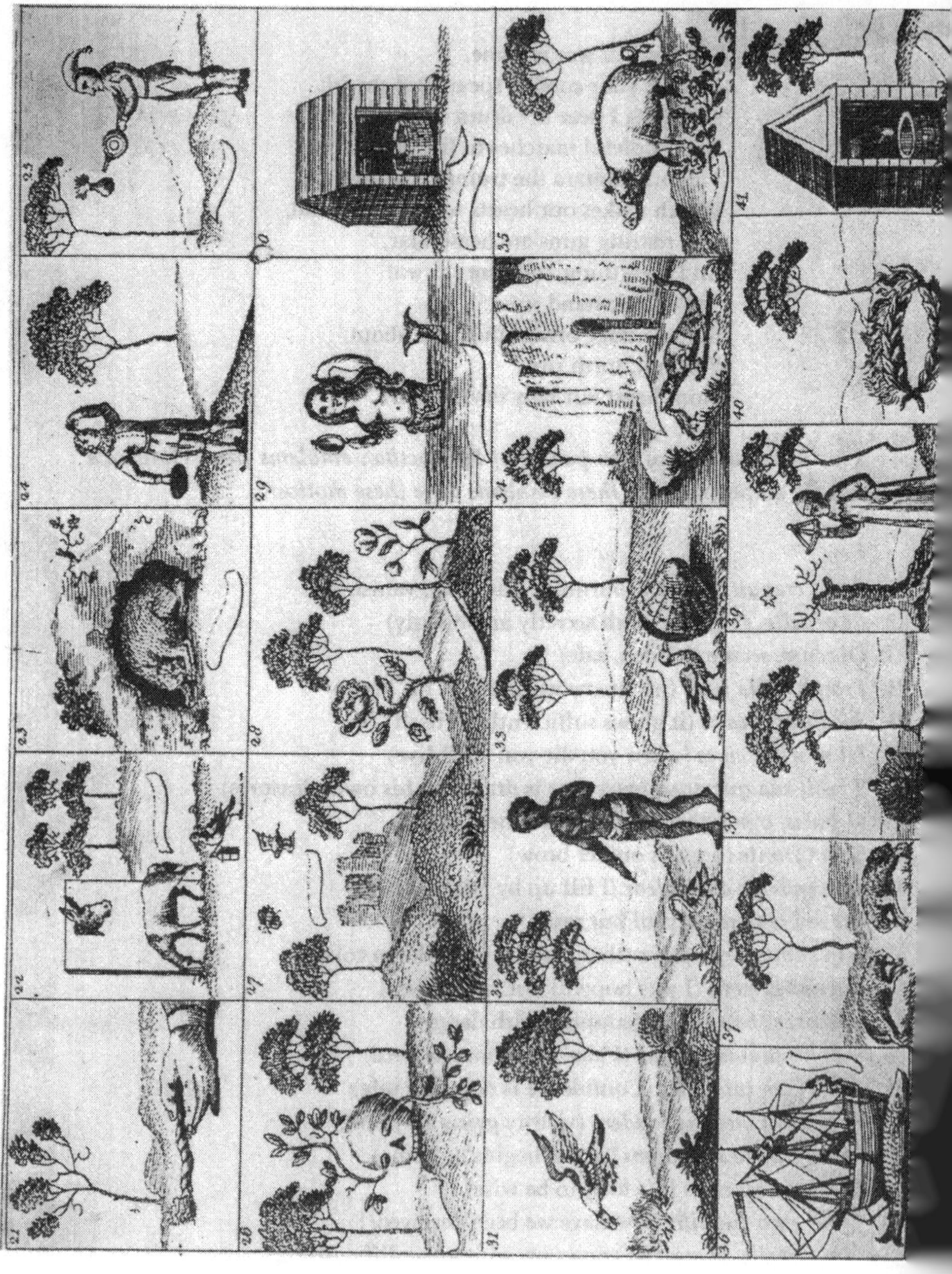

The successor to Tarleton as the favorite clown of the Elizabethans was Robert Armin (*c.* 1568—*c.* 1611), who worked at The Curtain and (in *Much Ado about Nothing, King Lear,* and other plays) at The Globe. He wrote a play *(Two Maids of Morelake)* and *Fool upon Fool, or Six Sorts of Sorts* (1600), which reappeared under his real name as *A Nest of Ninnies in an expanded edition (1608).* He was also probably the author of the quatrains on improvisations on subjects suggested by his audiences, *Quips upon Questions* (1600). This is the only extant picture of him.

TOWN AND COUNTRY.
From Greene's "Quip for an Upstart Courtier."

Jests and Merry Tales

George Clifford, third Earl of Cumberland (1558-1605) was the Queen's Champion and a court favorite but also fitted out 10 privateering expeditions against the Spanish and Spanish America and sailed with four of them himself.

Many are the little stories the folk have told about Elizabethan greats. John Manningham's diary (ed. Bruce, 1868) has this jest:

Upon a time when Burbage played Richard III, there was a citizen grew so far in liking him that before she went from the play she appointed him to come that night unto her by the name of Richard the Third. Shakespeare overhearing their conclusion went before, was entertained, and at his game ere Burbage came. Then message being brought that Richard the Third was at the door, Shakespeare caused to be made return that William the Conqueror was before Richard the Third.

John Aubrey's gossipy Brief Lives *informs us of the amorous adventures of Sir Walter Ralegh:*

He loved a wench well; and one time getting one of the Maids of Honour up against a tree in a wood ('twas his first lady) who seemed at first boarding to be something fearful of her honour, and modest, she cried, 'Sweet Sir Walter, what do you me ask? Will you undo me? Nay, Sweet Sir Walter! Sweet Sir Walter! Sir Walter!' At last, as the danger and the pleasure at the same time grew higher, she cried in the ecstasy, 'Swisser Swatter, Swisser Swatter!' She proved with child, and I doubt not but this hero took care of them both, as also that the product was more than an ordinary mortal.

The Lives of the Poets *(1753) long after the event, for Spenser died before 1600, has this tale:*

It is said that upon presenting some poems to the Queen she ordered him a gratuity of one hundred pounds, but the Lord Treasurer Burghley objecting to it, said with some scorn of the poet, of whose merit he was totally ignorant, 'What, all this for a song?' The Queen replied, 'Then give him what is reason.' Spenser for some time waited but had the mortification to find himself disappointed of Her Majesty's bounty. Upon this he took a proper opportunity to present a paper to Queen Elizabeth, in which he reminded her of the order she had given, in the following lines:

I was promised on a time
To have reason for my rhime.
From that time, unto this season,
I received nor rhime, nor reason.

The paper produced the intended effect, and the Queen, after sharply reproving the Treasurer, immediately directed the payment of the hundred pounds she had first ordered.

Sir James Prior's manuscript anecdotes tell of an inscription that was still to be seen in 1749 at Losely Hall:

Dr. Donne, the poet, in 1602 married An[ne], daughter of Sir George Moore, privately against her father's consent, who was so enraged that he not only turned him and his wife out of his house, but got Lord Chancellor Egerton to turn him out of his office as Secretary to the Great Seal. Donne and his wife took refuge in a house in Pyrford, in the neighbourhood of his father-in-law, who lived at Losely, in the country of Surrey, where the first thing he did was to write on a pane of glass [scratching it with a diamond ring]—

John Donne
An Donne
Undone.

It is said that when Ben Jonson asked Charles I for a square foot to be buried in in Westminster Abbey that is all he got. "He was buried in an upright position in order to take up no more space than he had bargained for," reports one writer. Another adds: "A certain Sir John Young, who happened to be in Westminster Abbey when Jonson's grave was being covered over, paid the mason eighteen pence to inscribe upon the gravestone Orare *(pray for, in Latin) Ben Jonson.*

In 1866 Hermann Oesterley brought out an edition of A Hundred Merry Tales *(1526), for (with works such as Thomas Berthelet's* Tales and Quick Answers *of 1535 and others of their own day) such books of amusing stories were well-known to Elizabeth and her contemporaries. In 1970 I wrote an introduction to a Scholars' Facsimiles & Reprints edition of what we called* Shakespeare's Jest Book, *"one of the treasuries of the humor of the common man that Shakespeare certainly knew and enjoyed."*

Perhaps you may, this once, enjoy trying to decipher the old-fashioned text of a small selection of the stories. it is not as difficult as at first it looks! An accent over a vowel means it is followed by an n: lõdõ) *The stories are, however, hardly kneeslappers. . . .*

XXIV

CERTAYN man there was dwellynge in a towne callyd Gotam which went to a fayre .iii. myle of to by ſhepe/ & as he cam ouer a brydge he met wt one of hys neybours & told him whether he went/ & he aſkyd hym whych way he wold bryng thẽ/ whych ſayd he wold brĩg thẽ ouer the ſame brydge/ nay quod the other mã but thou ſhalt not/ by god quod he but I wyll/ ye other agayn ſaid he ſhuld not/ & he agayn ſaid he wold bryng them ouer ſpyte of his teth & ſo fell at wordys/ & at the laſt to buffertys that eche one knokkyd other well about the heddys wt theyre fyſtys. To whom there cam a thyrd man which was a mylner wyth a ſak of mele vppõ a horſe a neybour of theyrs & partyd them & aſkyd thẽ what was the cauſe of theyr varyaunce/ whych then ſhewyd hym the matter & cauſe as ye haue harde/ Thys thyrd man the mylner thought to rebuke theyr folyſſhnes with a famylyer example & toke hys ſak of mele from his hors bak & openyd it & pouryd all the mele in the ſak ouer the bridge into the ronyng riuer wherby all the mele was loſt & ſayd thus. By my trouth neybors becauſe ye ſtryue for dryuyng ouer the brydge thoſe ſhepe which be not yet bought nor wot not wher they be/ me thynkyth therfore there is euyn as mych wyt in your heddys as there is mele in my ſak.

¶ Thys tale ſhewyth you that ſome man takyth vppõ hym to ſhew other men wyſdome when he is but a fole hym ſelf.

XL

A SCOLER of Oxford lately made master of arte come to the cyte of lōdon & in polys met with the sayd mery gētylmā of essex which was euer dysposyd to playe many mery paieantys with whome before he had bene of famylier accoyntance and prayd hym to geue hym a sercenet typet. This gentylman more lyberall of promys than of gyft grantyd hym he sholde haue one yf he wolde come to his lodgynge to the signe of the bulle without byshops gate in the next mornynge at vi of the cloke. Thys scoler thanked hym & for that nyght departed to hys lodgynge in flete strete/ & in the mornynge erely as he poynted cam to hym to the sygne of the bull/ Anon as this gentylman saw hym he bad hym go with hym in to the Cite & he sholde be sped anone/ which incontynent went togeder tyll they cam in to seynt laurence churche in the Jury wher the gentylman espyed a prest raueshyd to masse & tolde the scoler that yonder is the preste that hathe the typet for you & bade hym knele down in the pewe & he wolde[4] speke to hym for it/ And incontynent this gentilman went to the prest and sayd Syr here is a scoler and kynsman of myne greatly dyseased with the chyncowgh. I pray yow when masse ys done gyue hym iij draughtys of your chales. The prest grāūted hym & turned hym to the scoler and sayd Syr I shall serue you as son as I haue sayd masse. the scoler thē taryed styl & hard the masse trustīg then whan the masse was done that the preste wolde geue hym his typet of sarcenet. Thys gentylman in the meane whyle departed out of the churche. This prest whan masse was don put wyne in the chalice & cam to the scoler knelyng in the pew profferyng hym to drink of the chales. this ſcoler lokyd vpon hym & muſed & ſayd/ maſter perſon wherfore profer ye me the chalyce mary quod the preſte for the gentylman tolde me ye were dyſeſyd with the chĩcough & prayd me therfore that for a medcyn ye myght drynk of the chalis. Nay by ſeynt mary quod the ſkolar he promyſyd me ye ſholdd delyuer me a typet of ſercenet. Nay ſayde the preſte he ſpake to me of no typet/ but he deſyryd me to gyue you drynk of the chales for the chyncough. By goddys body quod the ſcoler he is as he was euer wont to be but a mockyng wrech/ & euer I lyue I ſhall quyte it hym & ſo departyd out of the churche ĩ gret ãger.

¶ By thys tale ye may perceyue it were no wyſdom for a man to truſt to a man to do a thynge that ys contrary to hys olde accuſtumyd condycyons.

LXXIX

TWO knyghtes there were whiche went to a ſtondyng felde wᵗ theyr prynce. But one of them was cõfeſſyd before he went/ but the other wẽt into the felde wᵗout ſhryſt or repẽtaũce/ afterward this prĩce wã yᵉ feld & had yᵉ vyctorye yᵗ day/ wherfore he yᵗ was cõfeſſyd came to yᵉ prĩce & aſkyd an offyce & ſayd he had deſeruyd[1] it for he had don good ſeruyce & aduẽtured that day as far as ony man in yᵉ felde/ to whõ the other yᵗ was vncõfeſſyd anſweryd and ſayd nay by the mas I am more worthy to haue a rewarde than he/ for he aduenturyd but his body for your ſake for he durſt not go to yᵉ felde tyl he was cõfeſſyd/ but as for me I dyd iupd both body lyfe & ſoule for your ſake/ for I went to the felde without cõfeſſyon or repentañce.

These are amusing little anecdotes or jokes that filled the anonymous A Sackful of News, *one of many inexpensive anthologies of gross wit of the sort Elizabethans loved. In these popular if trashy publications were established many trends and techniques of the literature of the common man.*

There was a friar in London which did use to go often to the house of an old woman; but ever when he came to her house, she hid all the meat [food] she had. On a time this friar came to her house, bringing certain company with him, and demanded of the wife if she had any meat. And she said, "Nay."

"Well," quoth the friar, "have you not a whetstone?"

"Yea," quoth the woman, "what will you do with it?"

"Marry," quoth he, "I would make meat thereof."

Then she brought a whetstone. He asked her likewise if she had not a frying pan. "Yea," said she, "but what the devil will ye do therewith?"

"Marry," said the friar, "you shall see by and by what I will do with it." And when he had the pan, he set it on the fire and put the whetstone therein.

"Cock's [God's] body," said the woman, "you will burn the pan."

"No, no," quoth the friar, "if you will give me some eggs, it will not burn at all." But she would have had the pan from him when that she saw it was in danger; yet he would not let her but still urged her to fetch him some eggs, which she did.

"Tush," said the friar, "here are not enow, go fetch ten or twelve." So the good wife was constrained to fetch more for fear lest the pan should burn. And when he had them, he put them in the pan.

"Now," quoth he, "if you have no butter, the pan will burn and the eggs too." So the good wife, being very loath to have her pan burnt and her eggs lost, she fetched him a dish of butter, the which he put into the pan and made good meat thereof and brought it to the table, saying, "Much good may it do you, my masters; now may you say you have eaten of a buttered whetstone."

Whereat all the company laughed, but the woman was exceeding angry because the friar had subtly beguiled her of her meat.

* * *

There was an old man that could not well see, who had a fair young wife, and with them dwelt a young man which had long wooed his mistress to have his pleasure of her, who at the last consented to him; but they knew not how to bring it to pass, for she did never go abroad but in her husband's company, and led him always. At last she devised a very fine shift, and bade her servant that he should that night about midnight come into her chamber where her husband and she lay, and she would find some device for him.

Night came, and the old man and wife went to bed, but she slept not a wink, but thought still upon her pretended purpose; but a little before the time prefixed, she awakened her husband and said thus unto him, "Sir, I will tell you a thing in secret which your servant was purposed to do; when I am alone, I can never be at quiet for him, but he is always enticing me to have me at his will; and so at the last to be quiet with him, I consented to meet him in the garden, but for mine honesty's sake I will not. Wherefore I pray you put on my clothes and go meet him; so when he comes to you, beat him well and chide him, for I know well he will not strike you because you are his master, and then he may amend himself and prove a good servant."

And the man was well pleased therewith. So the good man put on his wife's clothes and took a good cudgel in his hand and went into the garden. At length there came the servant to his mistress where she lay in bed and did what he would with her, and she was content; and then she told him how she had sent her husband into the garden in her apparel, and wherefore, and to what purpose.

So her servant arose and, as she bade him, took a good staff with him and went into the garden, as though he knew not it was his master, and said unto him, "Nay, you whore, I did this but only to prove thee, whether thou wouldest be false to my good master, and not that I would do such a vile thing with thee." Whereupon he fell upon his master, giving him many sore stripes, and beating him most cruelly, still calling him nothing but, "Out, you whore, will you offer this abuse to my good master?"

"Alas," quoth his master, "good John, I am thy master; strike me no more, I pray thee."

"Nay, whore," quoth he, "I know who thou art well enough." And so he struck him again, beating him most grievously.

"Good John," said his master, "feel, I have a beard." Then the servant felt, knowing well who it was, who presently kneeled down and cried his master mercy. "No, thanks be to God," quoth his master, "I have as good a servant of thee as a man can have, and I have as good a wife as the world affords."

Afterwards the master went to bed and his servant also. When the old man came to bed to his wife, she demanded of him how he sped. He answered and said, "By my troth, wife, I have the trustiest servant in the world, and as faithful a wife; for my servant came thither with a great staff, and did beat me right sore, thinking it had been you; wherefore I was well pleased therewith."

But ever after the servant was well beloved of his master but better of his mistress; for his master had no mistrust of him, though he had made him a cuckold. So the poor man was cruelly beaten and made a summer's bird [cuckoo] nevertheless.

* * *

There was once a country man which came to London where he had never been before; and as he went over London Bridge, he saw certain ships sailing, being the first time he had seen any, and perceiving the sails made of cloth, he thought to assay if his plow would go so; and when he came home, he caused his wife to give him a large new sheet and went and set it on the plow like a sail, thinking the plow would go with the wind; but it removed not, which when he saw, he said, "What the devil, have I spoiled my sheet about nothing?" So he set his horses to the plow again.

* * *

There was a man born in Essex that had been brought up in Norfolk from a child, and on a time he was purposely minded to see his father and mother in Essex; and as he went, he heard a cow cry.

"Thanked be God," said he, "that once before I die, I hear my mother's tongue."

* * *

There was a man and his wife lying in bed together, and the good man laid his buttocks on his wife's knees, and so they lay sleeping, and the man dreamed that he was dead and, as he thought, was carried into heaven; and being there, he dreamed that he did shit through the moon into the world, but he did shit into his wife's lap. And when he awaked, he told his wife his dream; and as she would have turned on the other side, she felt that she was all to-beshitten.

"Cock's body," quoth she, "you have dreamed fair, for you have all to-beshitten my knees." And so they were both fain to rise to make themselves clean.

* * *

There was a lady dwelt in the country which had a fool that did use to go with her to church; and on a time as his lady sat in the church, she let a great fart escape so that all the people heard it; and they looked on the fool that stood by her, thinking that it was he; which when the fool perceived, he said, "Truly, it was not I that let the fart; it was my lady." Whereat she was ashamed and went out of the church and chid the fool because he said it was not himself.

Then the fool ran into the church again and said aloud, "Masters, the fart which my lady let I will take it upon me, for she commanded me to say so." Whereat all the people laughed more than they did before, and the lady was much more ashamed.

For this story, you have to know that Sir Edward Coke (1552-1634), who was attorney general under Elizabeth and chief justice under James I, had his surname pronounced "cook." In 1598 he married, as his second wife, the widow of Sir William Hatton and grand-daughter of the great Lord Burghley. There was a considerable amount of public speculation: why should so great a lady marry a man who, at that time at least, had not attained great rank himself. John Aubrey says he learned the reason: "In bed with his new wife, Coke put his hand on her belly and felt a child stir."

'What? Flesh in the pot?' he exclaimed. 'Yes,' said the lady, 'or else I would not have married a cook.' "

Sir Walter Ralegh scratched on a windowpane at the palace the story of his ambition in one line:

Fain would I climb yet fear I to fall.

The Queen read the line and completed the couplet:

If thy heart fail thee, climb not at all.

Of course the most famous story of Sir Walter is that of a time in 1581 when the Queen "hesitated in front of a particularly large puddle, Ralegh sprang forward and, taking off his new plush cloak, laid it on the ground for his sovereign to step on."

Another, probably equally famous, story of a dashing Elizabethan concerns Sir Philip Sidney's death at the battle of Zutphen. He was badly wounded and needed water but, just as he was handed some, he caught the eye of another casualty, a "humble soldier," looking longingly at the water. Sidney at once passed the bottle to him with the words, "Thy need is yet greater than mine."

The repetition of this story had something to do with Sidney being regarded in his day as the flower of chivalry. However, Alexander the Great had already long since capped it. Once on a thirsty march with his armies he was offered a helmet full of water. "Is there enough," he asked the servant, "for ten thousand men?" Then "when the soldier shook his head, Alexander poured the water out on the ground."

Long Meg (a tall girl from Lancashire) had the sort of career that made her famous with the common folk. She was a barmaid who knew Henry VIII's fool, Will Somers, and the poet laureate John Skelton, and many another Londoner. Then she donned men's clothes and went off to the wars. Marrying another soldier, she returned to London's suburbs and opened a popular public house in Islington. People had all sorts of amusing tales to tell of her in verse and prose, ballads and pamphlets.

The Whole Life and Death of Long Meg of Westminster *appeared in 1582, and more was published about her in 1590, 1594, 1625, etc. Thomas Middleton and Thomas Dekker collaborated on a comedy about her,* The Roaring Girl, or Moll Cut-Purse *(1611), but even before that Thomas Nashe and Gabriel Harvey, among others, capitalized on her public recognition.*

These are some stories from the 1582 pamphlet:

Where Meg Was Born, her Coming up to London, and her Usage to the Honest Carrier

In the reign of Henry VIII was born in Lancashire a maid called Long Meg. At eighteen years old she came to London to get her a service. Father Willis the carrier, being the wagoner and her neighbour, brought her up with some other lasses. After a tedious journey, being in sight of the desired city she demanded the cause why they looked sad. 'We have no money,' said one, 'to pay our fare.' So Meg replies, 'If that be all, I shall answer your demands,' and this put them in some comfort. But as soon as they came to St. John's Street, Willis demanded their money. 'Say what you will have,' quoth she. 'Ten shillings a piece,' said he. 'But we have not so much about us,' said she. 'Nay, then I will have it out of your bones.' 'Marry, content,' replied Meg; and taking a staff in her hand, so belaboured him and his man, that he desired her for God's sake to hold her hand. 'Not I,' said she, 'unless you bestow an angel on us for good luck, and swear ere we depart to get us good mistresses.'

The carrier having felt the strength of her arm, though it best to give her the money, and promised not to go till he had got them good places.

Usage of the Bailiff of Westminster, Who Came into her Mistress's and her Laws

After marriage she kept a house at Islington. The constable coming at night, he would needs search Meg's house, whereupon she came down in her shift, with a cudgel, and said, 'Mr. Constable, take care you go not beyond your commission, for if you do I'll so cudgel you as never since in Islington has been.' The constable seeing her frown, told her he would take her word, and so departed.

Meg, because in her house there should be a good decorum, hung up a table [placard], containing these principles:

First, if a gentleman or yeoman had a charge about him [was caring valuables] and told her of it, she would repay him if he lost it, but if he did not reveal it, and said he was robbed, he should have ten bastinadoes, and afterwards be turned out of doors.

Secondly, whoever called for meat, and had no money to pay, should have a box on the ear and a cross on the back that he might be marked and trusted no more.

Thirdly, if any good fellow came in and said he wanted [lacked] money, he should have his bellyful of meat and two pots of drink.

Fourthly, if any wrastler came in, and made a quarrel, and would not pay his reckoning, to turn into the fields and try a bout or two with Meg; the maiden of the house should dry beat him, and thrust him out of doors.

These and many such principles, she established in her house, which she kept still and quiet.

The Pleasant Conceits of Old Hobson, The Merry Londoner *by Richard Johnson (1607) recalled a colorful character of the previous age in stories like this:*

In the beginning of Queen Elizabeth's most happy reign, our late deceased sovereign, under whose peaceful government long flourished this our country of England, there lived in the city of London a merry citizen, named old Hobson, a haberdasher of small wares, dwelling at the lower end of Cheapside, in the Poultry, as well-known through this part of England as a sergeant knows the Counter gate. He was a homely plain man, most commonly wearing a buttoned cap close to his ears, a short gown girt hard about his middle, and a pair of slippers upon his feet of an ancient fashion; as for his wealth, it was answerable to the better sort of our citizens, but of so merry a disposition that his equal therein is hardly to be found.

* * *

In Christmas holidays, when Master Hobson's wife had many pies in the oven, one of his servants had stole one of them out and at the tavern had merrily eaten it. It fortuned that same day some of his friends dined with him, and one of the best pies were missing, the stealer whereof at after dinner he found out in this manner. He called all his servants in friendly sort together into the hall, and caused each of them to drink one to another both wine, ale and beer, till they were all drunk; then caused he a table to be furnished with very good cheer, whereat he likewise pleased them. Being set all together, he said, 'Why sit you not down, fellows?' 'We be set already,' quoth they. 'Nay,' quoth Master Hobson, 'He that stole the pie is not yet set.' 'Yes, that I do [am],' quoth he that stole it; by which means he knew what was become of the pie; for the poor fellow being drunk could not keep his own secrets.

Scogin's Jests *(1565) always pointed a moral. Witness a true word added to a jest:*

On a time a poor man did come to London to speak with Scogin, and Scogin had him to Paul's church to talk with him, and both walked round about the church. The poor man said, 'Here is a godly church.' 'Yea,' said Scogin, 'what do you think it cost making?' The poor husbandman said, 'I trow it cost forty shilling.' 'Yea,' said Scogin, 'that it did, and forty shilling thereto.' '' Ho there,' said the poor man. Here a man may see that a little portion of money is a great sum in a poor man's purse; and he that is ignorant in a matter, should be no judge.

The people of Gotham were all said to be fools, likewise the inhabitants of Chelm. Country people have traditionally been "hicks" to "city slickers." The Elizabethans liked to hear of jokes played on naive visitors to London, such as this one in The Sackful of News, *published 1557 and still popular a century and more later.*

There was an Essex man came to London, who had a pair of shoes full of nails, and as he went along Cheapside he passed by a merchant's house where many young men were at the door, and among the rest one of them perceived that the man had nails in his shoes, whereupon he said to him: 'Thou churl, why comest thou hither with thy nailed shoes, and breakest the stones of our streets? Indeed I will show my Lord Mayor of it.' When the countryman heard him, he put off his shoes, and carried them in his hand,

and went in his hose till he came to Paul's; whereat everybody laughed. And when he perceived that the people laughed at him, he put on his shoes again.

The smart riposte, especially from the underdog, is beloved of common people. Here's a typical one from Pasquil's Jests, *a little later than Elizabethan but much in the spirit of their humor in that period, a kind of humor we see exploited especially by clever servants, whether in Marlowe, Shakespeare, Jonson, or lesser dramatists.*

A poor beggar that was foul, black and loathsome to behold come to a rich citizen and asked his alms. To whom the citizen said, 'I pray thee get thee hence from me, for thou lookest as though thou camest out of hell.' The poor man, perceiving he could get nothing, answered: 'Forsooth, sir, you say troth, I came out of hell indeed.' 'Why didst thou not tarry there still?' quoth the citizen. 'Marry, sir,' quoth the beggar, 'there is no room for such a poor beggars as I am; all is kept for such gentlemen as you are.'

Professor Manley, who prints that in his anthology London in the Age of Shakespeare *(1986), has a number of other jests, conceits, clinches, flashes, and anecdotes from the great and the not-so-great. This one is attributed to Sir Francis Bacon and mentions 1588:*

In eighty-eight, when the queen went from Temple Bar along Fleet Street, the lawyers were ranked on one side [where the Inns of Court stand], and the companies [merchants' guilds, livery companies] and the companies of the city on the other. Said Master Bacon to a lawyer that stood next to him, 'Do but observe the courtiers; if they bow first to the citizens, they are in debt; if first to us, they are in law [litigation]."

Besides comic tales, there were tall tales. We'll notice but one. It is not just the Germans, with their Baron Munchausen, who delight in tall tales. Elizabethan England was full of travelers who were ready to tell of strange beasts and men with their heads below their shoulders, of monsters and giants and other marvels encountered in far-off and exotic locales. Elizabethans believed the wonders they read in such ancient authors as Pliny and what they heard from sailors in port. It is no exaggeration to say that their belief in dragons and such was at least as strong as modern belief in Bigfoot or Flying Saucers, yetis and UFOs. This from A Dialogue against the Fever Pestilence *(1564) by Dr. William Bullein, author of a* Book of Simples *that is one of the earliest English herbals and of this, mocking the simple.* Civis *means "citizen" and* Mendax *is Latin for "liar."*

Civis. Gentle master, I cannot tell what to call you, nor of what country you are.

Mendax. Sir, I was born near unto Tunbridge, where fine knives are made; my name is Mendax, a younger brother lineally descended of an ancient house before the conquest. We give three whetstones in gules, with no difference, and upon our crest a left hand, with a horn upon the thumb, and a knife in the hand. The supporters are a fox on the one side, and a friar on the other side. And of late I travelled into Terra Florida, whereas I felt both wealth and woe; the black ox never trod upon my foot before; a dog hath but a day. We are born all to travail, and as for me I have but little to lose. yet I am a gentleman, and cannot find it in my heart to play the slave, or go to cart; I never could abide it, by the mass.

Civis. You speak like a wise man. I perceive by your behaviour that you have been well brought up. I pray you, where is that land?

Mendax. Many thousand miles beyond Torrida Zona, on the equinocitial line, in the longitude near unto the pole antarctic; it is an hundred thousand miles long, and is in the part named America; and by the way are the islands called Fortunato or Canaria, whose west parts be situated in the third climate.

Civis. It was a dangerous travel into that country. Where landed you? At what place?

Mendax. We sailed to the islands of Portum Sanctum, and then to Madeira, in which were sundry countries and islands, as Eratelenty, Magnefortis, Grancanary, Teneriffe, Palme Ferro, etc. And our captain went with his soldiers to land. And at our first coming near unto the river in one of these islands, as we refreshed ourselves among the date trees, in the land of the palms, by the sweet wells, we did, to the great fear of us all, see a great battle between the dragon and the unicorn; and, as God would, the unicorn thrust the dragon to the heart; and, again, the dragon with his tail stung the unicorn to death. Here is a piece of his horn; the blood of dragons is rich; that battle was worth two hundred marks to our captain. Then we travelled further into Teneriffe, into an exceeding high mountain, above the middle region, whereas we had great plenty of rock alum, and might well hear an heavenly harmony among the stars. The moon was near hand us with marvellous heat; and when we came down at the hill-foot grew many gross herbs, as lovage, laserpitium, acanthus and solanum: and whether it was by the eating of solanum or no, there was a great mighty man naked and hairy, in a deep sleep, whom we gently suffered to lie still. He had a great beard in which a bird did breed, and brought her young ones meat; this man slept half a year and waked not. Our captain declared unto us that the spials had viewed the land, and how that our enemies were at hand. The next day most fearful people painted with sundry colours approached in strange beasts' skins, with flint so were their shafts and darts made, with whom we fought and slew and took some, and yet the people so assaulted us, that with much difficulty we recovered our barks. And then we sailed forth, and chanced to let fall our sounding-lead new-tallowed, whereupon did stick gold. With all speed we sent down our divers, and so within three days we gathered thirty hogsheads of fine gold, besides two butts of orient pearls; all the shore was full of coral. From thence we sailed to the great isle called Madagastat, in Scorea, where were kings,

Mahometans by religion, black as devils. Some had no heads, but eyes in their breasts. Some, when it rained, covered all the whole body with one foot. That land did abound in elephants' teeth; the men did eat camels' and lions' flesh. Musk and civet in every place did abound, and the mother of pearl, whereof the people made their platters to put in their meat; they dwell among spice; the ground is moist with oil of precious trees. Plenty of wine out of grapes as big as this loag; much pepper; they cannot tell what to do with sugar; but that their merchants of Maabar, twenty days' journey off, do come and take of their goods frankly for nothing; but some of them do bring iron to make edge tools, for which they have for one pound twenty pound of fine gold. Their pots, pans and all vessels are clean gold garnished with diamonds. I did see swine feed in them.

Civis. Did you see no strange fowls there and fishes?

Mendax. In the isle called Ruc, in the great Can's land, I did see mermaids and satyrs with other fishes by night came four miles from the sea, and climbed into trees, and did eat dates and nutmegs, with whom the apes and baboons had much fighting, yelling and crying. The people of that land do live by eating the flesh of women. In this land did I see an ape play at tick-tack and after at Irish on the tables with one of that land; and also a parrot give one of their gentlewomen a checkmate at chess. There geese dance trenchmore.

Civis. God keep us from those cruel people.

Mendax. But, sir, as for birds, they are not only infinite in numbers, but also in kinds; some voices most sweet and some most fearful; nightingales as big as geese, owls greater than some horse; and there are birds that do lie in a rock where dragons are, whose feathers on their wings are thirty foot long, the quill as big as a cannon royal. Also I heard parrots dispute in philosophy, fresh [?] in Greek, and sing descant. Also there are a people called Astomii, which live very long, and neither eat or drink, but only live by air and the smell of fruits. In Selenetide there are women, contrary to the nature of other women, do lay eggs and hatch them, from whom do children come fifty times greater than those which are born of women. There did I see Scipodes having but one foot, which is so broad that they cover all their bodies for the rain and the sun.

Item, I did see men having feet like horse, called Ippopodes.

Item, I did see the Satyrs, half men and half goats, playing upon cornets.

Item, I did see Apothami, half horse and half man.

Item, I played at tables with the people called Fanesii, whose ears were as long as cloaks, covering all their bodies; near them is the great city called O, four hundred miles within the wall; the wall was brass, two thousand gates, six hundred bridges as big as London Bridge; the city paved with gold. Naked men dwell there with two heads and six hands every man. There did I see apes play at tennis.

Civis. I pray you is there any plenty of precious stones?

Mendax. Very many, but hard to come by; but in the island Zanzibar is much plenty of ambergris, that they make clay for their houses withal; there, if we had holden together like friends, we might have gotten a world. When I do remember it, alas, alas, every man is but for himself; you may consider what division is; emeralds, rubies, turkies, diamonds, and sapphires were sold when we came thither first for the weight of iron; a thousand rich turkesses were sold for three shillings four pence a peck. Our men gathered up carbuncles and diamonds with rakes under the spice trees.

Civis. How chance you brought none home in to this realm?

Mendax. Oh, sir, we filled two ships with fine gold, three ships with ambergris, musk and unicorns' horns, and two tall barks with precious stones, and sailed by the adamant stones, which will draw iron unto them, and so cast away the greatest riches in Heathenness or Christendom.

From 'The Norfolke Gentleman' (*Roxburghe Ballads* I. 284).

Elizabeth and Her Court

The expression in this 1575 portrait of Queen Elizabeth well suggests the monar[illegible] who quashed 48 bills of her Parliament.

Nicolò Machiavelli's Il Principe *("The Prince") was mangled in translation but still had an immense effect on the Elizabethan English. It was taken as a bible of villainy. It gave the stage and popular thought in general the stereotype of the Machiavellian consummate and crafty villain, all "policy" and no heart. Queen Elizabeth had to reign and rule in an atmosphere haunted by this devious image of the prince from Machiavelli:*

A prince...should seem to be all mercy, faith, integrity, humanity, and religion. And nothing is more necessary than to seem to have this last quality, for men in general judge more by the eyes than by the hands, for every one can see, but very few have to feel. Everybody sees what you appear to be, few feel what you are, and those few will not dare to oppose themselves to the many, who have the majesty of the state to defend them; and in the actions of men, and especially of princes, from which there is no appeal, the end justifies the means. Let a prince therefore aim at conquering and maintaining the state, and the means will always be judged honorable and praised by every one, for the vulgar is always taken by appearances and the issue of the event; and the world consists only of the vulgar, and the few who are not vulgar are isolated when the many have a rallying point in the prince.

Praise of Queen Elizabeth, practically a major industry in "Good Queen Bess' golden days," sounds more rhetorical than real in the style of Lyly's Euphues and His England, *a work which in typically Elizabethan style shows off its rhetoric and uses as many classical allusions as it can, like raisins in a rice pudding:*

This queen [Mary] being deceased, Elizabeth, being of the age of twenty-two years [actually, 25], of more beauty than honor, and yet of more honor than any earthly creature, was called from a prisoner to be a prince, from the castle to the crown, from the fear of losing her head, to be supreme head. And here, ladies, it may be you will move a question, why this noble lady was either in danger of death, or cause of distress, which, had you thought to have passed in silence, I would, notwithstanding, have revealed.

This lady all the time of her sister's reign was kept close, as one that tendered not those proceedings which were contrary to her conscience, who, having divers enemies, endured many crosses, but so patiently as in her deepest sorrow she would rather sign for the liberty of the Gospel than her own freedom. Suffering her inferiors to triumph over her, her foes to threaten her, her dissembling friends to undermine her, learning in all this misery only the patience that Zeno taught Eretricus to bear and forbear, never seeking revenge, but, with good Lycurgus, to lose her own eye rather than to hurt another's eye.

But being now placed in the seat royal, she first of all established religion, banished popery, advanced the Word, that before was so much defaced, who having in her hand the sword to revenge, used rather bountifully to reward, being as far from rigor when she might have killed, as her enemies were from honesty when they could not, giving a general pardon when she had cause to use particular punishments, preferring the name of pity before the remembrance of perils, thinking no revenge more princely than to spare when she might spill [spoil], to stay when she might strike, to proffer to save with mercy when she might have destroyed with justice. Here is the clemency worthy commendation and admiration, nothing inferior to the gentle disposition of Aristides, who, after his exile, did not so much as note them that banished him, saying with Alexander that there can be nothing more noble than to do well to those that deserve ill.

This mighty and merciful queen, having many bills of private persons that sought beforetime to betray her, burnt them all, resembling Julius Caesar, who, being presented with the like complaints of his commons, threw them into the fire, saying that he had rather not know the names of rebels than have occasion to revenge, thinking it better to be ignorant of those that hated him than to be angry with them.

This clemency did her Majesty not only show at her coming to the throne, but also throughout her whole government, when she hath spared to shed their bloods that sought to spill hers, not tacking the laws to extremity, but mitigating the rigor with mercy, insomuch as it may be said of that royal monarch as it was of Antoninus, surnamed the godly Emperor, who reigned many years without the effusion of blood. What greater virtue can there be in a prince than mercy; what greater praise than to abate the edge which she should whet, to pardon where she should punish, to reward where she should revenge?

I myself being in England when her Majesty was for her recreation in her barge upon the Thames, heard of a gun that was shot off, though of the party unwittingly, yet to her noble person dangerously, which fact she most graciously pardoned, accepting a just excuse before a great amends, taking more grief for her poor barge-man, that was a little hurt, than care for herself that stood in greatest hazard. O rare example of pity, O singular spectacle of piety.

Divers besides have there been which by private conspiracies, open rebellions, close wiles, cruel witchcrafts, have sought to end her life, which saveth all their lives, whose practices by the divine providence of the Almighty, have ever been disclosed, insomuch that he hath kept her safe in the whale's belly when her subjects went about to throw her into the sea, preserved her in the hot oven [like the Hebrews in the fiery furnace in *Daniel* 3] when her enemies increased the fire, not suffering a hair to fall from her, much less any harm to fasten upon her. These injuries and treasons of her subjects, these policies and undermining of foreign nations so little moved her, that she would often say, 'Let them know that, though it be not lawful for them to speak what they list, yet it is lawful for us to do with them what we list,' being always of that merciful mind, which was in Theodosius, who wished rather that he might call the dead to life than put the living to death, saying with Augustus when she should set her hand to any condemnation, 'I would to God we could not write.' Infinite were the examples that might be alleged, and almost incredible, whereby she hath shown herself a lamb in meekness, when she had cause to be a lion in might, proved to be an eagle in fierceness, requiting injuries with benefits, revenging grudges with gifts, in highest majesty bearing the lowest mind, forgiving all that sued for mercy, and forgetting all that deserved justice.

O divine nature, O heavenly nobility, what thing can there more be required in a prince, than in greatest power to show greatest patience, in chiefest glory to bring forth chiefest grace, in abundance of all earthly pomp to manifest abundance of all heavenly piety? O fortunate England that hath such a Queen, ungrateful if thou pray not for her, wicked if thou do not love her, miserable if thou lose her.

Just before she began her procession from The Tower through the city for her coronation, Elizabeth prayed aloud:

O Lord, Almighty and Everlasting God, I give Thee most hearty thanks that Thou hast been so merciful unto me as to spare me to behold this joyful day. And I acknowledge that Thou hast dealt as wonderfully and as mercifully with me as Thou didst with Thy true and faithful servant, Daniel, Thy prophet, whom Thou deliveredst out of the den from the cruelty of the greedy and raging Lions: even so was I overwhelmed and only by Thee delivered. To Thee therefore only be thanks, honor, and praise for ever. Amen.

When the procession was met by the Lord Mayor of London, who welcomed her, Elizabeth said:

I thank my Lord Mayor, his brethren, and you all. And whereas your request is that I should continue your good lady and queen, be ye ensured that I will be as good unto you as ever queen was to her people. No will in me can lack, neither do I trust shall there lack any power. And persuade yourselves that for the safety and quietness of you all I will not spare if need be to spend my blood. God thank you all.

Queen Elizabeth herself wrote this poem some time around 1561:

When I was fair and young, and favour gracèd me,
Of many was I sought, their mistress for to be:
But I did scorn them all, and answered them therefore,
'Go, go, go, seek some otherwhere!

Importune me no more!'

How many weeping eyes I made to pine with woe,
How many sighing hearts, I have no skill to show:
Yet I the prouder grew, and answered them therefore,
'Go, go, go, seek some otherwhere!
Importune me no more!'

Then spake fair Venus' son, that proud victorious boy,
And said, 'Fine Dame, since that you be so coy,
I will so pluck your plumes that you shall say no more,
"Go, go, go, seek some otherwhere!
Importune me no more!" '

When he had spake these words, such change grew in my breast
That neither night nor day since that, I could take any rest.
Then, lo! I did repent that I had said before,
'Go, go, go, seek some otherwhere!
Importune me no more!'

Thirty years later, the man who was to become her successor, James I, wrote this sonnet in The Lepanto:

The azured vault, the crystal circles bright,
The gleaming fiery torches powdered there;
The changing round, the shining beamy light,
The sad and bearded fires, the monsters fair;
The prodigies appearing in the air;
The rearing thunders and the blustering winds;
The fowls in hue and shape and nature rare,
The pretty notes that winged musicians finds;
In earth, the savoury flowers, the metalled minds,
The wholesome herbs, the hautie pleasant trees,
The silver streams, the beasts of sundry kinds,
The bounded roars and fishes of the seas,—
All these, for teaching man, the Lord did frame
To do his will whose glory shines in thame.

The Virgin Queen had at least two reasons not to submit to a husband: first, she was a sovereign and taking a husband in those days meant subjecting oneself; second, if the gossip that Ben Jonson told William of Hawthornden was correct, she was born with a membrane that made sexual penetration painful or impossible (though she is said to have "tried with many," such as Essex and Leicester). She now and then seemed to encourage this or that favorite or such foreign suitors as the Duc d'Alençon, but privately she had decided to rule alone. This proved to be a very successful if difficult decision and produced many benefits for the English, not the least of which was that she was available as Virgin Queen to be the Protestant replacement for the cult of The Blessed Virgin.

The Parliament and people, nonetheless, worried about the succession and early in her reign there was considerable concern that she would die (as eventually she did, a couple of generations later) childless.

Succession was always a problem with any monarch and the House of Commons grew uneasy when the Virgin Queen continued long in that state. On 4 February 1559 the House decided to ask her to marry and soon after a delegation presented her with the petition. Her reply to the Commons was characteristic:

As I have good cause, so do I give you all my hearty thanks for the good zeal and loving care you seem to have—as well towards me as to the whole estate of your country. Your petition, I perceive, consisteth of three parts, and my answer to the same shall depend of two.

And to the first part, I may say unto you that from my years of understanding sith I first had consideration of myself to be born a servant of Almighty God, I happily chose this kind of life in the which I yet live: which, I assure you, for mine own part hath hitherto best contented myself and, I trust, hath been most acceptable unto God. From the which, if either ambition of high estate offered to me in marriage by the pleasure and appointment of my Prince—whereof I have some record in the presence, as you, our Treasurer, well know—or if eschewing the danger of mine enemies or the avoiding of the peril of death, whose messenger or rather a continual watchman, the Prince's indignation, was no little time daily before mine eyes (by whose means—although I know or justly may suspect—yet I will not now utter, or if the whole cause were in my sister herself, I will not now burthen her therewith because I will not charge the dead), if any of these, I say, could have drawn or dissuaded me from this kind of life, I had not now remained in this estate wherein you see me. But so constant have I always continued in this determination (although my youth and words may seem to some hardly to agree together, yet is it most true), that at this day I stand free from any other meaning that either I had had in times past or have at this present; with which trade of life I am so thoroughly acquainted that I trust God, who hath hitherto therein preserved and led me by the hand, will not of His goodness suffer me to go alone.

For the other part, the manner of your petition I do well like and take it in good part because it is simple and containeth no limitation of place or person. If it had been otherwise, I must needs have misliked it very much and thought it in you a very great presumption: being unfit and altogether unmeet for you to require them that may command; or those to appoint, whose parts are to desire; or such to bind and limit, whose duties are to obey; or to take upon you to draw my love to your liking, or to frame my will to

God to incline my heart to another kind of life, you may very well assure yourselves, my meaning is not to determine anything wherewith the realm may or shall have just cause to be discontented. And therefore put that clean out of your heads. For I assure you but what credit my assurance may have you, I cannot tell; but what credit it shall deserve to have, the sequel shall declare), I will never in that matter conclude anything that shall be prejudicial to the realm. For the well, good, and safety whereof, I will never shun to spend my life. And whomsoever my chance shall be to light upon, I trust he shall be such as shall be as careful for the realm and you—I will not say as myself because I cannot so certainly determine of any other, but by my desire he shall be such as shall be as careful for the preservation of the realm, and you, as myself. And albeit it might please Almighty God to continue me still in this mind to live out of the state of marriage, yet is it not to be feared; but He will so work in my heart and in your wisdom, as good provision by His help may be made whereby the realm shall not remain destitute of an heir that may be a fit governor and peradventure more beneficial to the realm that such offspring as may come of me. For though I be never so careful of your well doing, and mind ever so to be, yet may my issue grow out of kind and become perhaps ungracious. And in the end, this shall be for me sufficient: that a marble stone shall declare that a queen, having reigned such a time, lived and died a virgin. And here I end and take your coming to me in good part and give unto you all my hearty thanks—more yet for your zeal and good meaning than for your petition.

Of course Elizabeth, like any ruler, had her enemies and detractors. It was her constant care and her triumph that she was able to hold her nation together, put down rebellion, and create an atmosphere of unity and general peace. But one laborer of Great Wenden (Essex) spoke for some when he dared to say in 1591:

Let us pray for a King. We shall never have merry world while the Queen liveth, and had we but one that would rise [in rebellion], I would be the next.

Discussing with her ladies in waiting a possible epitaph, Queen Elizabeth said:

I am no lover of pompous title, but only desire that my name may be recorded in a line or two, which shall briefly express my name, my virginity, the years of my reign, the reformation of religion under it, and my preservation of peace.

Elizabeth ruled her Parliament and Lords as well as her common people but that was not because the English had no ideas about a more democratic monarchy. Here is Thomas Starkey (1499?-1538) who opposed not only papal supremacy but also absolute monarchy of the type that Henry VIII and his daughter Elizabeth imposed by force of personality.

This is a startling idea for its time from a Dialogue *Starkey wrote a year or so before his death but which, obviously, could not be published for a very long time thereafter.*

That country cannot long be well governed, nor maintained with good policy, where all is ruled by the will of one not chosen by election but cometh to it by natural succession, for seldom seen it is that they which have by succession come to kingdoms and realms are worthy of such high authority.... What is more repugnant to nature than a whole nation to be governed by the will of a prince...? What is more contrary to reason than all the whole people to be ruled by him which commonly lacketh all reason...? It is not man that can make a wise prince of him that lacketh wit by nature.... But this is in man's power, to elect and choose him that is both wise and just, and make him a prince, and him that is a tyrant so to depose.

On 30 November 1601, Elizabeth spoke to the last Parliament of her long reign in a moving address known as "The Golden Speech." As her subjects knelt, the frail little woman addressed them in royal fashion:

Mr. Speaker: we have heard your declaration and perceive your care of our estate, by falling into a consideration of a grateful acknowledgment of such benefits as you have received; and that your coming is to present thanks to us, which I accept with no less joy than your loves can have desire to offer such a present.

I do assure you there is no prince that loves his subjects better, or whose love can countervail our love. There is no jewel, be it of never so rich a price, which I set before this jewel: I mean your love. For I do esteem it more than any treasure or riches; for that we know how to prize, but love and thanks I count unvaluable. And, though God hath raised me high, yet this I count the glory of my crown, that I have reigned with your loves. This makes me that I do not so much rejoice that God hath made me to be a Queen, as to be a Queen over so thankful a people. Therefore, I have cause to wish nothing more than to content the subject; and that is a duty which I owe. Neither do I desire to live longer days than I may see your prosperity; and that is my only desire. And as I am that person that still yet under God hath delivered you, so I trust, by the almighty power of God, that I shall be His instrument to preserve you from every peril, dishonor, shame, tyranny, and oppression; partly by means of your intended helps [subsidies they were granting] which we take very acceptably, because it manifesteth the largeness of your good loves and loyalties unto your sovereign.

Of myself I must say this: I never was any greedy, scraping grasper, nor a strait, fast-holding Prince, nor yet a waster. My heart was never set on any worldly goods, but only for my subjects' good. What you bestow on me, I will not hoard it up, but receive it to bestow on you again. Yea, mine own properties I account yours, to be expended for your good; and your eyes shall see the bestowing of all for your good. Therefore, render unto them, I beseech you, Mr. Speaker, such thanks as you imagine my heart yieldeth, but my tongue cannot express.

Mr. Speaker, I would wish you and the rest to stand up, for I shall yet trouble you with longer speech.

They rose, and she continued:

Mr. Speaker, you give me thanks, but I doubt me I have a greater cause to give you thanks than you me, and I charge you to thank them of the Lower House from me. For, had I not received a knowledge from you, I might have fallen into the lapse of an error, only for lack of true information.

Since I was Queen, yet did I never put my pen to any grant but that, upon pretext and semblance made unto me, it was both good and beneficial to the subject in general, though a private profit to some of my ancient servants who had deserved well at my hands. But the contrary being found by experience, I am exceedingly beholding to such subjects as would move the same at the first. And I am not so simple to suppose, but that there be some of the Lower House whom these grievances never touched: and for them, I think they spake out of zeal to their countries, and not out of spleen or malevolent affection as being parties grieved; and I take it exceeding gratefully from them, because it gives us to know that no respects or interest had moved them, other than the minds they have to suffer no diminution of our honor and our subjects' love unto us. The zeal of which affection, tending to ease my people and knit their hearts unto me, I embrace with a princely care, for above all earthly treasure I esteem my people's love, more than which I desire not to merit.

That my grants should be grievous to my people and oppressions privileged under color of our patents, our kingly dignity shall not suffer it. Yea, when I heard it, I could give no rest unto my thoughts until I had reformed it. Shall they, think you, escape unpunished that have thus oppressed you, and have been respectless of their duty, and regardless of our honor? No, I assure you, Mr. Speaker, were it not more for conscience sake than for any glory or increase of love that I desire, these errors, troubles, vexations, and oppressions, done by these varlets and lewd persons, not worthy the name of subjects, should not escape without condign punishment. But I perceive they dealt with me like physicians who, ministering a drug, make it more acceptable by giving it a good aromatical savor, or when they give pills do gild them all over.

I have ever used to set the Last Judgment Day before mine eyes, and so to rule as I shall be judged to answer before a higher Judge, to whose judgment seat I do appeal, that never thought was cherished in my heart that tended not unto my people's good. And now, if my kingly bounties have been abused, and my grants turned to the hurt of my people, contrary to my will and meaning, and if any in authority under me have neglected or perverted what I have committed to them, I hope God will not lay their culps and offenses to my charge; who, though there were danger in repealing our grants, yet what danger would I not rather incur for your good, than I would suffer them still to continue?

I know the title of a King is a glorious title; but assure yourself that the shining glory of princely authority hath not so dazzled the eyes of our understanding, but that we well know and remember that we also are to yield an account of our actions before the great Judge. To be a King and wear a crown is a thing more glorious to them that see it, than it is pleasant to them that bear it. For myself, I was never so much enticed with the glorious name of a King or royal authority of a Queen, as delighted that God hath made me His instrument to maintain His truth and glory, and to defend this Kingdom (as I said) from peril, dishonor, tyranny, and oppression.

There will never Queen sit in my seat with more zeal to my country, care for my subjects, and that will sooner with willingness venture her life for your good and safety, than myself. For it is my desire to live nor reign no longer than my life and reign shall be for your good. And though you have had and may have many princes more mighty and wise sitting in this seat, yet you never had nor shall have any that will be more careful and loving.

Shall I ascribe anything to myself and my sexly weakness? I were not worthy to live then; and, of all, most unworthy of the mercies I have had from God, who hath given me a heart that yet never feared any foreign or home enemy. And I speak it to give God the praise, as a testimony before you, and not to attribute anything to myself. For, I oh Lord! what am I, whom practices and perils past should not fear? Or what can I do? That I should speak for any glory, God forbid.

This, Mr. Speaker, I pray you deliver unto the House, to whom heartily recommend me. And so I commit you all to your best fortunes and further counsels. And I pray you, Mr. Comptroller, Mr. Secretary, and you of my Council, that before these gentlemen go into their countries, you bring them all to kiss my hand.

And so she reigned and loved and came to be, truly, the living embodiment of the English spirit. Thomas Dekker in The Wonderful Year *speaks eloquently of the passing of Elizabeth:*

She came in with the fall of the leaf [November, 1558], and went away with the spring [March, 1603]: her life (which was dedicated to Virginity), both beginning and closing up a miraculous Maiden circle: for she was born upon a Lady Even, and died upon a Lady Eve: her Nativity and death being memorable by this wonder: the first and last years of her Reign by this, that a *Lee* was Lord Mayor when she came to the Crown, and a *Lee* Lord Mayor when she departed from it. Three places are made famous by her for three things, *Greenwich* for her birth, *Richmond* for her death, and *Whitehall* for her Funeral.

A number of old ballads and broadsides ended with this patriotic sentiment:

Lord, save our gracious sovereign,
Elizabeth, by name,
That long unto our comfort,
She may both rule and reign.

In the same reign of the second Elizabeth of England we can conclude in the same vein. Sir John Davies, Hymns to Astraea:

Reserve, sweet spring, this nymph of ours
Eternal garlands of thy flowers,
Green garlands never wasting;
In her shall last our state's fair spring,
Now and forever flourishing,
As long as heaven is lasting.

The bold signature of *Elizabeth R[egina].*